In the ~~~~~~~~~~~~~ my grandfather Fumiyasu Yamakawa passed away. My energetic grandpa was over ninety years old, swam in the ocean every morning and participated in the masters race. His spirit of inquiry led him to try new things and have many hobbies. He always aimed to improve at whatever he tried. I wish we could have drank together, played go and talked together even more. My beloved grandpa. (My current weight...70 kg!! Huuuh?!)

–Mitsutoshi Shimabukuro, 2015

Mitsutoshi Shimabukuro made his debut in **Weekly Shonen Jump** in 1996. He is best known for **Seikimatsu Leader Den Takeshi!**, for which he won the 46th Shogakukan Manga Award for children's manga n 2001. His current series **Toriko**, began serialization in Japan in 2008

TORIKO

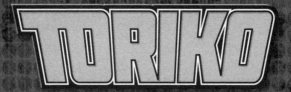

TORIKO VOL. 35
SHONEN JUMP Manga Edition

STORY AND ART BY **MITSUTOSHI SHIMABUKURO**

Translation/Christine Dashiell
Weekly Shonen Jump Lettering/Erika Terriquez
Graphic Novel Touch-Up Art & Lettering/Elena Diaz
Design/Veronica Casson
Weekly Shonen Jump Editor/Hope Donovan
Graphic Novel Editor/Marlene First

Printed in the U.S.A.

Published by VIZ Media, LLC
P.O. Box 77010
San Francisco, CA 94107

10 9 8 7 6 5 4 3 2 1
First printing, August 2016

www.viz.com

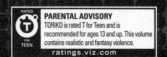

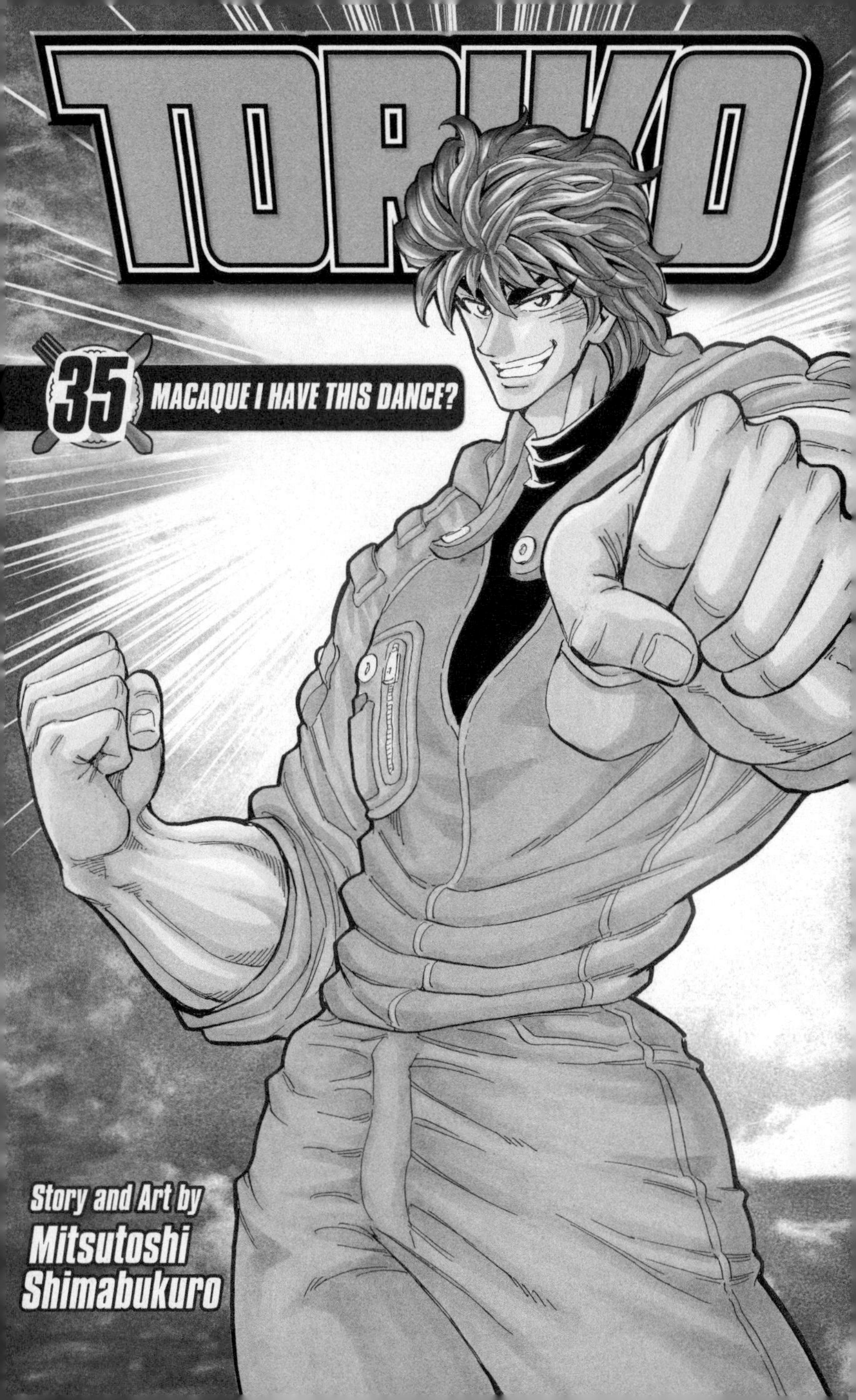

TORIKO

35 MACAQUE I HAVE THIS DANCE?

Story and Art by
Mitsutoshi Shimabukuro

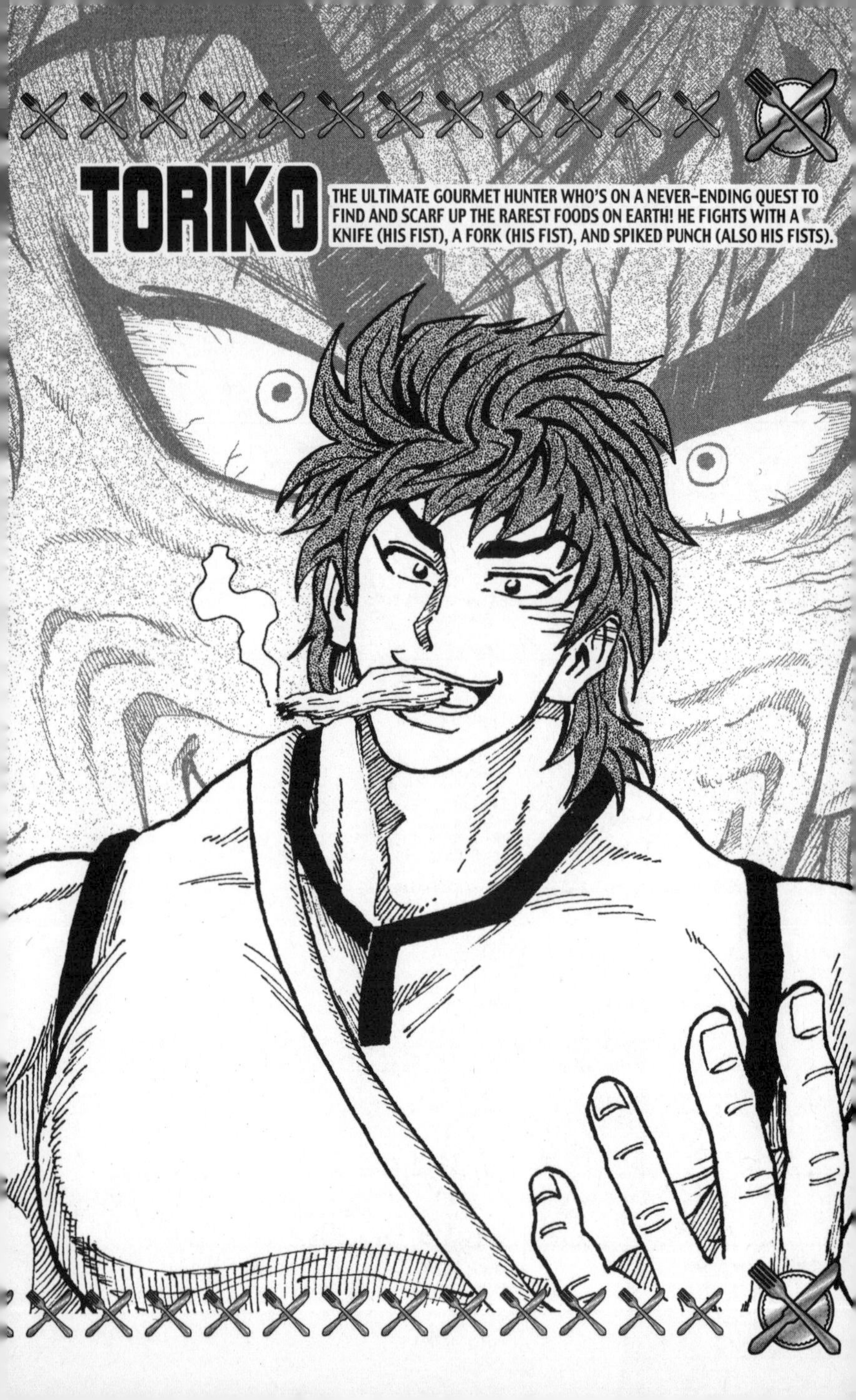
TORIKO
THE ULTIMATE GOURMET HUNTER WHO'S ON A NEVER-ENDING QUEST TO FIND AND SCARF UP THE RAREST FOODS ON EARTH! HE FIGHTS WITH A KNIFE (HIS FIST), A FORK (HIS FIST), AND SPIKED PUNCH (ALSO HIS FISTS).

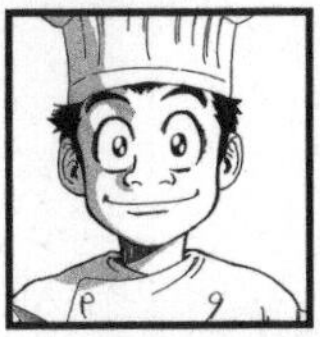

● **KOMATSU**
TALENTED IGO HOTEL CHEF AND TORIKO'S #1 FAN.

● **COCO**
ONE OF THE FOUR KINGS, THOUGH HE IS ALSO A FORTUNETELLER. SPECIAL ABILITY: POISON FLOWS IN HIS VEINS.

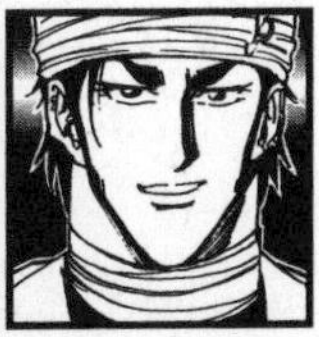

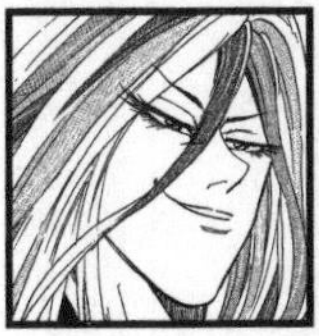

● **SUNNY**
ONE OF THE FOUR KINGS. SENSORS IN HIS LONG HAIR ENABLE HIM TO "TASTE" THE WORLD. OBSESSED WITH ALL THAT IS BEAUTIFUL.

● **ZEBRA**
ONE OF THE FOUR KINGS. A DANGEROUS INDIVIDUAL WITH SUPERHUMAN HEARING AND VOCAL POWERS.

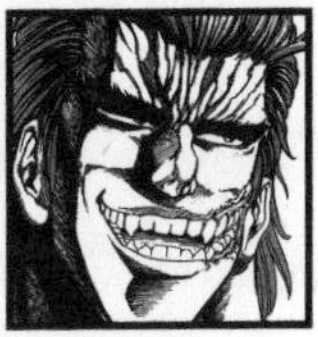

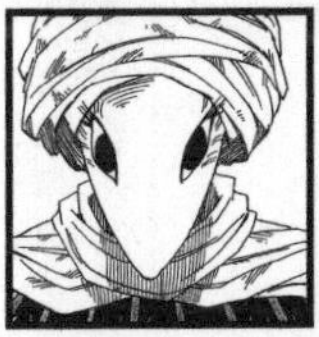

● **KAKA**
A TASTE HERMIT NITRO WHO AWOKE FROM DROUGHT DORMANCY. SHE MET TORIKO AND THE GANG IN AREA 7 AND BECAME THEIR GUIDE.

● **MONKEY KING BAMBINA**
ONE OF THE EIGHT KINGS AND THE RULER OF AREA 7. HE'S THE GREATEST PRACTITIONER OF MONKEY MARTIAL ARTS.

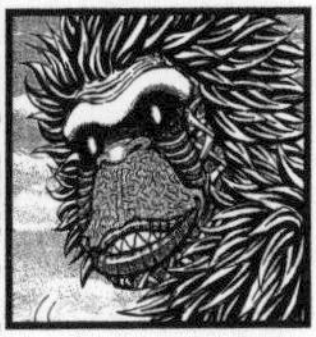

WHAT'S FOR DINNER

THE AGE OF GOURMET IS DECLARED OVER. IN ORDER TO GET KOMATSU BACK FROM GOURMET CORP., TORIKO VENTURES INTO THE GOURMET WORLD ON HIS OWN. EIGHTEEN MONTHS LATER, THE PAIR RETURNS HOME ALONG WITH A MASSIVE AMOUNT OF PROVISIONS TO FEED THE HUMAN WORLD. UPON THEIR RETURN, THE TWO ARE COMMISSIONED BY THE NEW IGO PRESIDENT, MANSOM, TO SEARCH FOR THE REMAINDER OF ICHIRYU'S FULL-COURSE MEAL. JOINING FORCES WITH THE OTHER FOUR KINGS, COCO, SUNNY AND ZEBRA, THEY SUCCEED IN RETRIEVING THE MIRACLE INGREDIENT THAT WILL SAVE HUMANITY FROM STARVATION: THE BILLION BIRD.

IN ORDER TO REVIVE THE AGE OF GOURMET, THE FIVE OF THEM ACCEPT AN ENORMOUS ORDER. THEY MUST TRAVEL TO THE GOURMET WORLD AND FIND ACACIA'S FULL-COURSE MEAL. ARMED WITH THE INFORMATION AND THE OCTOMELON CAMPER MONSTER GIVEN TO THEM BY ICHIRYU'S MYSTERIOUS FRIEND CHICHI, THE FIVE MEN SET THEIR SIGHTS ON THE GOURMET WORLD.

THEIR FIRST STOP IS AREA 8, WHERE TORIKO MUST FACE OFF AGAINST THE RULER OF THE CONTINENT, NIGHTMARE HERACLES, IN ORDER TO OBTAIN ACACIA'S SALAD, AIR. BUT THE OVERWHELMING DIFFERENCE IN STRENGTH LEAVES TORIKO ON THE BRINK OF DEATH.

MEANWHILE, KOMATSU REACHES AIR AND USES HIS MASTERFUL CULINARY SKILLS TO PREPARE IT. THIS MAGNIFICENT FEAT SAVES THE NIGHTMARES AND ALL OF AREA 8! AT LAST, TORIKO AND HIS FRIENDS SAMPLE AIR, WHICH GIVES TORIKO AND HIS FRIENDS THE POWER TO CONTROL THEIR GOURMET CELLS, AND HE EVEN ADDS IT TO HIS OWN FULL-COURSE MEAL.

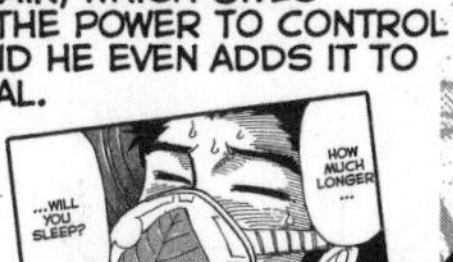
HOW MUCH LONGER ...
...WILL YOU SLEEP?

THAT'S WHEN THE REVIVER, TEPPEI, WHO HAD DEFECTED TO NEO, ATTACKS KOMATSU. TORIKO AND THE GANG HEAD TO AREA 7 TO CAPTURE ACACIA'S SOUP, PAIR, WHICH IS THE ONLY THING THAT CAN SAVE KOMATSU. THERE IS ONLY ONE VERY BIG PROBLEM THAT STANDS IN THEIR WAY... ONE OF THE EIGHT KINGS—THE MISCHIEVOUS MONKEY KING BAMBINA. AND TO MAKE MATTERS WORSE, THEY LEARN FROM THEIR GUIDE KAKA THAT THE FOOD TREASURE PAIR IS ACTUALLY A PART OF BAMBINA'S BODY! IN ORDER TO OBTAIN PAIR, TORIKO AND THE GANG MUST UNDERGO MONKEY MARTIAL ARTS TRAINING...AND THEN THE PRO WRESTLING MATCH BETWEEN THE MONKEY KING AND THE FOUR KINGS BEGINS!!

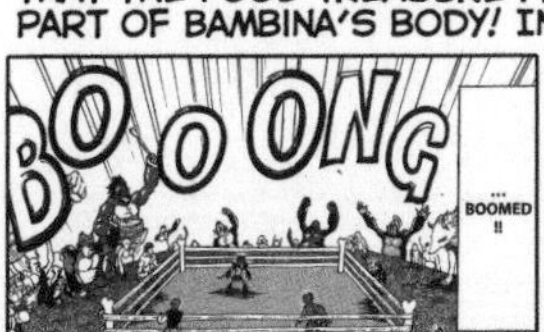
BOOONG
... BOOMED !!

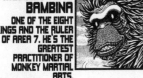

Contents

TORIKO

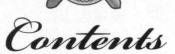

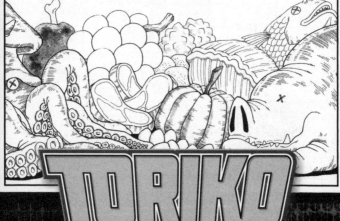

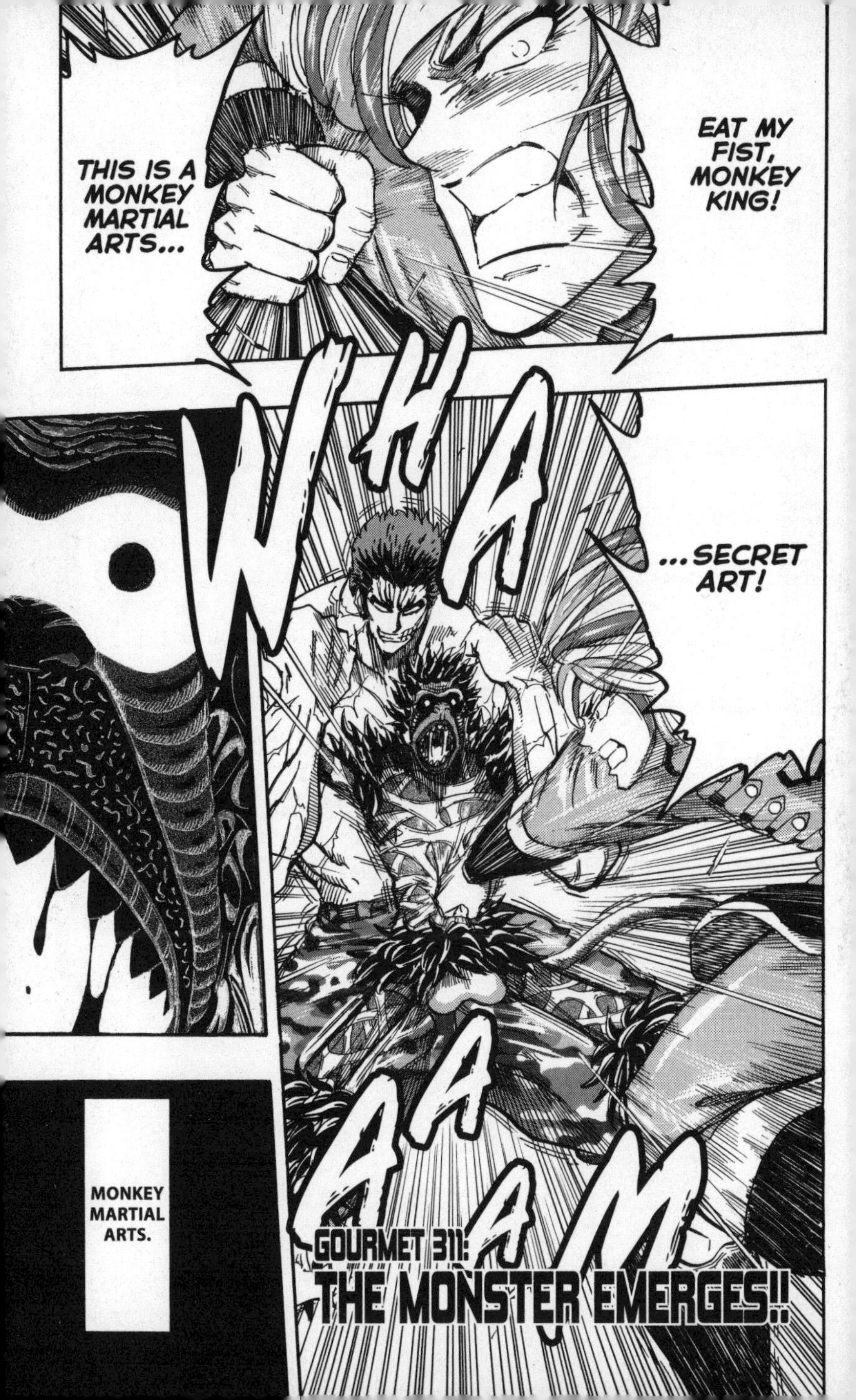
EAT MY FIST, MONKEY KING!
THIS IS A MONKEY MARTIAL ARTS...
...SECRET ART!
WHAAAAM
MONKEY MARTIAL ARTS.

GOURMET 311: THE MONSTER EMERGES!!

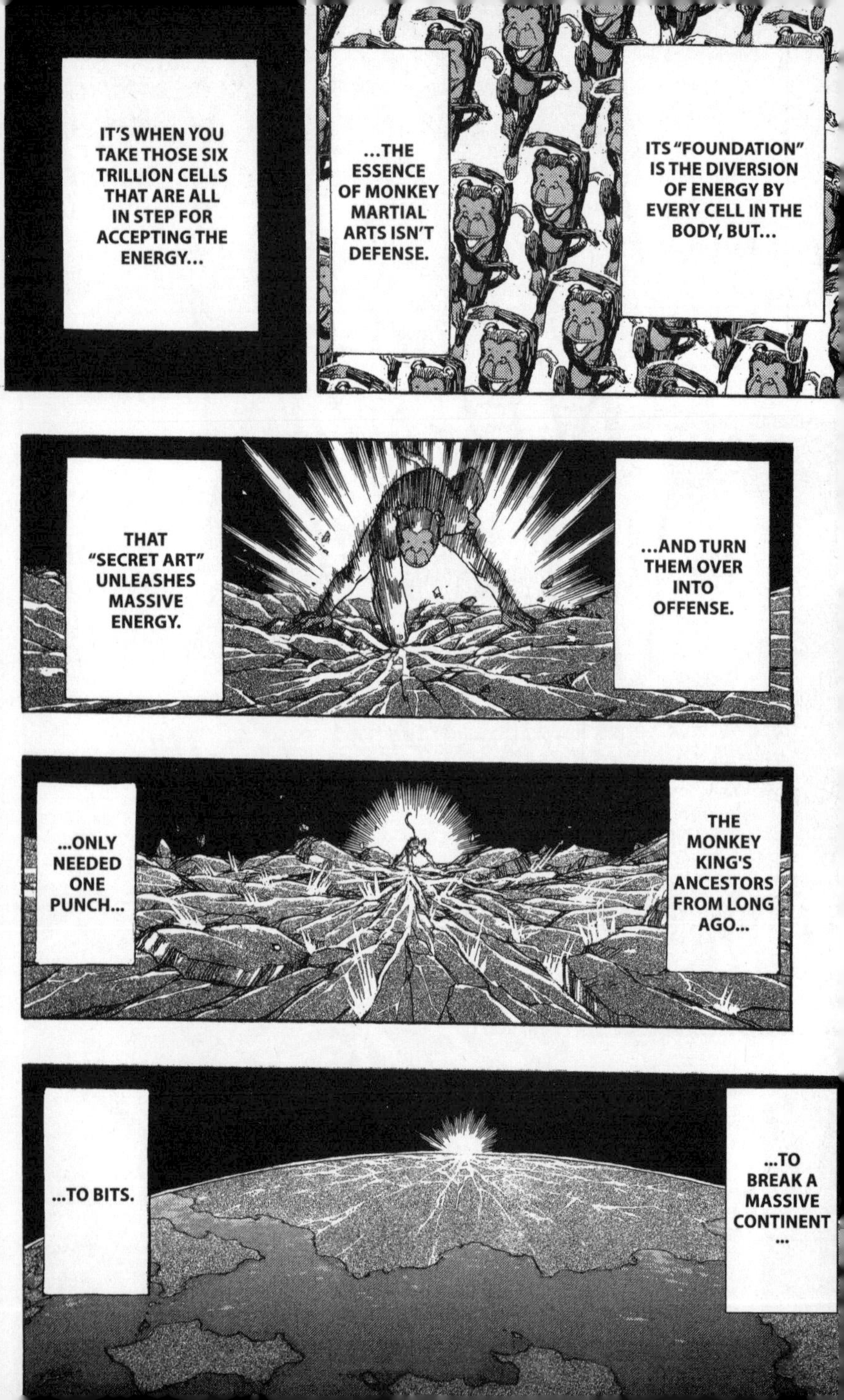
ITS "FOUNDATION" IS THE DIVERSION OF ENERGY BY EVERY CELL IN THE BODY, BUT...
...THE ESSENCE OF MONKEY MARTIAL ARTS ISN'T DEFENSE.
IT'S WHEN YOU TAKE THOSE SIX TRILLION CELLS THAT ARE ALL IN STEP FOR ACCEPTING THE ENERGY...
...AND TURN THEM OVER INTO OFFENSE.
THAT "SECRET ART" UNLEASHES MASSIVE ENERGY.
THE MONKEY KING'S ANCESTORS FROM LONG AGO...
...ONLY NEEDED ONE PUNCH...
...TO BREAK A MASSIVE CONTINENT ...
...TO BITS.

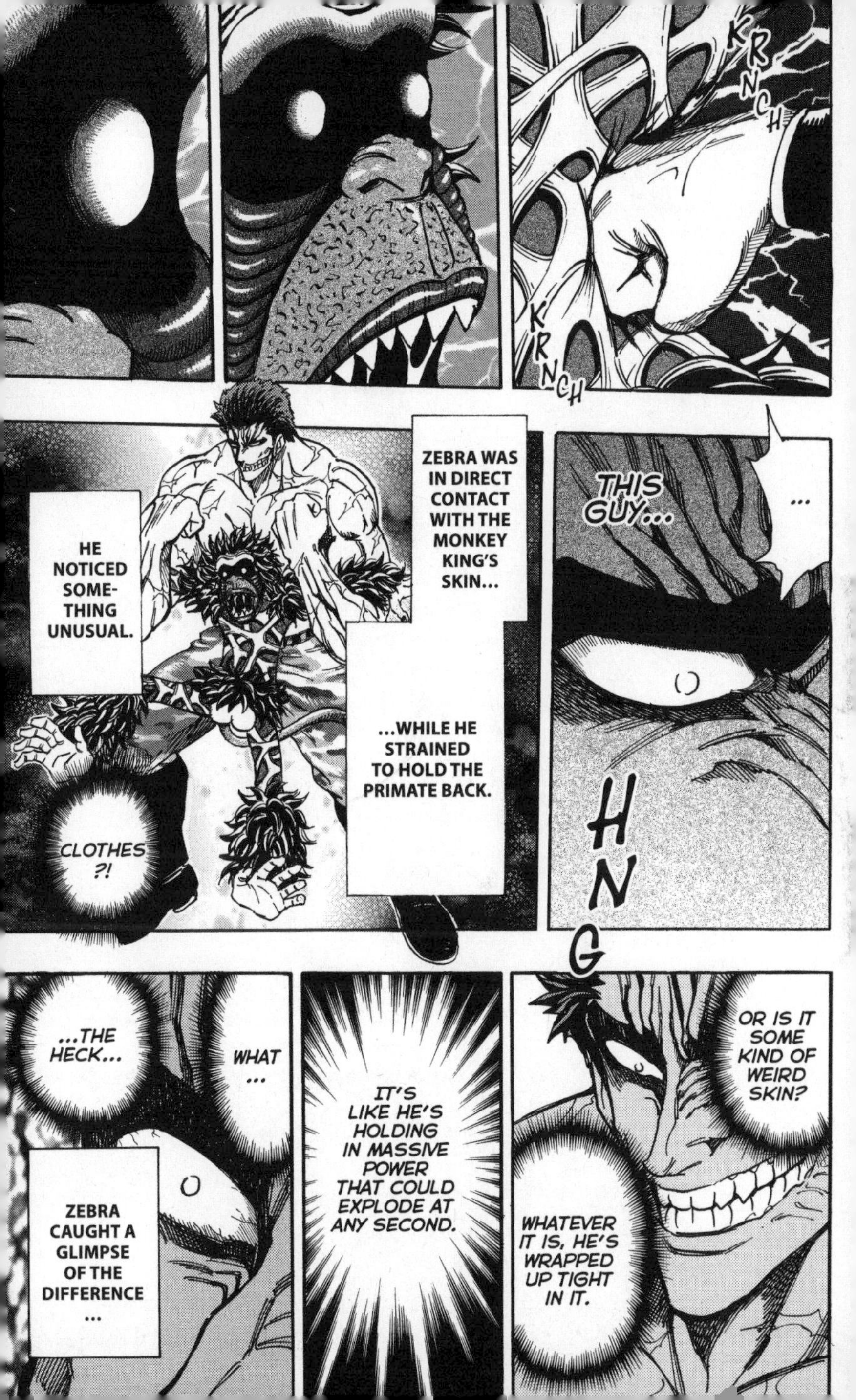
KRNCH
KRNCH
...
THIS GUY...
HNNG
ZEBRA WAS IN DIRECT CONTACT WITH THE MONKEY KING'S SKIN...
...WHILE HE STRAINED TO HOLD THE PRIMATE BACK.
HE NOTICED SOME-THING UNUSUAL.
CLOTHES?!
OR IS IT SOME KIND OF WEIRD SKIN?
WHATEVER IT IS, HE'S WRAPPED UP TIGHT IN IT.
IT'S LIKE HE'S HOLDING IN MASSIVE POWER THAT COULD EXPLODE AT ANY SECOND.
WHAT...
...THE HECK...
ZEBRA CAUGHT A GLIMPSE OF THE DIFFERENCE...

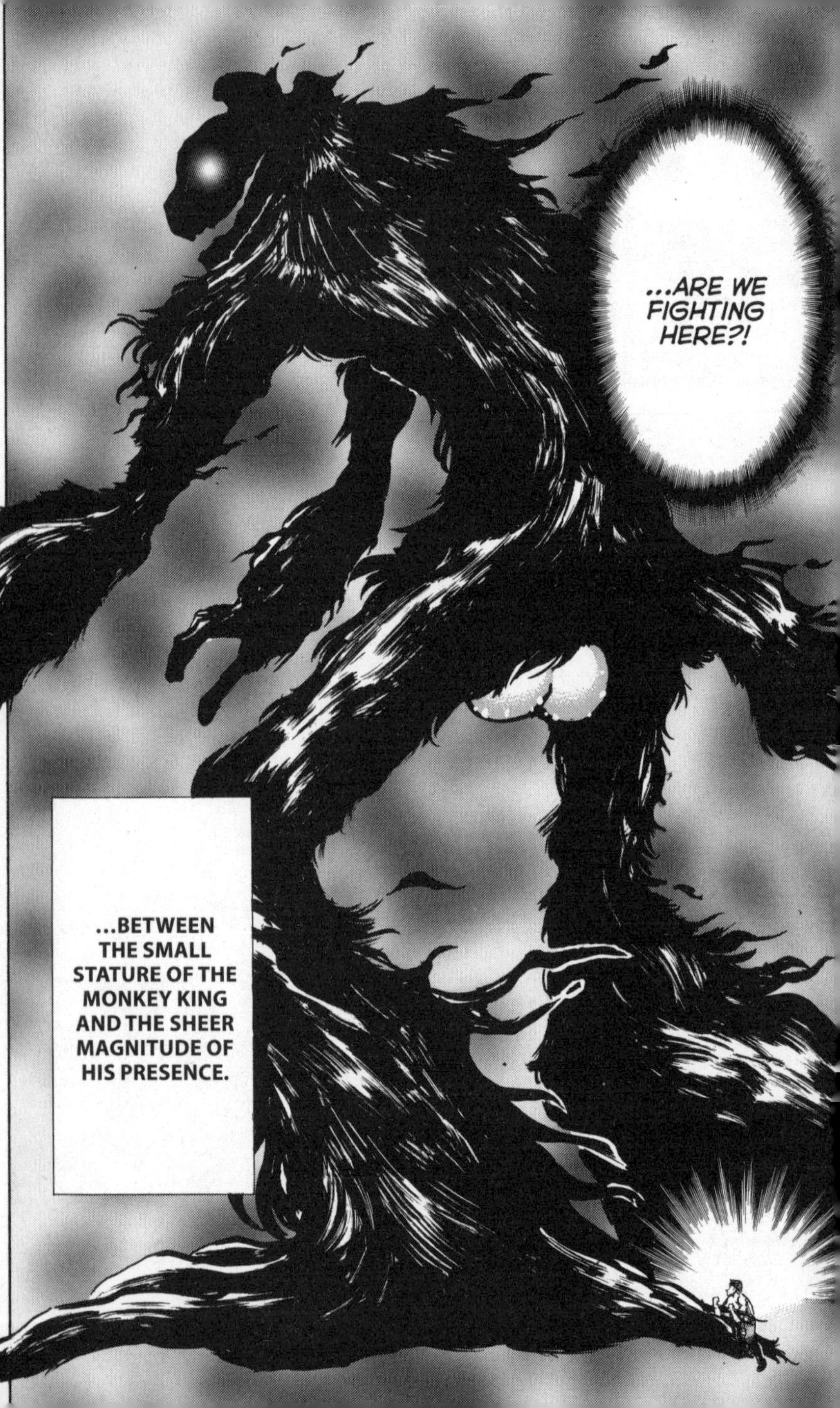
...ARE WE FIGHTING HERE?!
...BETWEEN THE SMALL STATURE OF THE MONKEY KING AND THE SHEER MAGNITUDE OF HIS PRESENCE.

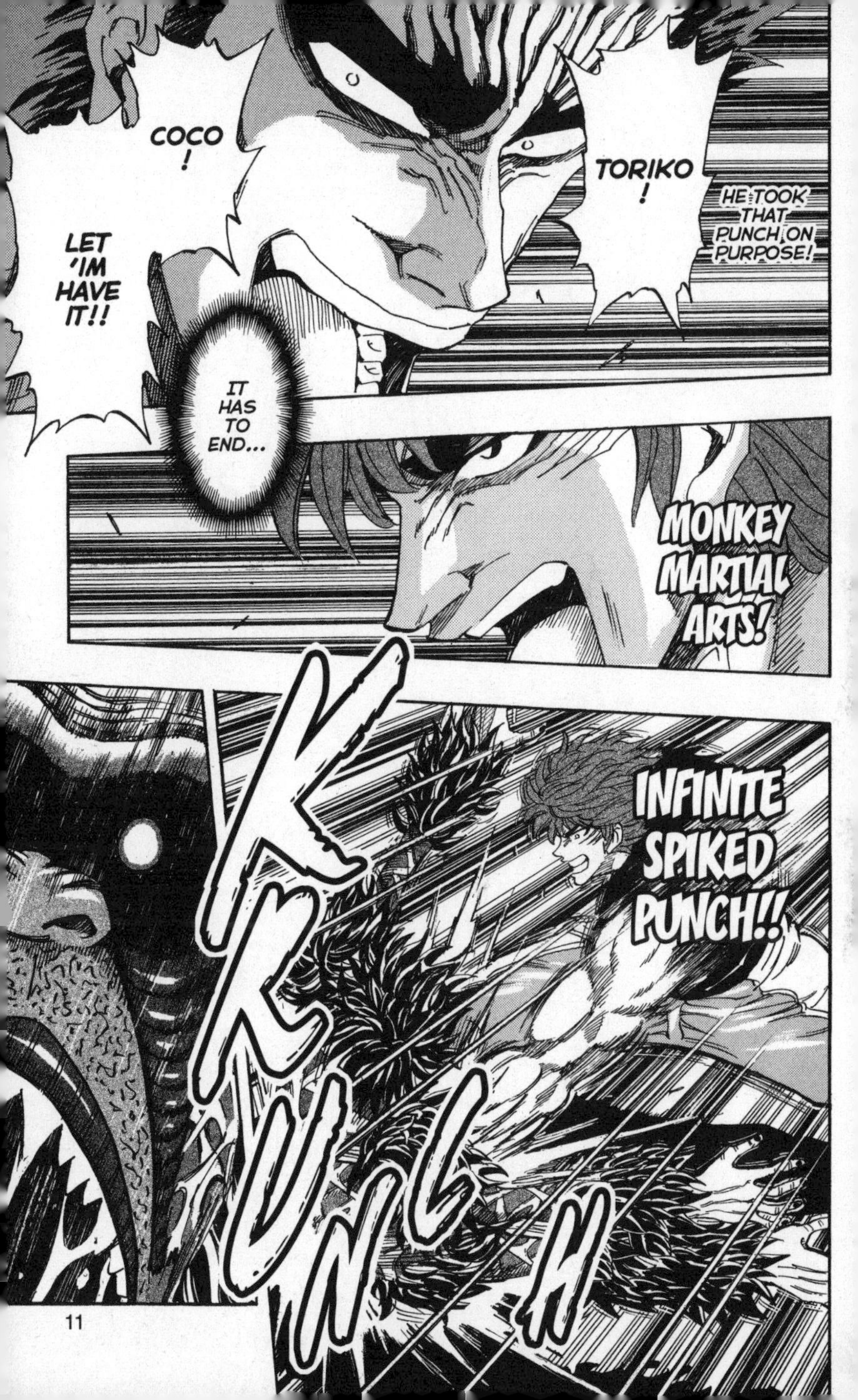
TORIKO!
HE TOOK THAT PUNCH ON PURPOSE!
COCO!
LET 'IM HAVE IT!!
IT HAS TO END...
MONKEY MARTIAL ARTS!
INFINITE SPIKED PUNCH!!

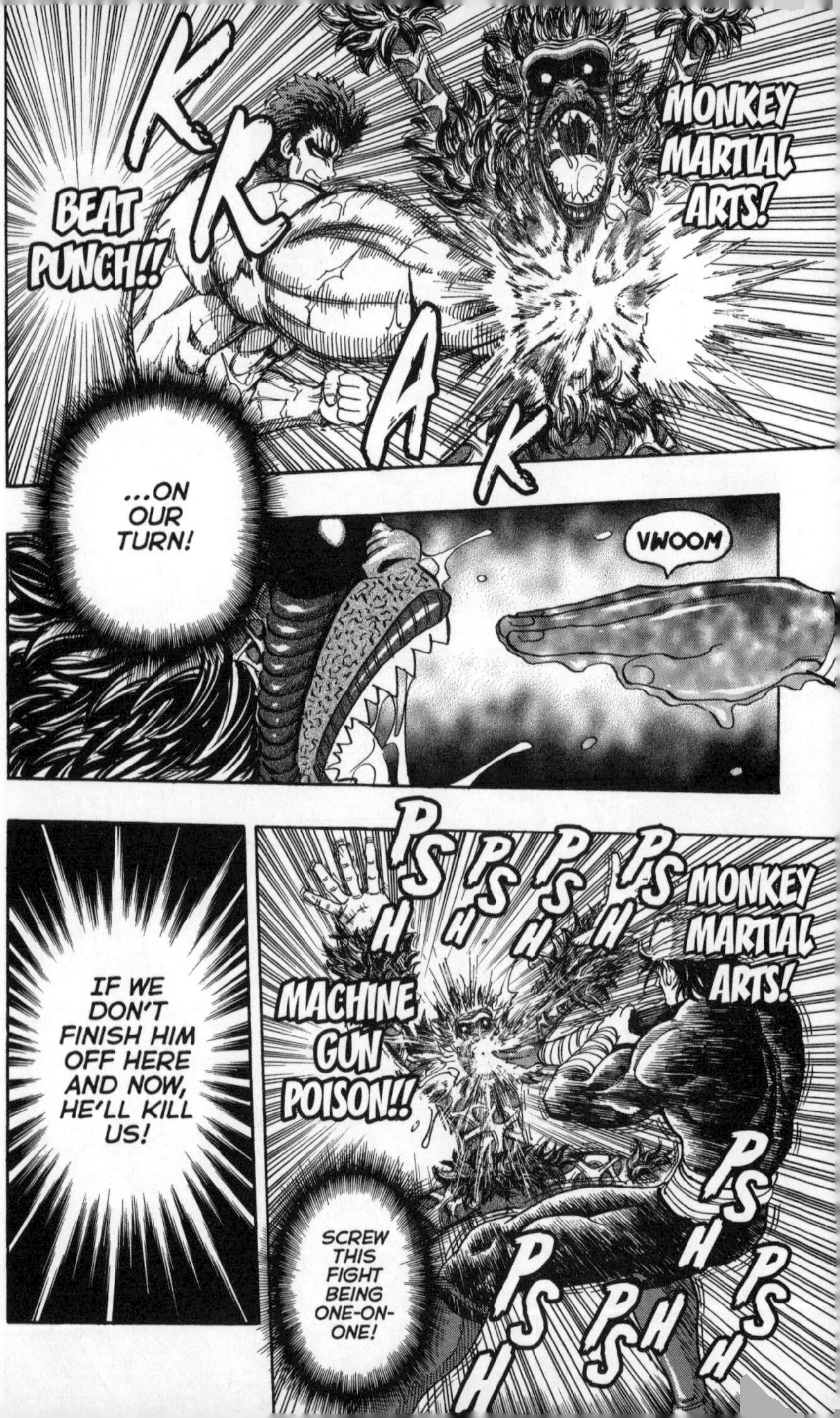
MONKEY MARTIAL ARTS!
BEAT PUNCH!!
KAK
...ON OUR TURN!
VWOOM
PSH PSH PSH PSH
MONKEY MARTIAL ARTS!
MACHINE GUN POISON!!
SCREW THIS FIGHT BEING ONE-ON-ONE!
PSH PSH PSH PSH
IF WE DON'T FINISH HIM OFF HERE AND NOW, HE'LL KILL US!

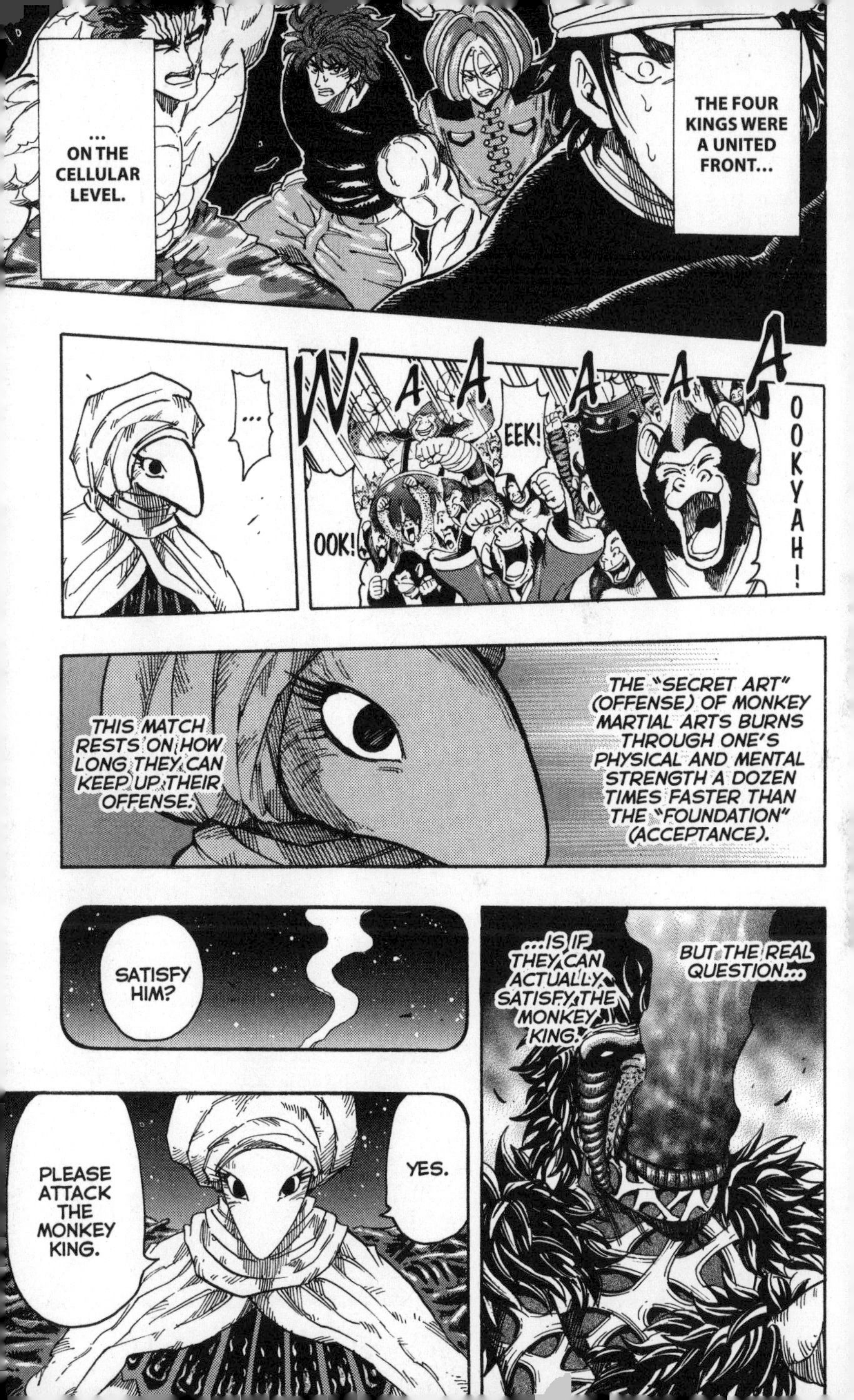
THE FOUR KINGS WERE A UNITED FRONT...
... ON THE CELLULAR LEVEL.
WAAAAAA
OOKYAH!
EEK!
OOK!
...
THE "SECRET ART" (OFFENSE) OF MONKEY MARTIAL ARTS BURNS THROUGH ONE'S PHYSICAL AND MENTAL STRENGTH A DOZEN TIMES FASTER THAN THE "FOUNDATION" (ACCEPTANCE).
THIS MATCH RESTS ON HOW LONG THEY CAN KEEP UP THEIR OFFENSE.
BUT THE REAL QUESTION...
...IS IF THEY CAN ACTUALLY SATISFY THE MONKEY KING.
SATISFY HIM?
YES.
PLEASE ATTACK THE MONKEY KING.

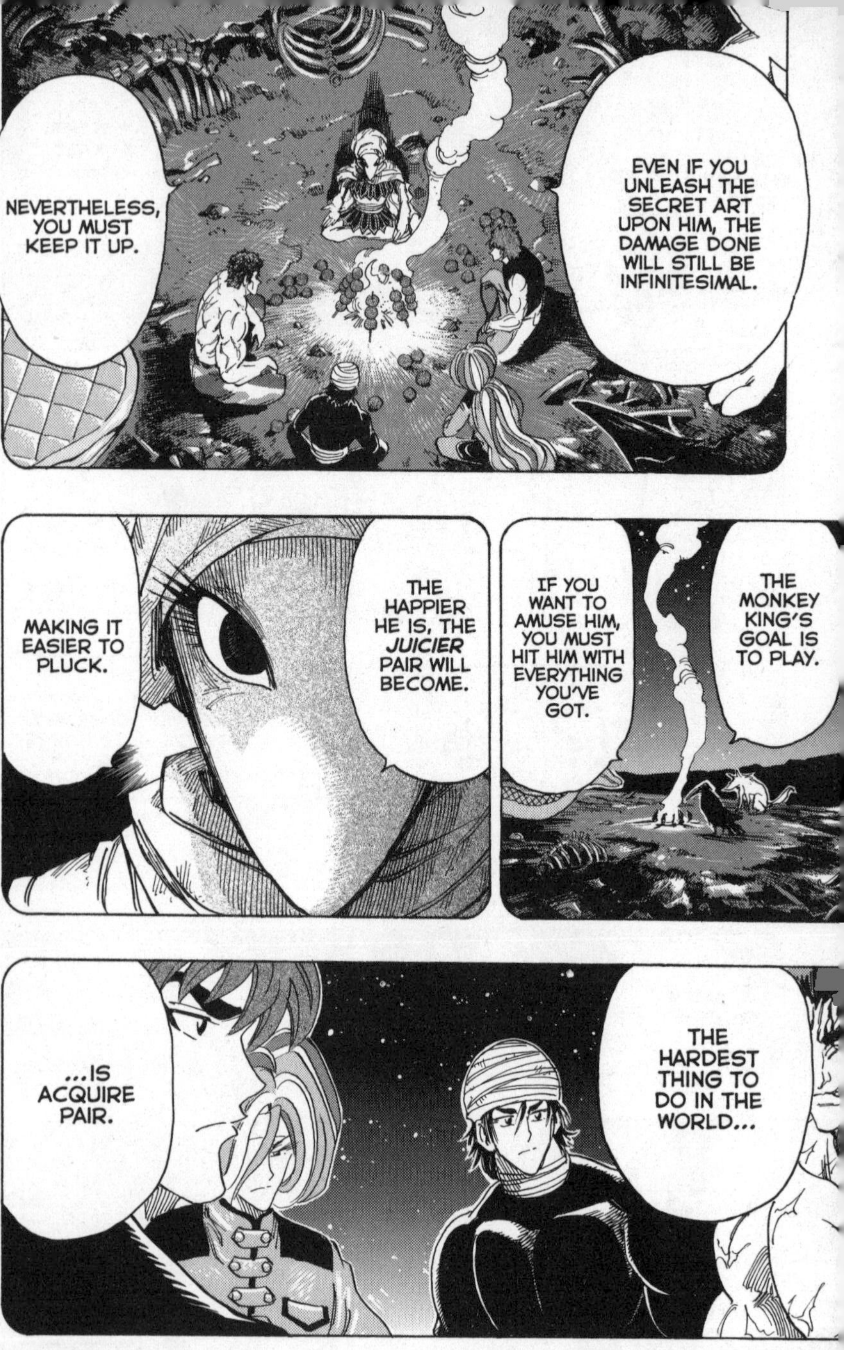
EVEN IF YOU UNLEASH THE SECRET ART UPON HIM, THE DAMAGE DONE WILL STILL BE INFINITESIMAL.
NEVERTHELESS, YOU MUST KEEP IT UP.
THE MONKEY KING'S GOAL IS TO PLAY.
IF YOU WANT TO AMUSE HIM, YOU MUST HIT HIM WITH EVERYTHING YOU'VE GOT.
THE HAPPIER HE IS, THE *JUICIER* PAIR WILL BECOME.
MAKING IT EASIER TO PLUCK.
THE HARDEST THING TO DO IN THE WORLD...
...IS ACQUIRE PAIR.

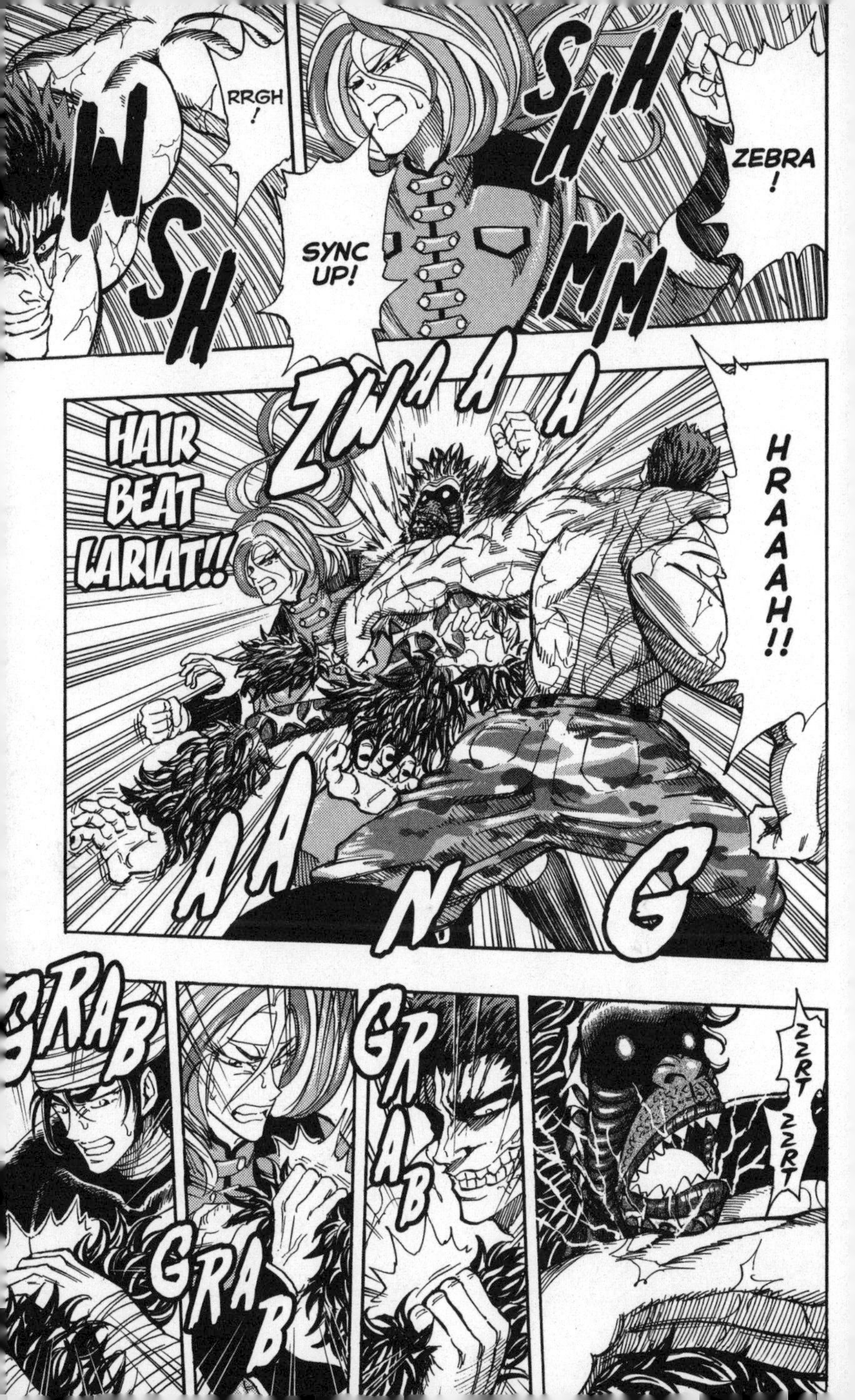
SHHMM
ZEBRA!
SYNC UP!
RRGH!
WSHSH
HRAAAAH!!
ZWAAAAAANG
HAIR BEAT LARIAT!!
ZZRT ZZRT
GRGRAB
GRAB
GRAB

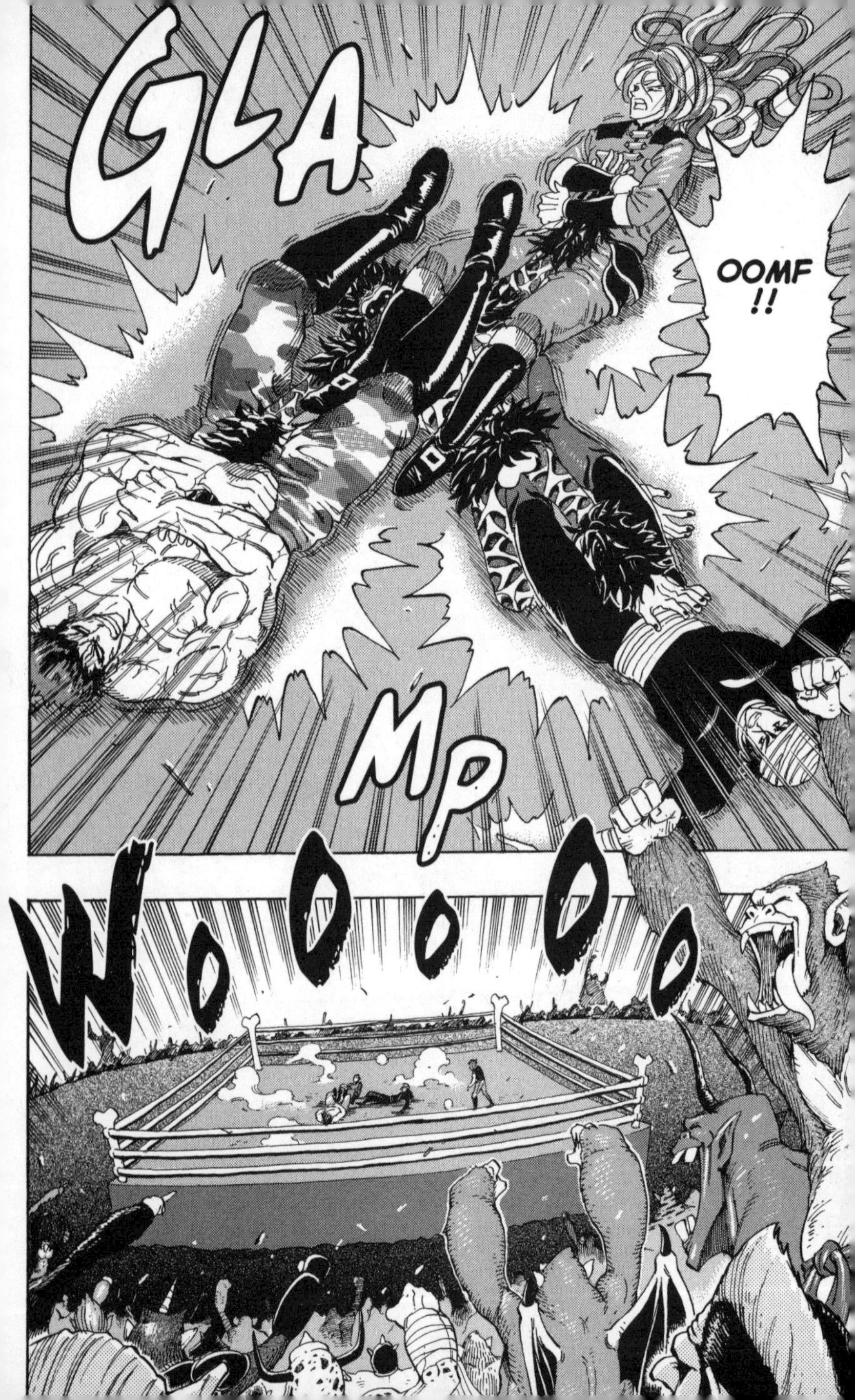
GLAMp
OOMF !!
WoOoOo

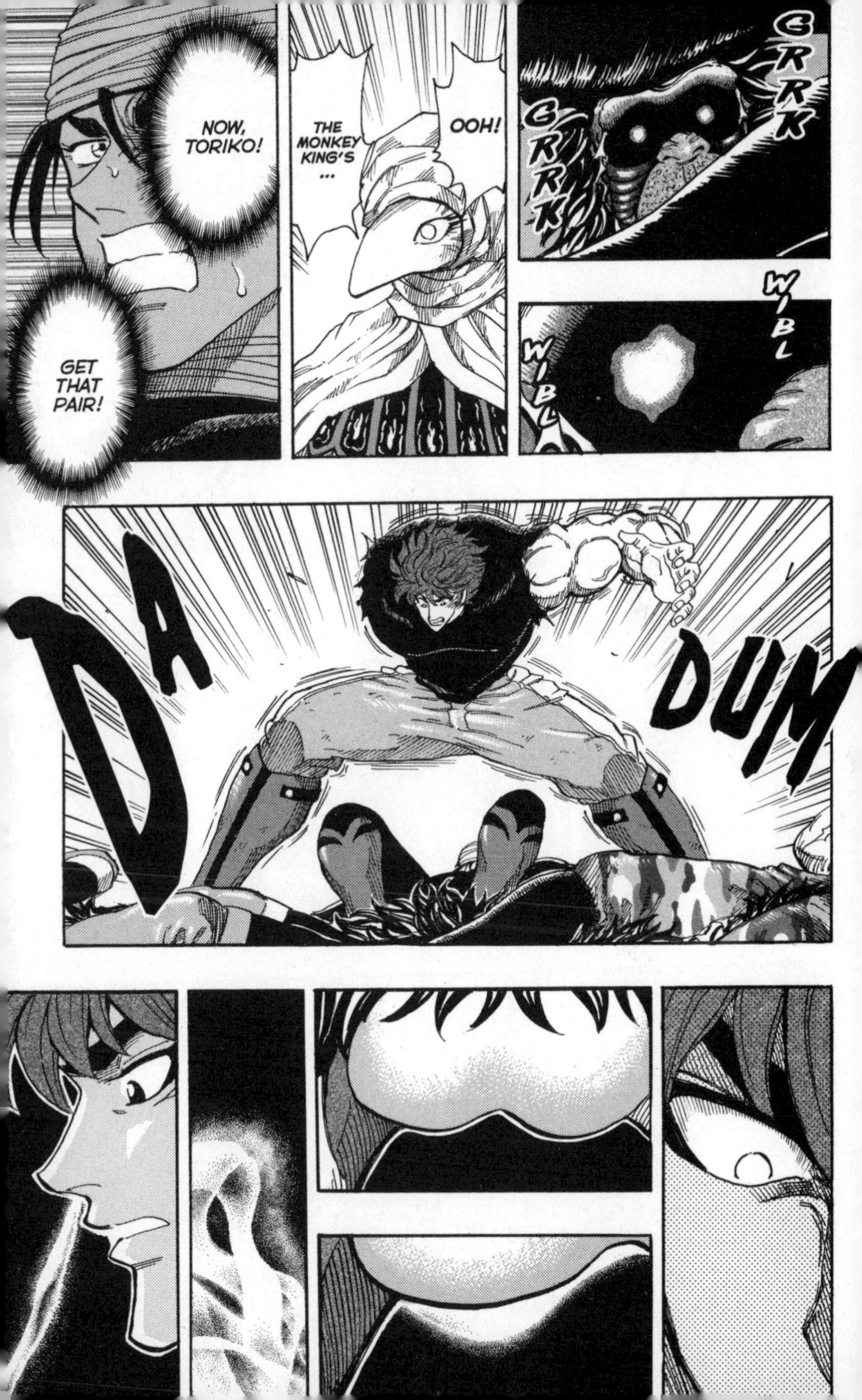
GRRK
GRRK
WIBL
WIBL
OOH!
THE MONKEY KING'S...
NOW, TORIKO!
GET THAT PAIR!
DA
DUM

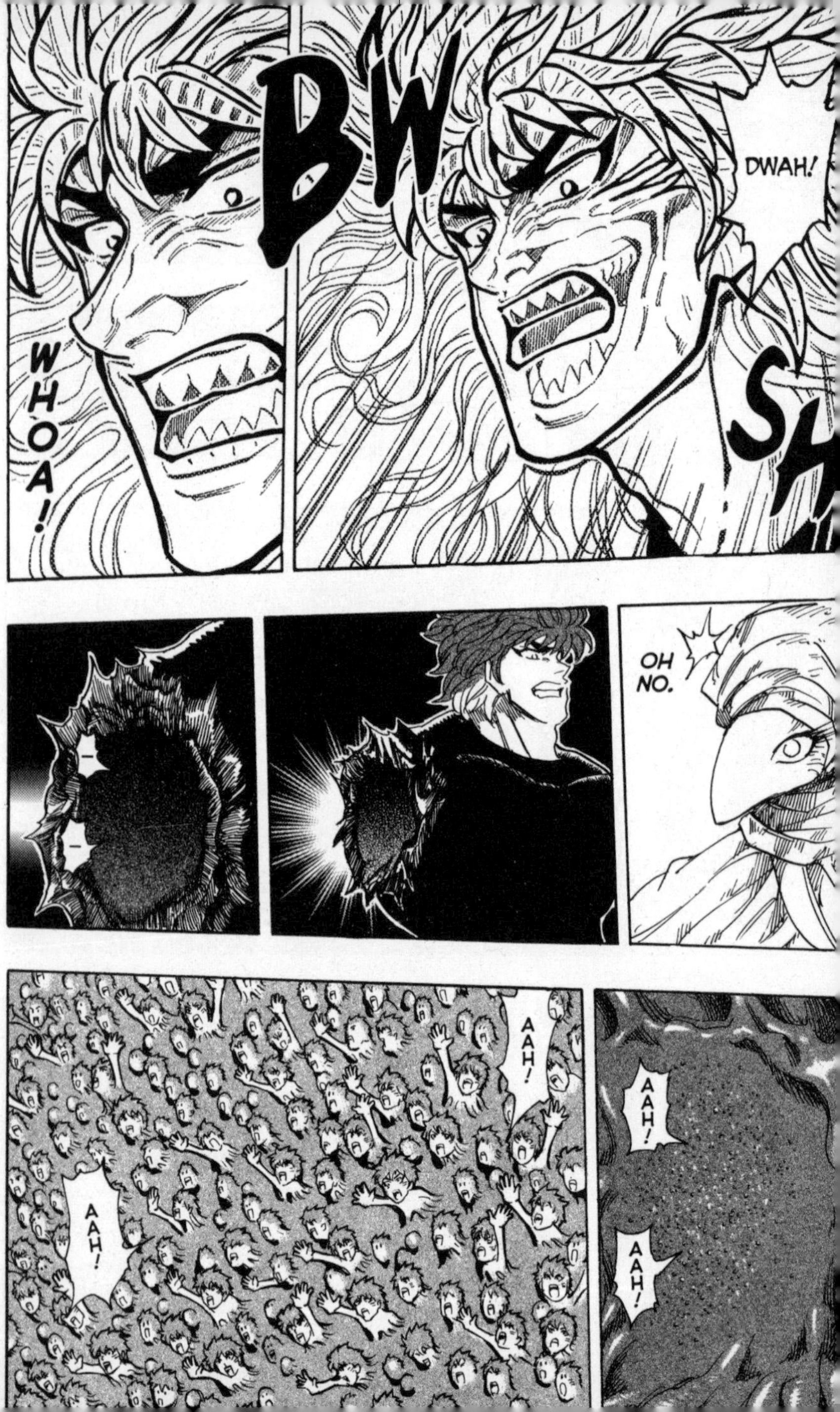
DWAH!
SH
BW
WHOA!
OH NO.
AAH!
AAH!
AAH!
AAH!

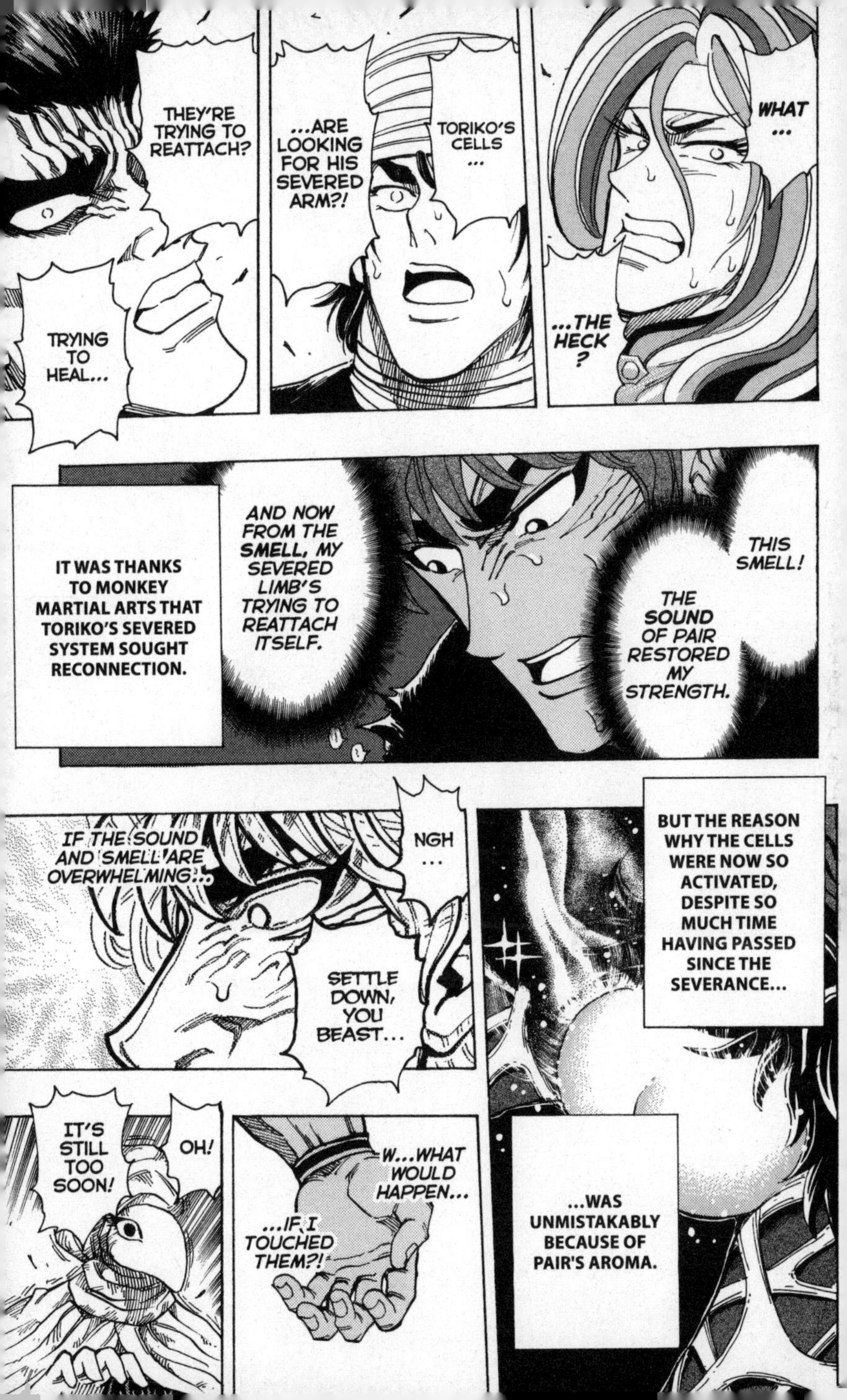
WHAT ...
...THE HECK ?
TORIKO'S CELLS ...
...ARE LOOKING FOR HIS SEVERED ARM?!
THEY'RE TRYING TO REATTACH?
TRYING TO HEAL...
THIS SMELL!
THE SOUND OF PAIR RESTORED MY STRENGTH.
AND NOW FROM THE SMELL, MY SEVERED LIMB'S TRYING TO REATTACH ITSELF.
IT WAS THANKS TO MONKEY MARTIAL ARTS THAT TORIKO'S SEVERED SYSTEM SOUGHT RECONNECTION.
BUT THE REASON WHY THE CELLS WERE NOW SO ACTIVATED, DESPITE SO MUCH TIME HAVING PASSED SINCE THE SEVERANCE...
...WAS UNMISTAKABLY BECAUSE OF PAIR'S AROMA.
NGH ...
IF THE SOUND AND SMELL ARE OVERWHELMING...
SETTLE DOWN, YOU BEAST...
W...WHAT WOULD HAPPEN...
...IF I TOUCHED THEM?!
OH!
IT'S STILL TOO SOON!

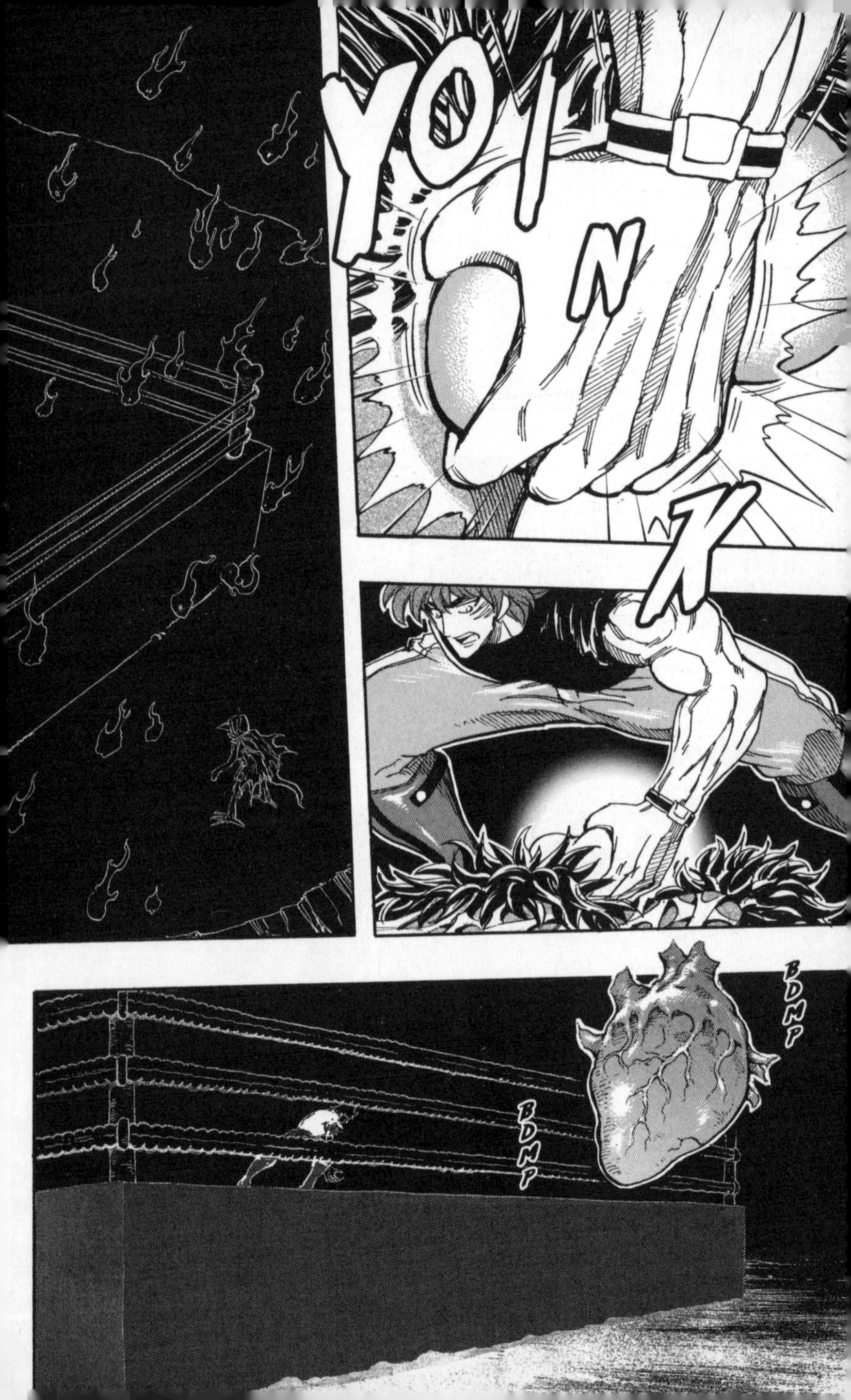
YOINK
BDMP
BDMP

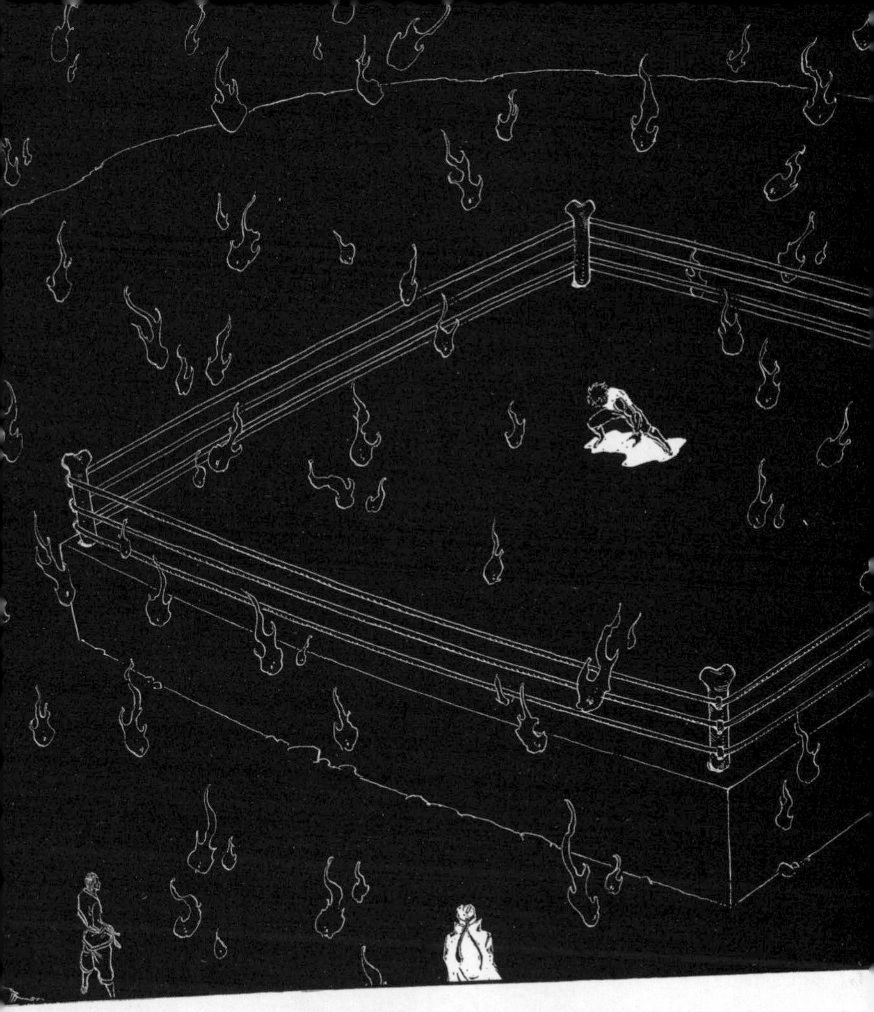

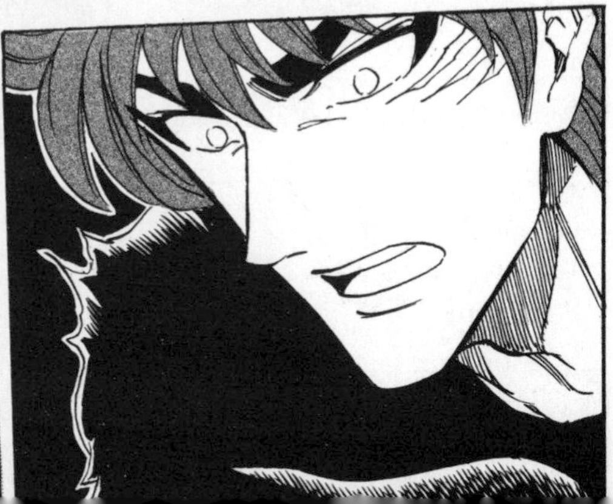

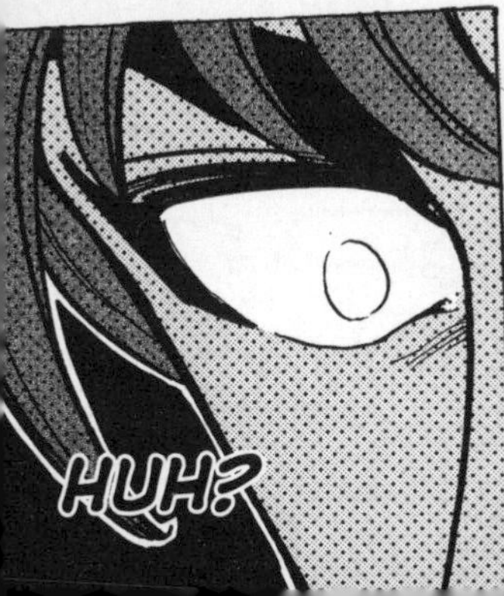
HUH?

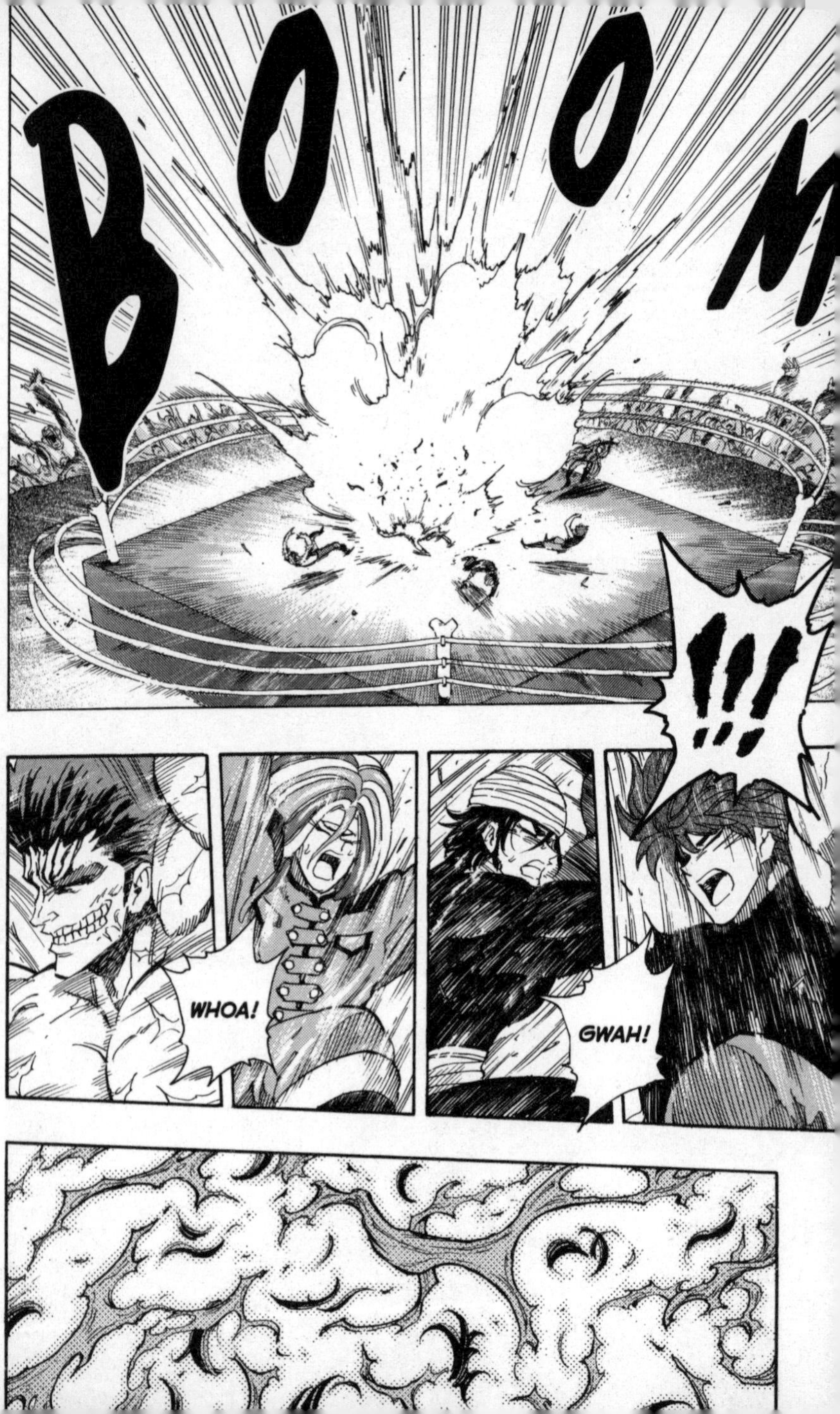
BOOM
!!!
GWAH!
WHOA!

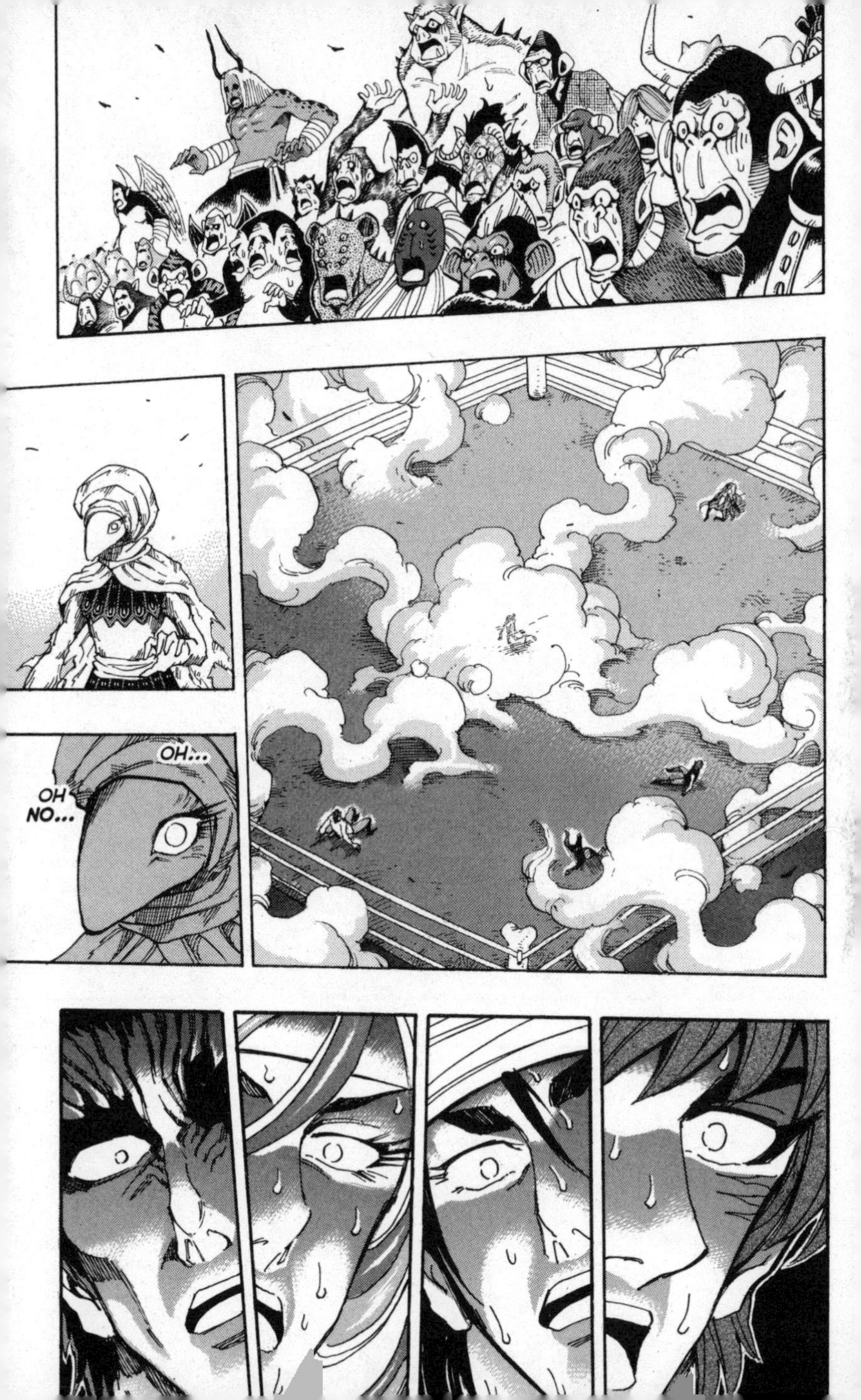
OH...
OH NO...

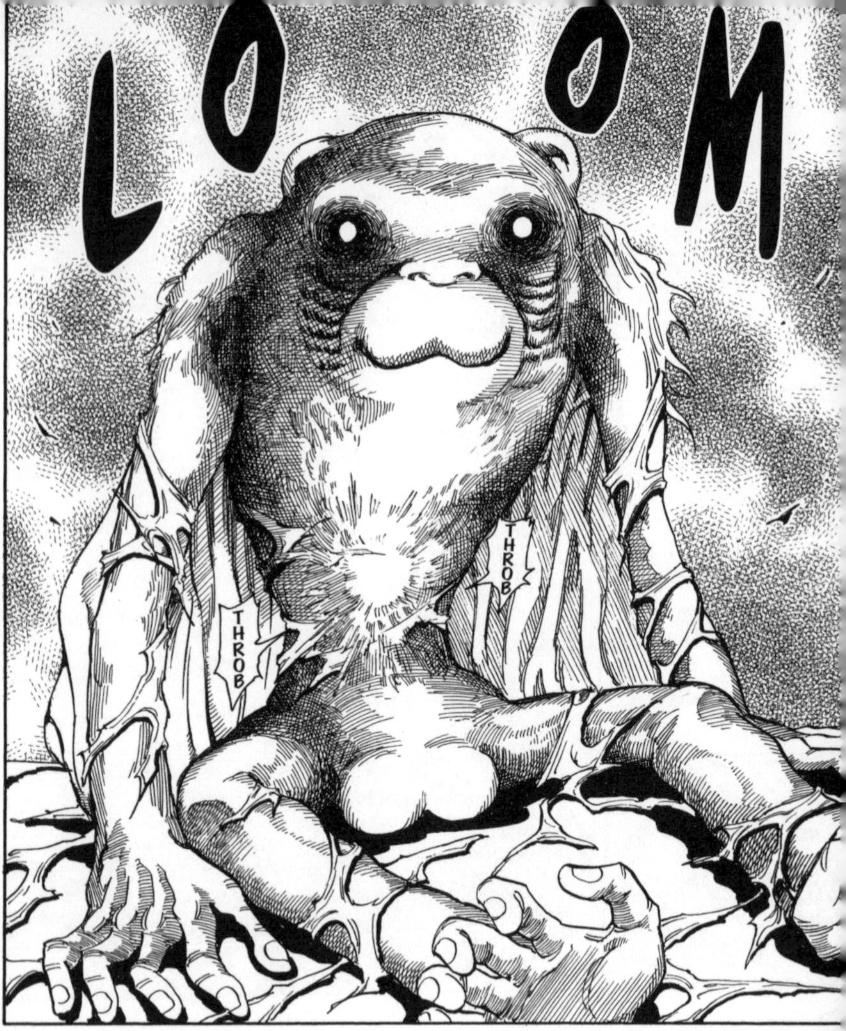
LOOM
THROB
THROB

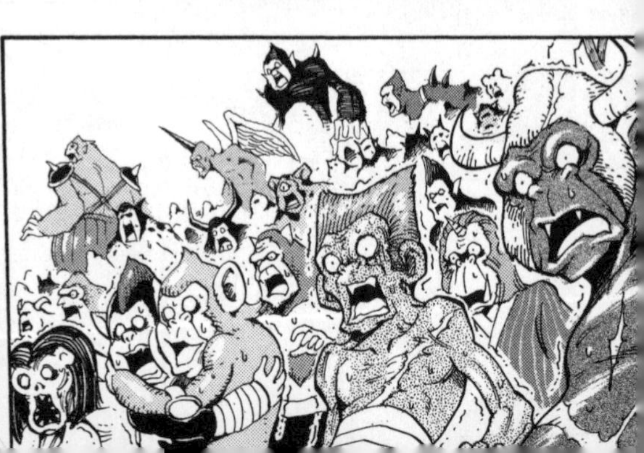

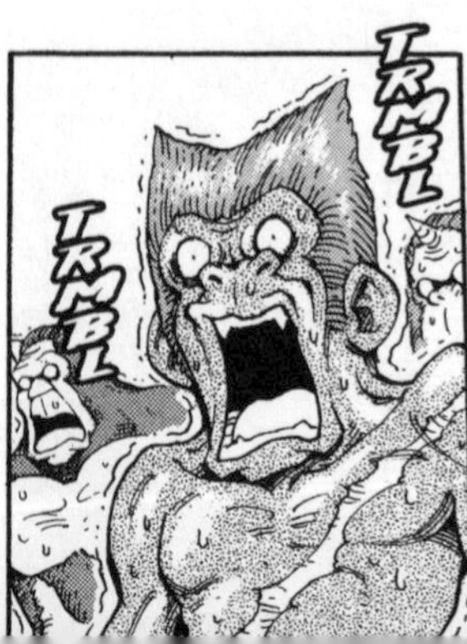
TRMBL
TRMBL

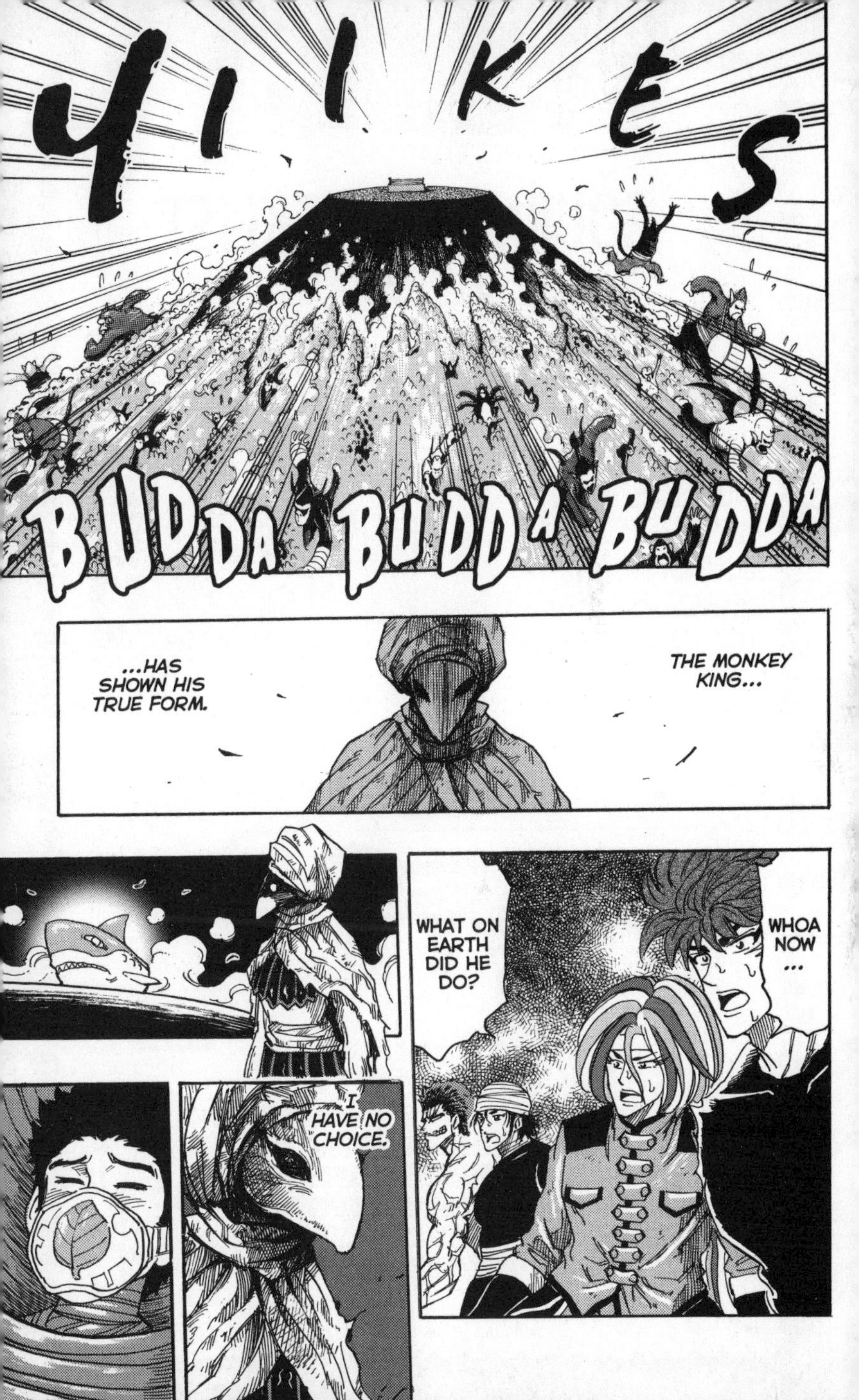
YIIKES
BUDDA BUDDA BUDDA
THE MONKEY KING...
...HAS SHOWN HIS TRUE FORM.
WHOA NOW ...
WHAT ON EARTH DID HE DO?
I HAVE NO CHOICE.

TORIKO

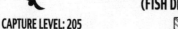

GOURMET CHECKLIST

Vol. 337

SALMON WYVERN
(FISH DRAGON)

CAPTURE LEVEL: 205

HABITAT: SLOW RAIN HILL

SIZE: 16 M

HEIGHT: ---

WEIGHT: 12 TONS

PRICE: 120,000 YEN PER 100 G

SCALE

A FLYING DRAGON WITH WINGS AKIN TO SLICED SALMON. THEY MOVE IN PACKS OF SEVERAL HUNDRED AND CAN BE SEEN SWIMMING OR FLYING IN A BEAUTIFUL FLOWING MOTION. EACH INDIVIDUAL SPECIMEN'S CAPTURE LEVEL IS NOT ALL THAT HIGH FOR THE GOURMET WORLD, BUT WHEN CONFRONTING AN ENEMY, THEY EXCEL AT FORMING GROUPS AND ATTACKING IN DROVES. THEY ARE NOT AS STRONG AS OTHER CREATURES IN THE GOURMET WORLD, BUT THEY ARE FRIGHTENINGLY INTELLIGENT.

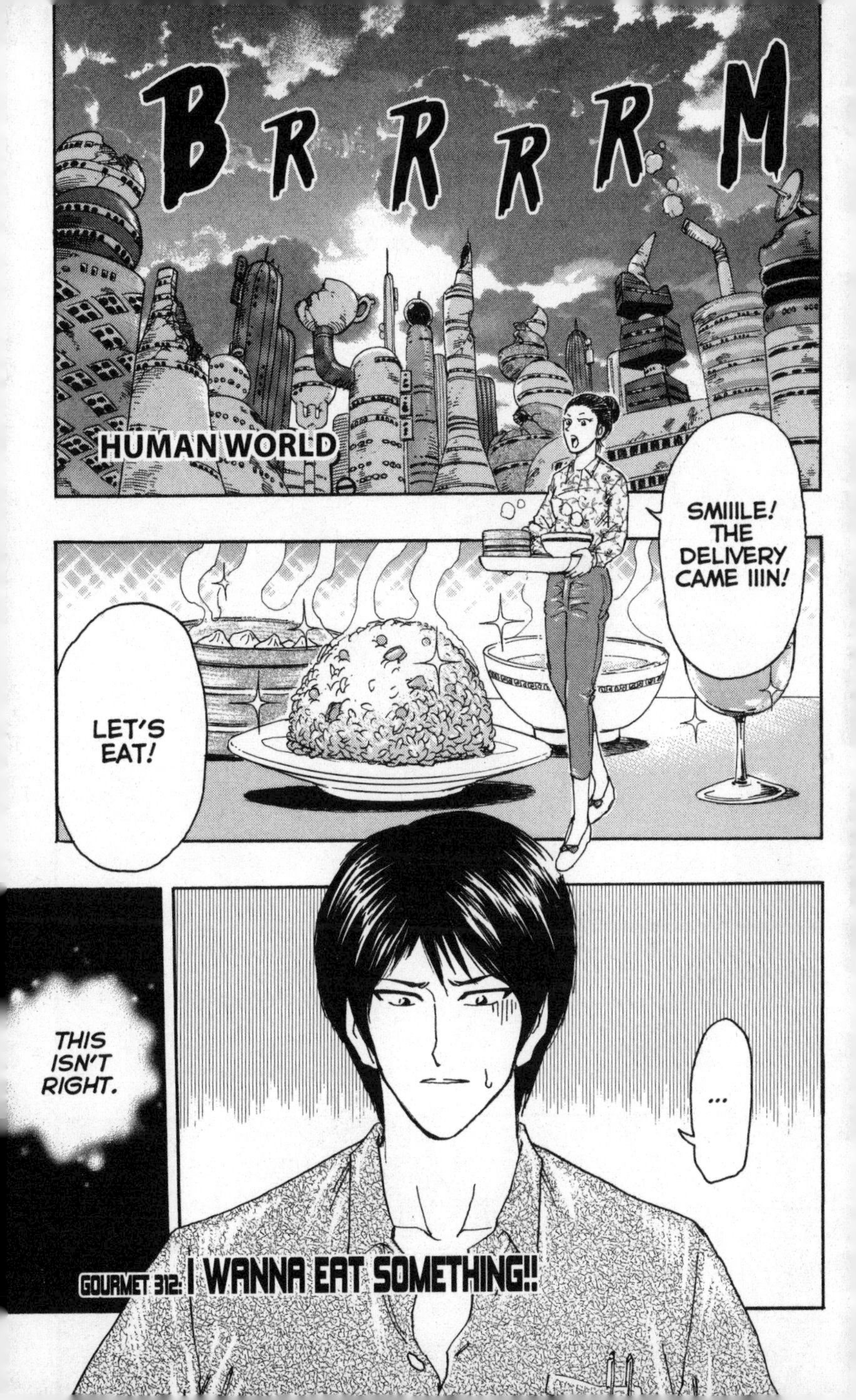
BRRRRM
HUMAN WORLD
SMIIILE! THE DELIVERY CAME IIIN!
LET'S EAT!
...
THIS ISN'T RIGHT.
GOURMET 312: I WANNA EAT SOMETHING!!

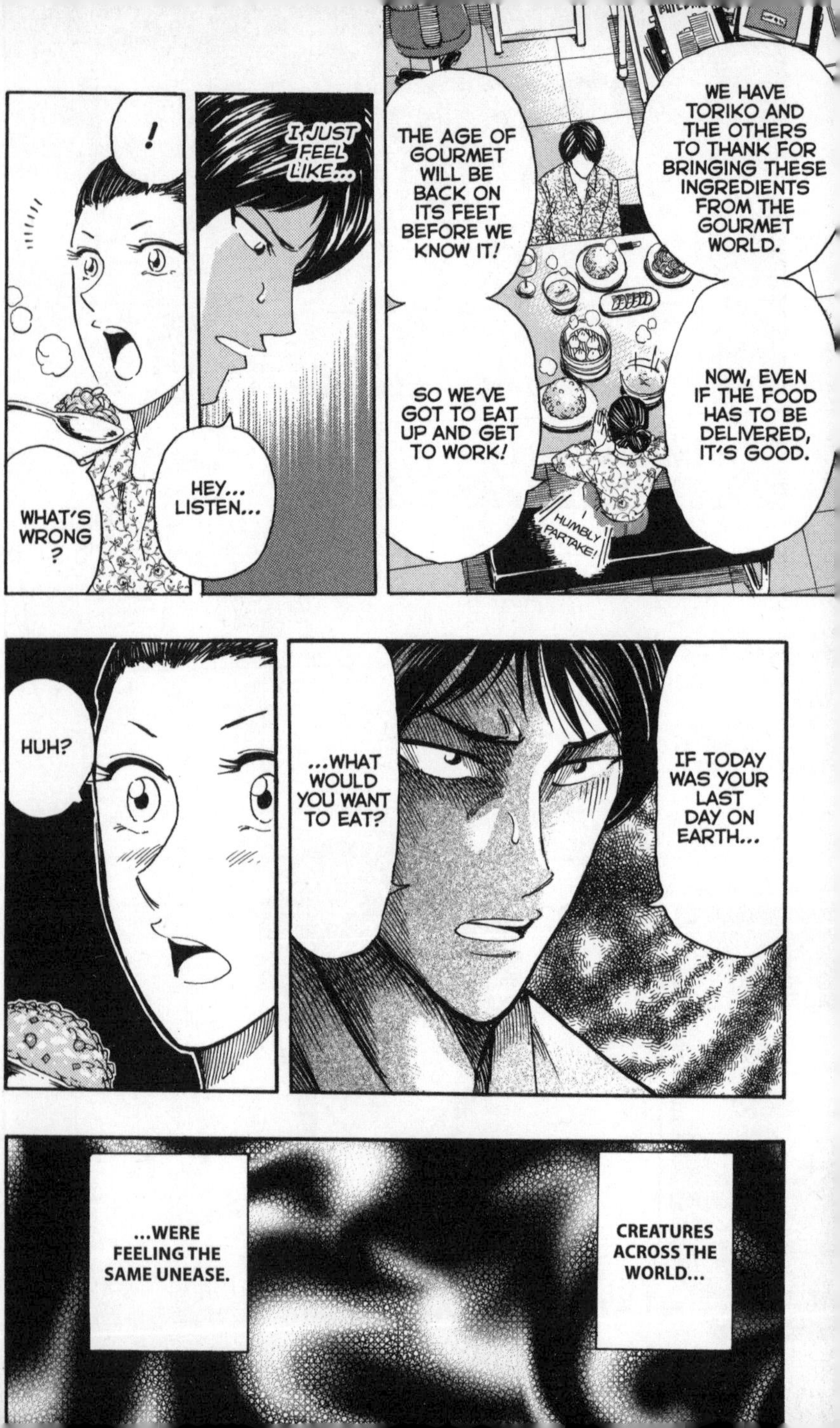
WE HAVE TORIKO AND THE OTHERS TO THANK FOR BRINGING THESE INGREDIENTS FROM THE GOURMET WORLD.
NOW, EVEN IF THE FOOD HAS TO BE DELIVERED, IT'S GOOD.
THE AGE OF GOURMET WILL BE BACK ON ITS FEET BEFORE WE KNOW IT!
SO WE'VE GOT TO EAT UP AND GET TO WORK!
I HUMBLY PARTAKE!
I JUST FEEL LIKE...
HEY... LISTEN...
!
WHAT'S WRONG?
IF TODAY WAS YOUR LAST DAY ON EARTH...
...WHAT WOULD YOU WANT TO EAT?
HUH?
CREATURES ACROSS THE WORLD...
...WERE FEELING THE SAME UNEASE.

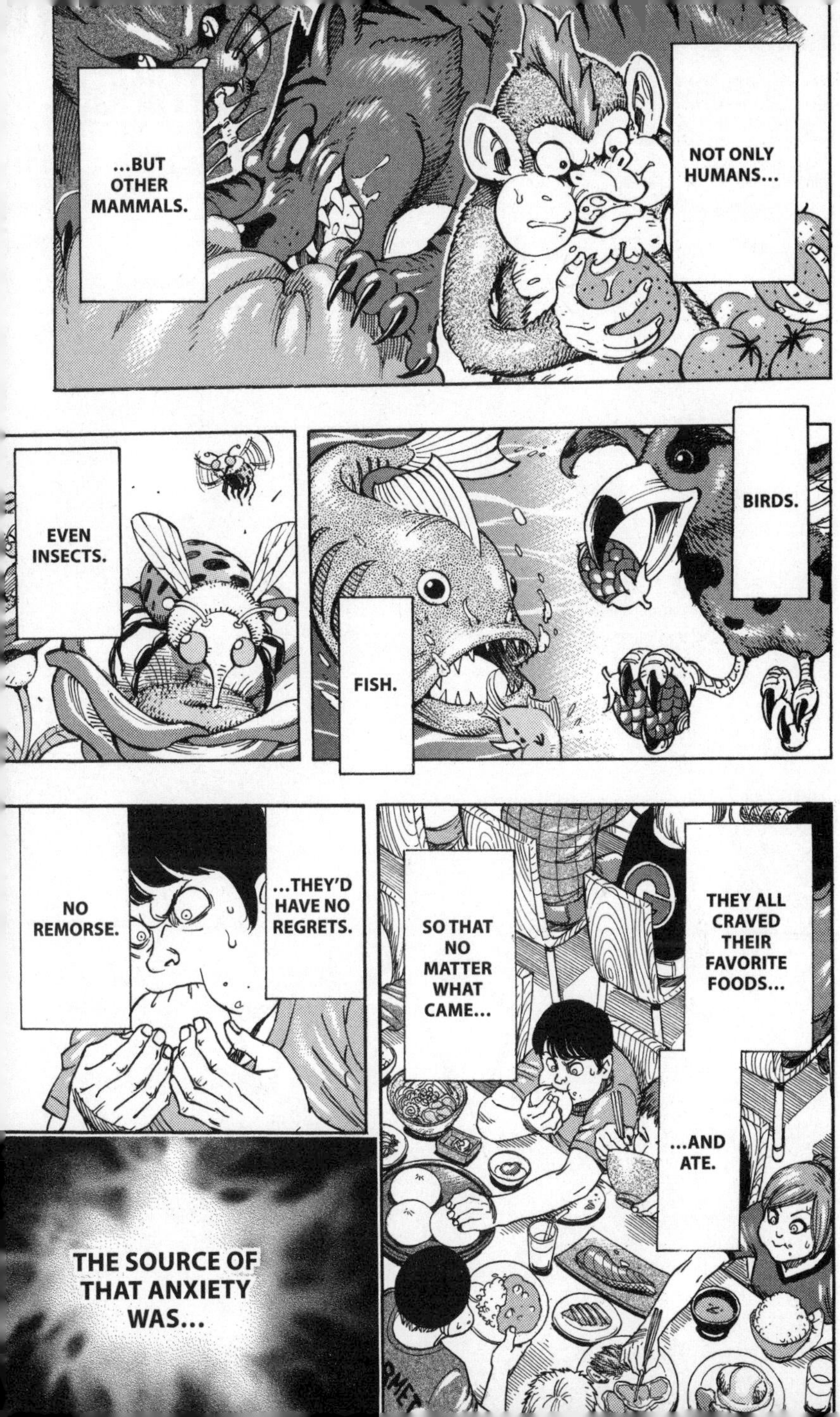
NOT ONLY HUMANS...
...BUT OTHER MAMMALS.
BIRDS.
FISH.
EVEN INSECTS.
THEY ALL CRAVED THEIR FAVORITE FOODS...
...AND ATE.
SO THAT NO MATTER WHAT CAME...
...THEY'D HAVE NO REGRETS.
NO REMORSE.
THE SOURCE OF THAT ANXIETY WAS...

GOURMET 312: I WANNA EAT SOMETHING!!

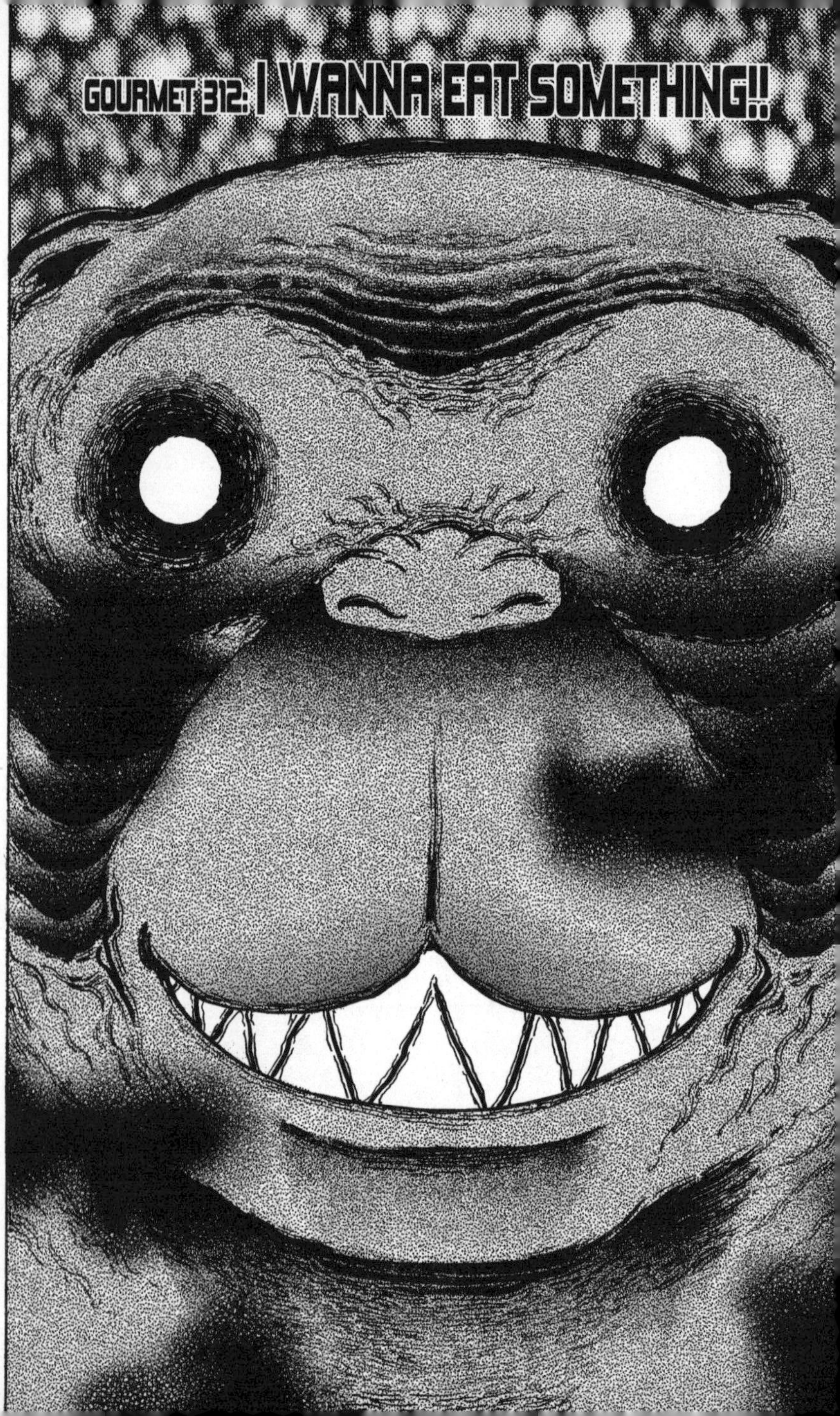

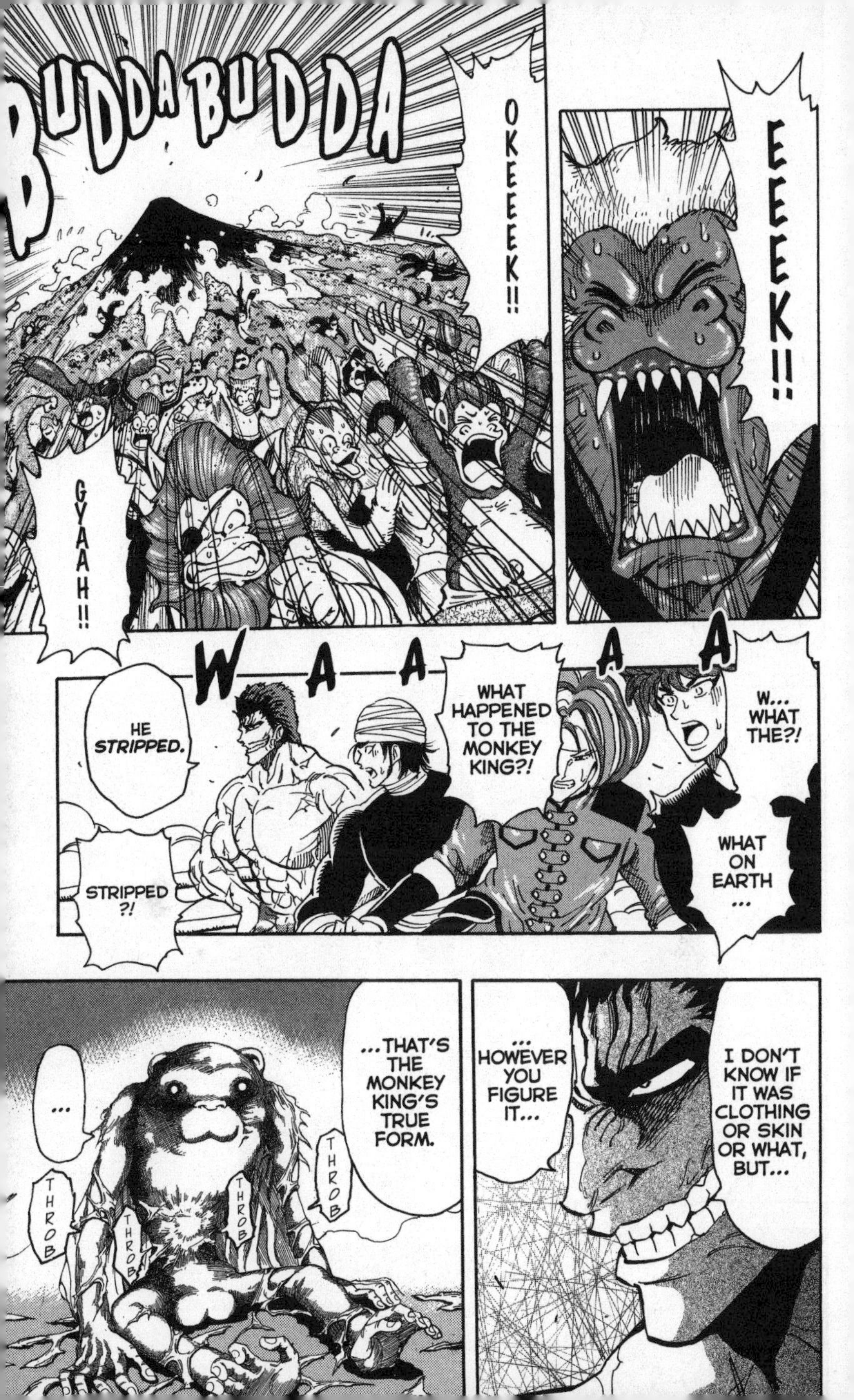
EEEEK!!
OKEEEEK!!
BUDDA BUDDA
GYAAH!!
WAAAA
W... WHAT THE?!
WHAT ON EARTH...
WHAT HAPPENED TO THE MONKEY KING?!
HE STRIPPED.
STRIPPED?!
I DON'T KNOW IF IT WAS CLOTHING OR SKIN OR WHAT, BUT...
...HOWEVER YOU FIGURE IT...
...THAT'S THE MONKEY KING'S TRUE FORM.
THROB
THROB
THROB
THROB
...

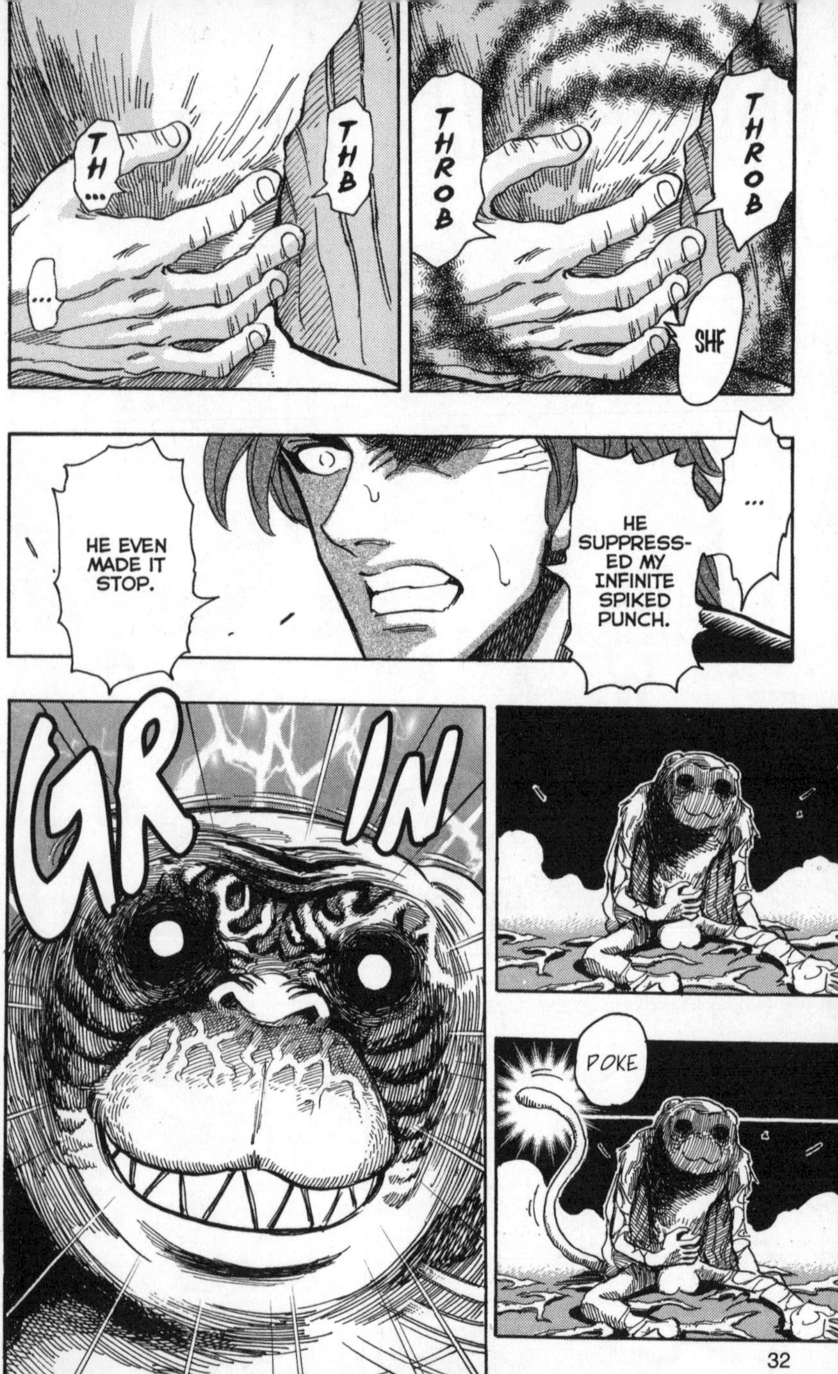
THROB
THROB
SHF
THB
TH...
....
...
HE SUPPRESS-ED MY INFINITE SPIKED PUNCH.
HE EVEN MADE IT STOP.
POKE
GR IN

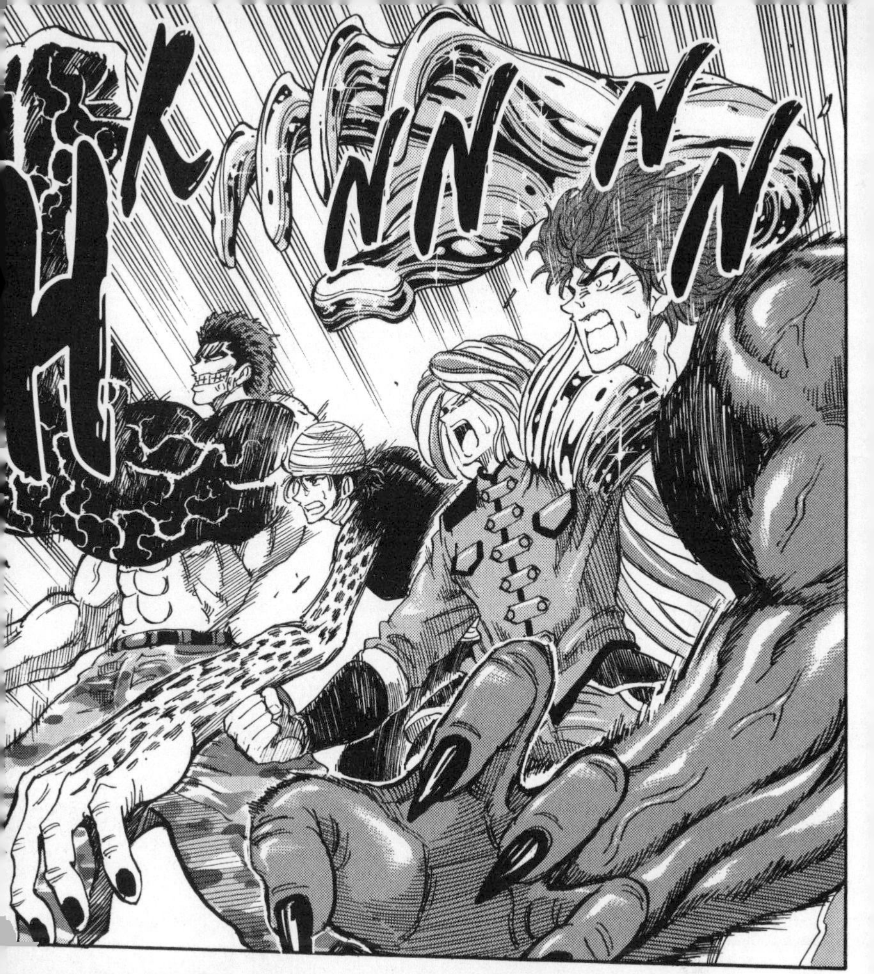

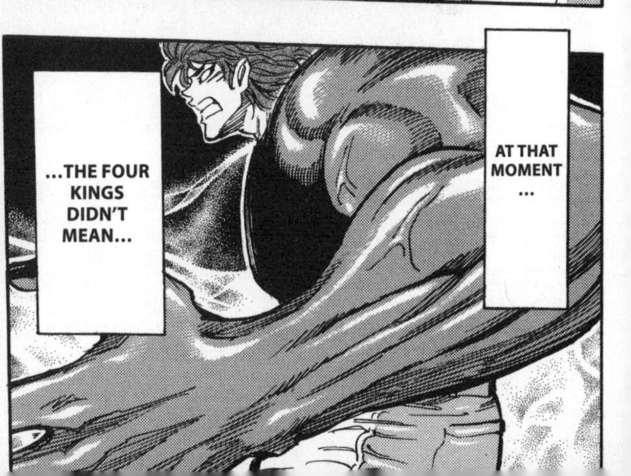
AT THAT MOMENT ...
...THE FOUR KINGS DIDN'T MEAN...

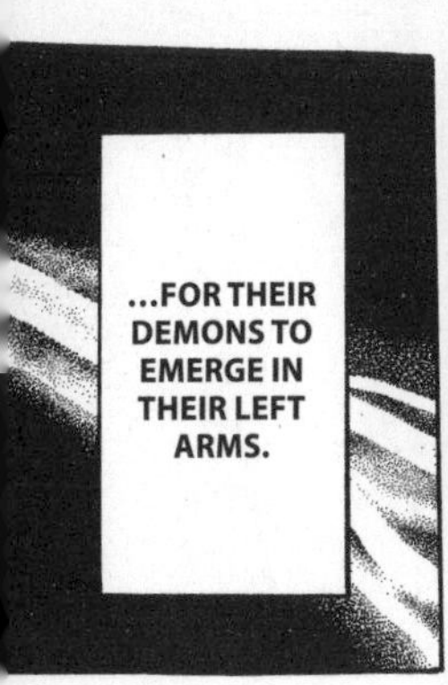
...FOR THEIR DEMONS TO EMERGE IN THEIR LEFT ARMS.

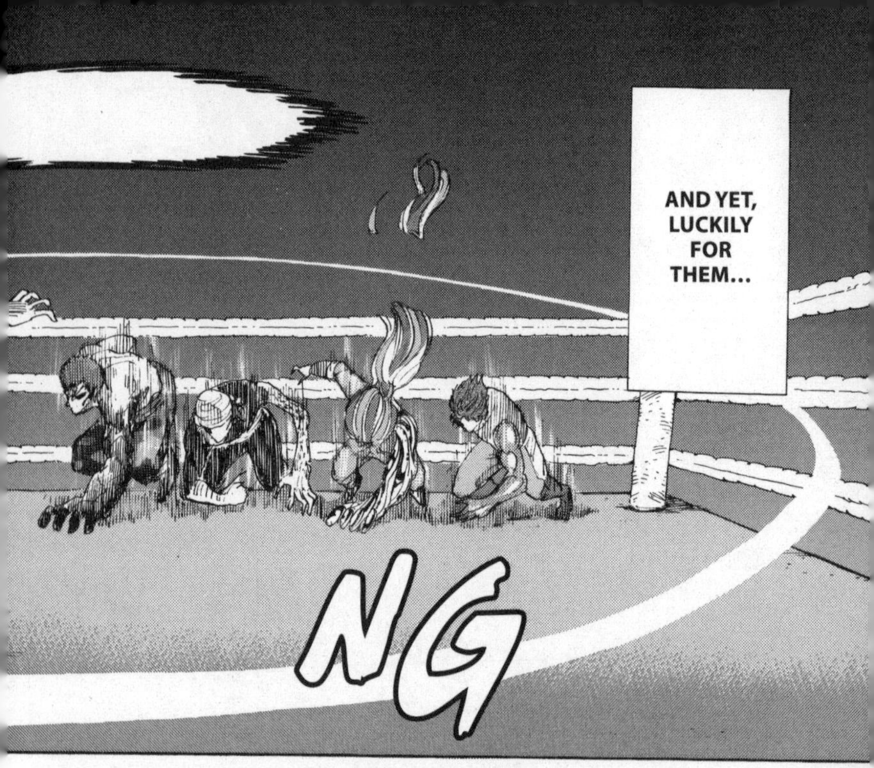
AND YET, LUCKILY FOR THEM...
NG

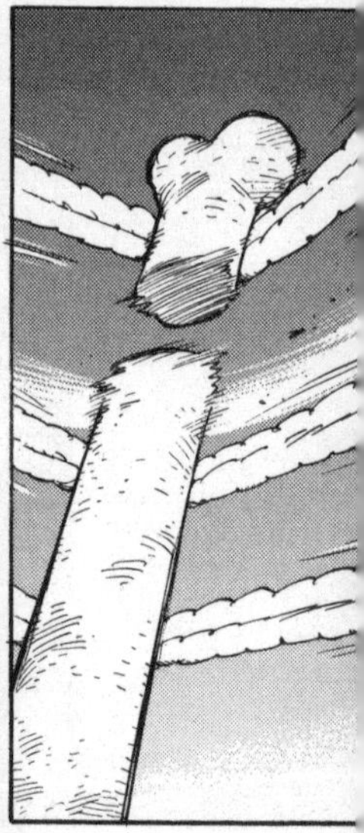

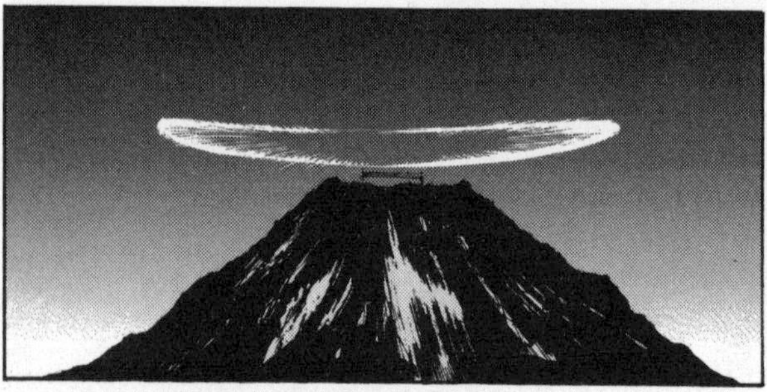

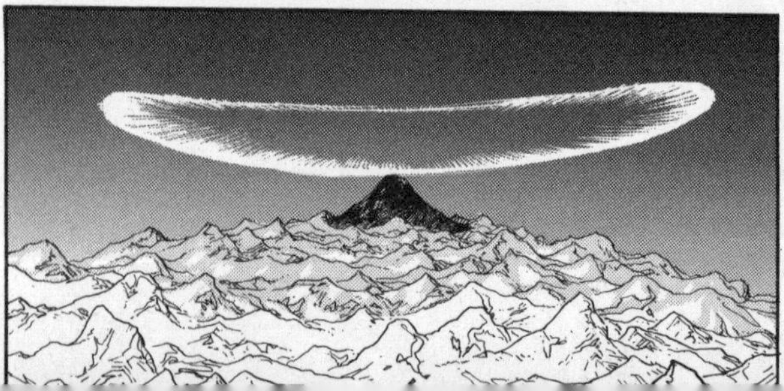

...THAT WAS WHAT PROTECTED THEM FROM THE MONKEY KING'S FIRST ATTACK.

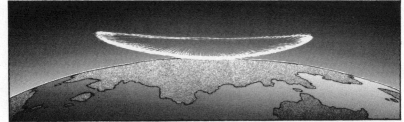

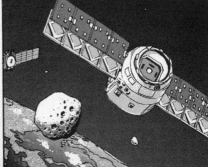

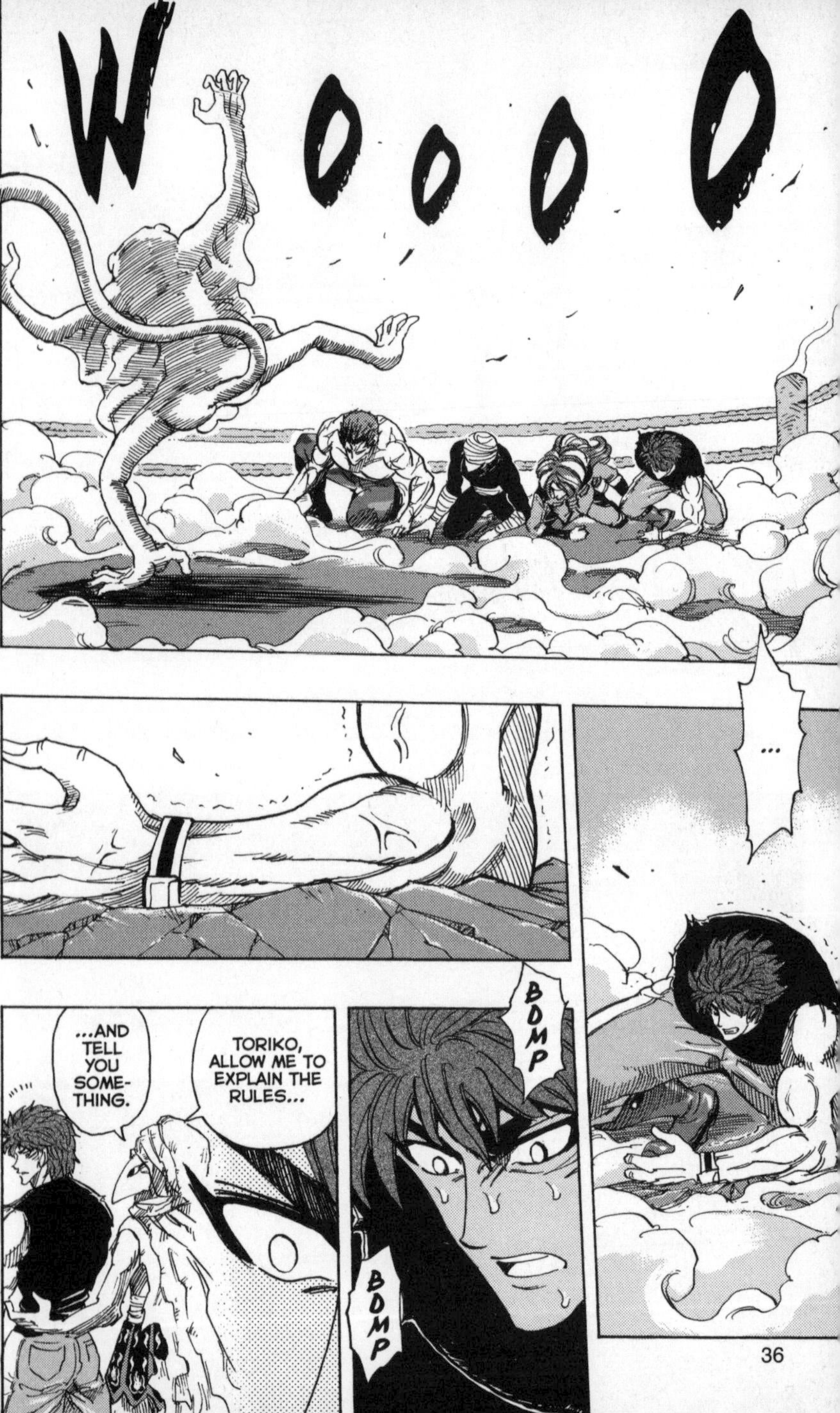
WOOOO
...
BDOMP
BDOMP
TORIKO, ALLOW ME TO EXPLAIN THE RULES...
...AND TELL YOU SOME-THING.

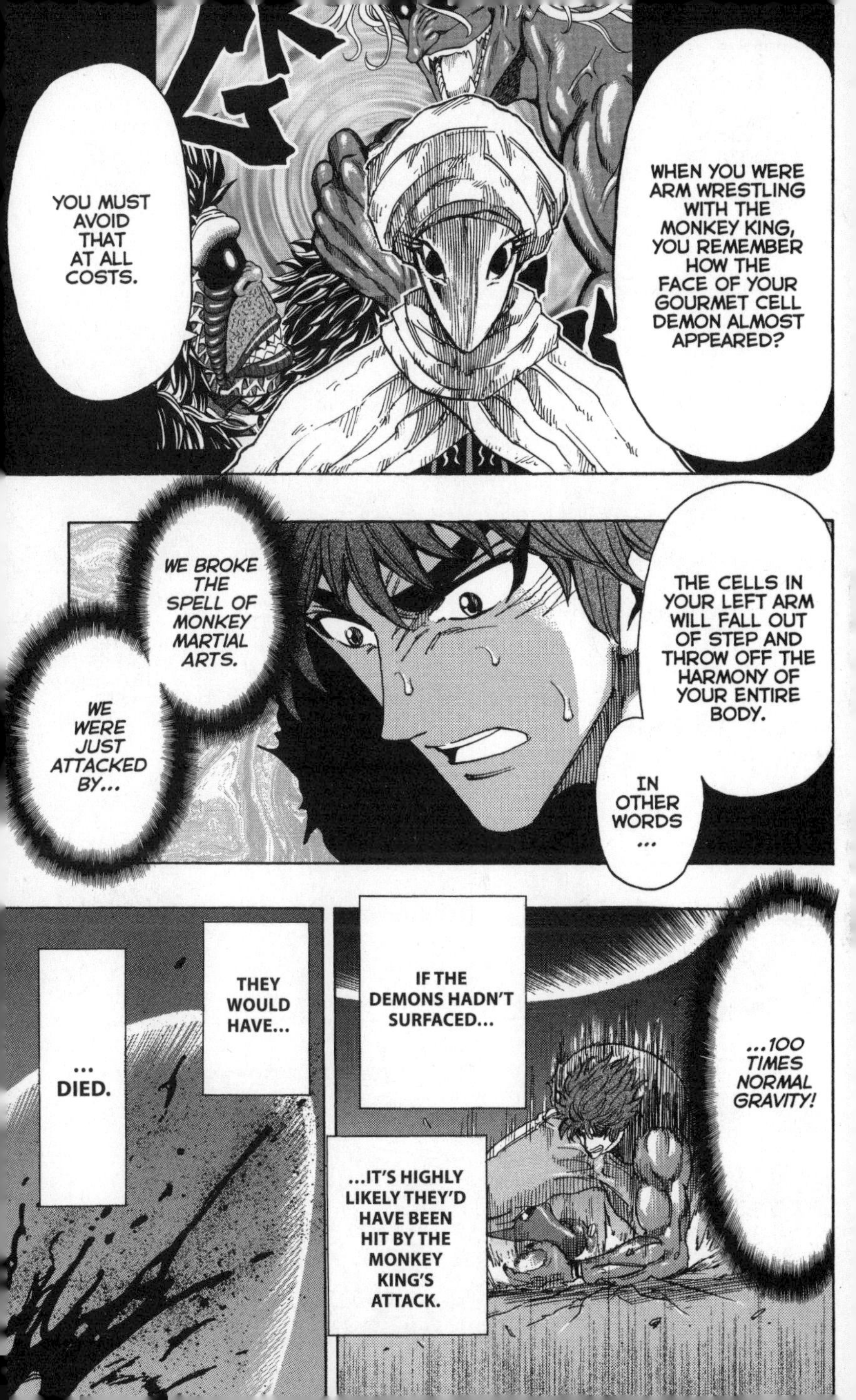
WHEN YOU WERE ARM WRESTLING WITH THE MONKEY KING, YOU REMEMBER HOW THE FACE OF YOUR GOURMET CELL DEMON ALMOST APPEARED?
YOU MUST AVOID THAT AT ALL COSTS.
THE CELLS IN YOUR LEFT ARM WILL FALL OUT OF STEP AND THROW OFF THE HARMONY OF YOUR ENTIRE BODY.
IN OTHER WORDS...
WE BROKE THE SPELL OF MONKEY MARTIAL ARTS.
WE WERE JUST ATTACKED BY...
...100 TIMES NORMAL GRAVITY!
IF THE DEMONS HADN'T SURFACED...
...IT'S HIGHLY LIKELY THEY'D HAVE BEEN HIT BY THE MONKEY KING'S ATTACK.
THEY WOULD HAVE...
... DIED.

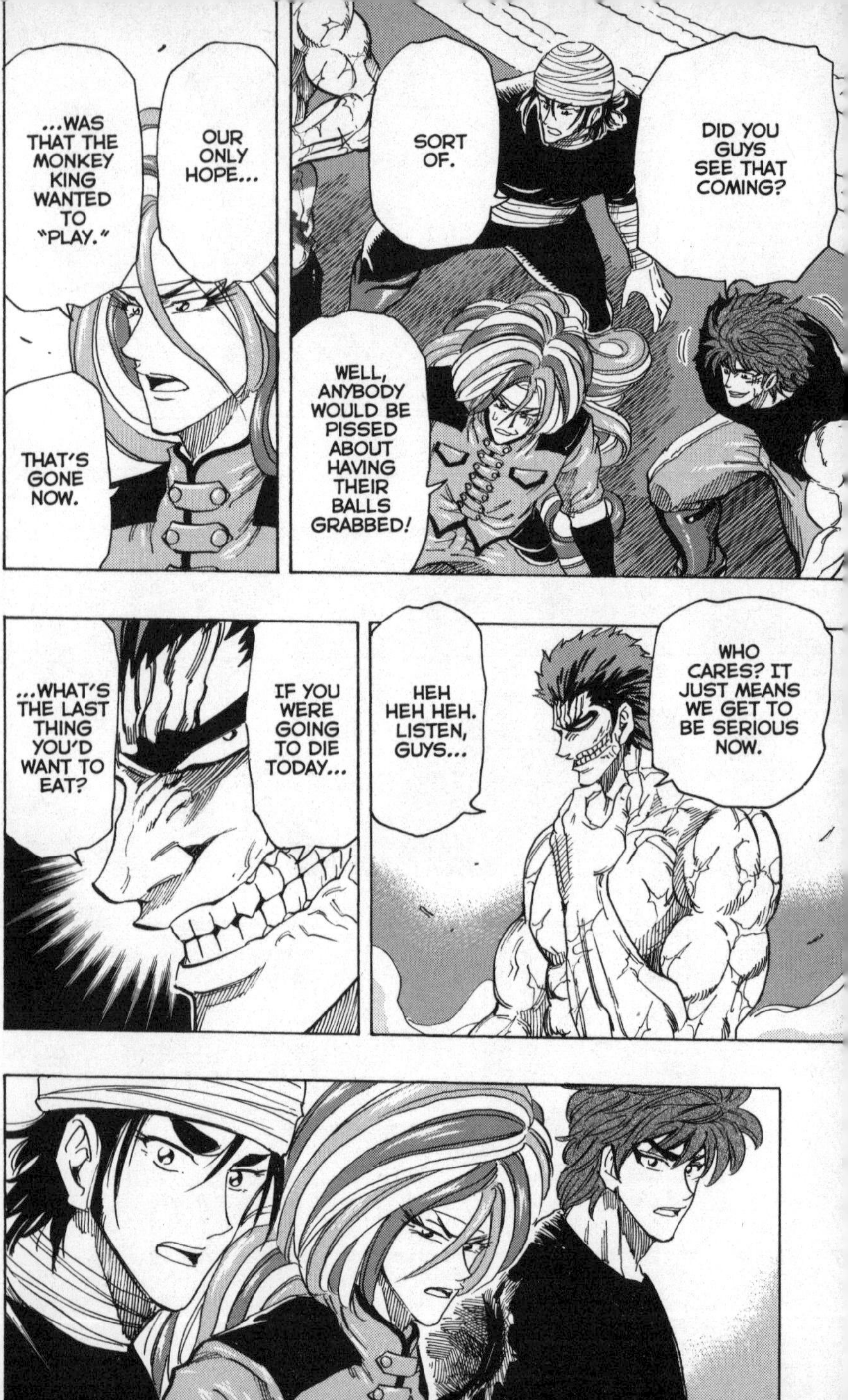
DID YOU GUYS SEE THAT COMING?
SORT OF.
WELL, ANYBODY WOULD BE PISSED ABOUT HAVING THEIR BALLS GRABBED!
OUR ONLY HOPE...
...WAS THAT THE MONKEY KING WANTED TO "PLAY."
THAT'S GONE NOW.
WHO CARES? IT JUST MEANS WE GET TO BE SERIOUS NOW.
HEH HEH HEH. LISTEN, GUYS...
IF YOU WERE GOING TO DIE TODAY...
...WHAT'S THE LAST THING YOU'D WANT TO EAT?

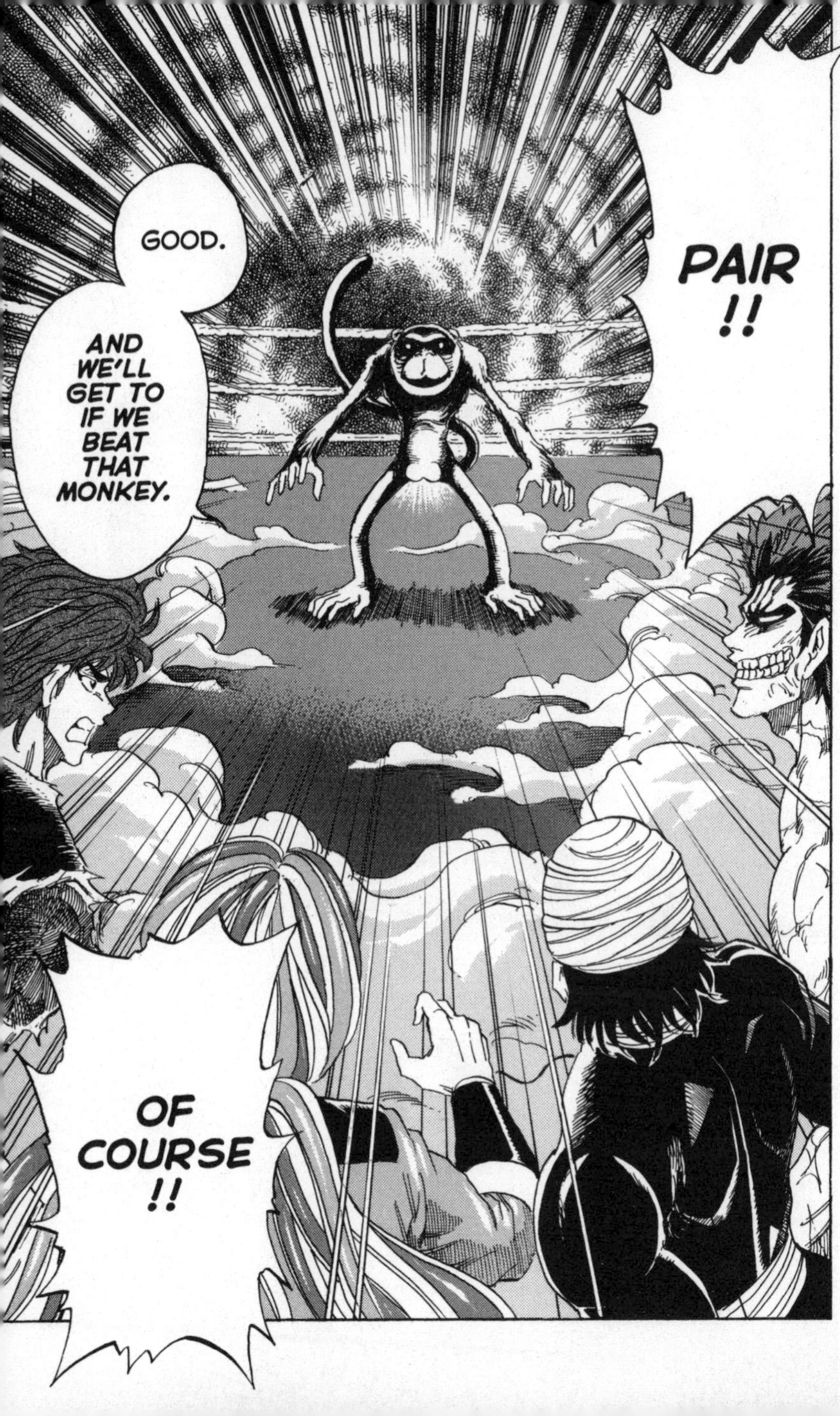
PAIR !!
GOOD.
AND WE'LL GET TO IF WE BEAT THAT MONKEY.
OF COURSE !!

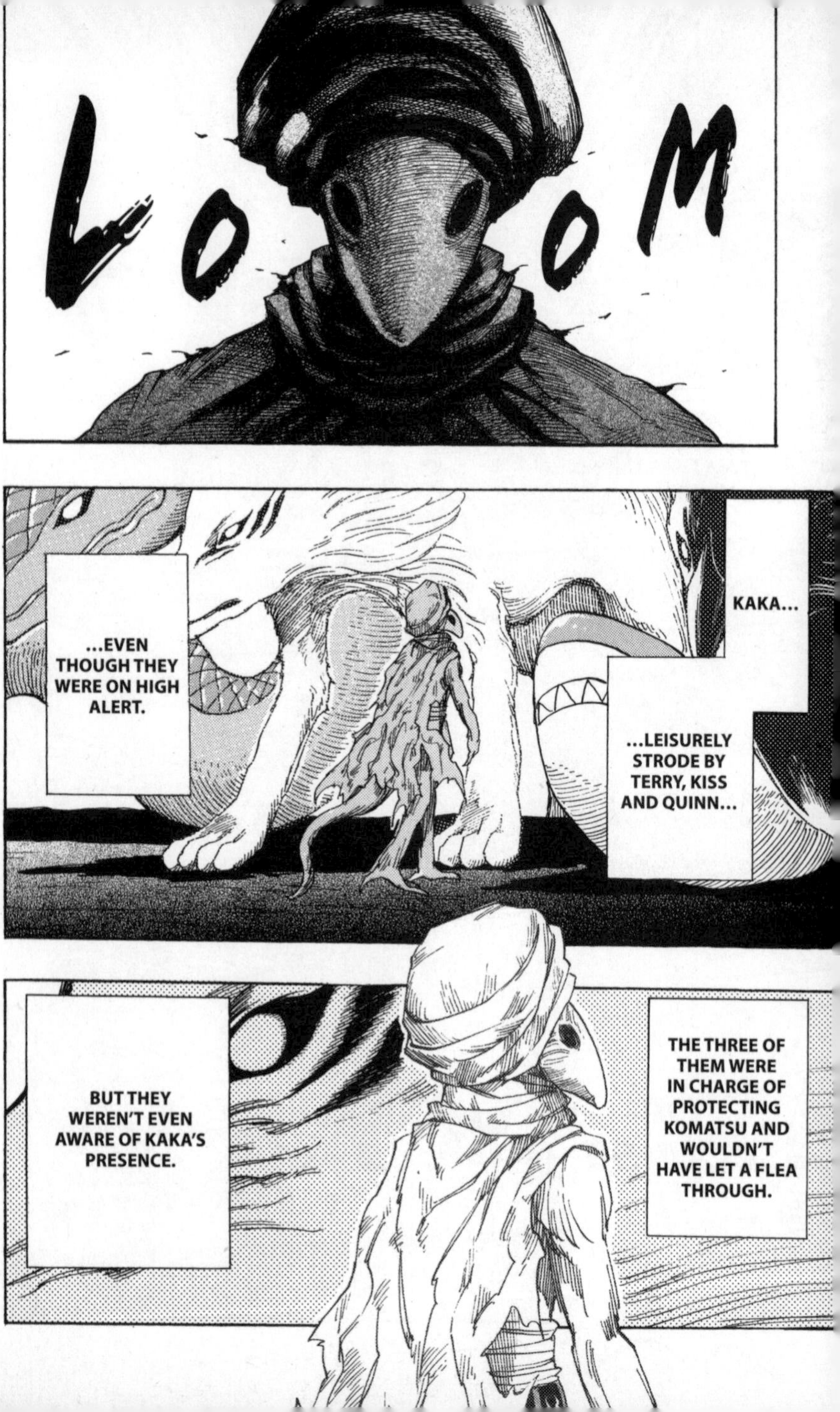
LOOM
KAKA...
...LEISURELY STRODE BY TERRY, KISS AND QUINN...
...EVEN THOUGH THEY WERE ON HIGH ALERT.
THE THREE OF THEM WERE IN CHARGE OF PROTECTING KOMATSU AND WOULDN'T HAVE LET A FLEA THROUGH.
BUT THEY WEREN'T EVEN AWARE OF KAKA'S PRESENCE.

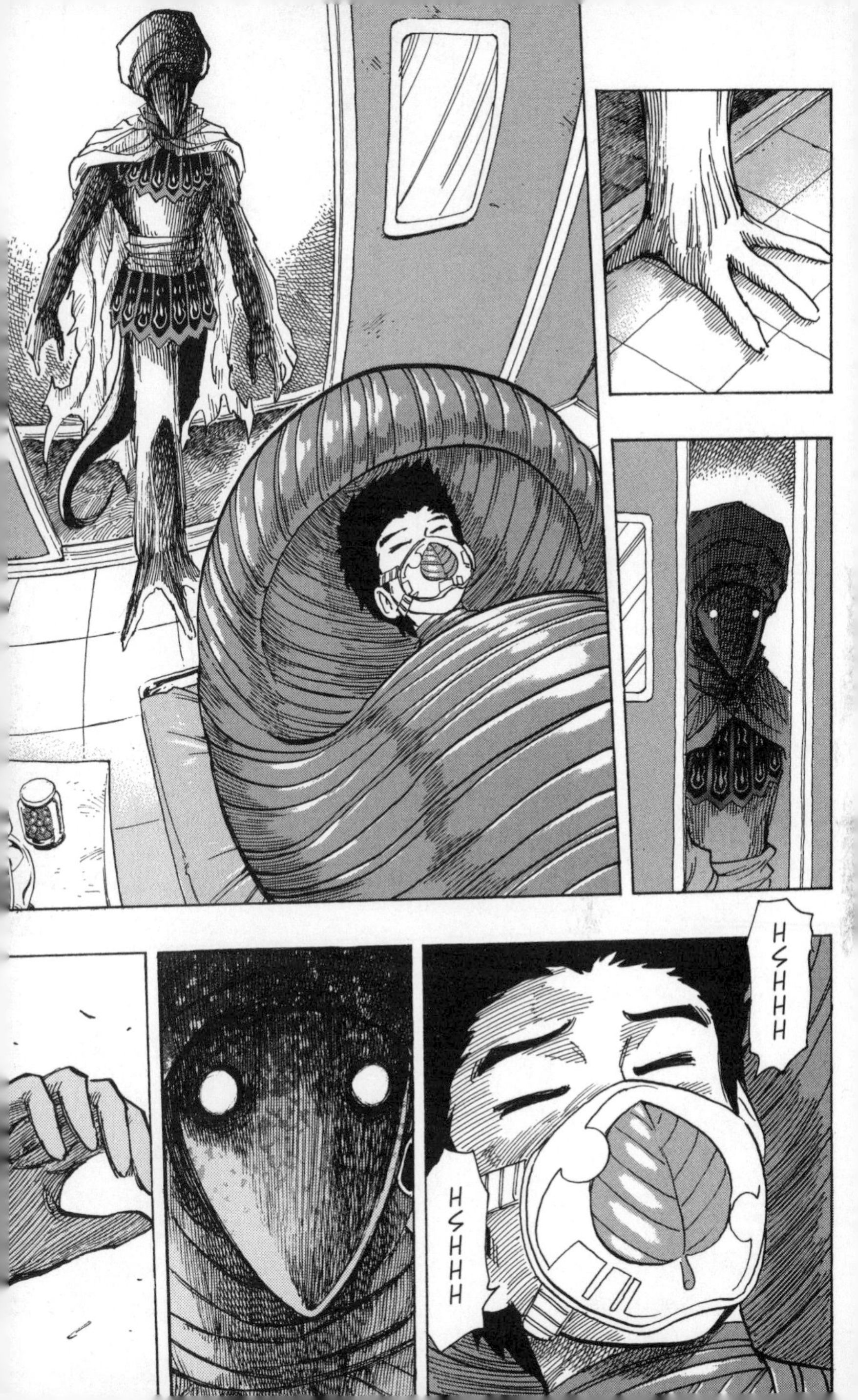
HSHHH
HSHHH

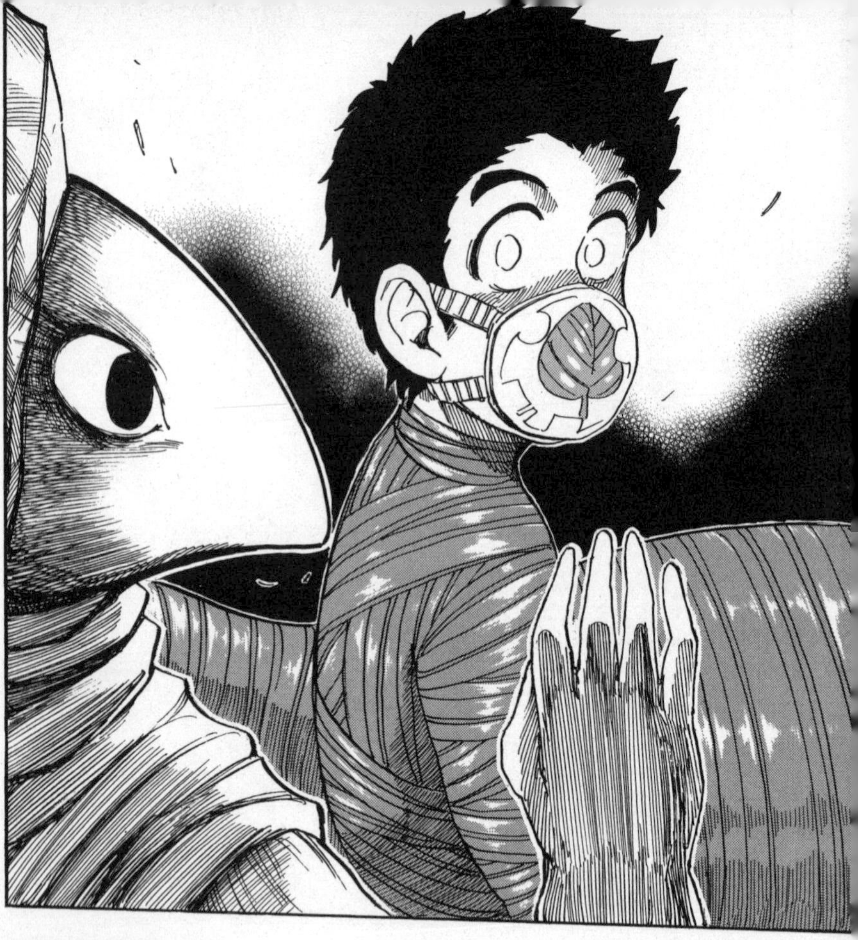
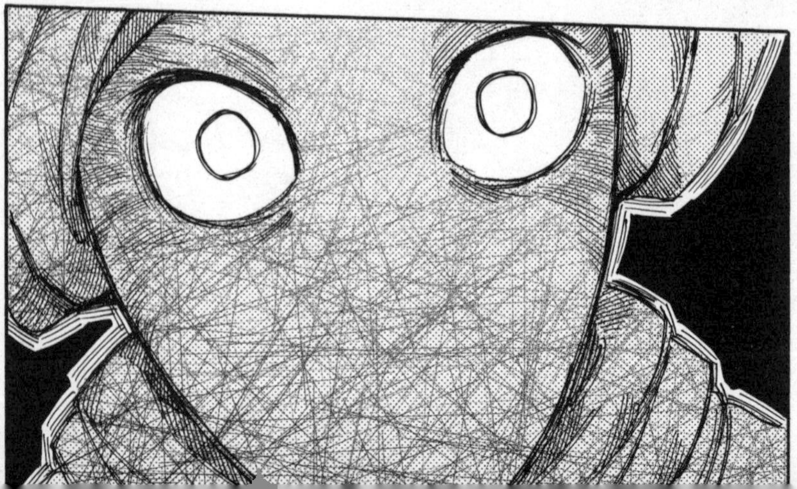

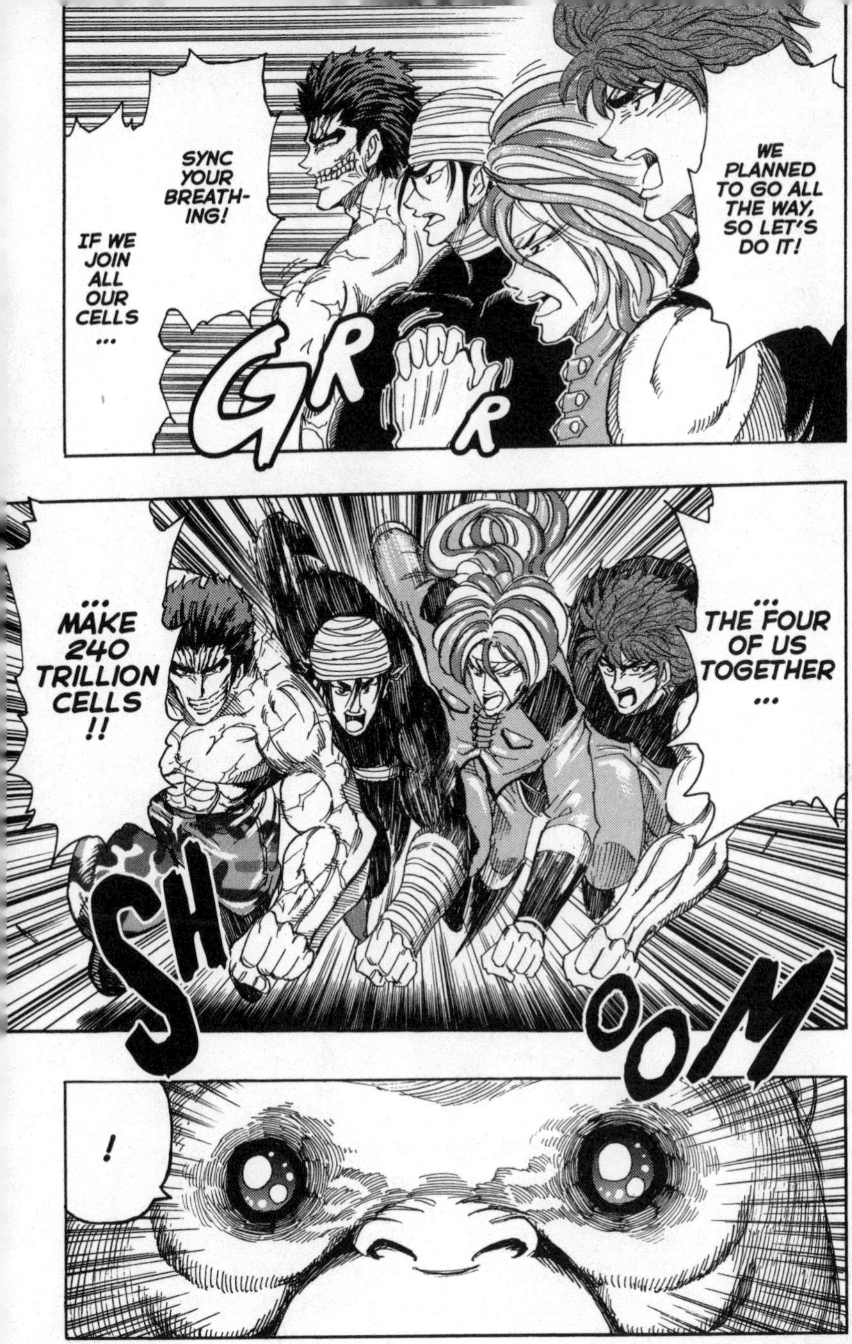
WE PLANNED TO GO ALL THE WAY, SO LET'S DO IT!
SYNC YOUR BREATH-ING!
IF WE JOIN ALL OUR CELLS ...
GRR
... THE FOUR OF US TOGETHER ...
... MAKE 240 TRILLION CELLS !!
SHOOM
!

TORIKO

GOURMET CHECKLIST
Vol. 338

RED-HAIRED PORK
(MAMMAL)

CAPTURE LEVEL: 1
HABITAT: FOUND EVERYWHERE
SIZE: 3.5 M
HEIGHT: 2.5 M
WEIGHT: 4 TONS
PRICE: 800 YEN PER 100 G

SCALE

THIS GIANT PIG CAN BE ARTIFICIALLY RAISED AND WAS A PRIZED INGREDIENT DURING THE GOURMET WAR WHEN FOOD WAS SCARCE. THEY HAVE VIOLENT PERSONALITIES BUT A LOW CAPTURE LEVEL. IT'S NOT THEIR FLAVOR SO MUCH AS THE GENEROUS AMOUNT OF MEAT THEY PROVIDE THAT MADE THEM SUCH A PRECIOUS INGREDIENT AT THE TIME. THE LIFE OF A RED-HAIRED PORK WAS EVEN MORE HIGHLY VALUED THAN A HUMAN LIFE DURING THAT TIME, WHICH GOES TO SHOW HOW DESPERATE AND DARK THE TIMES WERE.

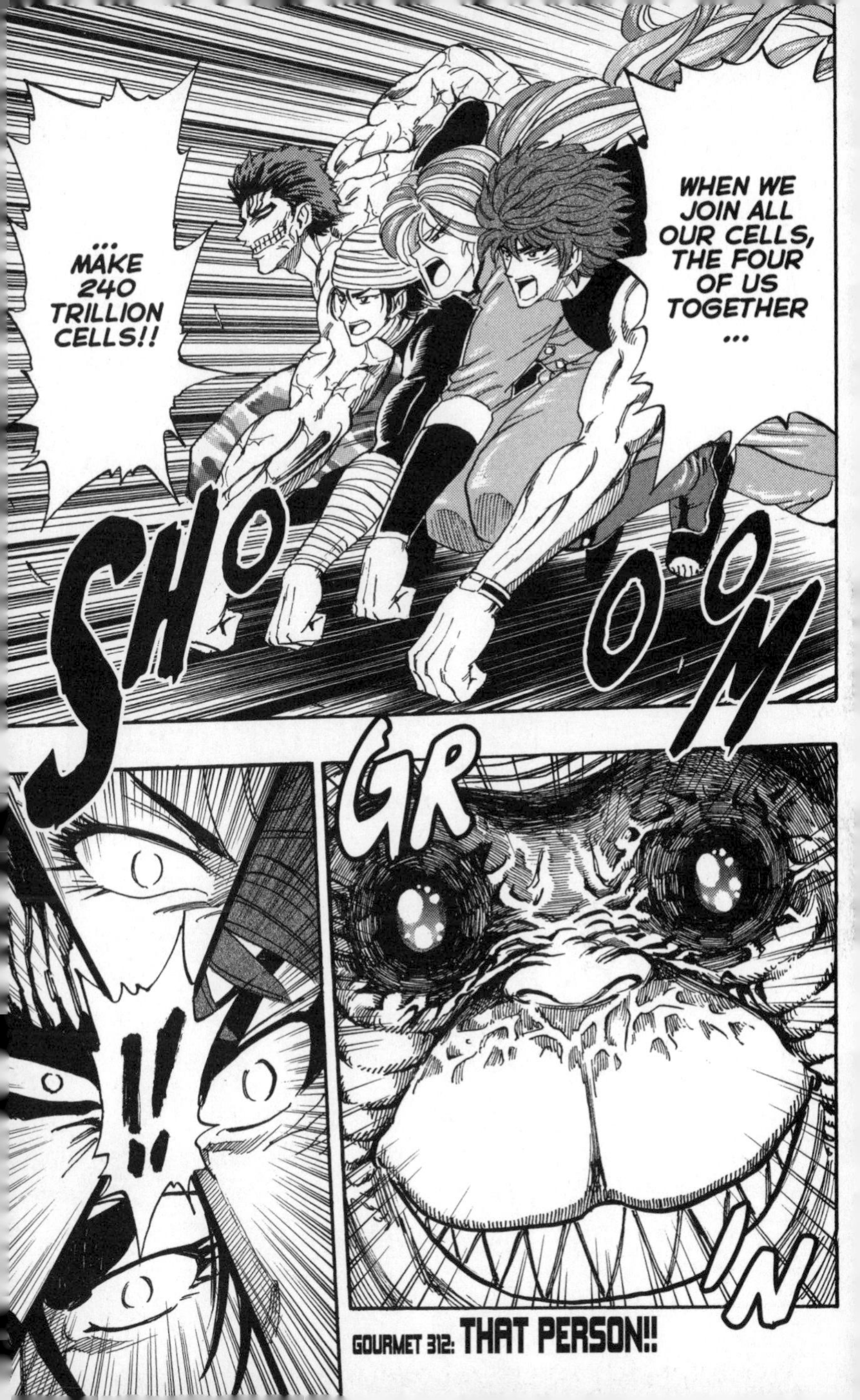
WHEN WE JOIN ALL OUR CELLS, THE FOUR OF US TOGETHER ...
... MAKE 240 TRILLION CELLS!!
SHOOOM
GRIN
!!

GOURMET 312: THAT PERSON!!

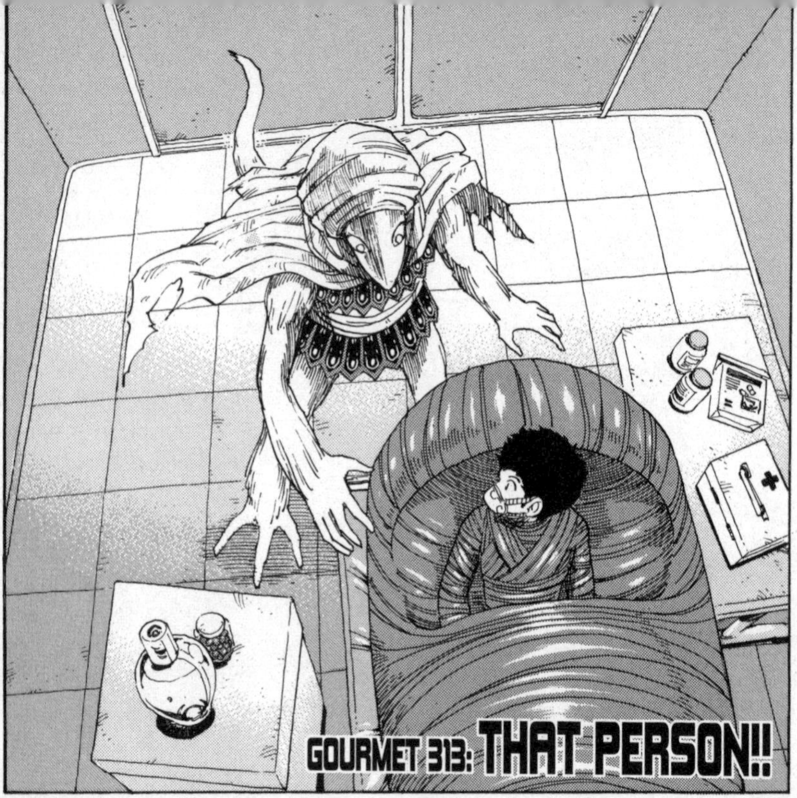

GOURMET 313: THAT PERSON!!

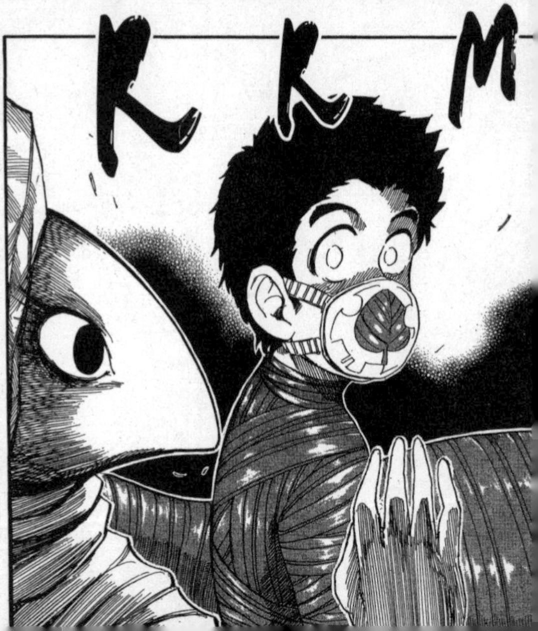
K K M

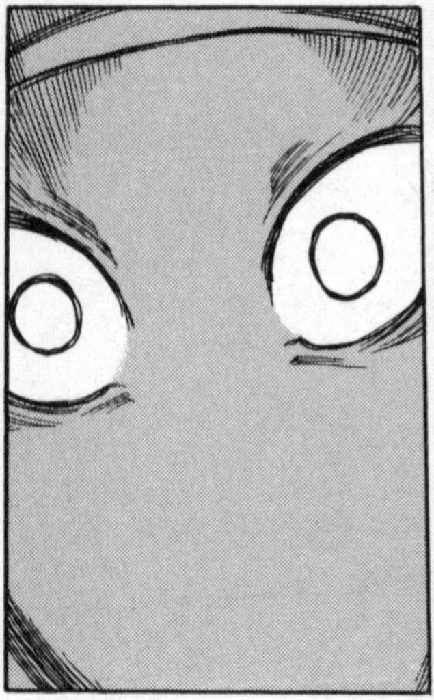

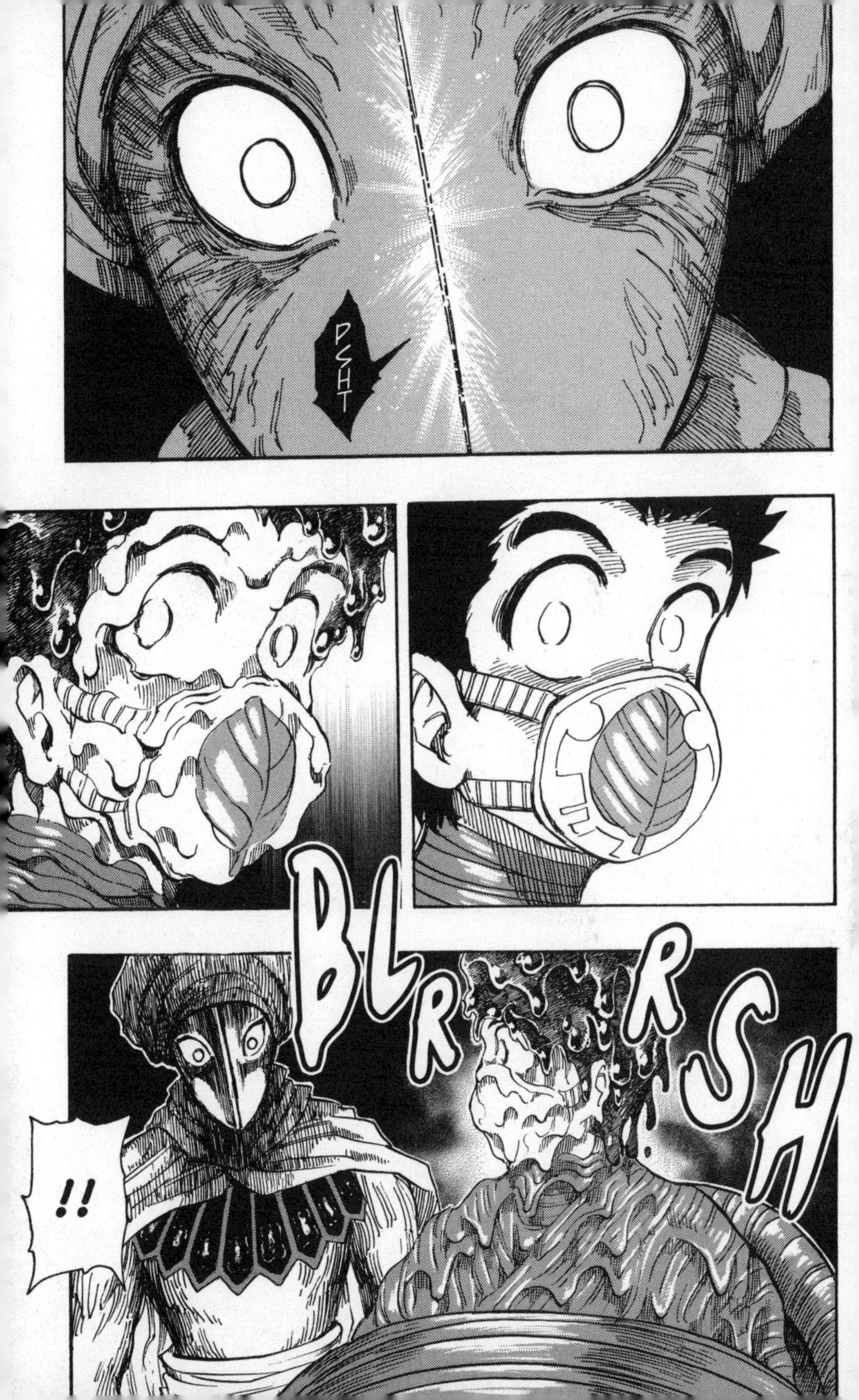
PSHT
BLRRRSH
!!

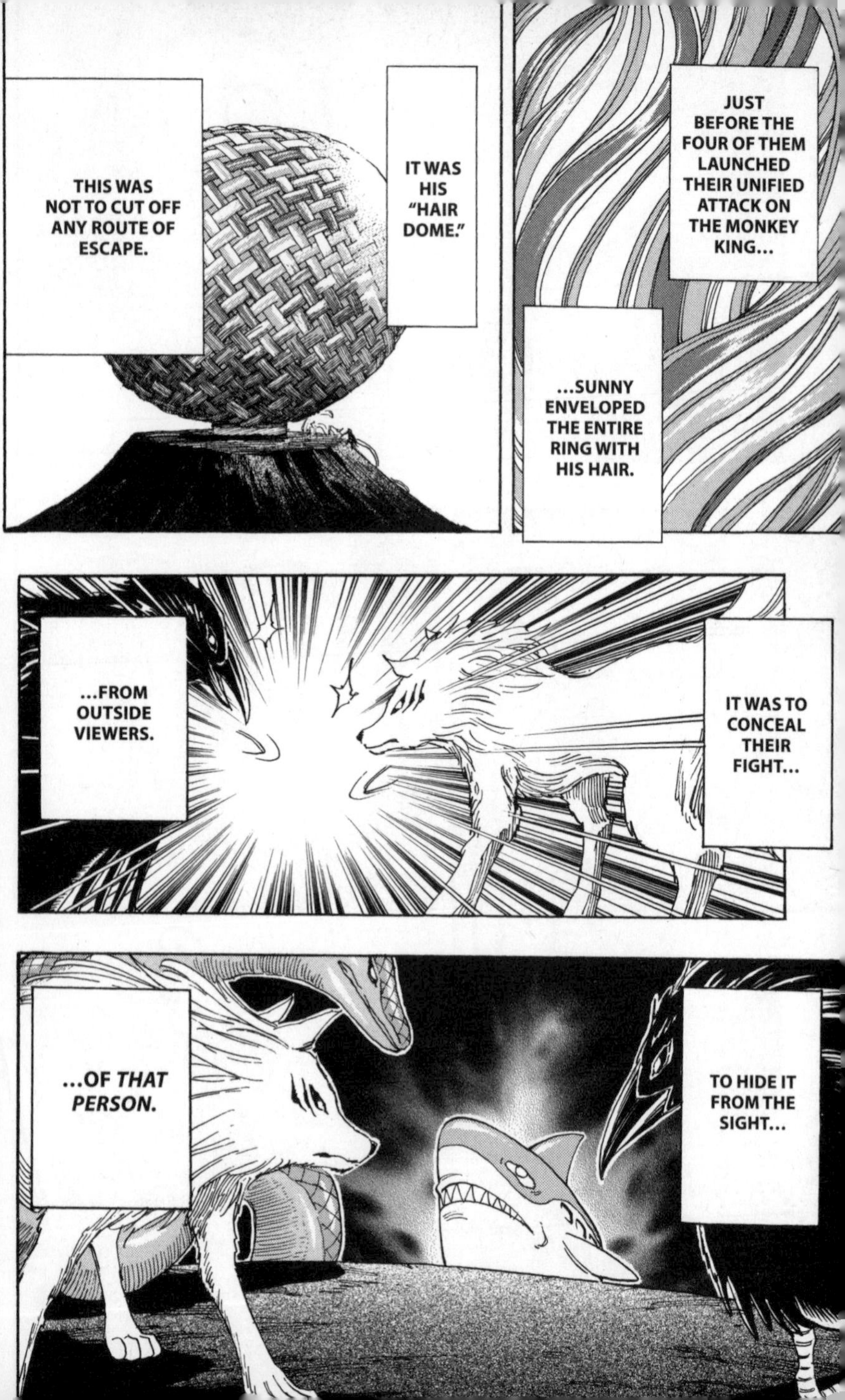
JUST BEFORE THE FOUR OF THEM LAUNCHED THEIR UNIFIED ATTACK ON THE MONKEY KING...
...SUNNY ENVELOPED THE ENTIRE RING WITH HIS HAIR.
IT WAS HIS "HAIR DOME."
THIS WAS NOT TO CUT OFF ANY ROUTE OF ESCAPE.
IT WAS TO CONCEAL THEIR FIGHT...
...FROM OUTSIDE VIEWERS.
TO HIDE IT FROM THE SIGHT...
...OF *THAT PERSON.*

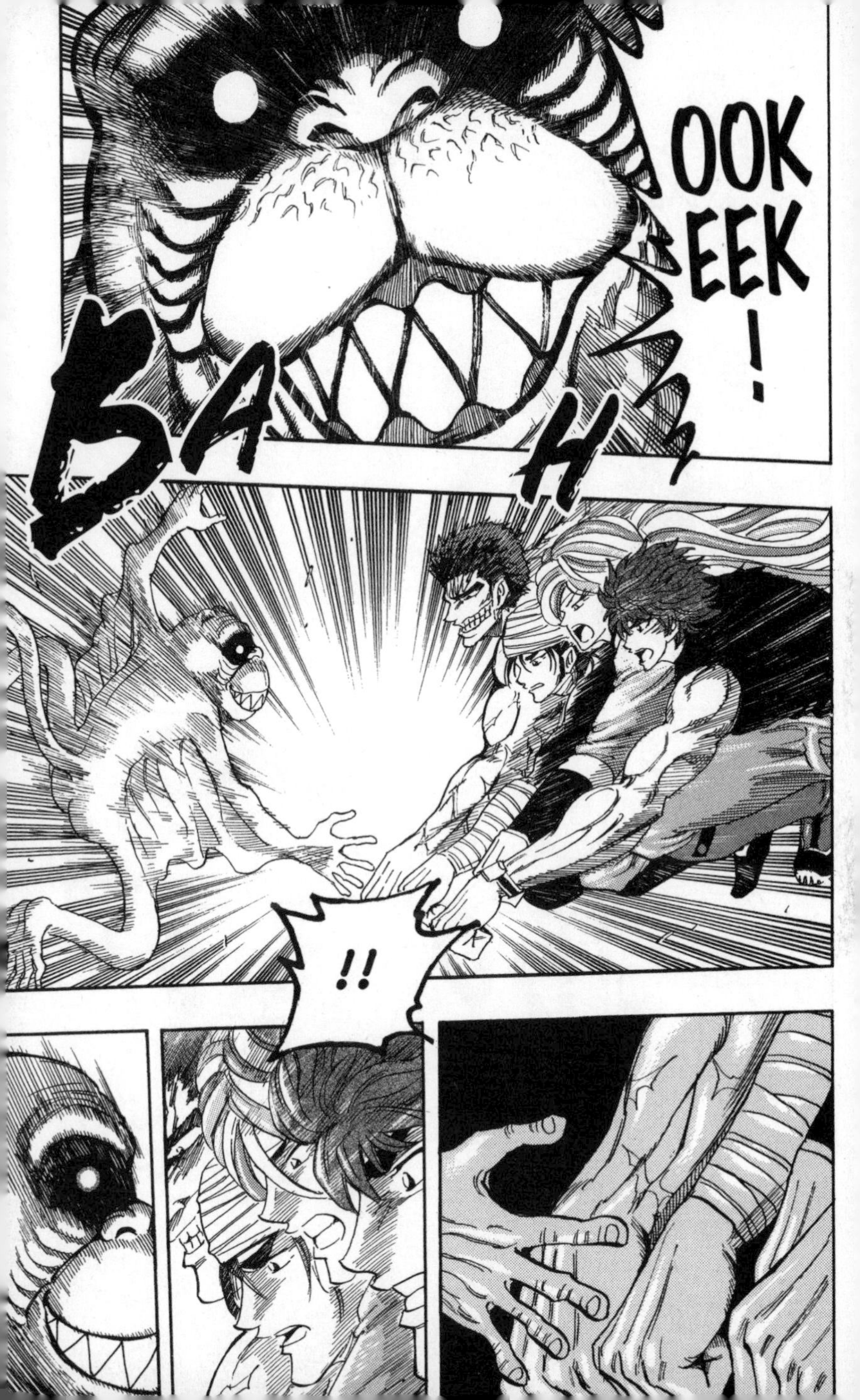
OOK EEK!
BAHM
!!

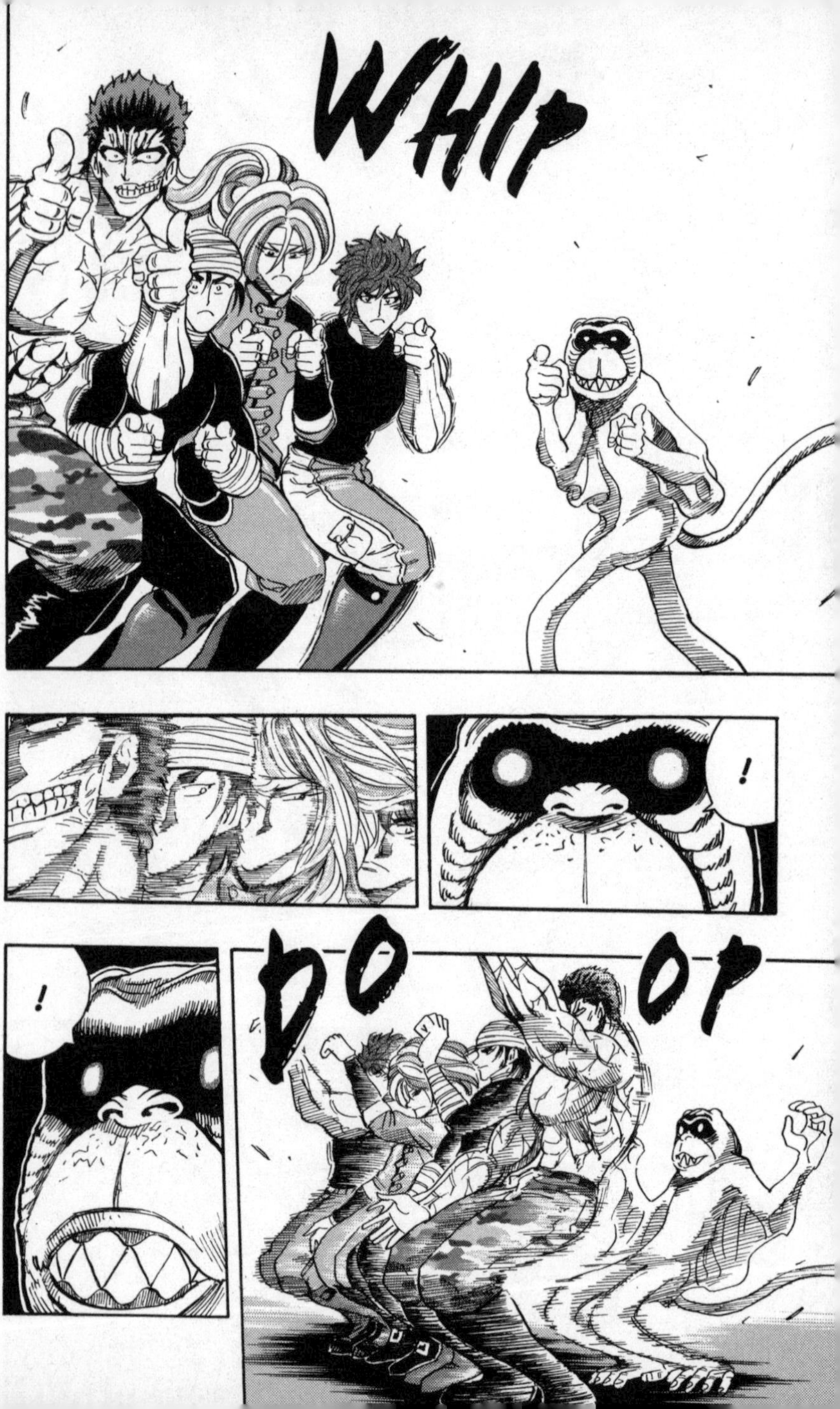
WHIP
!
DO-OP
!

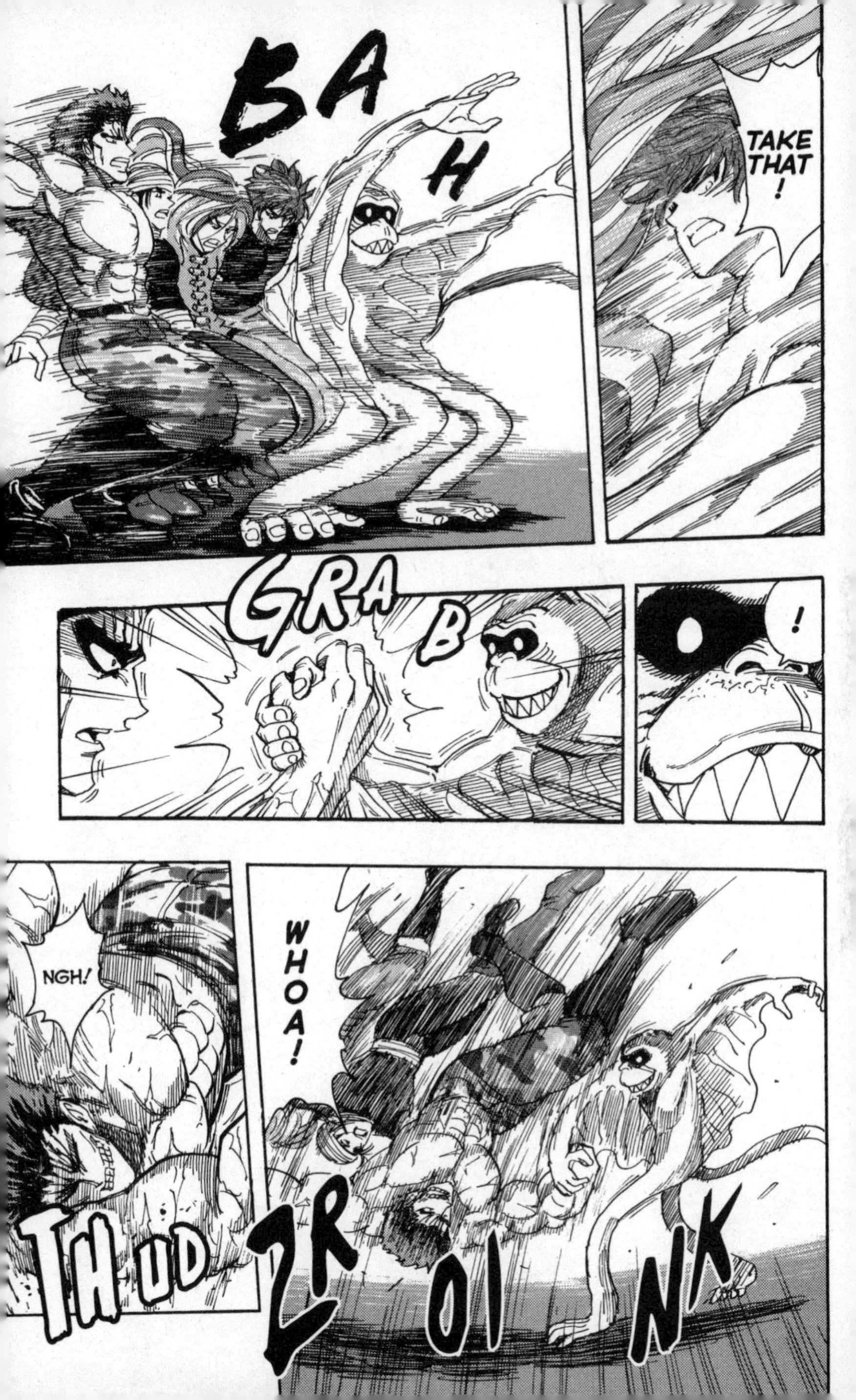
TAKE THAT!
BAH
!
GRAB
WHOA!
ZROINK
NGH!
THUD

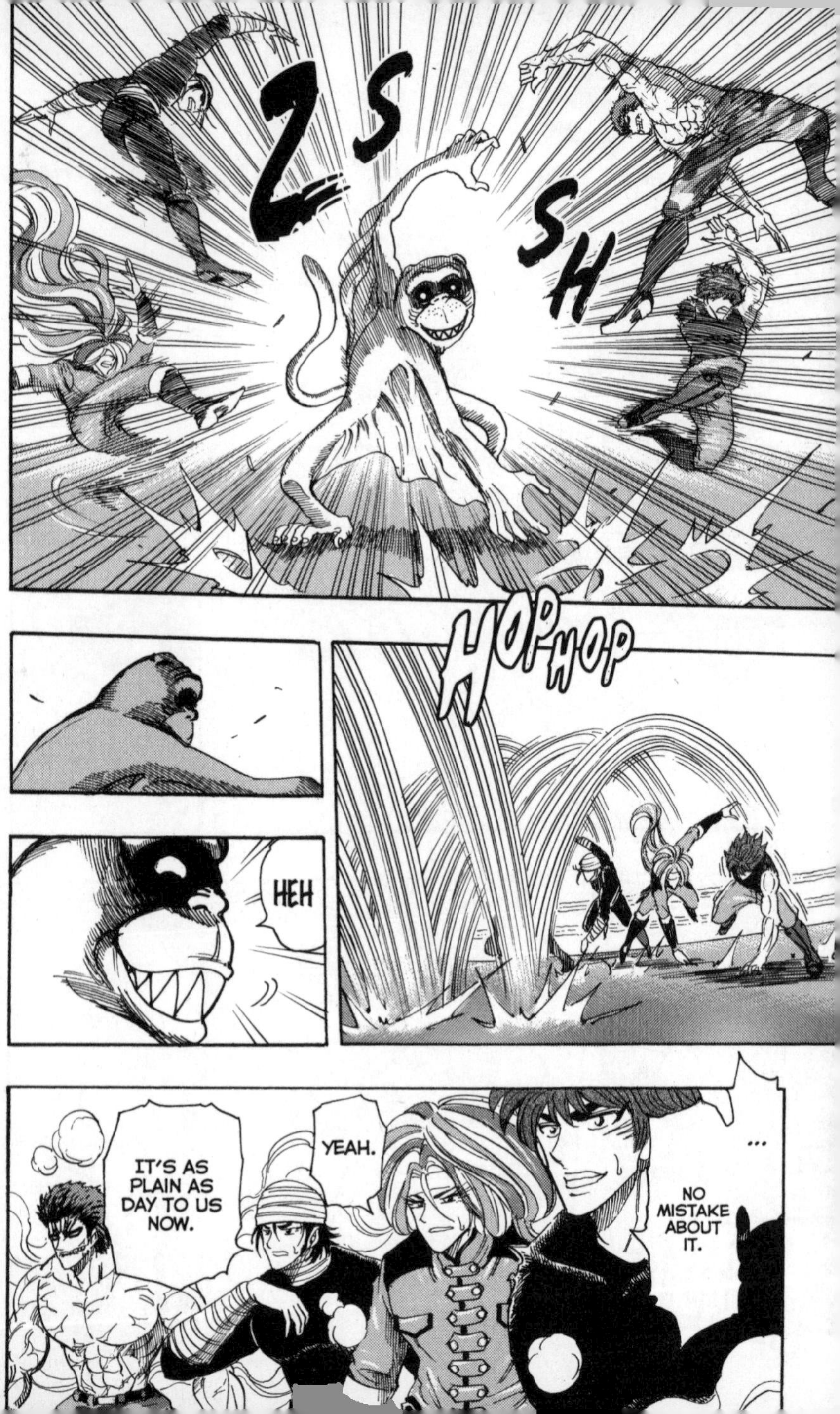
ZSSH
HOP HOP
HEH
...
NO MISTAKE ABOUT IT.
YEAH.
IT'S AS PLAIN AS DAY TO US NOW.

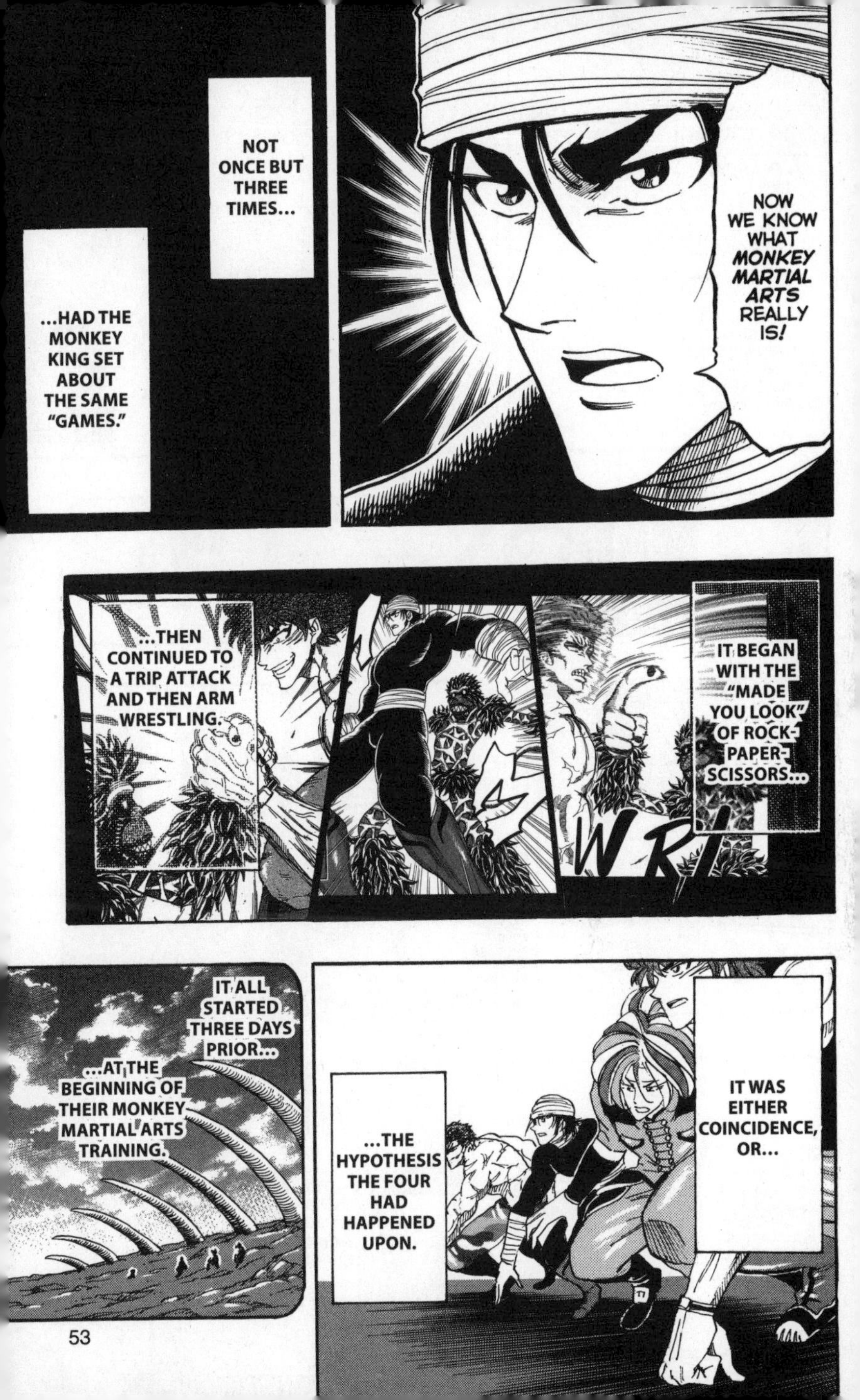
NOW WE KNOW WHAT *MONKEY MARTIAL ARTS* REALLY IS!
NOT ONCE BUT THREE TIMES...
...HAD THE MONKEY KING SET ABOUT THE SAME "GAMES."
IT BEGAN WITH THE "MADE YOU LOOK" OF ROCK-PAPER-SCISSORS...
WR
...THEN CONTINUED TO A TRIP ATTACK AND THEN ARM WRESTLING.
IT WAS EITHER COINCIDENCE, OR...
...THE HYPOTHESIS THE FOUR HAD HAPPENED UPON.
IT ALL STARTED THREE DAYS PRIOR...
...AT THE BEGINNING OF THEIR MONKEY MARTIAL ARTS TRAINING.

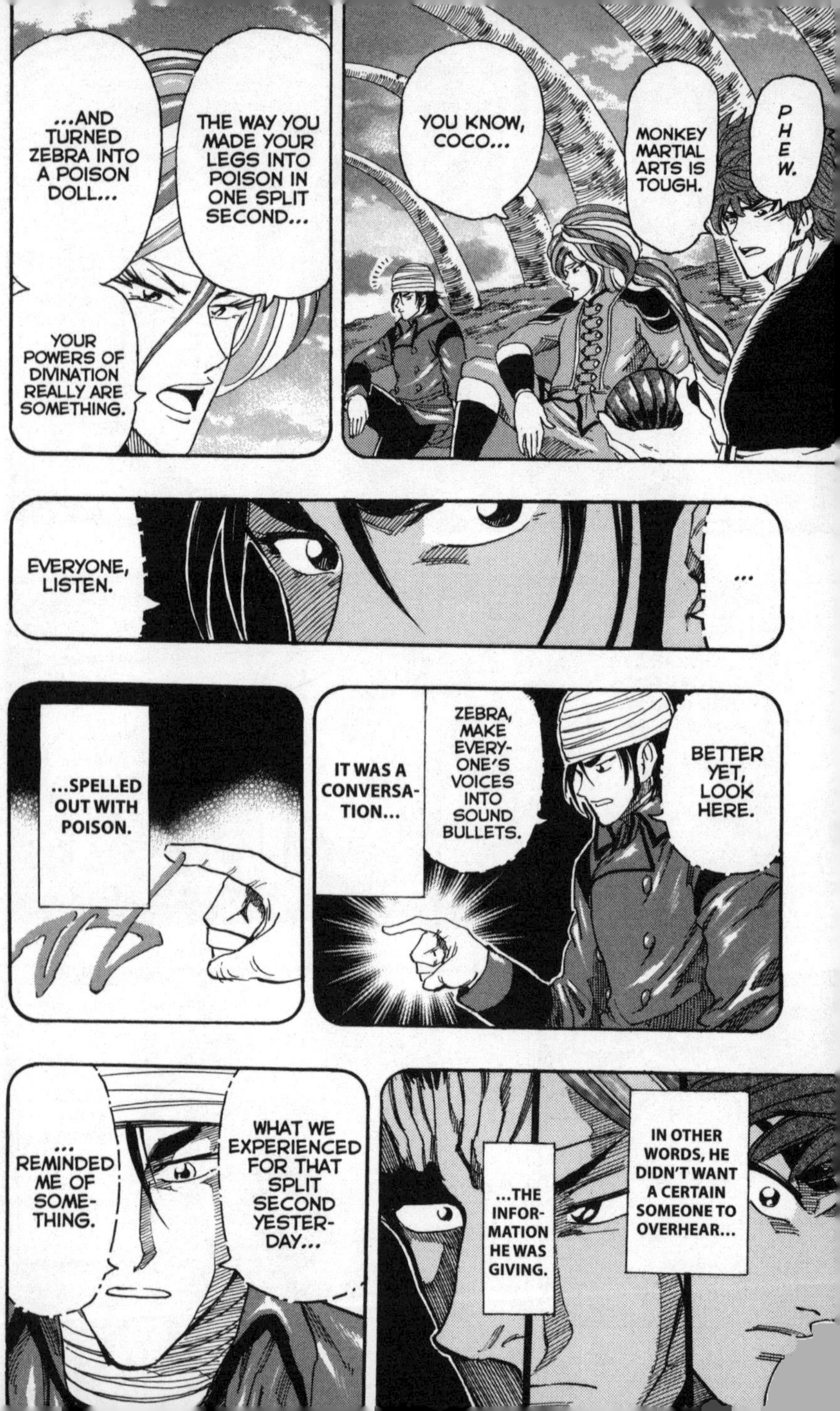
PHEW.
MONKEY MARTIAL ARTS IS TOUGH.
YOU KNOW, COCO...
THE WAY YOU MADE YOUR LEGS INTO POISON IN ONE SPLIT SECOND...
...AND TURNED ZEBRA INTO A POISON DOLL...
YOUR POWERS OF DIVINATION REALLY ARE SOMETHING.
...
EVERYONE, LISTEN.
BETTER YET, LOOK HERE.
ZEBRA, MAKE EVERYONE'S VOICES INTO SOUND BULLETS.
IT WAS A CONVERSATION...
...SPELLED OUT WITH POISON.
IN OTHER WORDS, HE DIDN'T WANT A CERTAIN SOMEONE TO OVERHEAR...
...THE INFORMATION HE WAS GIVING.
WHAT WE EXPERIENCED FOR THAT SPLIT SECOND YESTERDAY...
...REMINDED ME OF SOMETHING.

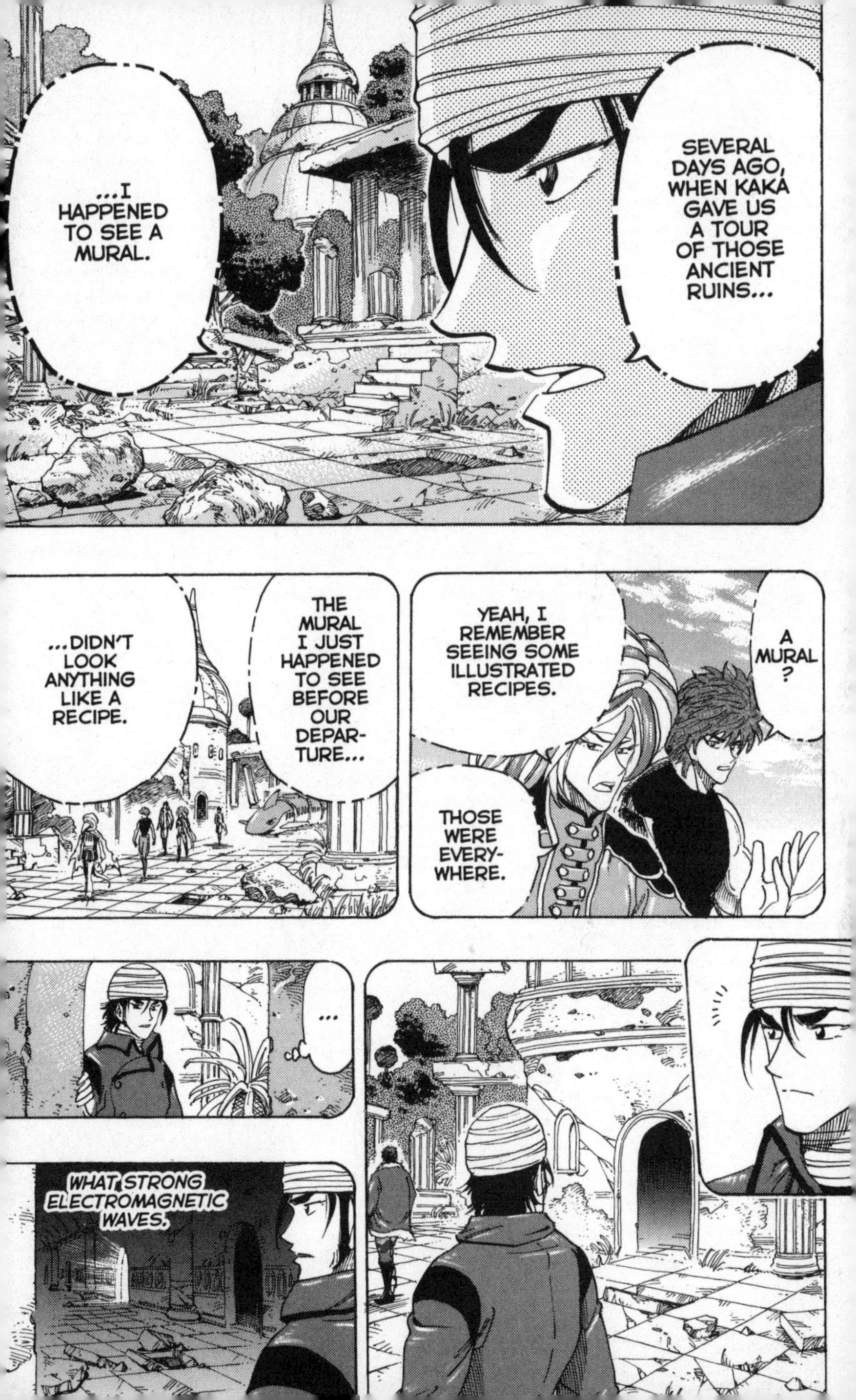
SEVERAL DAYS AGO, WHEN KAKA GAVE US A TOUR OF THOSE ANCIENT RUINS...
...I HAPPENED TO SEE A MURAL.
A MURAL?
YEAH, I REMEMBER SEEING SOME ILLUSTRATED RECIPES.
THOSE WERE EVERYWHERE.
THE MURAL I JUST HAPPENED TO SEE BEFORE OUR DEPARTURE...
...DIDN'T LOOK ANYTHING LIKE A RECIPE.
...
WHAT STRONG ELECTROMAGNETIC WAVES.

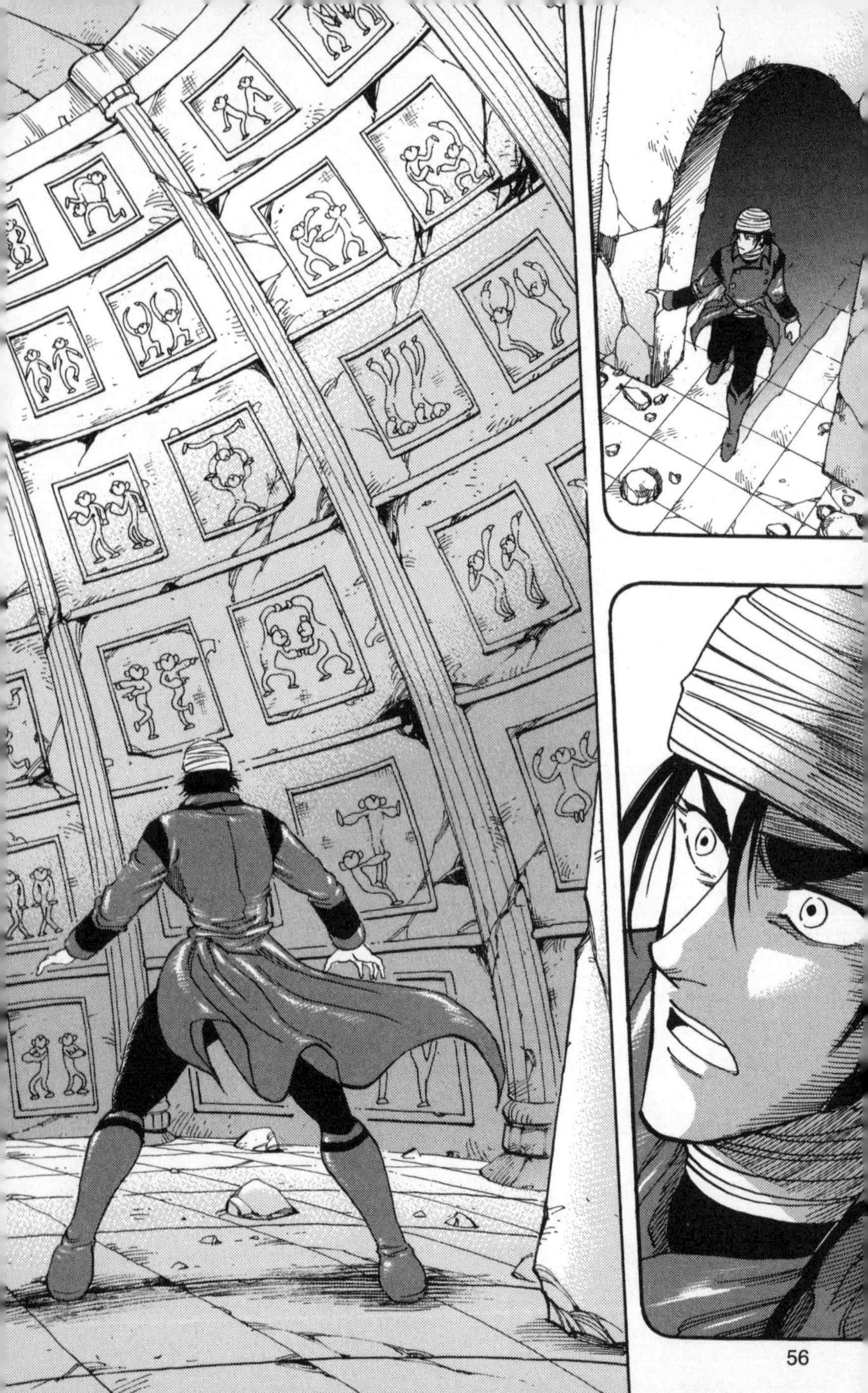

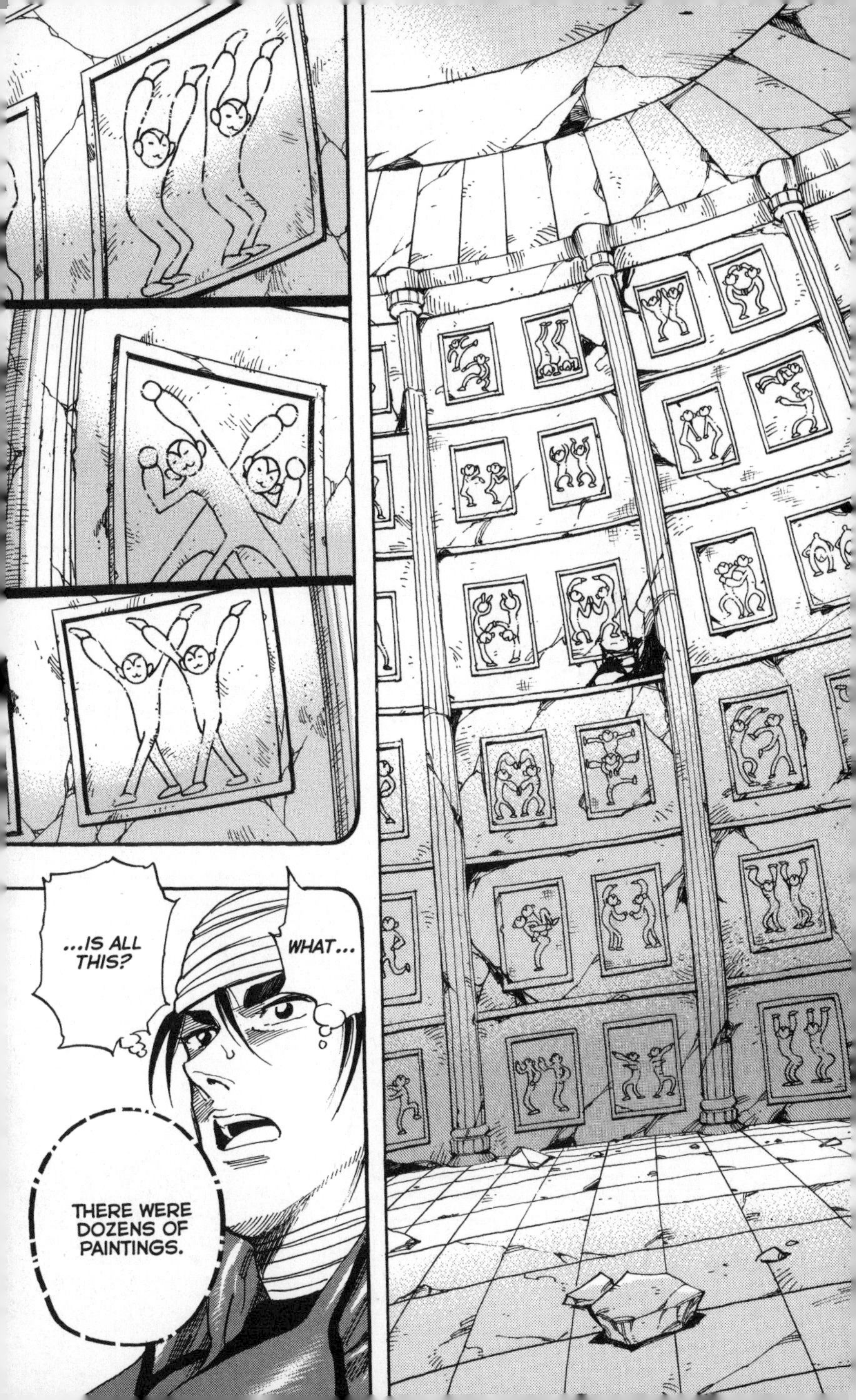
WHAT...
...IS ALL THIS?
THERE WERE DOZENS OF PAINTINGS.

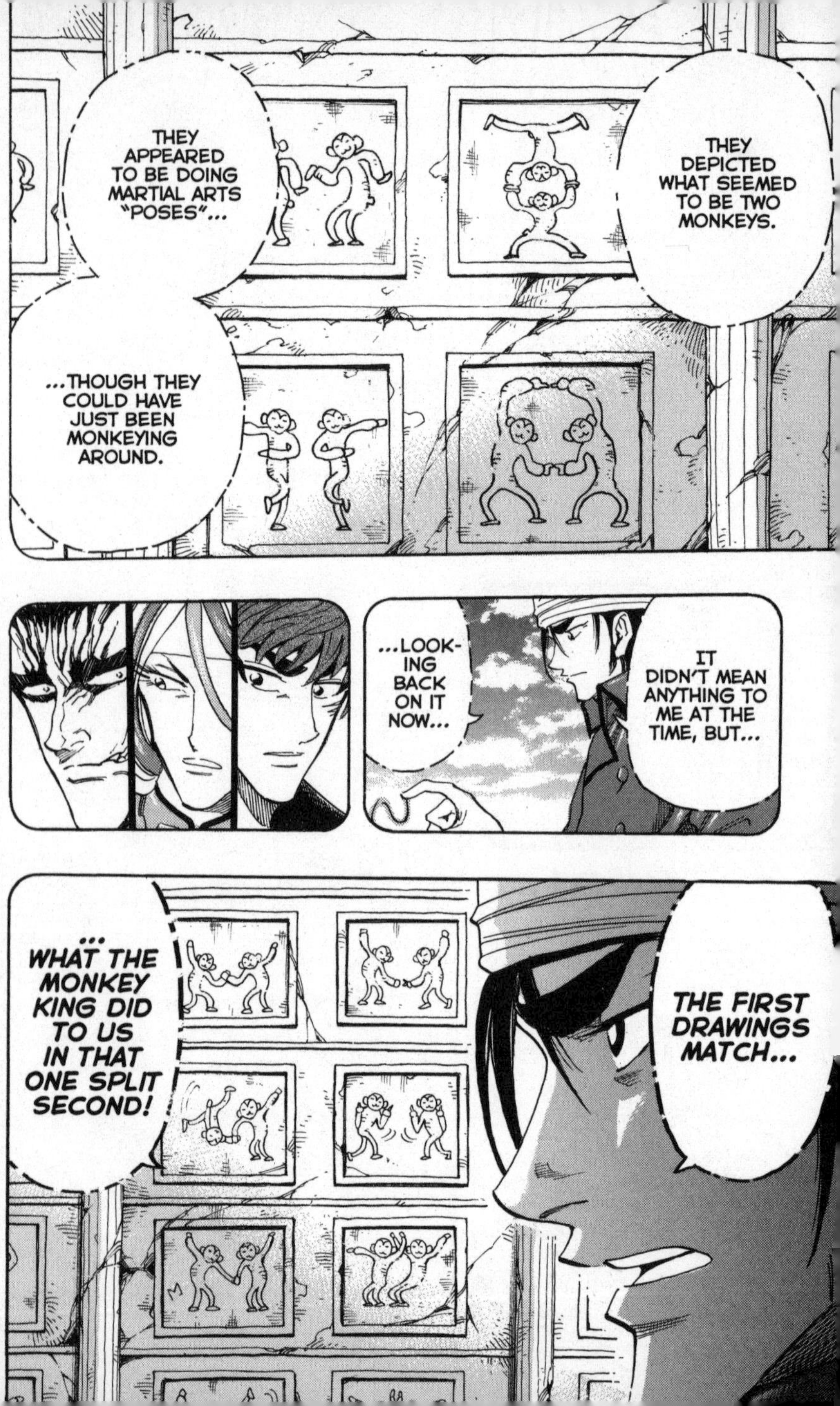
THEY DEPICTED WHAT SEEMED TO BE TWO MONKEYS.
THEY APPEARED TO BE DOING MARTIAL ARTS "POSES"...
...THOUGH THEY COULD HAVE JUST BEEN MONKEYING AROUND.
IT DIDN'T MEAN ANYTHING TO ME AT THE TIME, BUT...
...LOOKING BACK ON IT NOW...
THE FIRST DRAWINGS MATCH...
...WHAT THE MONKEY KING DID TO US IN THAT ONE SPLIT SECOND!

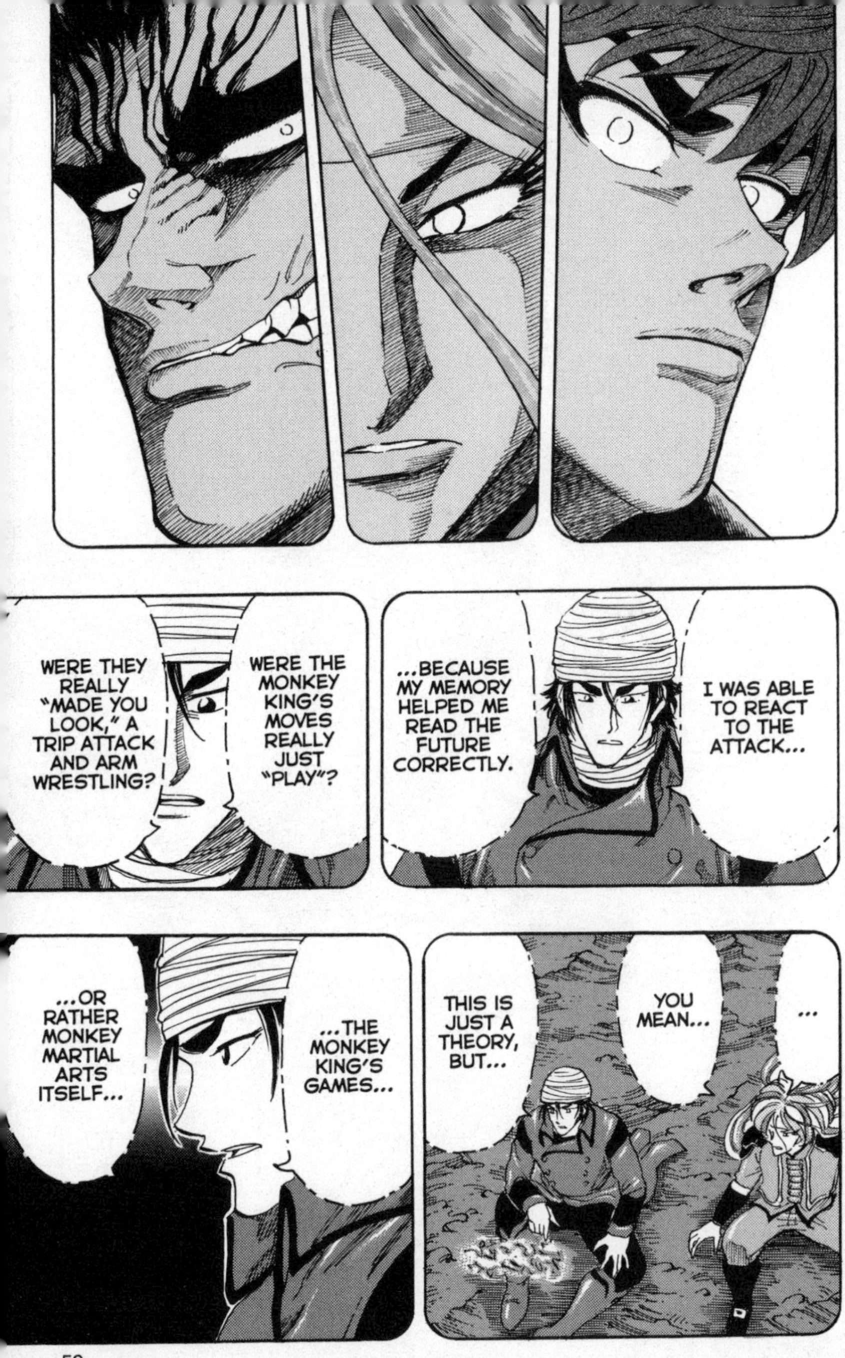
I WAS ABLE TO REACT TO THE ATTACK...
...BECAUSE MY MEMORY HELPED ME READ THE FUTURE CORRECTLY.
WERE THE MONKEY KING'S MOVES REALLY JUST "PLAY"?
WERE THEY REALLY "MADE YOU LOOK," A TRIP ATTACK AND ARM WRESTLING?
...
YOU MEAN...
THIS IS JUST A THEORY, BUT...
...THE MONKEY KING'S GAMES...
...OR RATHER MONKEY MARTIAL ARTS ITSELF...

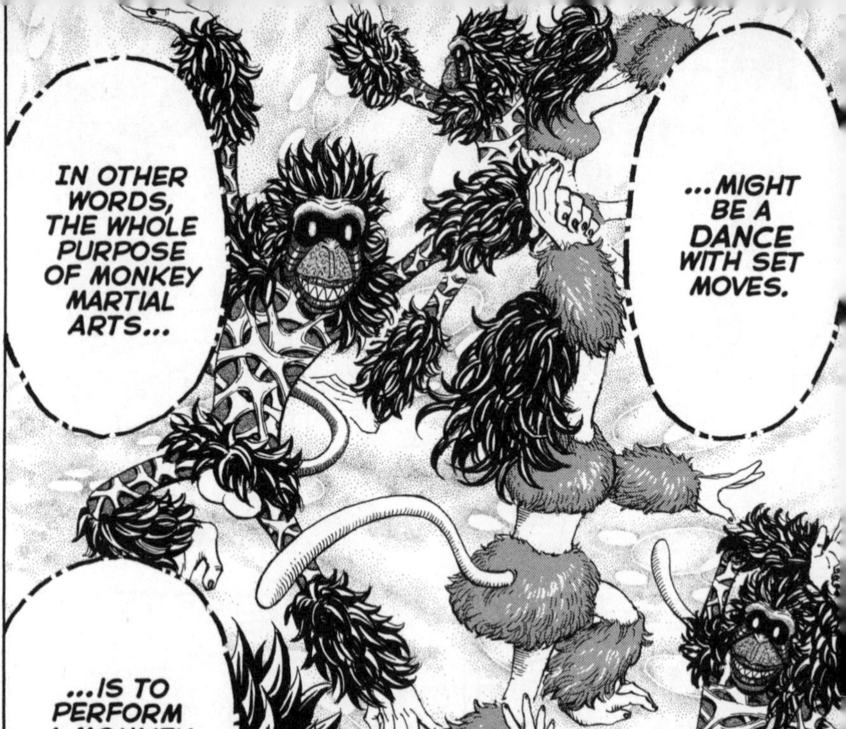
...MIGHT BE A DANCE WITH SET MOVES.
IN OTHER WORDS, THE WHOLE PURPOSE OF MONKEY MARTIAL ARTS...
...IS TO PERFORM A MONKEY DANCE.

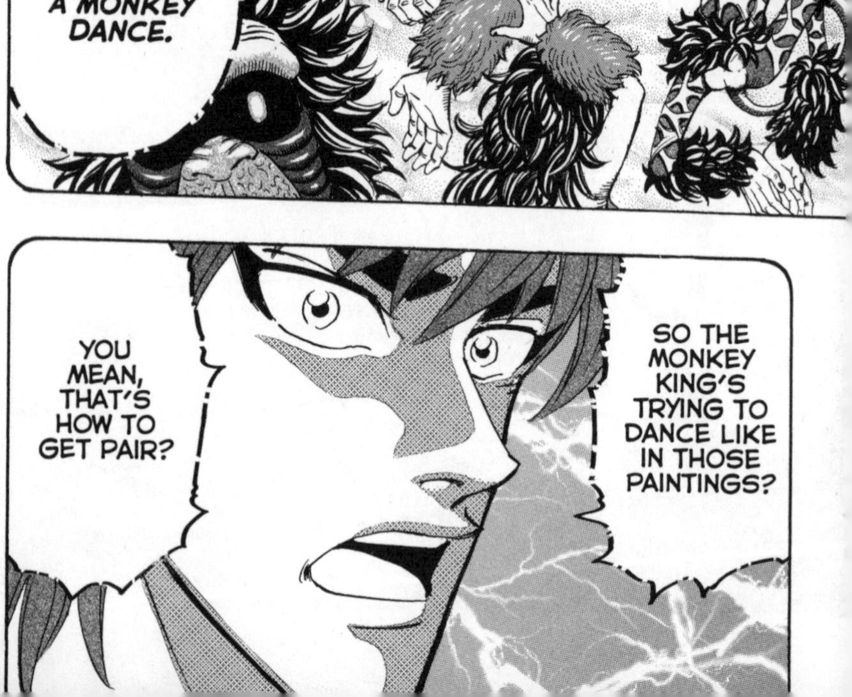
SO THE MONKEY KING'S TRYING TO DANCE LIKE IN THOSE PAINTINGS?
YOU MEAN, THAT'S HOW TO GET PAIR?

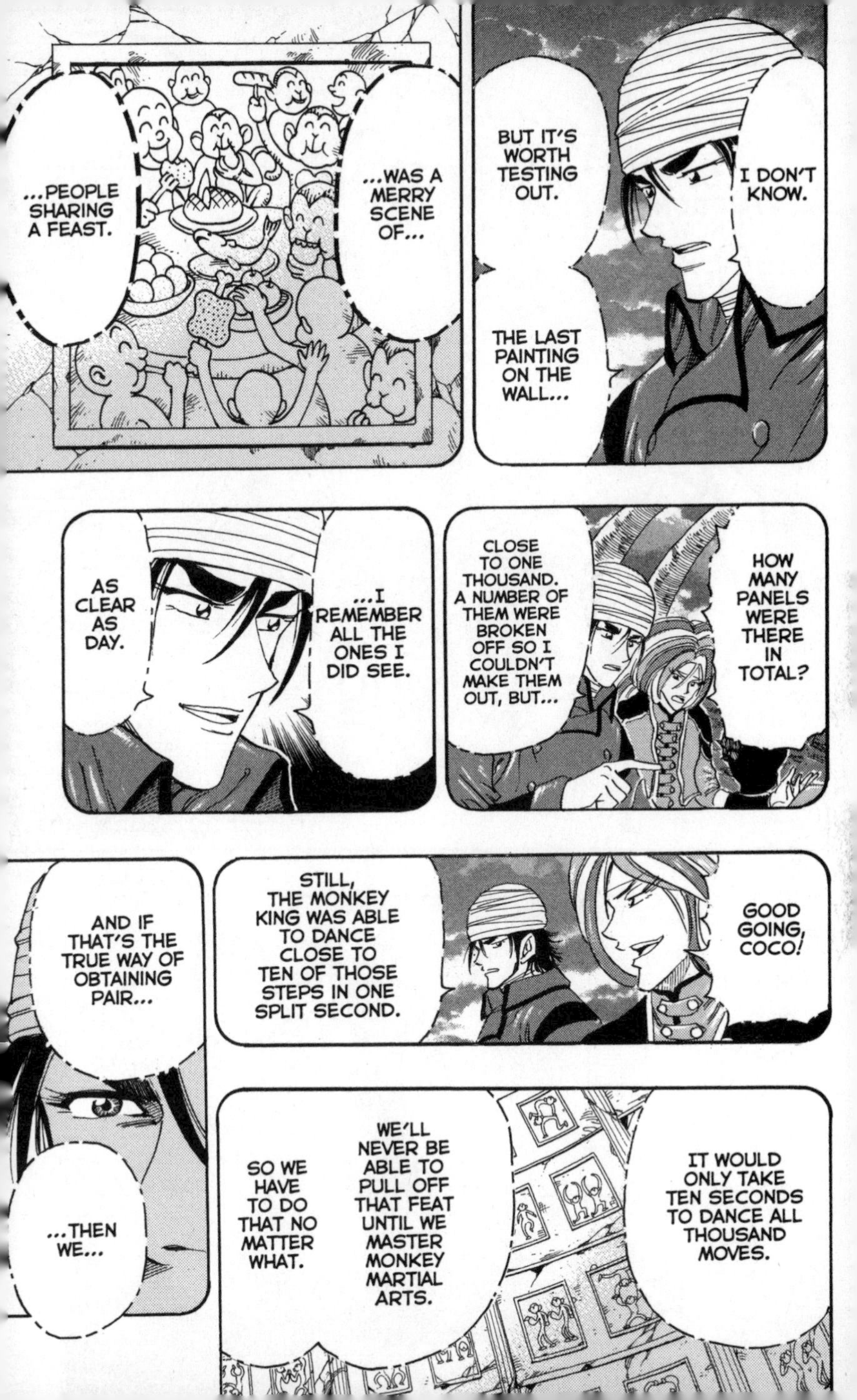
I DON'T KNOW.
BUT IT'S WORTH TESTING OUT.
THE LAST PAINTING ON THE WALL...
...WAS A MERRY SCENE OF...
...PEOPLE SHARING A FEAST.
HOW MANY PANELS WERE THERE IN TOTAL?
CLOSE TO ONE THOUSAND. A NUMBER OF THEM WERE BROKEN OFF SO I COULDN'T MAKE THEM OUT, BUT...
...I REMEMBER ALL THE ONES I DID SEE.
AS CLEAR AS DAY.
GOOD GOING, COCO!
STILL, THE MONKEY KING WAS ABLE TO DANCE CLOSE TO TEN OF THOSE STEPS IN ONE SPLIT SECOND.
IT WOULD ONLY TAKE TEN SECONDS TO DANCE ALL THOUSAND MOVES.
WE'LL NEVER BE ABLE TO PULL OFF THAT FEAT UNTIL WE MASTER MONKEY MARTIAL ARTS.
SO WE HAVE TO DO THAT NO MATTER WHAT.
AND IF THAT'S THE TRUE WAY OF OBTAINING PAIR...
...THEN WE...

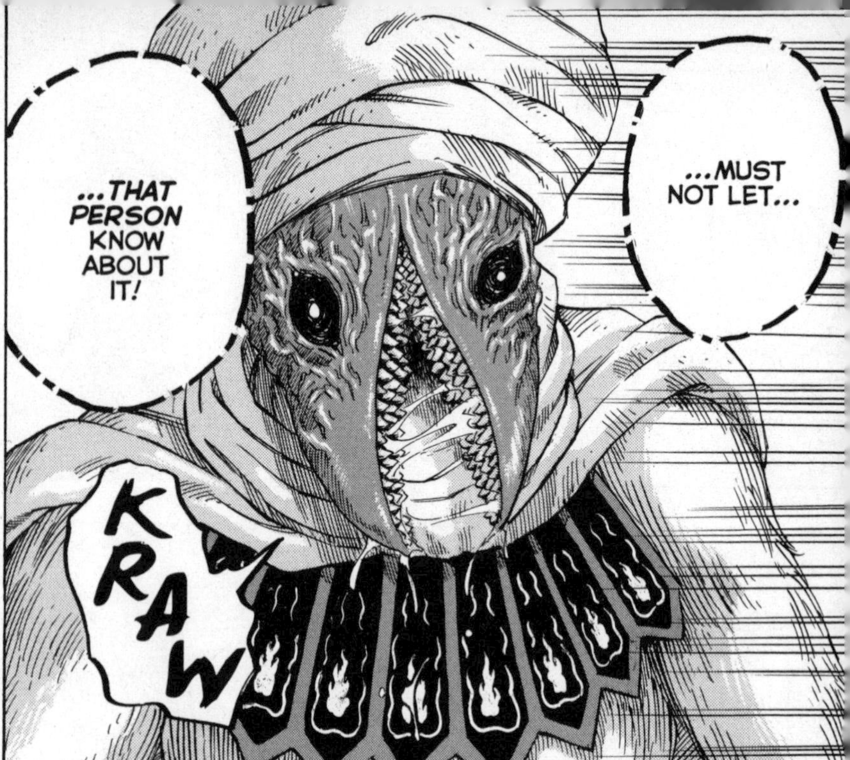
...MUST NOT LET...
...THAT PERSON KNOW ABOUT IT!
KRAW

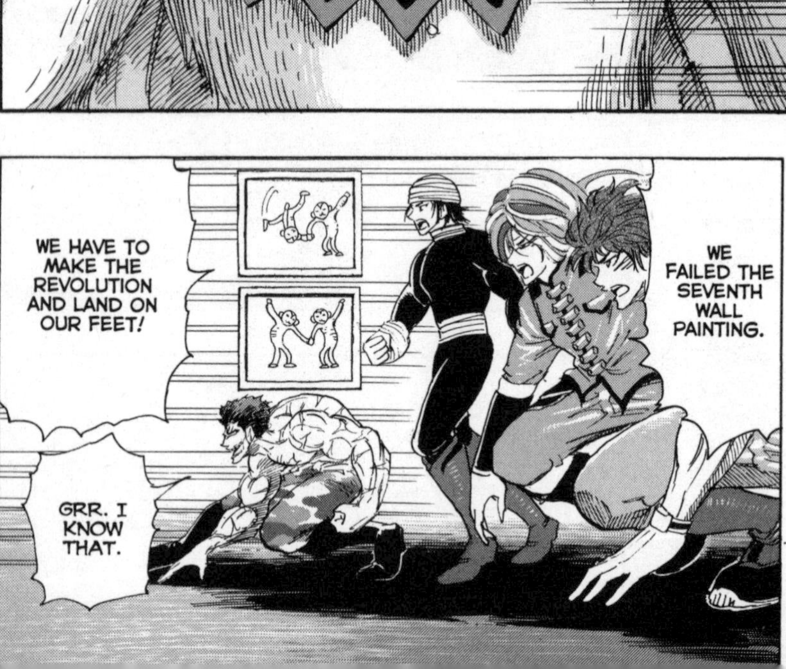
WE FAILED THE SEVENTH WALL PAINTING.
WE HAVE TO MAKE THE REVOLUTION AND LAND ON OUR FEET!
GRR. I KNOW THAT.

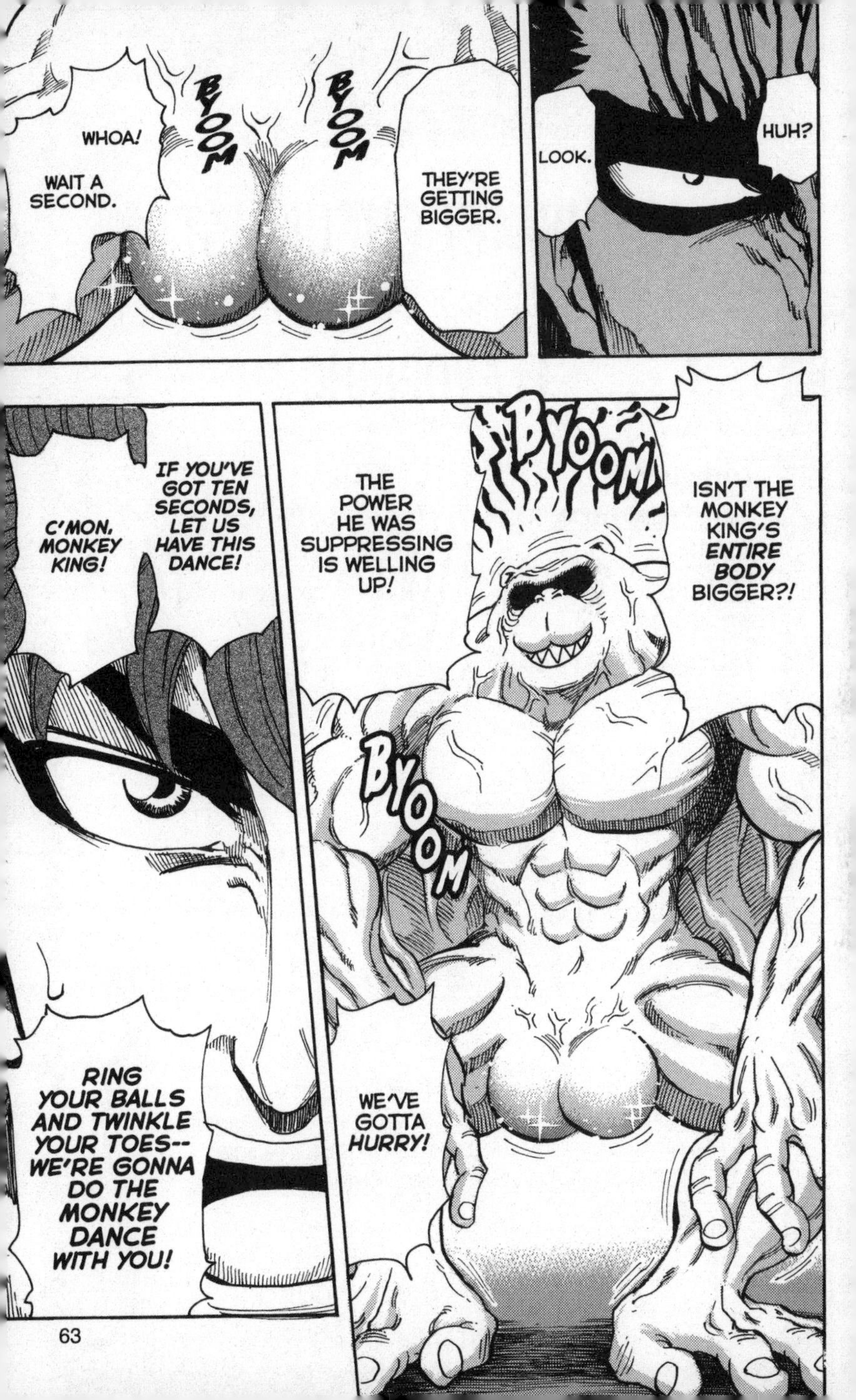
HUH?
LOOK.
THEY'RE GETTING BIGGER.
BYOOM
BYOOM
WHOA!
WAIT A SECOND.
BYOOM
ISN'T THE MONKEY KING'S ENTIRE BODY BIGGER?!
THE POWER HE WAS SUPPRESSING IS WELLING UP!
BYOOM
WE'VE GOTTA HURRY!
IF YOU'VE GOT TEN SECONDS, LET US HAVE THIS DANCE!
C'MON, MONKEY KING!
RING YOUR BALLS AND TWINKLE YOUR TOES-- WE'RE GONNA DO THE MONKEY DANCE WITH YOU!

TORIKO

GOURMET CHECKLIST

Vol. 339

FLAVORHINO
(MAMMAL)

CAPTURE LEVEL: 57
HABITAT: FOUND EVERYWHERE
SIZE: 8 M
HEIGHT: 4 M
WEIGHT: 25 TONS
PRICE: 2,000 YEN PER 100 GRAMS

SCALE

A UNIQUE RHINOCEROS WITH HYDRANGEA GROWING OUT OF ITS BACK. DESPITE SUCH AN APPEARANCE, THIS ROUGH FELLOW WILL RUSH HEAD-ON INTO ANYTHING. THIS WAS THE FIRST BEAST MIDORA CAPTURED WHEN HE WAS YOUNG DURING HIS TRAINING WITH ACACIA, ICHIRYU AND JIRO. HE CAPTURED IT FOR THE LOVING FROESE.

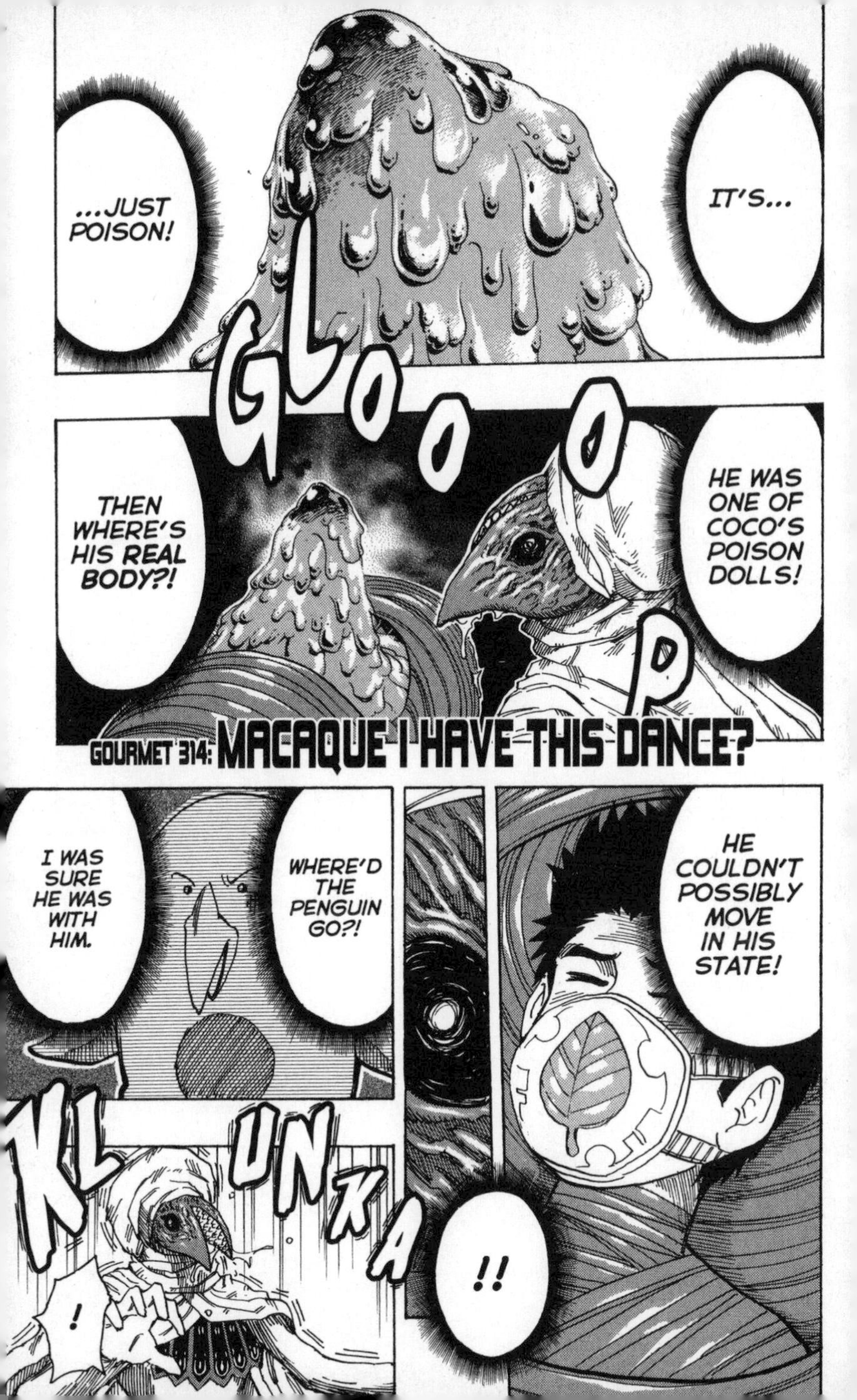
IT'S...
...JUST POISON!
GLOOOP
HE WAS ONE OF COCO'S POISON DOLLS!
THEN WHERE'S HIS REAL BODY?!
GOURMET 314: MACAQUE I HAVE THIS DANCE?
HE COULDN'T POSSIBLY MOVE IN HIS STATE!
WHERE'D THE PENGUIN GO?!
I WAS SURE HE WAS WITH HIM.
!!
KLUNKA
!

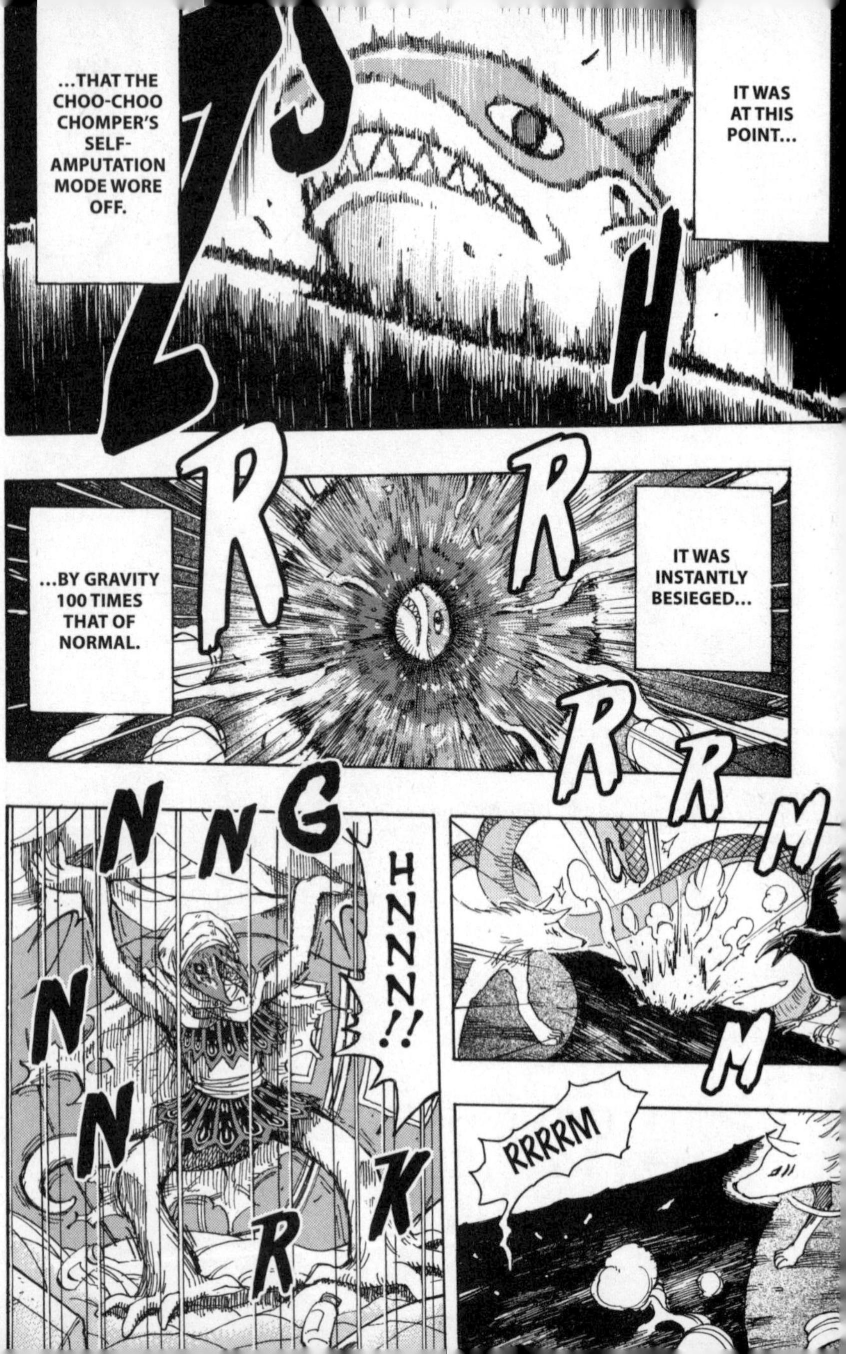
IT WAS AT THIS POINT...
...THAT THE CHOO-CHOO CHOMPER'S SELF-AMPUTATION MODE WORE OFF.
IT WAS INSTANTLY BESIEGED...
...BY GRAVITY 100 TIMES THAT OF NORMAL.
RRRRRMM
RRRRM
NNNG
HNNN!!
NNRK

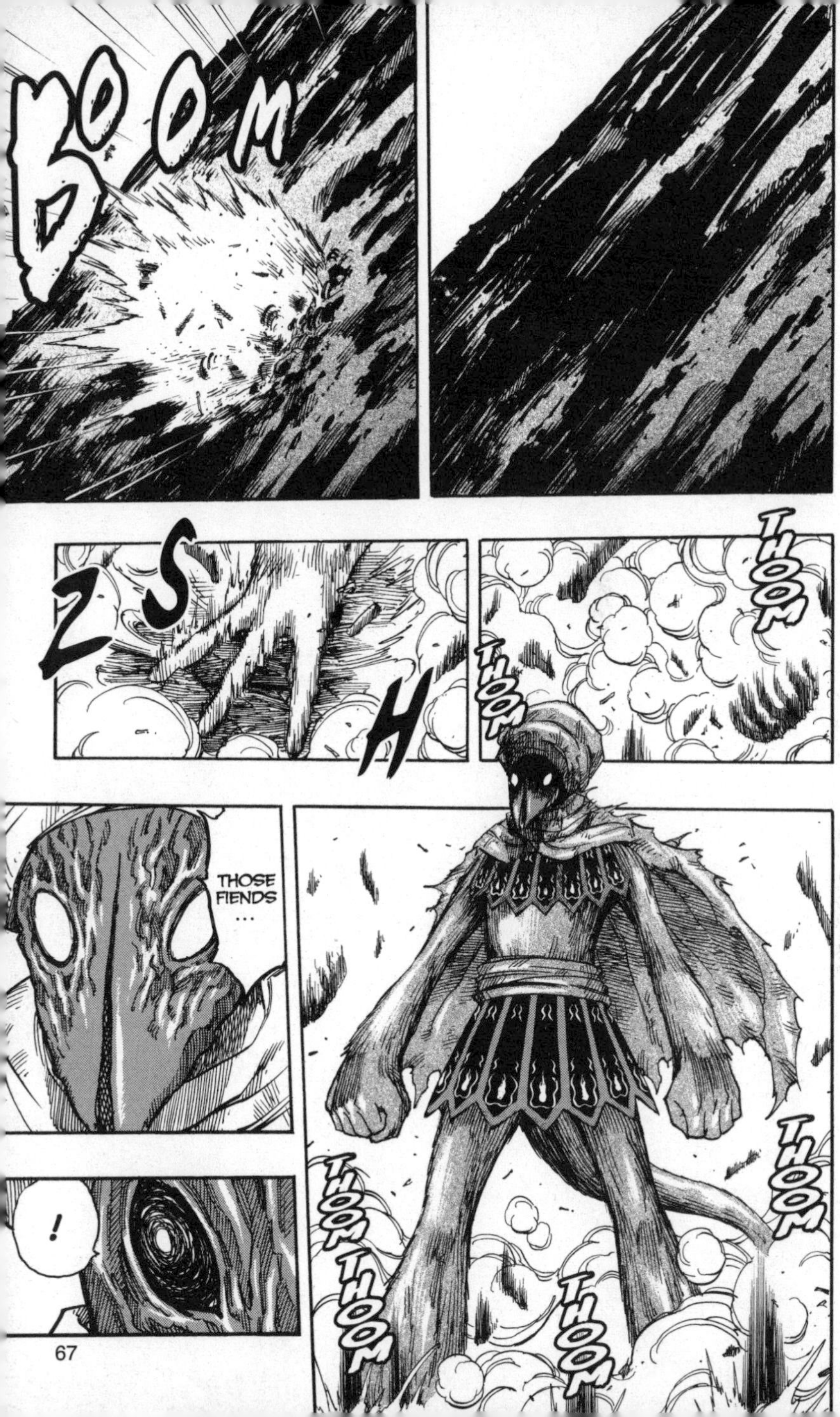
BOOM
THOOM
THOOM
ZSH
THOOM
THOOM
THOOM
THOOM
THOSE FIENDS ...
!

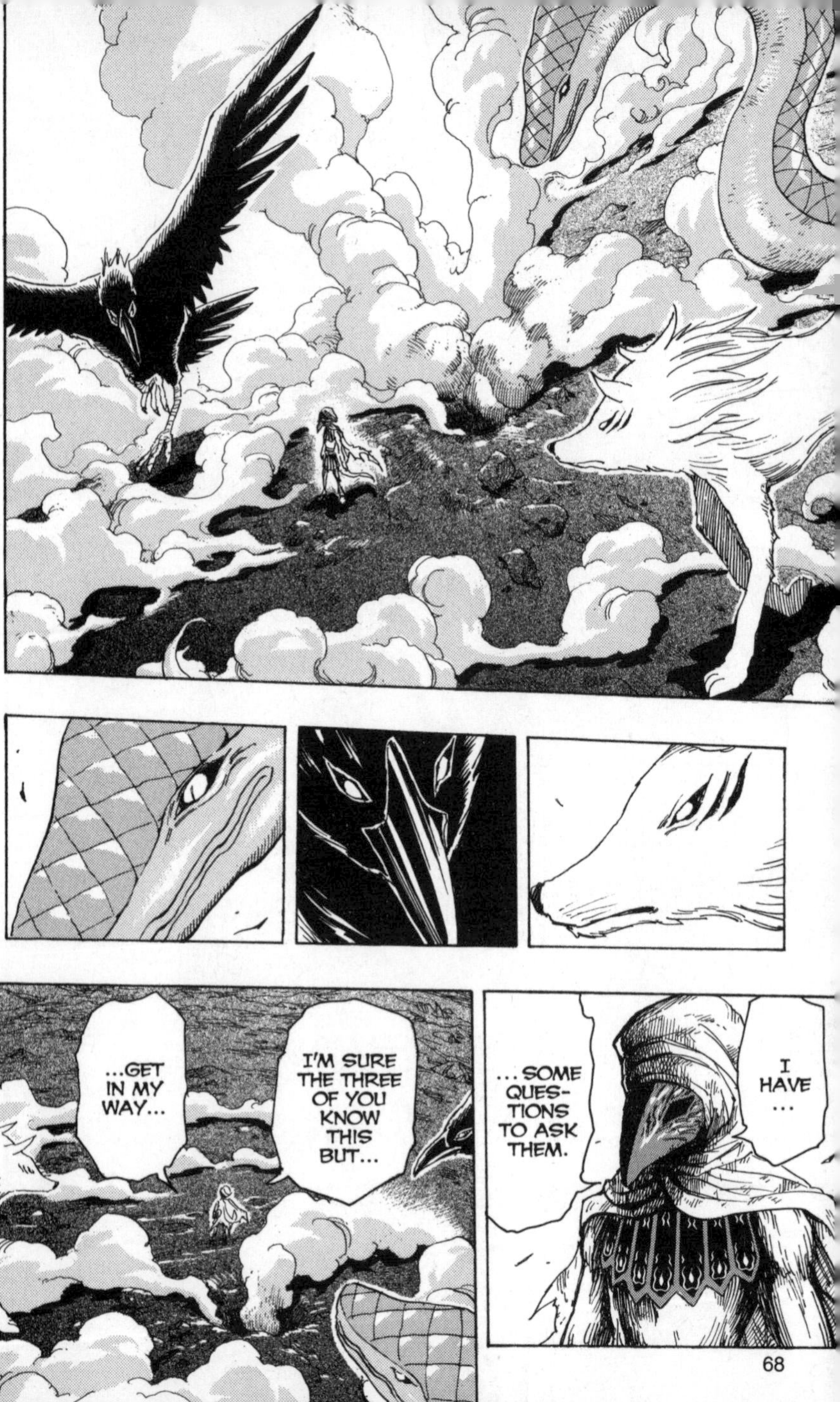
I HAVE ...
... SOME QUES-TIONS TO ASK THEM.
I'M SURE THE THREE OF YOU KNOW THIS BUT...
...GET IN MY WAY...

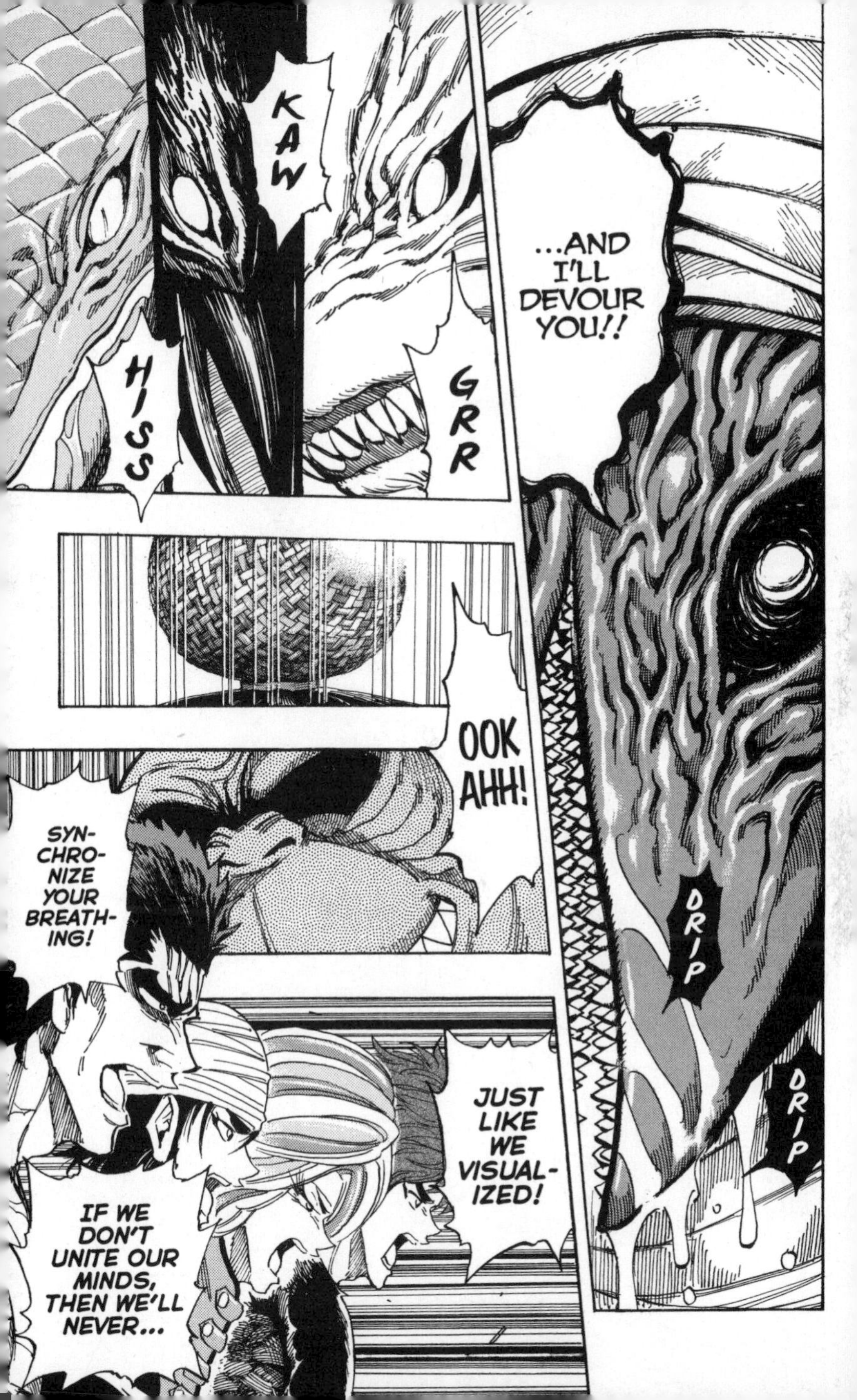
...AND I'LL DEVOUR YOU!!
DRIP
DRIP
KAW
GRR
HISS
OOK AHH!
SYN-CHRO-NIZE YOUR BREATH-ING!
JUST LIKE WE VISUAL-IZED!
IF WE DON'T UNITE OUR MINDS, THEN WE'LL NEVER...

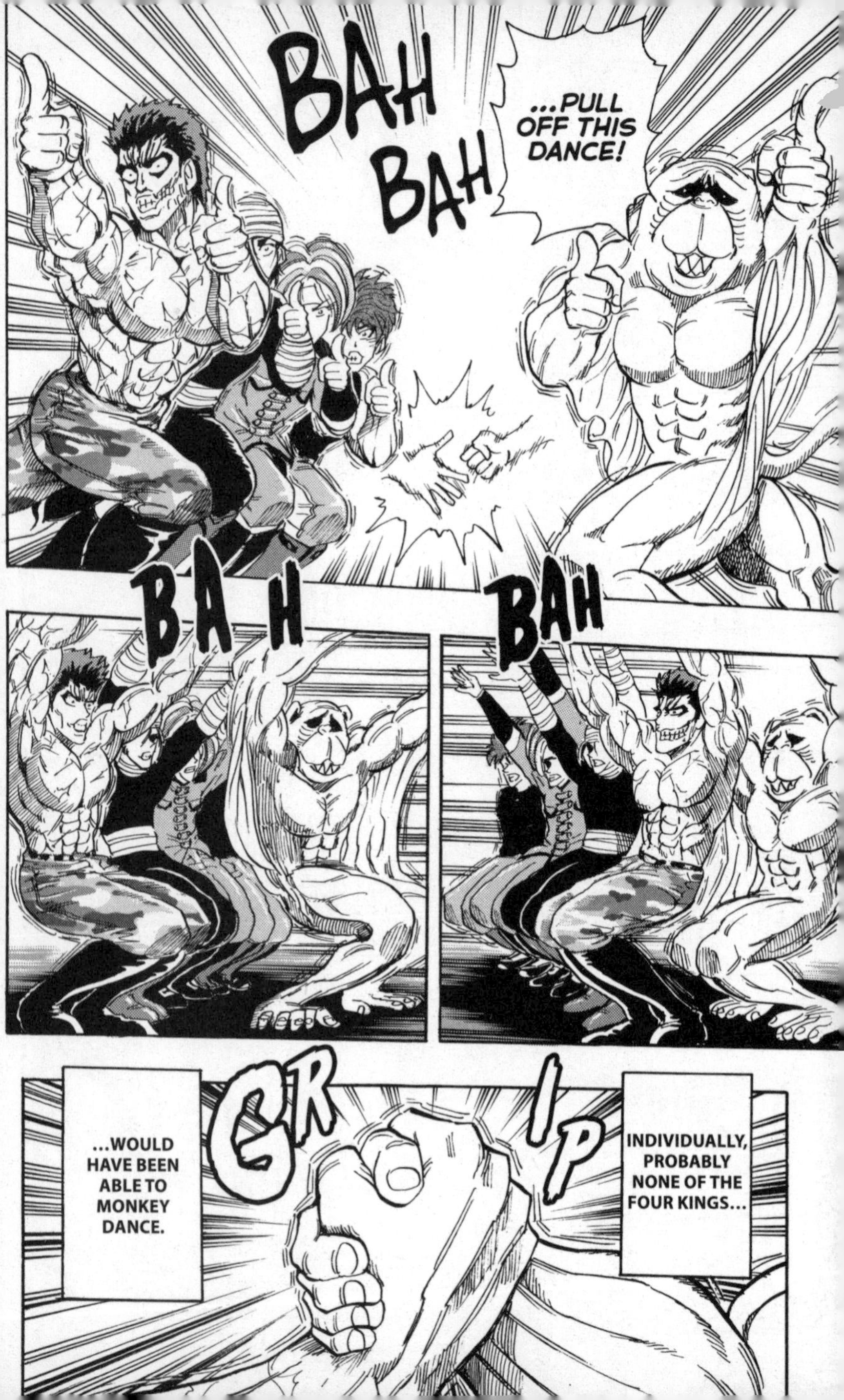
...PULL OFF THIS DANCE!
BAH BAH
BAH
BAH
INDIVIDUALLY, PROBABLY NONE OF THE FOUR KINGS...
GRIP
...WOULD HAVE BEEN ABLE TO MONKEY DANCE.

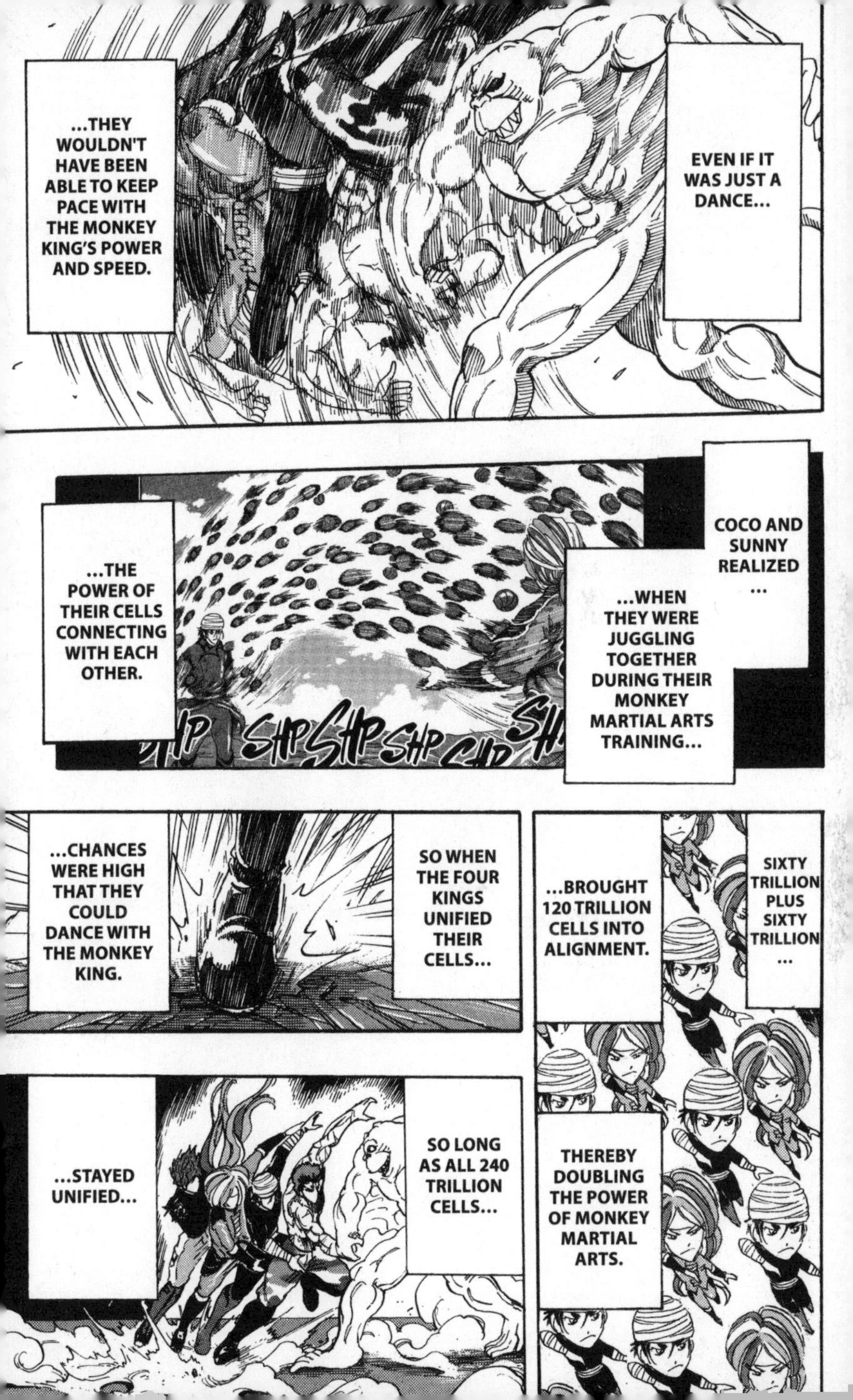
EVEN IF IT WAS JUST A DANCE...
...THEY WOULDN'T HAVE BEEN ABLE TO KEEP PACE WITH THE MONKEY KING'S POWER AND SPEED.
COCO AND SUNNY REALIZED ...
...WHEN THEY WERE JUGGLING TOGETHER DURING THEIR MONKEY MARTIAL ARTS TRAINING...
...THE POWER OF THEIR CELLS CONNECTING WITH EACH OTHER.
SHP SHP SHP SHP
SIXTY TRILLION PLUS SIXTY TRILLION ...
...BROUGHT 120 TRILLION CELLS INTO ALIGNMENT.
THEREBY DOUBLING THE POWER OF MONKEY MARTIAL ARTS.
SO WHEN THE FOUR KINGS UNIFIED THEIR CELLS...
...CHANCES WERE HIGH THAT THEY COULD DANCE WITH THE MONKEY KING.
SO LONG AS ALL 240 TRILLION CELLS...
...STAYED UNIFIED...

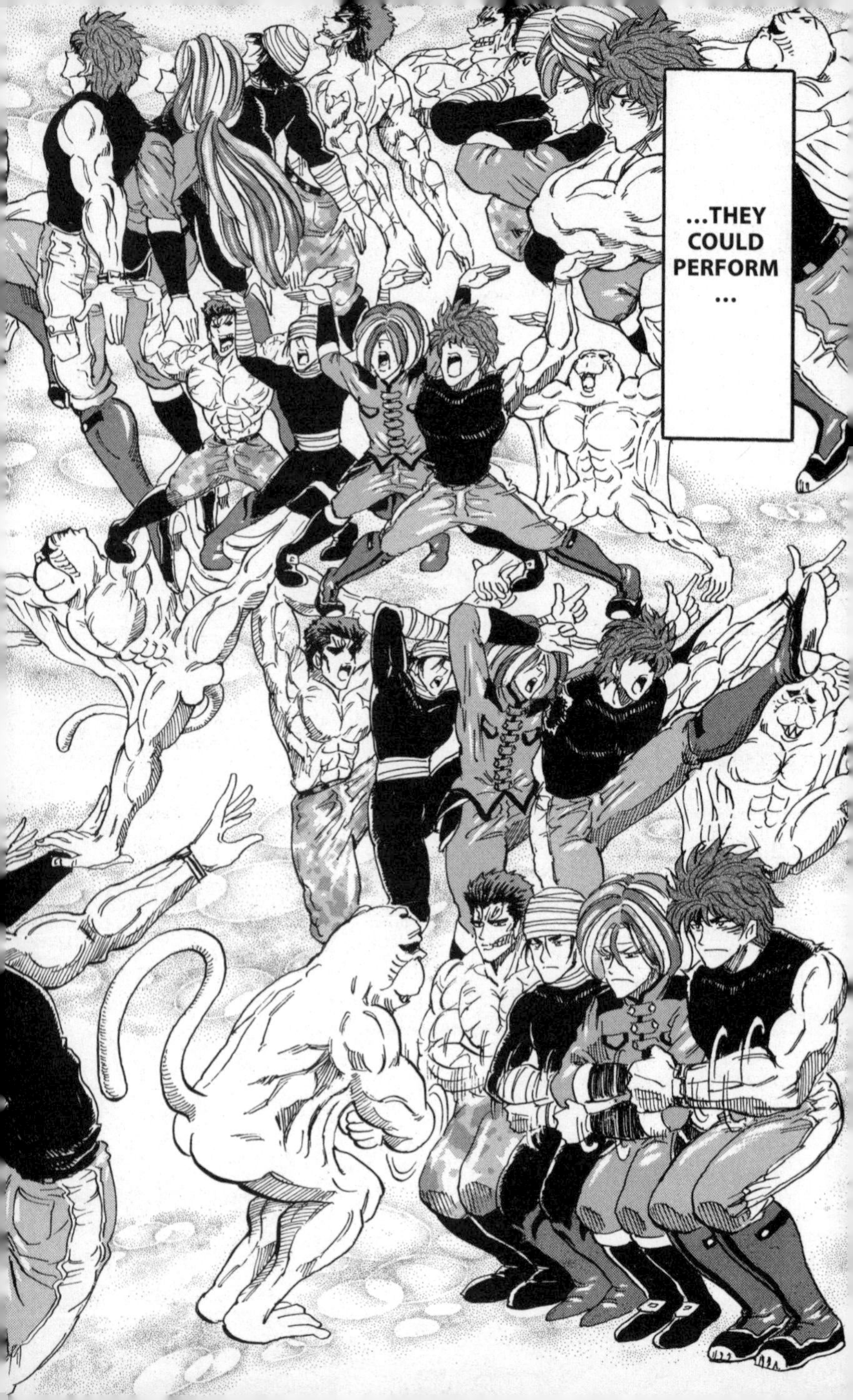
...THEY COULD PERFORM ...

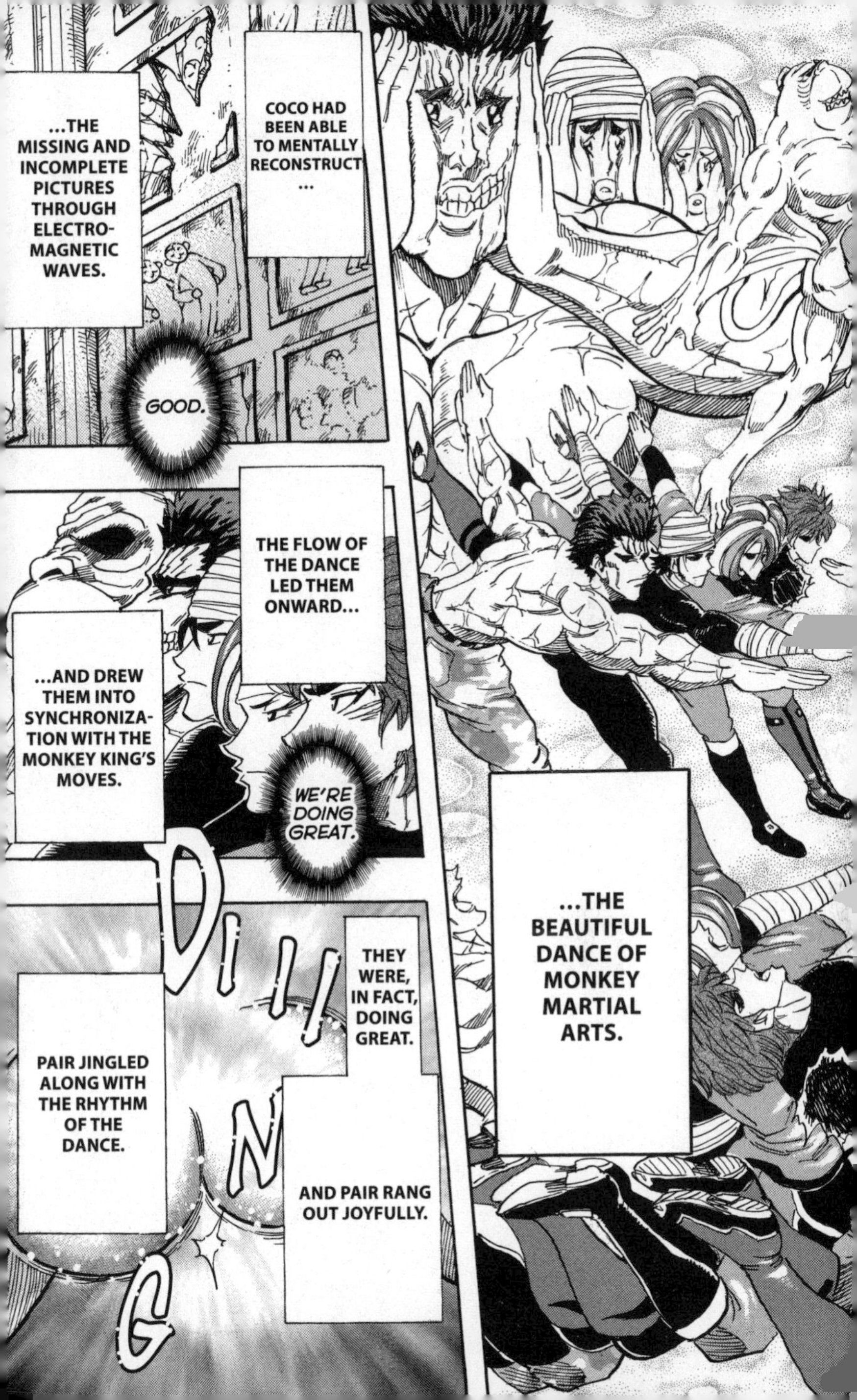
...THE BEAUTIFUL DANCE OF MONKEY MARTIAL ARTS.
COCO HAD BEEN ABLE TO MENTALLY RECONSTRUCT...
...THE MISSING AND INCOMPLETE PICTURES THROUGH ELECTRO-MAGNETIC WAVES.
GOOD.
THE FLOW OF THE DANCE LED THEM ONWARD...
...AND DREW THEM INTO SYNCHRONIZA-TION WITH THE MONKEY KING'S MOVES.
WE'RE DOING GREAT.
THEY WERE, IN FACT, DOING GREAT.
AND PAIR RANG OUT JOYFULLY.
PAIR JINGLED ALONG WITH THE RHYTHM OF THE DANCE.
DIIING

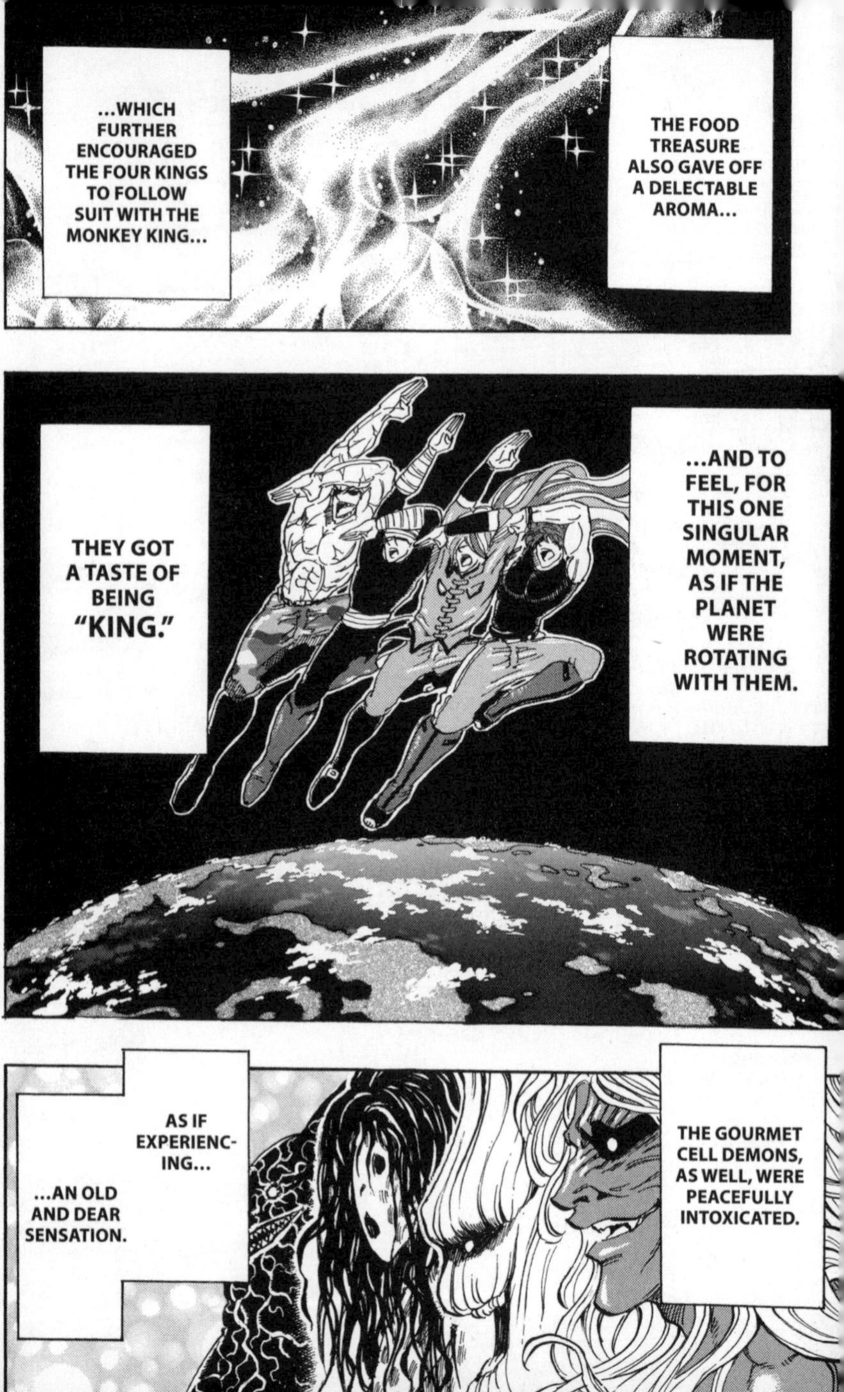
THE FOOD TREASURE ALSO GAVE OFF A DELECTABLE AROMA...
...WHICH FURTHER ENCOURAGED THE FOUR KINGS TO FOLLOW SUIT WITH THE MONKEY KING...
THEY GOT A TASTE OF BEING "KING."
...AND TO FEEL, FOR THIS ONE SINGULAR MOMENT, AS IF THE PLANET WERE ROTATING WITH THEM.
THE GOURMET CELL DEMONS, AS WELL, WERE PEACEFULLY INTOXICATED.
AS IF EXPERIENC-ING...
...AN OLD AND DEAR SENSATION.

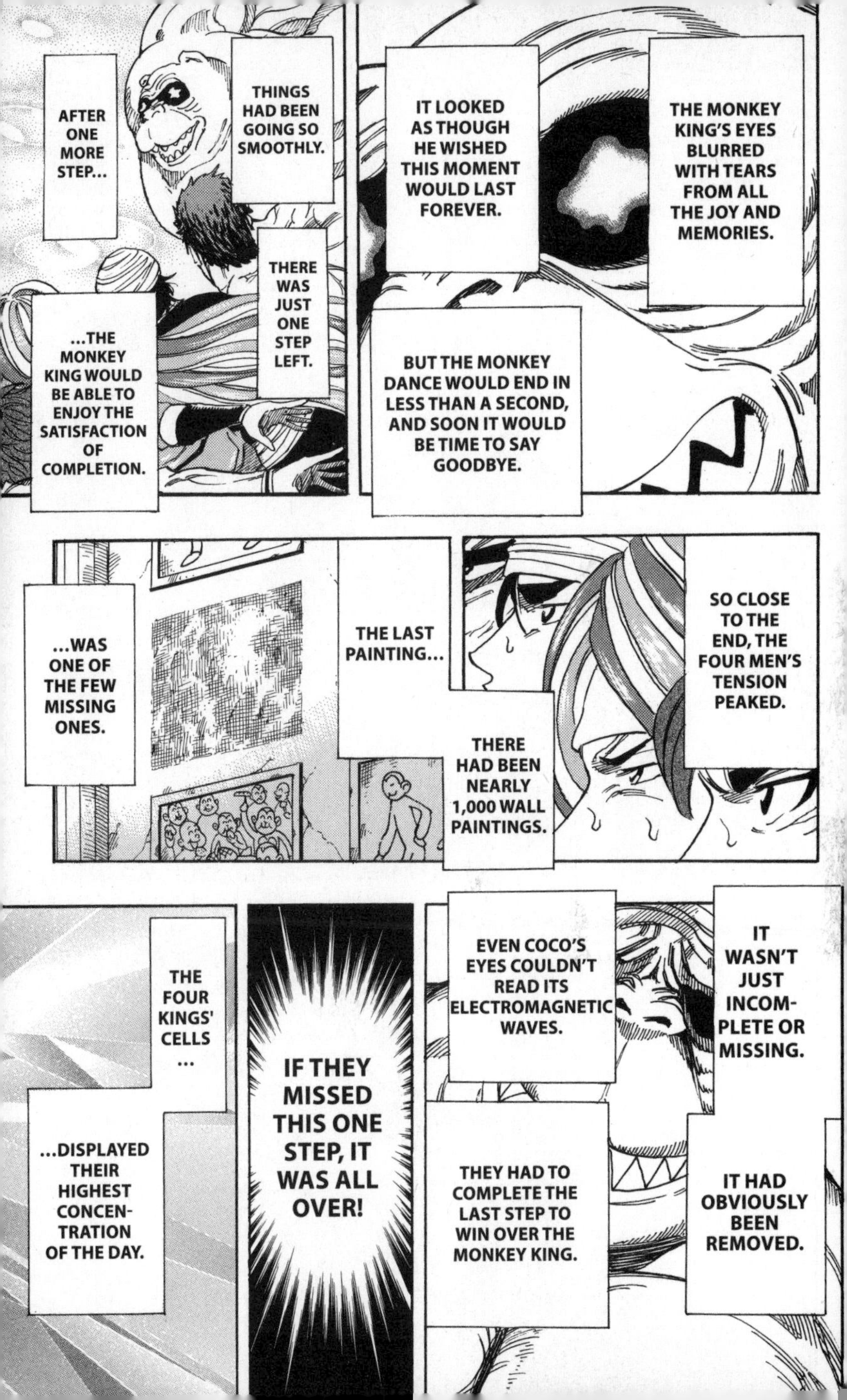
THE MONKEY KING'S EYES BLURRED WITH TEARS FROM ALL THE JOY AND MEMORIES.
IT LOOKED AS THOUGH HE WISHED THIS MOMENT WOULD LAST FOREVER.
BUT THE MONKEY DANCE WOULD END IN LESS THAN A SECOND, AND SOON IT WOULD BE TIME TO SAY GOODBYE.
THINGS HAD BEEN GOING SO SMOOTHLY.
THERE WAS JUST ONE STEP LEFT.
AFTER ONE MORE STEP...
...THE MONKEY KING WOULD BE ABLE TO ENJOY THE SATISFACTION OF COMPLETION.
SO CLOSE TO THE END, THE FOUR MEN'S TENSION PEAKED.
THERE HAD BEEN NEARLY 1,000 WALL PAINTINGS.
THE LAST PAINTING...
...WAS ONE OF THE FEW MISSING ONES.
IT WASN'T JUST INCOMPLETE OR MISSING.
EVEN COCO'S EYES COULDN'T READ ITS ELECTROMAGNETIC WAVES.
IT HAD OBVIOUSLY BEEN REMOVED.
THEY HAD TO COMPLETE THE LAST STEP TO WIN OVER THE MONKEY KING.
IF THEY MISSED THIS ONE STEP, IT WAS ALL OVER!
THE FOUR KINGS' CELLS...
...DISPLAYED THEIR HIGHEST CONCENTRATION OF THE DAY.

NOW FOR THE LAST ONE.

OKAY.

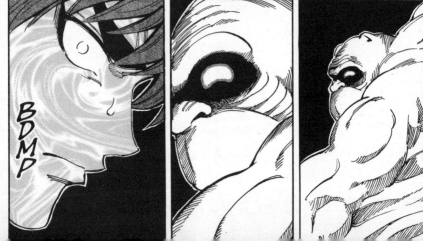

BDMP

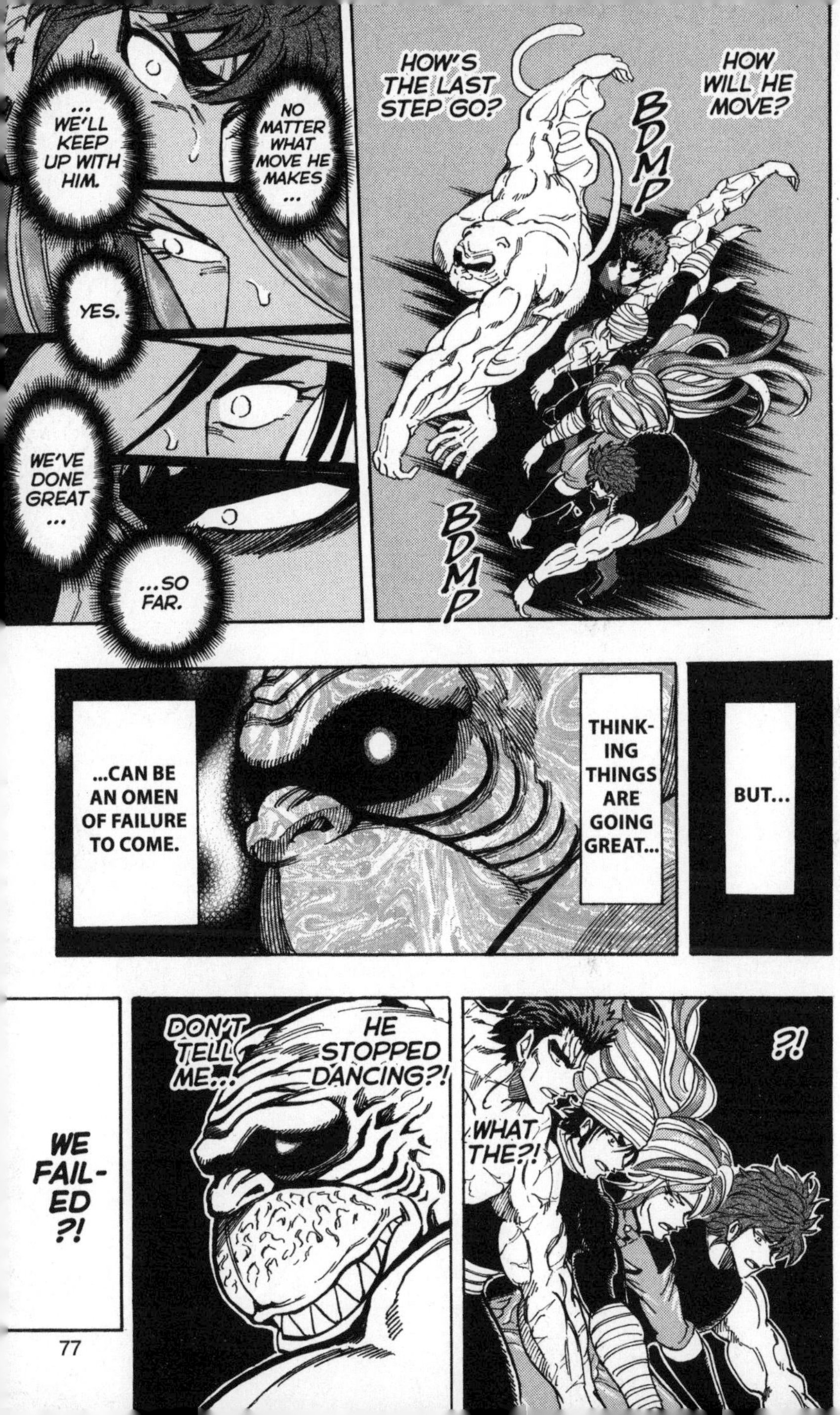
HOW WILL HE MOVE?
HOW'S THE LAST STEP GO?
BDMP
BDMP
NO MATTER WHAT MOVE HE MAKES...
...WE'LL KEEP UP WITH HIM.
YES.
WE'VE DONE GREAT...
...SO FAR.
BUT...
THINKING THINGS ARE GOING GREAT...
...CAN BE AN OMEN OF FAILURE TO COME.
?!
WHAT THE?!
HE STOPPED DANCING?!
DON'T TELL ME...
WE FAILED?!

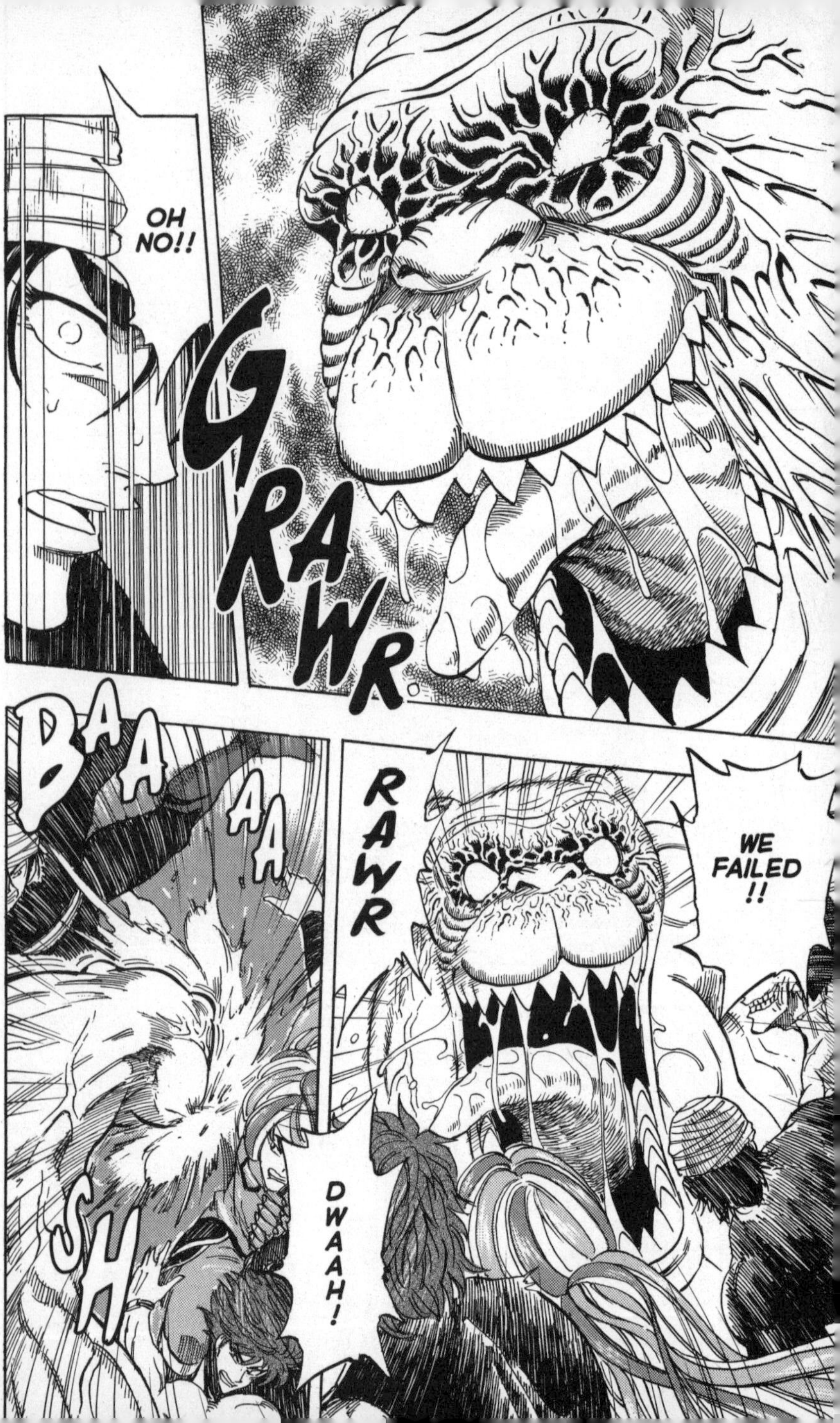
GRAWR
OH NO!!
WE FAILED!!
RAWR
DWAAAH!
BAAAA
SH

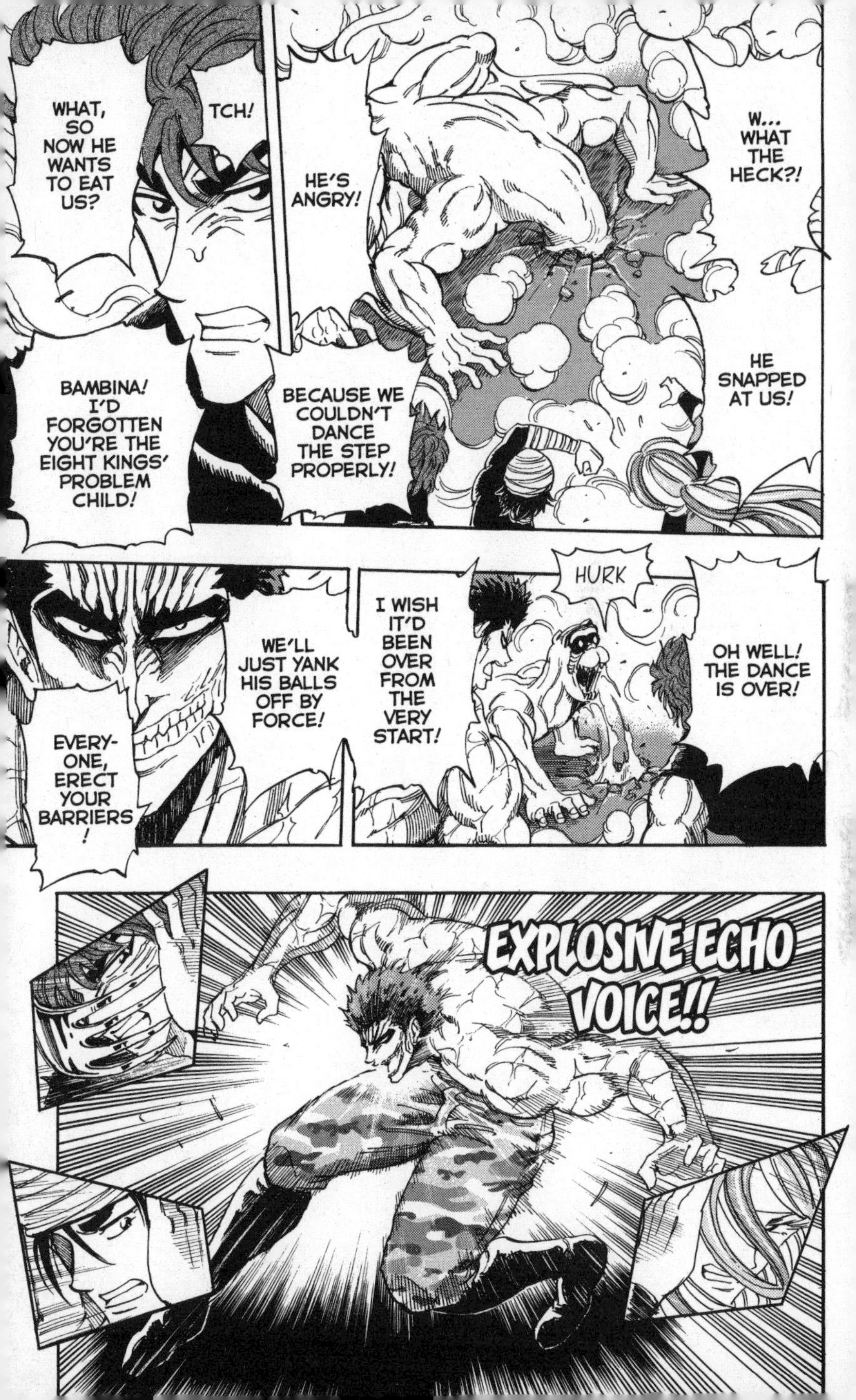
W... WHAT THE HECK?!
HE'S ANGRY!
HE SNAPPED AT US!
BECAUSE WE COULDN'T DANCE THE STEP PROPERLY!
TCH!
WHAT, SO NOW HE WANTS TO EAT US?
BAMBINA! I'D FORGOTTEN YOU'RE THE EIGHT KINGS' PROBLEM CHILD!
HURK
OH WELL! THE DANCE IS OVER!
I WISH IT'D BEEN OVER FROM THE VERY START!
WE'LL JUST YANK HIS BALLS OFF BY FORCE!
EVERYONE, ERECT YOUR BARRIERS!
EXPLOSIVE ECHO VOICE!!

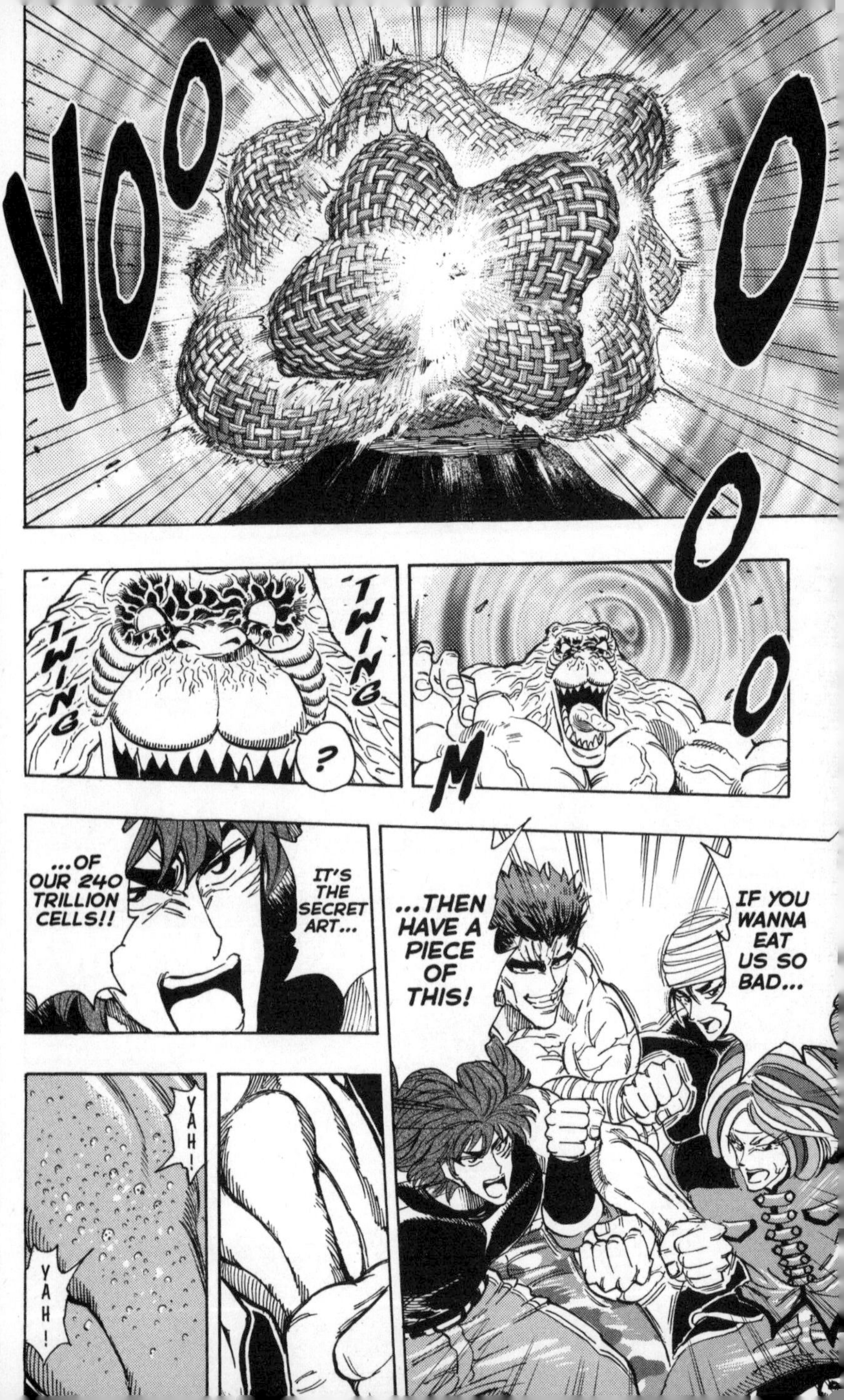
VOOOOOM
TWING
TWING
?
IF YOU WANNA EAT US SO BAD...
...THEN HAVE A PIECE OF THIS!
IT'S THE SECRET ART...
...OF OUR 240 TRILLION CELLS!!
YAH!
YAH!

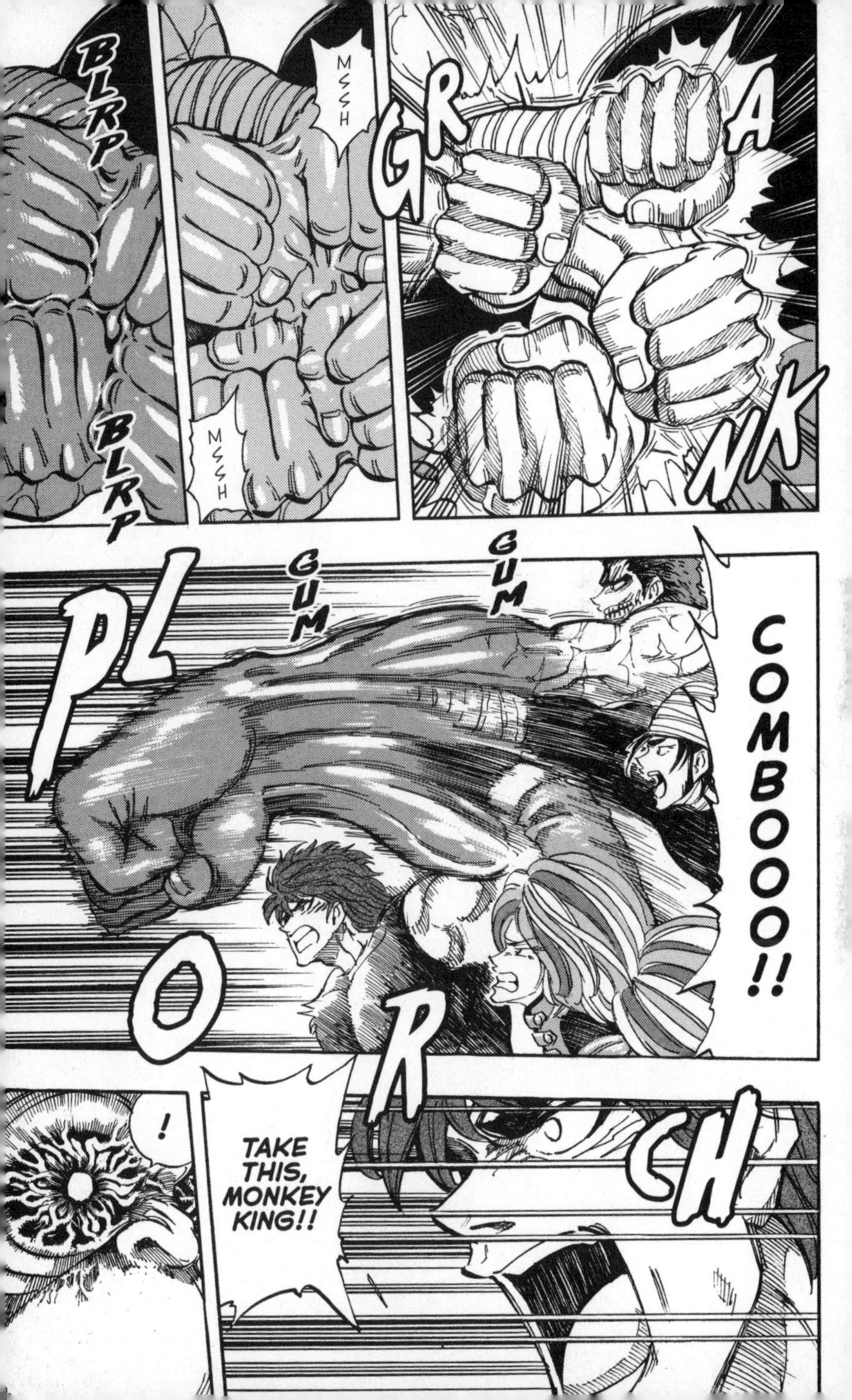
GRANK
MSSH
MSSH
BLRP
BLRP
COMBOOOO!!
GUM
GUM
PLORCH
TAKE THIS, MONKEY KING!!
!

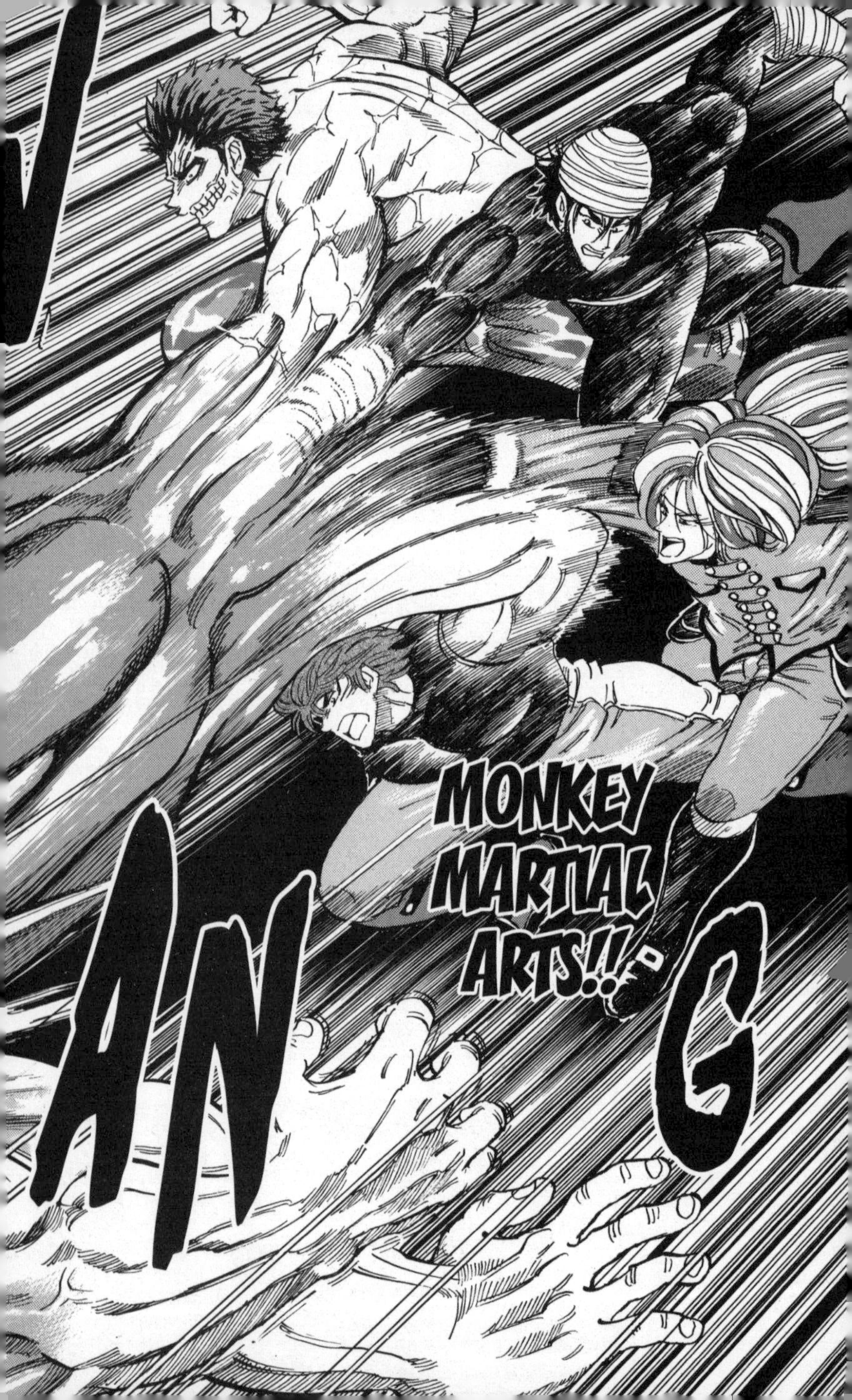
MONKEY MARTIAL ARTS!!
AN
G

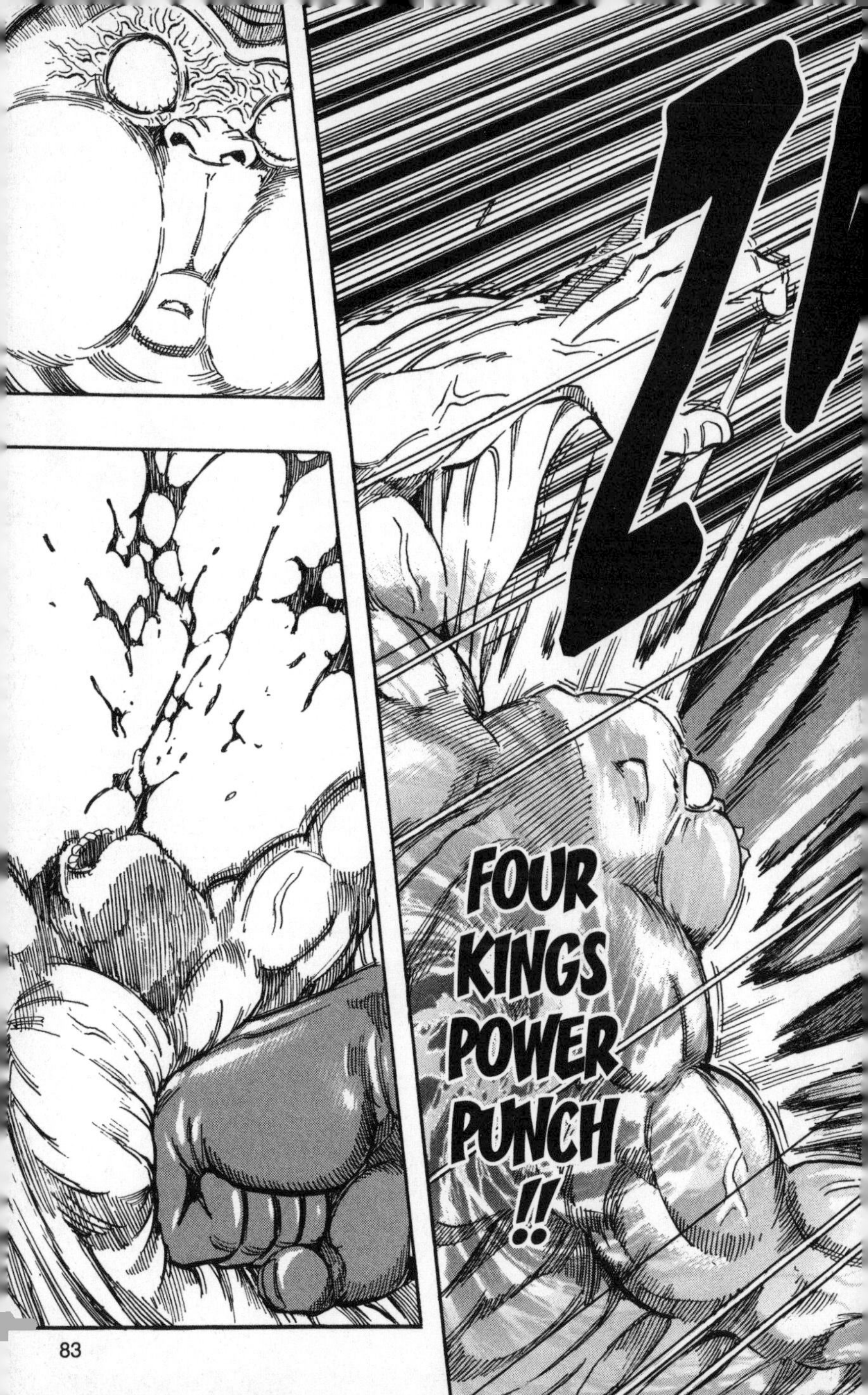
FOUR KINGS POWER PUNCH!!

GOURMET CHECKLIST

Vol. 340

 ## POISON BOAR
(MAMMAL)

CAPTURE LEVEL: 25
HABITAT: FOUND EVERYWHERE
SIZE: 7 M
HEIGHT: 3.5 M
WEIGHT: 15 TONS
PRICE: 1.2 MILLION YEN PER 100G

SCALE

THIS CREATURE DOESN'T HAVE MUCH COMBAT ABILITY, BUT IF CAPTURED THE WRONG WAY IT WILL IMMEDIATELY TURN TOXIC. ICHIRYU, JIRO AND MIDORA SPENT DAYS TRAINING WITH ACACIA TO HONE THEIR SKILLS, AND THIS MONSTER IS ONE OF MANY THEY GRAPPLED WITH ON A DAILY BASIS.

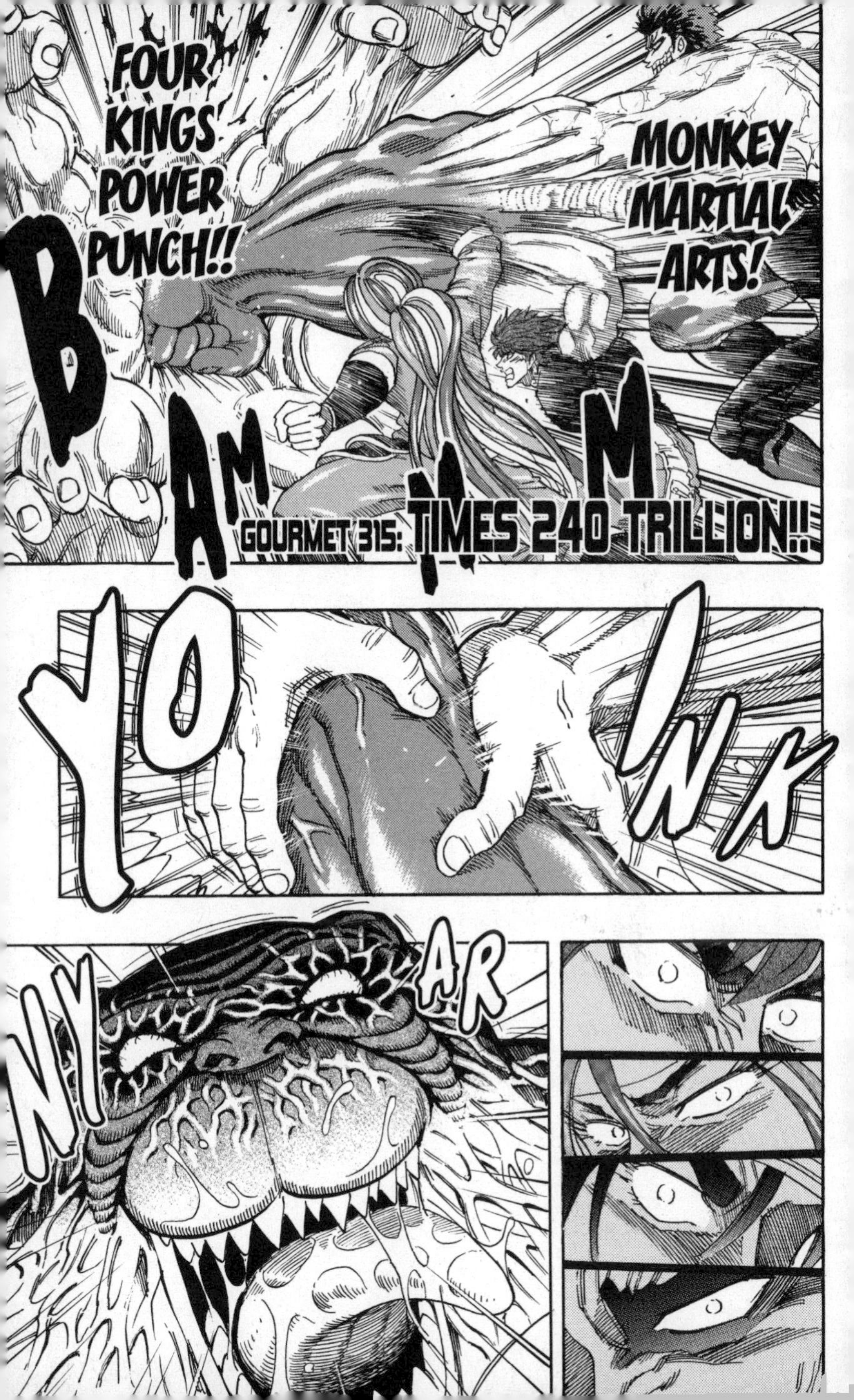
MONKEY MARTIAL ARTS!
FOUR KINGS POWER PUNCH!!
BAMMM
GOURMET 315: TIMES 240 TRILLION!!
YOINK
NY
AR

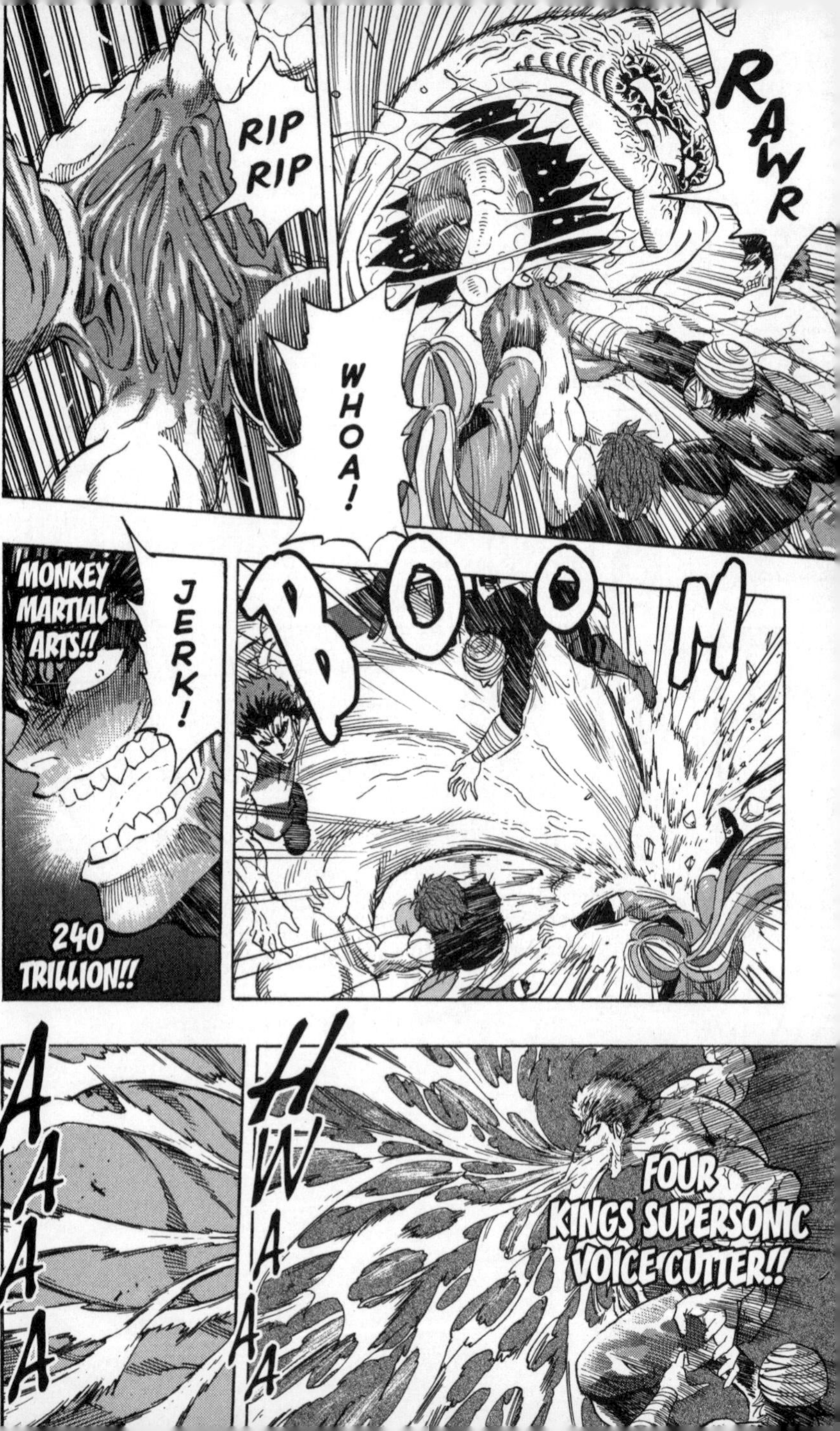
RAWR
RIP RIP
WHOA!
BOOM
JERK!
MONKEY MARTIAL ARTS!!
240 TRILLION!!
HWAAAA
AAAAA
FOUR KINGS SUPERSONIC VOICE CUTTER!!

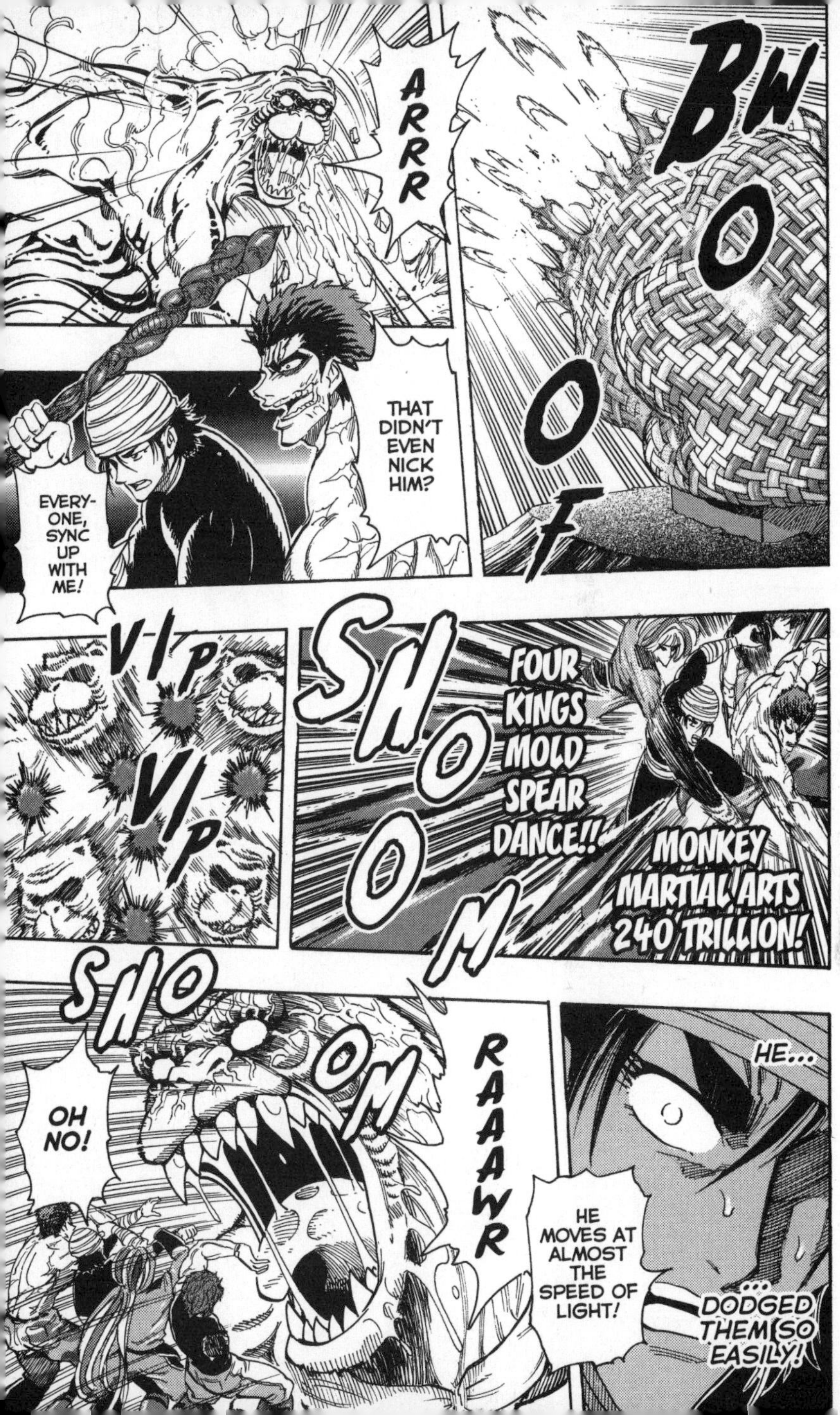
BWOOOF
ARRR
THAT DIDN'T EVEN NICK HIM?
EVERY-ONE, SYNC UP WITH ME!
SHOOOM
FOUR KINGS MOLD SPEAR DANCE!!
MONKEY MARTIAL ARTS 240 TRILLION!
VIP VIP VIP
HE...
HE MOVES AT ALMOST THE SPEED OF LIGHT!
...DODGED THEM SO EASILY!
SHOOOM
RAAAAWR
OH NO!

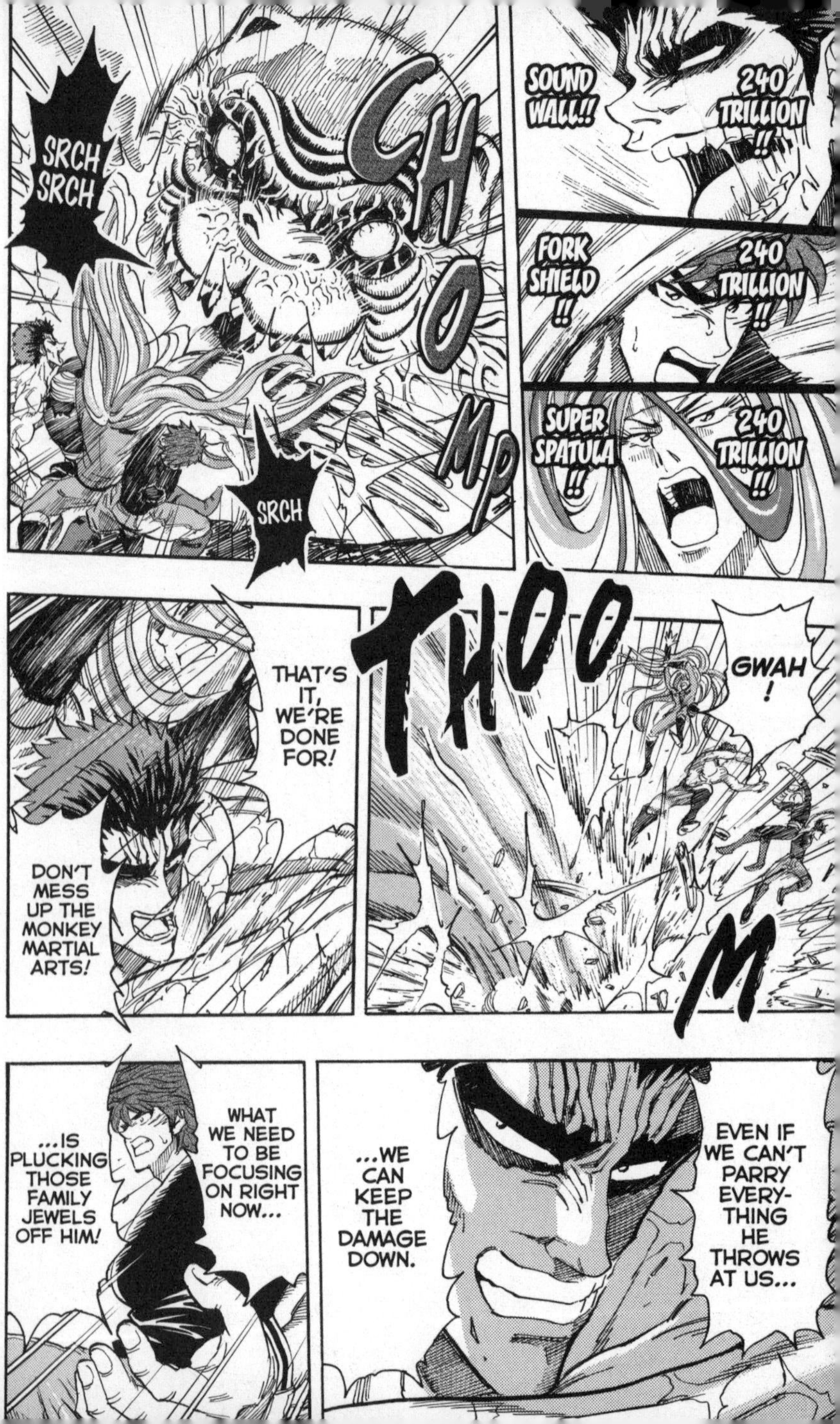
240 TRILLION!!
SOUND WALL!!
240 TRILLION!!
FORK SHIELD!!
240 TRILLION!!
SUPER SPATULA!!
CHOMP
SRCH SRCH
SRCH
THOOM
GWAH!
THAT'S IT, WE'RE DONE FOR!
DON'T MESS UP THE MONKEY MARTIAL ARTS!
EVEN IF WE CAN'T PARRY EVERY-THING HE THROWS AT US...
...WE CAN KEEP THE DAMAGE DOWN.
WHAT WE NEED TO BE FOCUSING ON RIGHT NOW...
...IS PLUCKING THOSE FAMILY JEWELS OFF HIM!

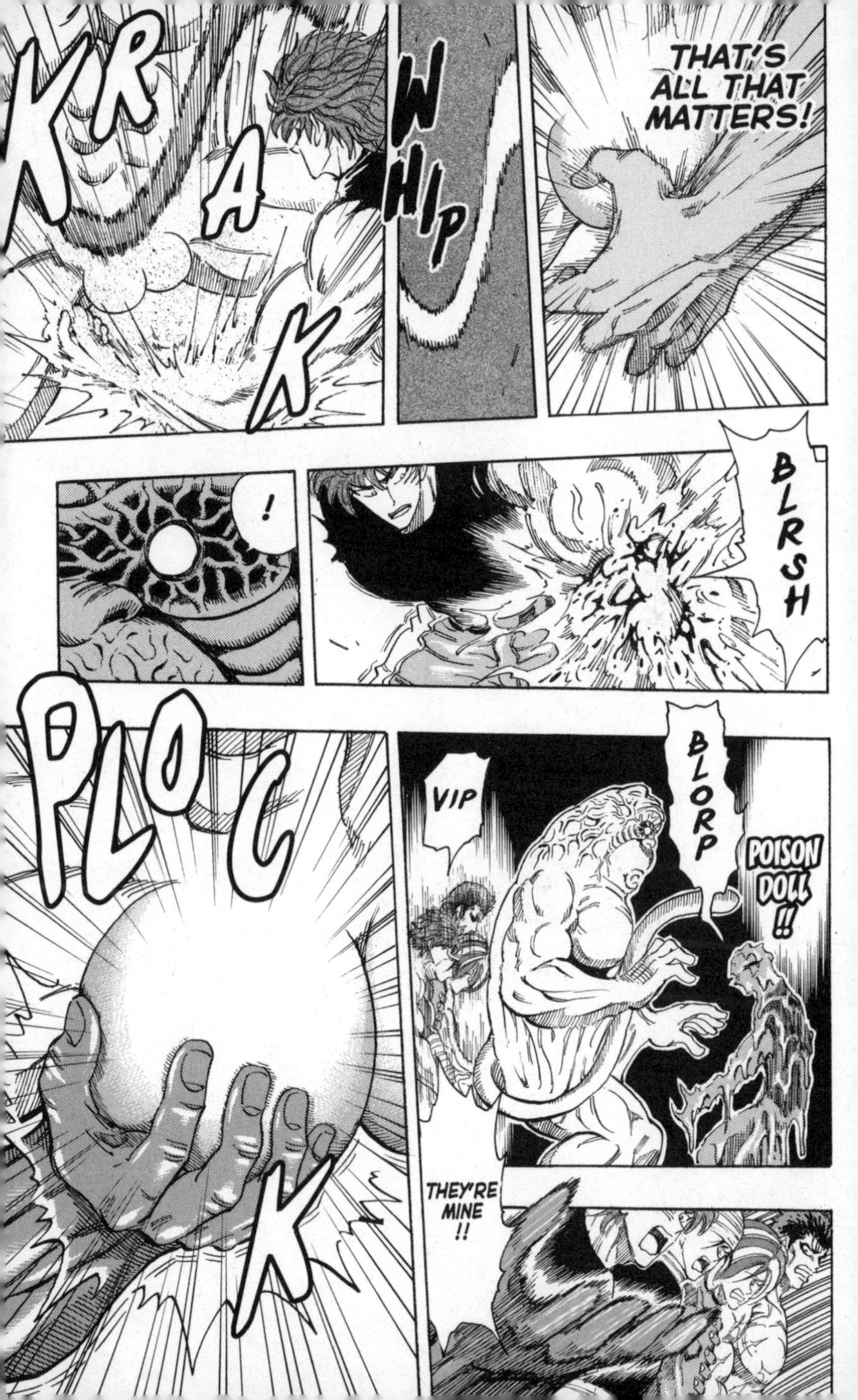
THAT'S ALL THAT MATTERS!
WHIP
KRAK
BLRSH
!
BLORP
POISON DOLL!!
VIP
THEY'RE MINE!!
PLOCK

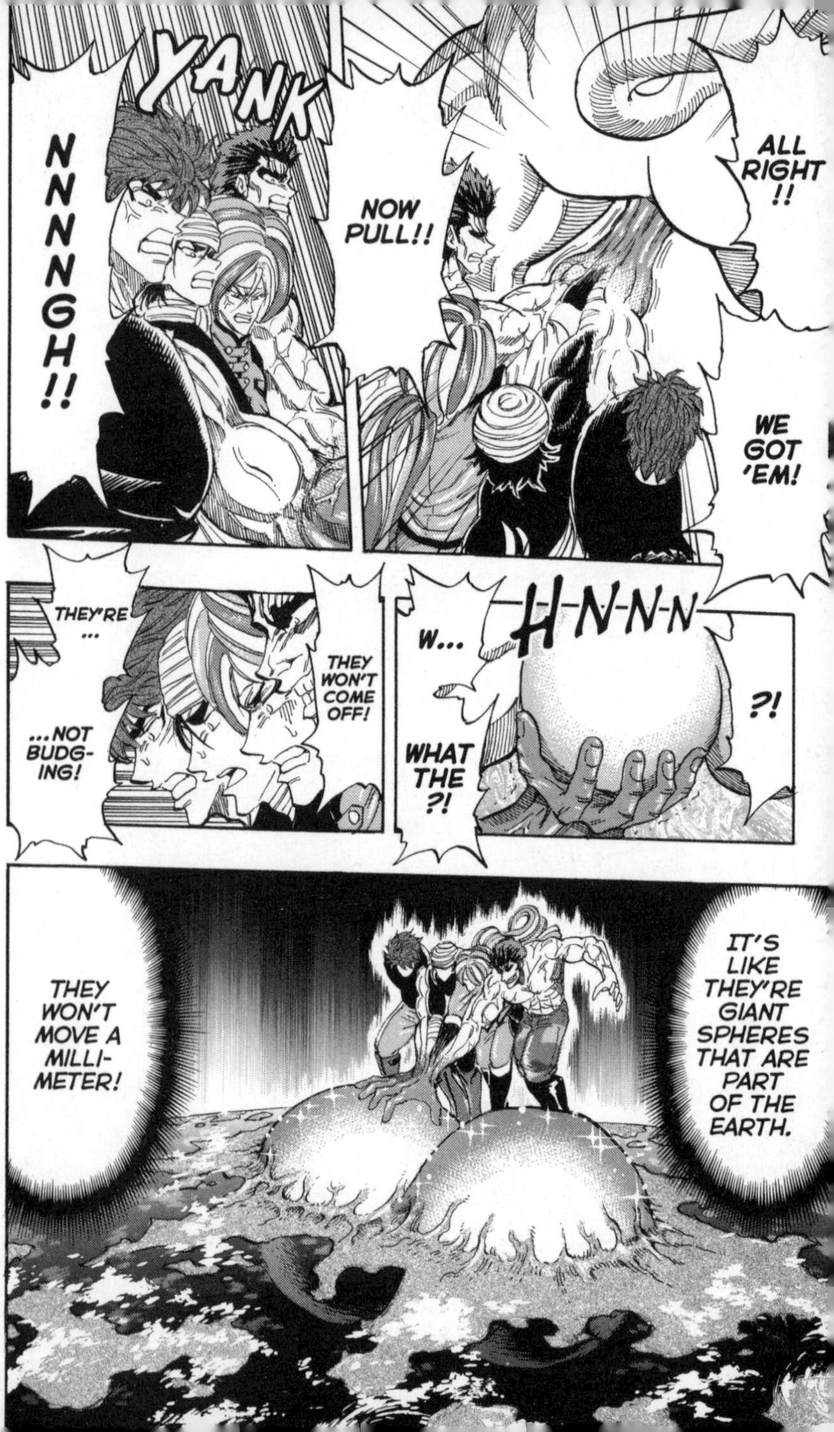
ALL RIGHT!!
NOW PULL!!
WE GOT 'EM!
YANK
NNNNNGH!!
H-N-N-N
?!
W...
WHAT THE?!
THEY WON'T COME OFF!
THEY'RE...
...NOT BUDGING!
IT'S LIKE THEY'RE GIANT SPHERES THAT ARE PART OF THE EARTH.
THEY WON'T MOVE A MILLIMETER!

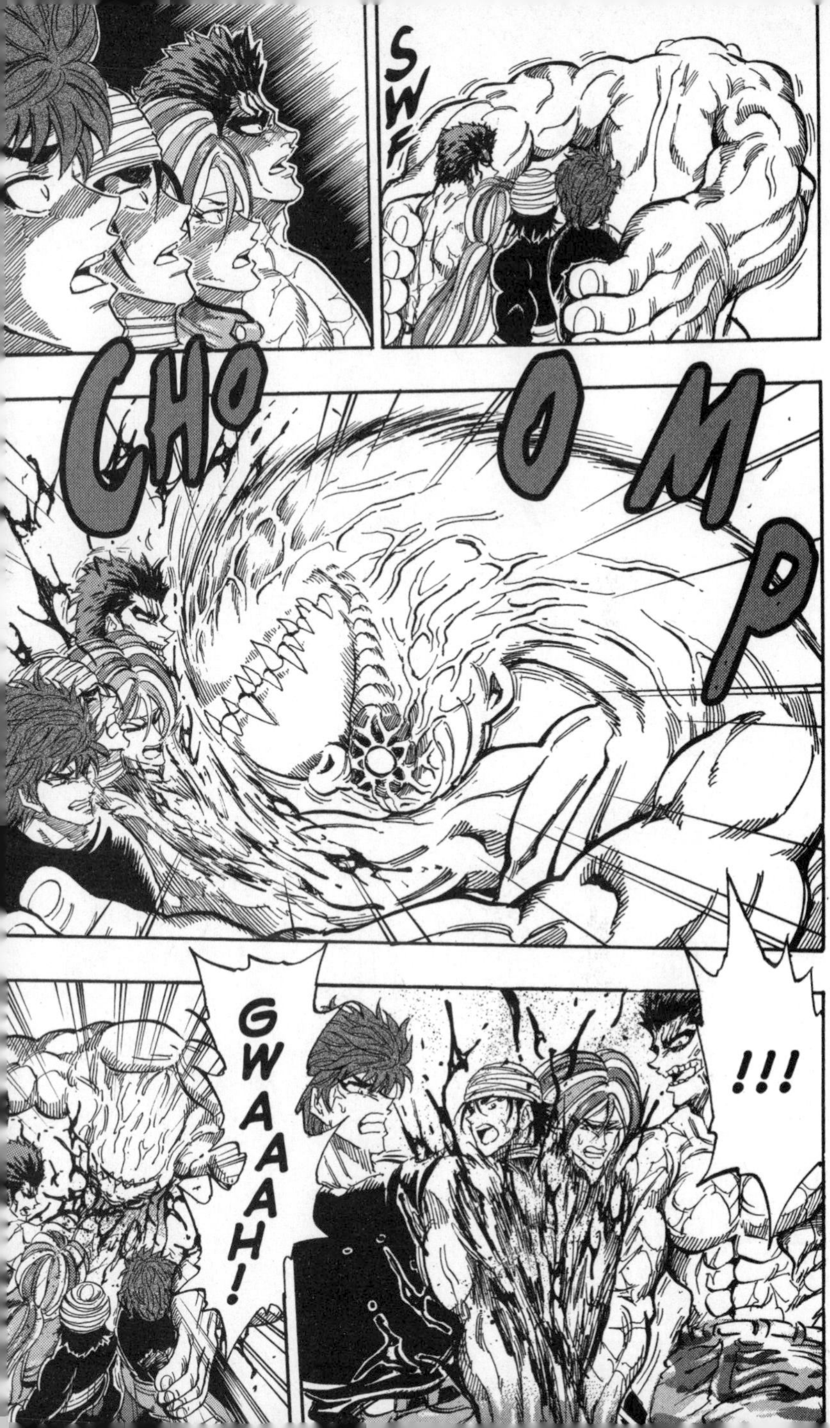
SWF
CHOMP
!!!
GWAAAAH!

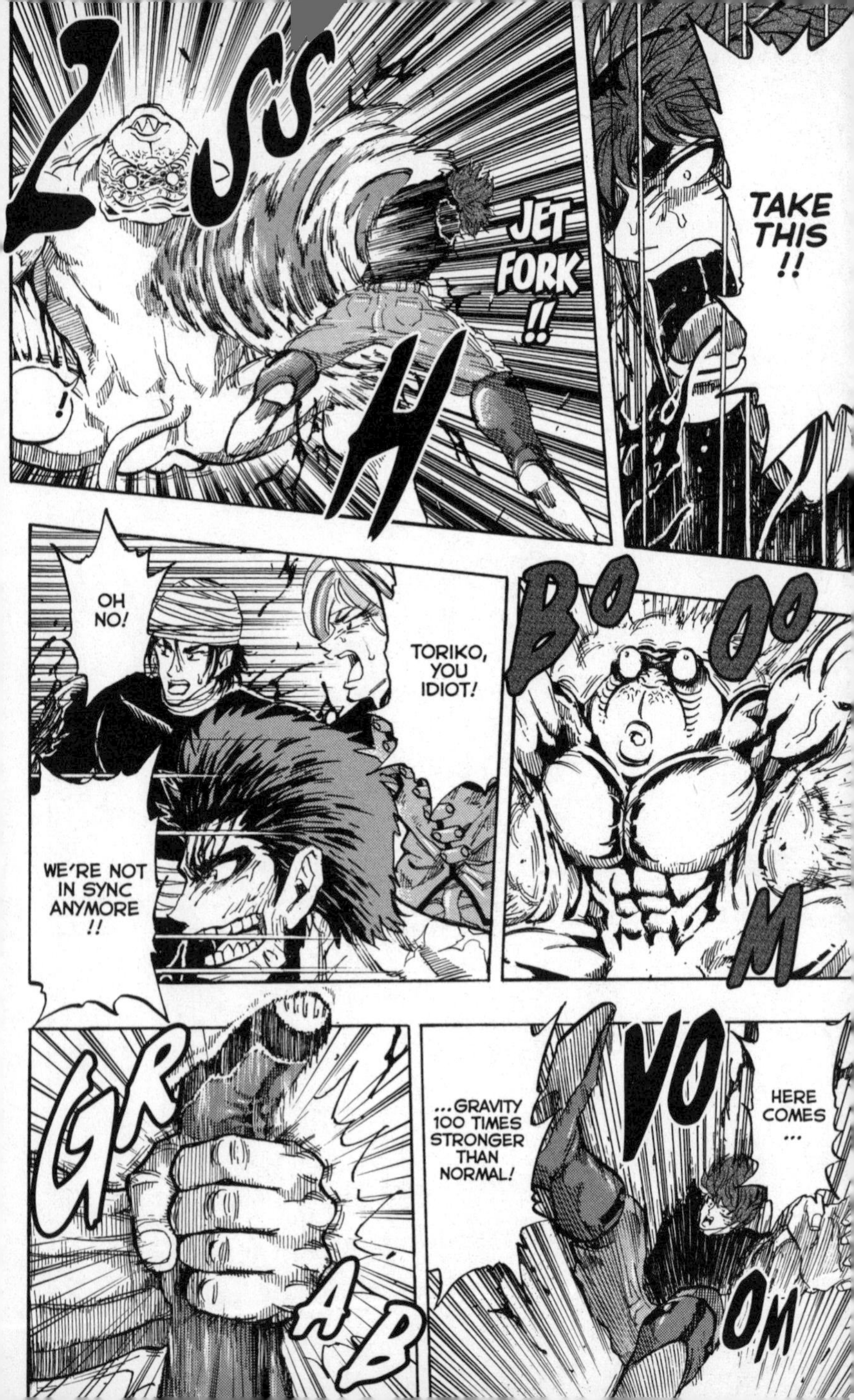
TAKE THIS !!
JET FORK !!
ZUSSH
!
BOOOOM
TORIKO, YOU IDIOT!
OH NO!
WE'RE NOT IN SYNC ANYMORE !!
HERE COMES ...
...GRAVITY 100 TIMES STRONGER THAN NORMAL!
VOOM
GRAB

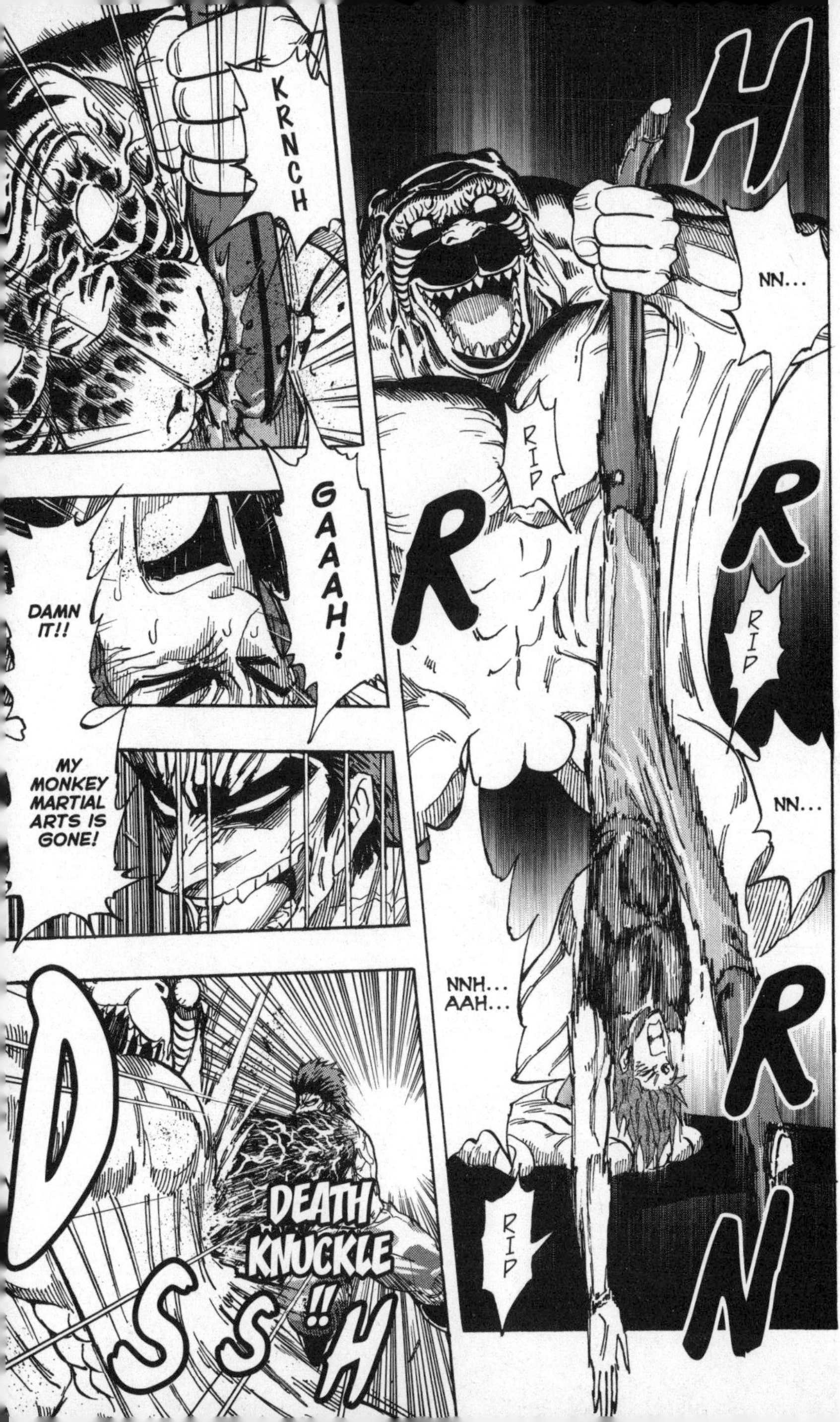
HRRRN
NN...
RIP
RIP
NN...
NNH... AAH...
RIP
KRNCH
GAAAAH!
DAMN IT!!
MY MONKEY MARTIAL ARTS IS GONE!
DSSH
DEATH KNUCKLE!!

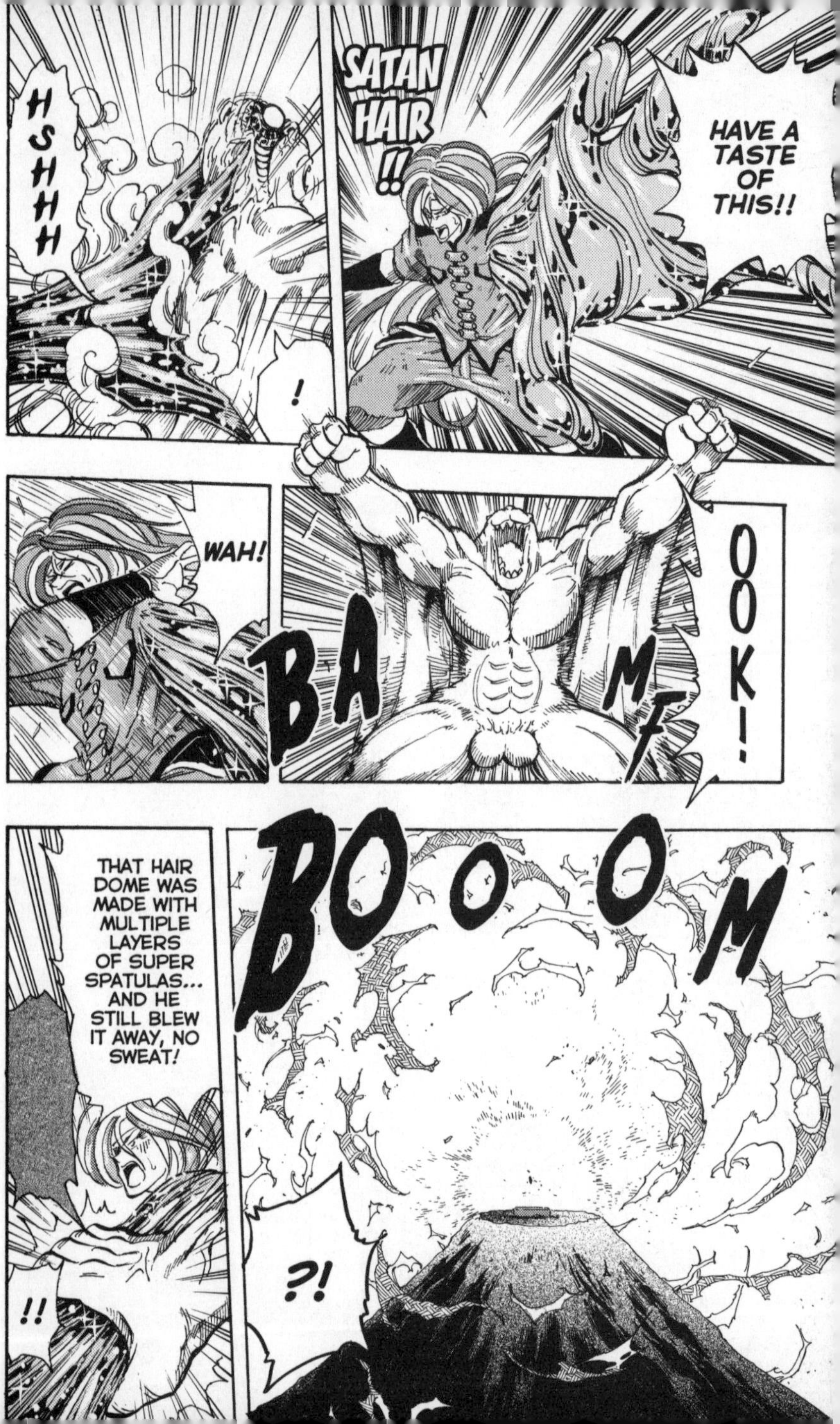
HAVE A TASTE OF THIS!!
SATAN HAIR!!
HSHHH
!
OOK!!
BAMF
WAH!
BOOOOM
?!
THAT HAIR DOME WAS MADE WITH MULTIPLE LAYERS OF SUPER SPATULAS... AND HE STILL BLEW IT AWAY, NO SWEAT!
!!

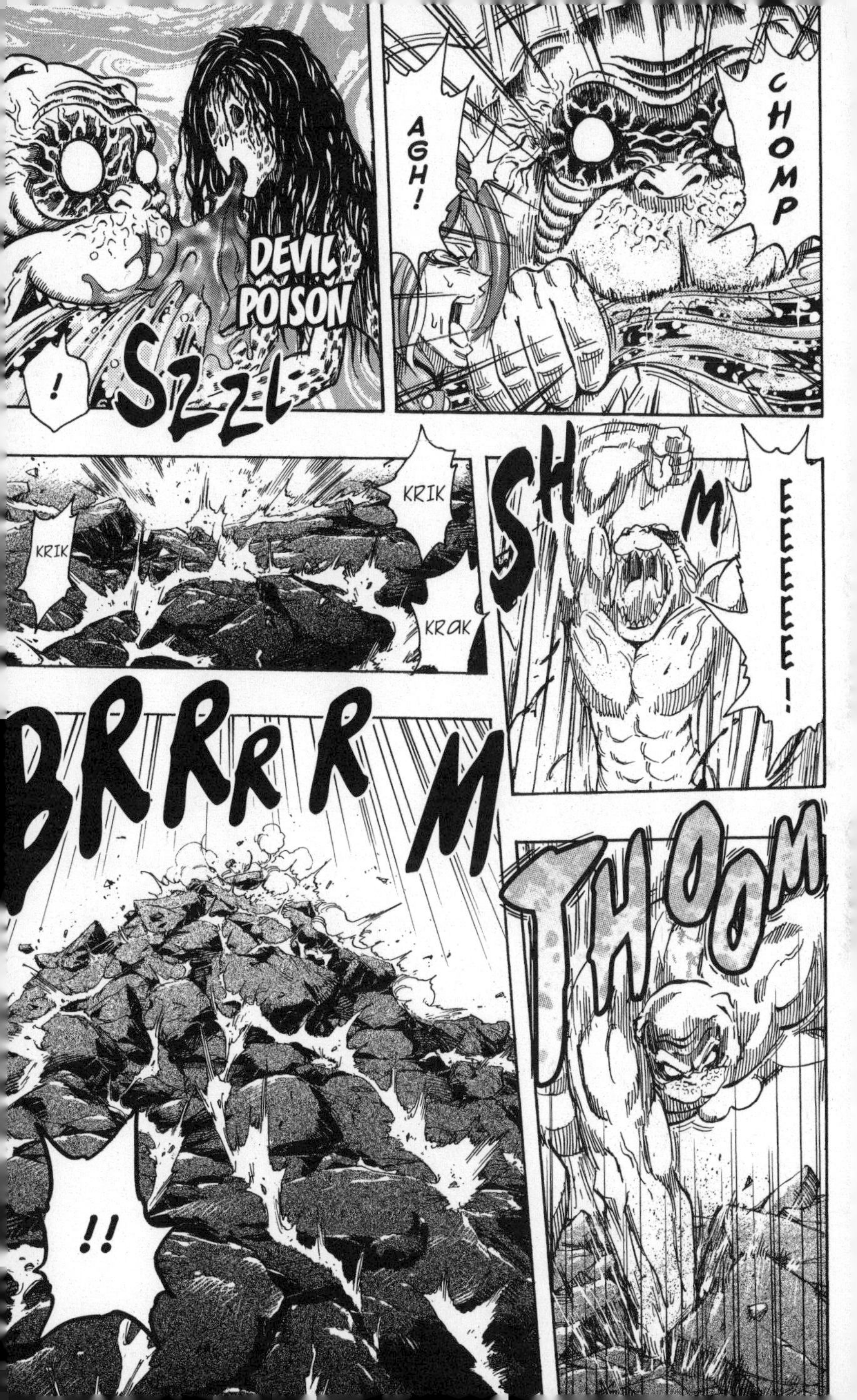

CHOMP
AGH!
DEVIL POISON
SZZL
!
SHM
EEEEEEE!
KRIK
KRAK
KRIK
THOOM
BRRRRM
!!

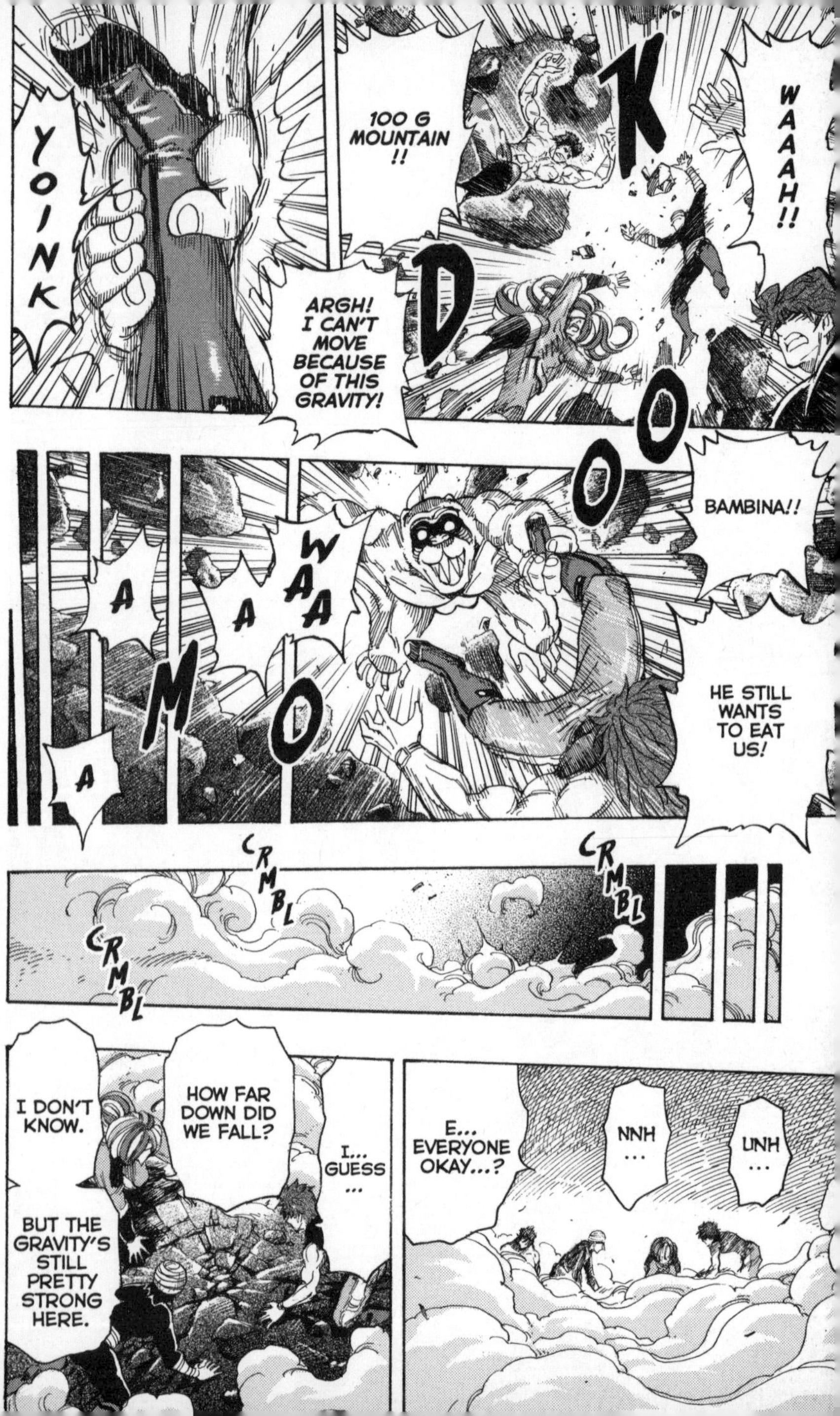
WAAAAH!!
100 G MOUNTAIN !!
ARGH! I CAN'T MOVE BECAUSE OF THIS GRAVITY!
YOINK
BAMBINA!!
HE STILL WANTS TO EAT US!
WAAA
CRMBL
CRMBL
CRMBL
UNH ...
NNH ...
E... EVERYONE OKAY...?
I... GUESS ...
HOW FAR DOWN DID WE FALL?
I DON'T KNOW.
BUT THE GRAVITY'S STILL PRETTY STRONG HERE.

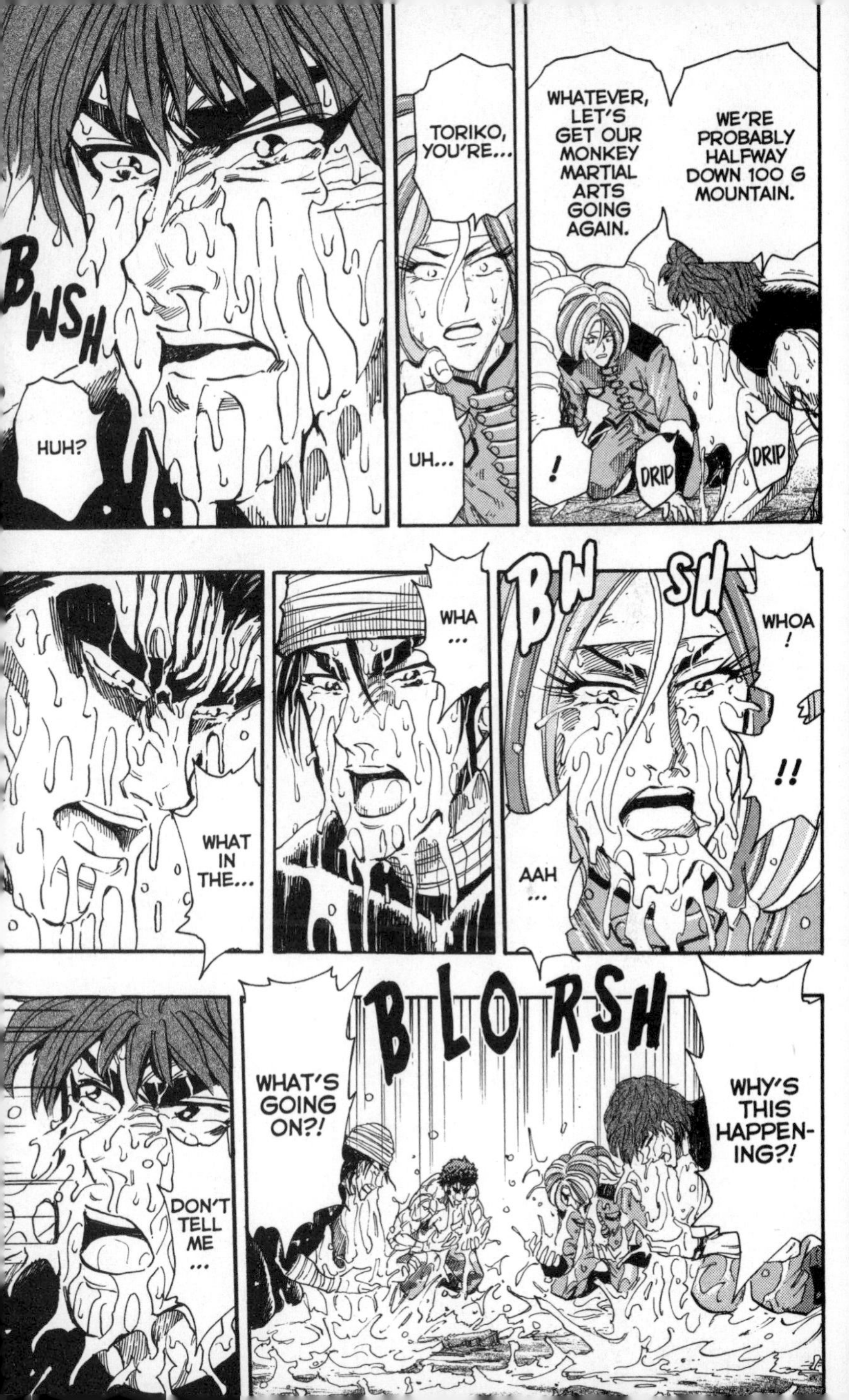
WE'RE PROBABLY HALFWAY DOWN 100 G MOUNTAIN.
WHATEVER, LET'S GET OUR MONKEY MARTIAL ARTS GOING AGAIN.
DRIP
DRIP
!
TORIKO, YOU'RE...
UH...
BWSH
HUH?
BWSH
WHOA!
!!
AAH...
WHA...
WHAT IN THE...
BLORSH
WHY'S THIS HAPPENING?!
WHAT'S GOING ON?!
DON'T TELL ME...

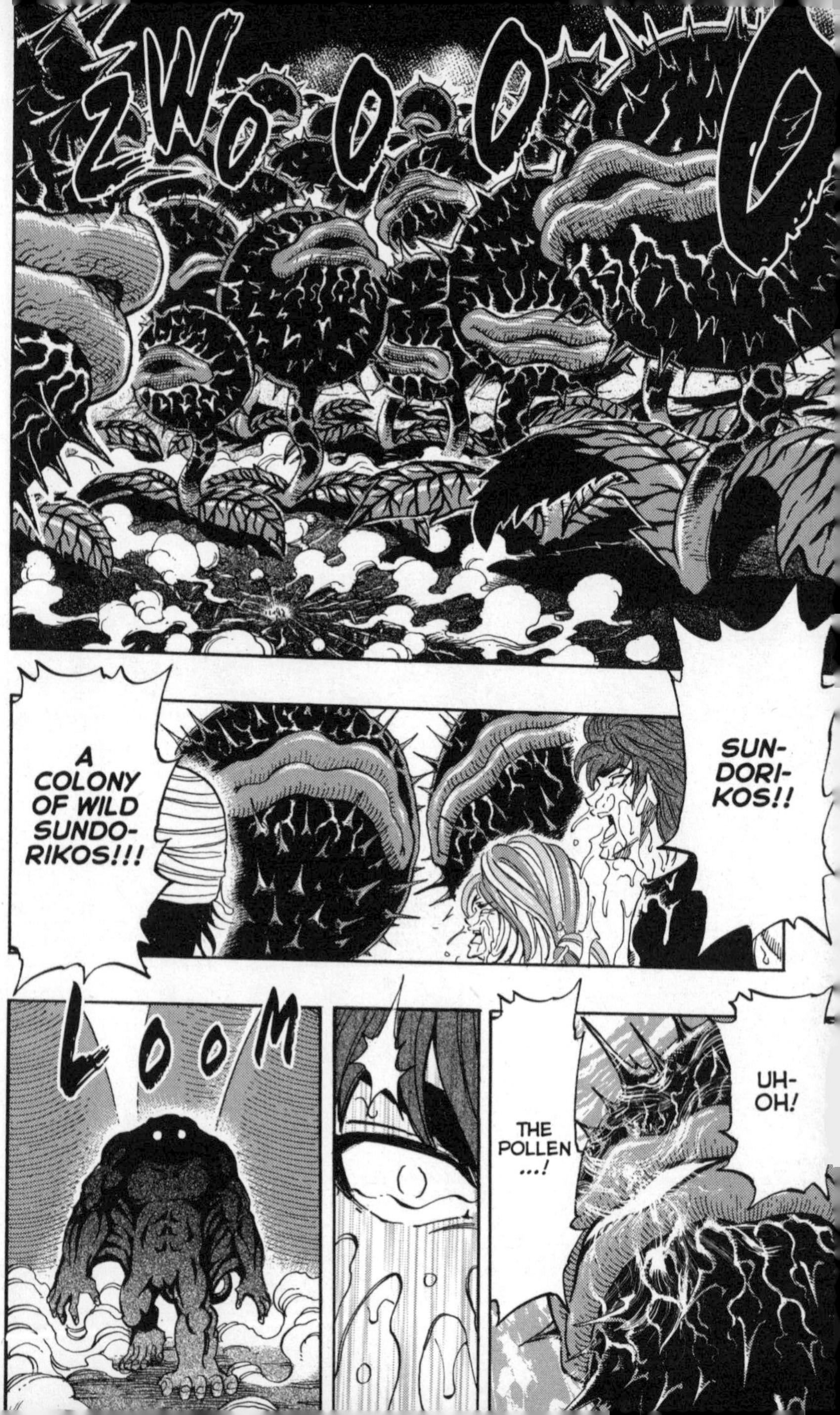
ZWOOOOO
SUN-DORI-KOS!!
A COLONY OF WILD SUNDORIKOS!!!
UH-OH!
THE POLLEN ...!
LOOM

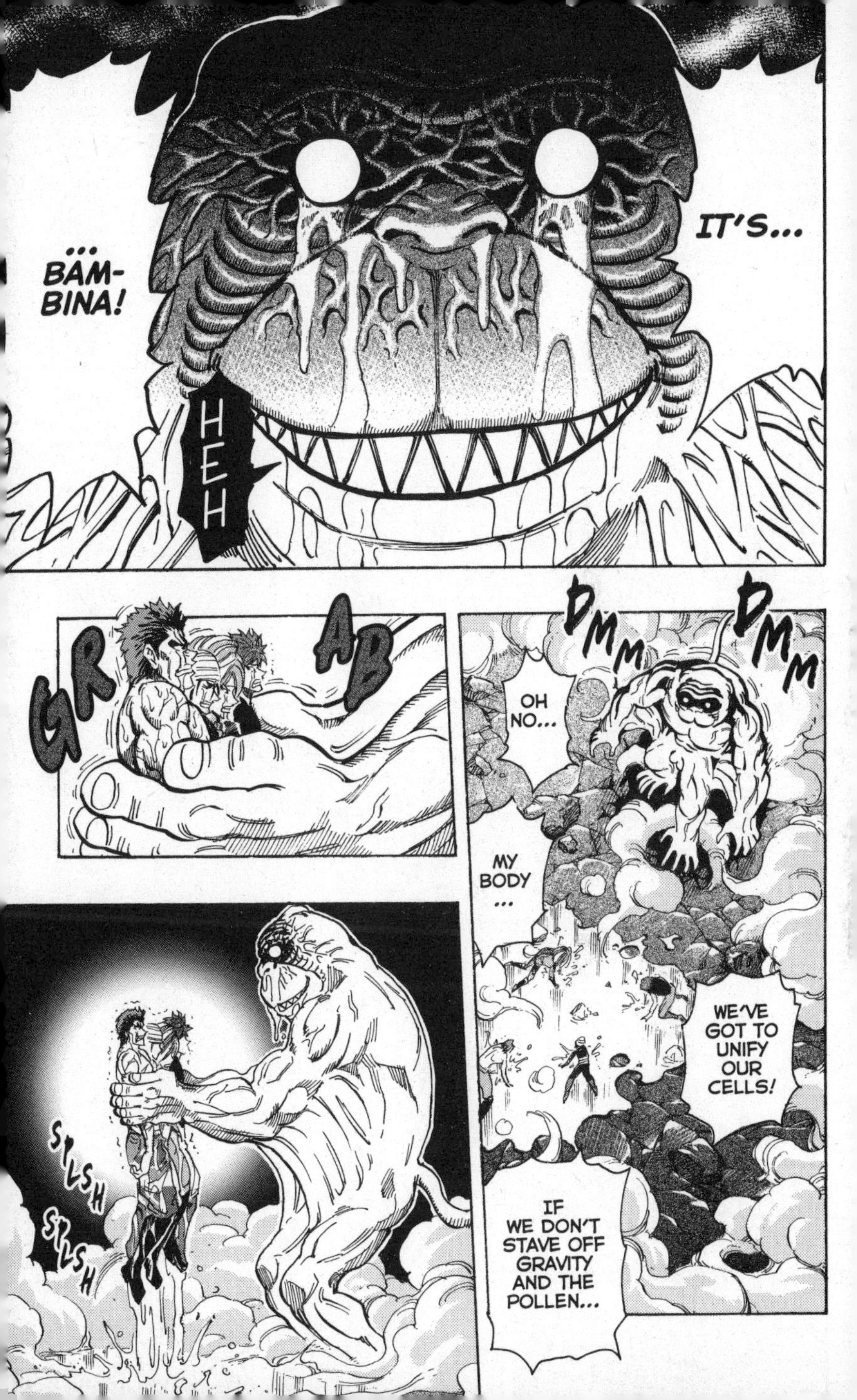
IT'S...
... BÄMBINA!
HEH
DMM DMM
OH NO...
MY BODY ...
GRAB
WE'VE GOT TO UNIFY OUR CELLS!
IF WE DON'T STAVE OFF GRAVITY AND THE POLLEN...
SHLSH SHLSH

OUR BODIES' FLUIDS...

N... NOT GOOD....

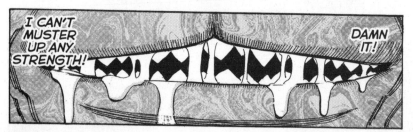

I CAN'T MUSTER UP ANY STRENGTH!

DAMN IT!

...THEN I'LL...

IF YOU'RE GOING TO EAT ME...

...ALL OVER.

IT'S...

DAMN IT!

I'LL...

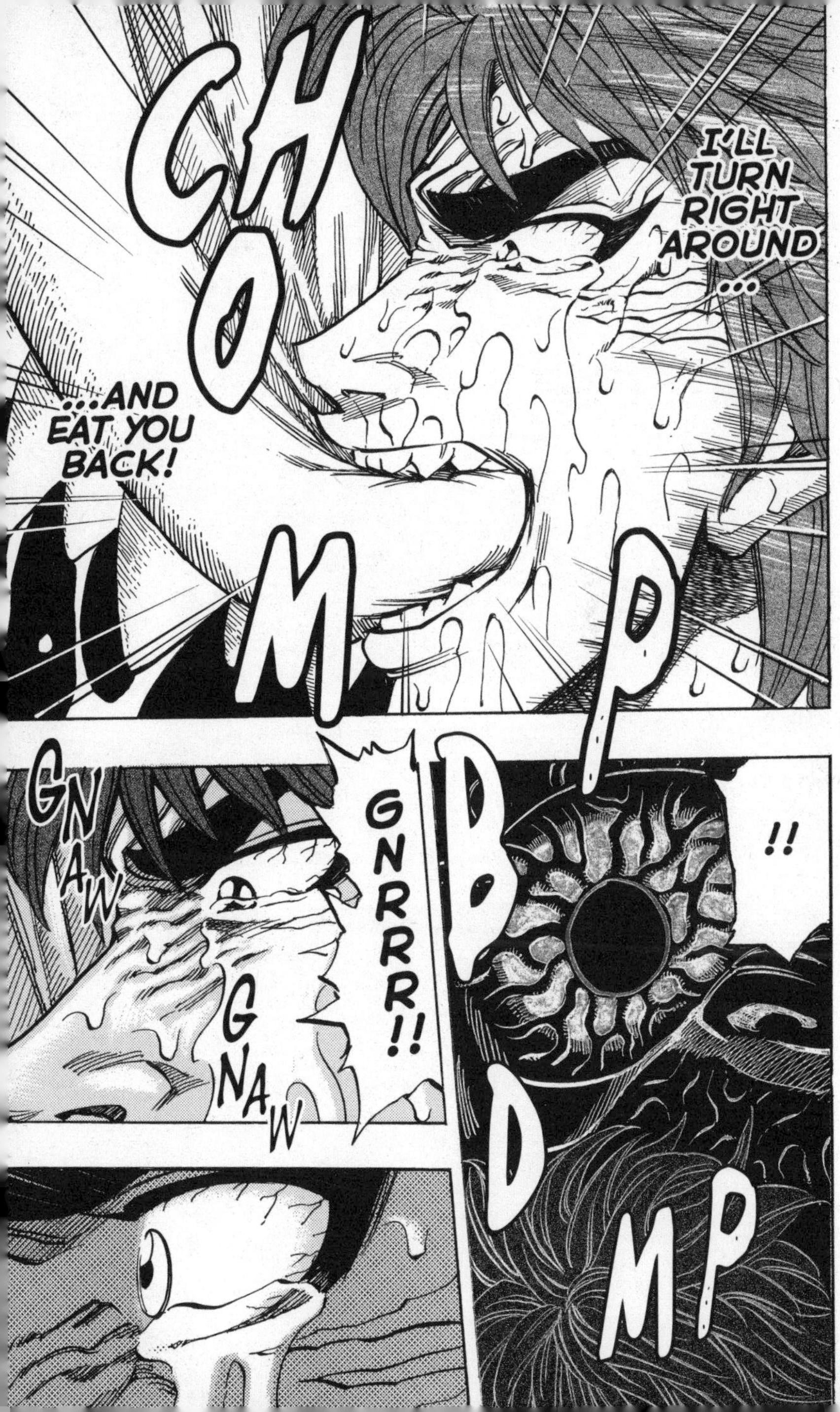
I'LL TURN RIGHT AROUND...
...AND EAT YOU BACK!
CHOMP
!!
BDMP
GNAW
GNRRR!!
GNAW

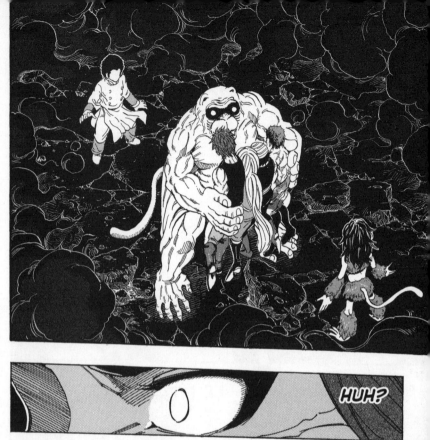

HUH?

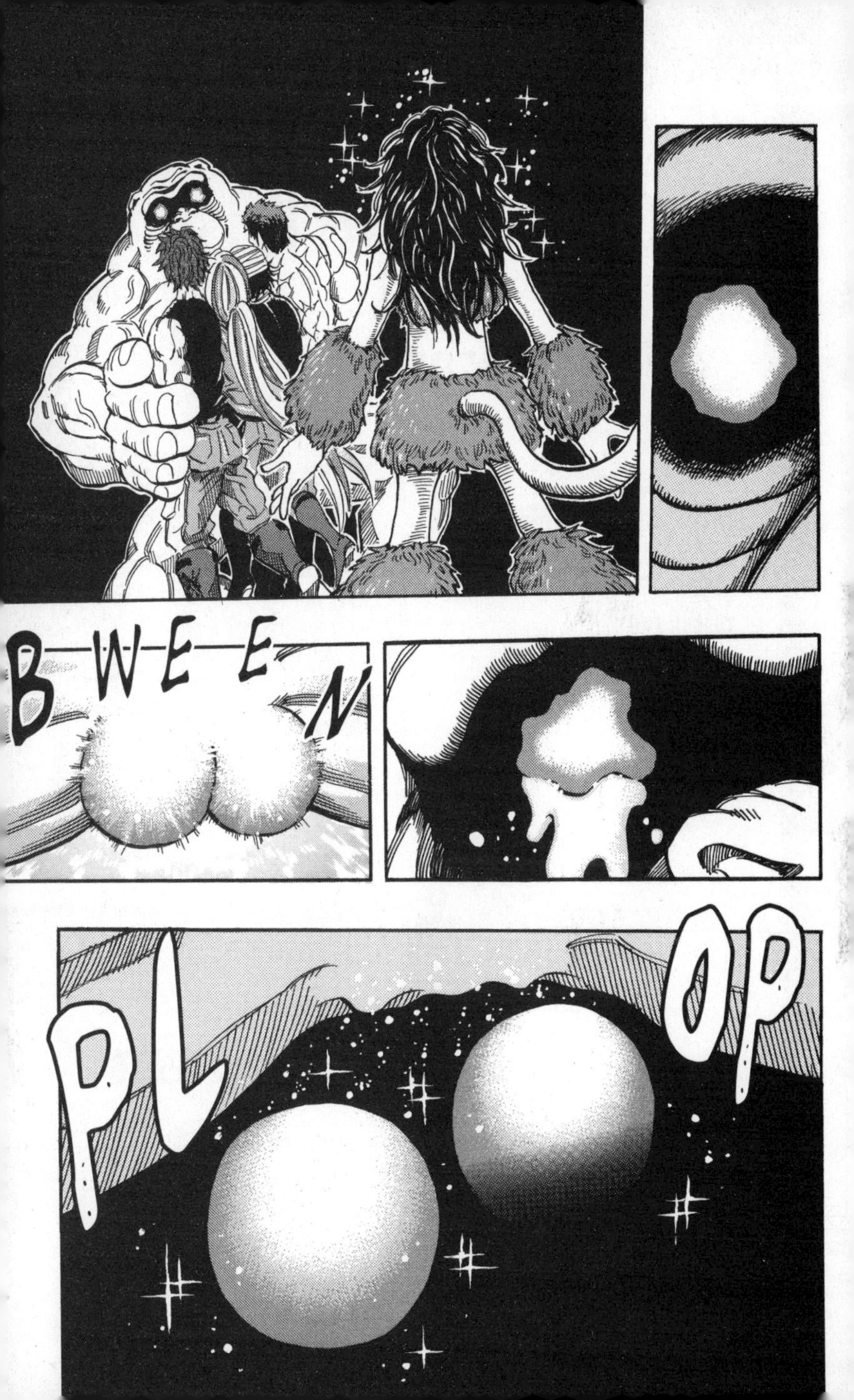
BWEEN
PLOP

TORIKO

GOURMET CHECKLIST

Vol. 341

CENTIPEDEMIA NUTS
(INSECT)

CAPTURE LEVEL: 1
HABITAT: FOUND EVERYWHERE
SIZE: 80 CM
HEIGHT: ---
WEIGHT: 2 KG
PRICE: 5,000 YEN PER INSECT

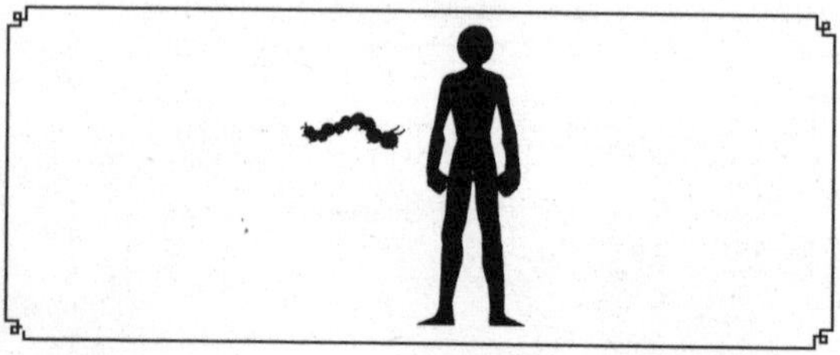

KLAK

CENTI-PEDEMIA NUTS.*

HERE YA GO.

SCALE

THESE NUTS COMPLEMENT THE ALCOHOL THAT JIRO SERVED TO TORIKO TO CHEER HIM UP AFTER HE LOST TO STARJUN. IT'S A CENTIPEDE-LIKE MACADAMIA NUT WHOSE MEAT IS SURROUNDED BY A HARD SHELL. IT'S NOT PARTICULARLY PRICEY NOR A DELICACY, BUT IT GOES PERFECTLY WITH A DRINK BECAUSE OF ITS SMOOTH TASTE.

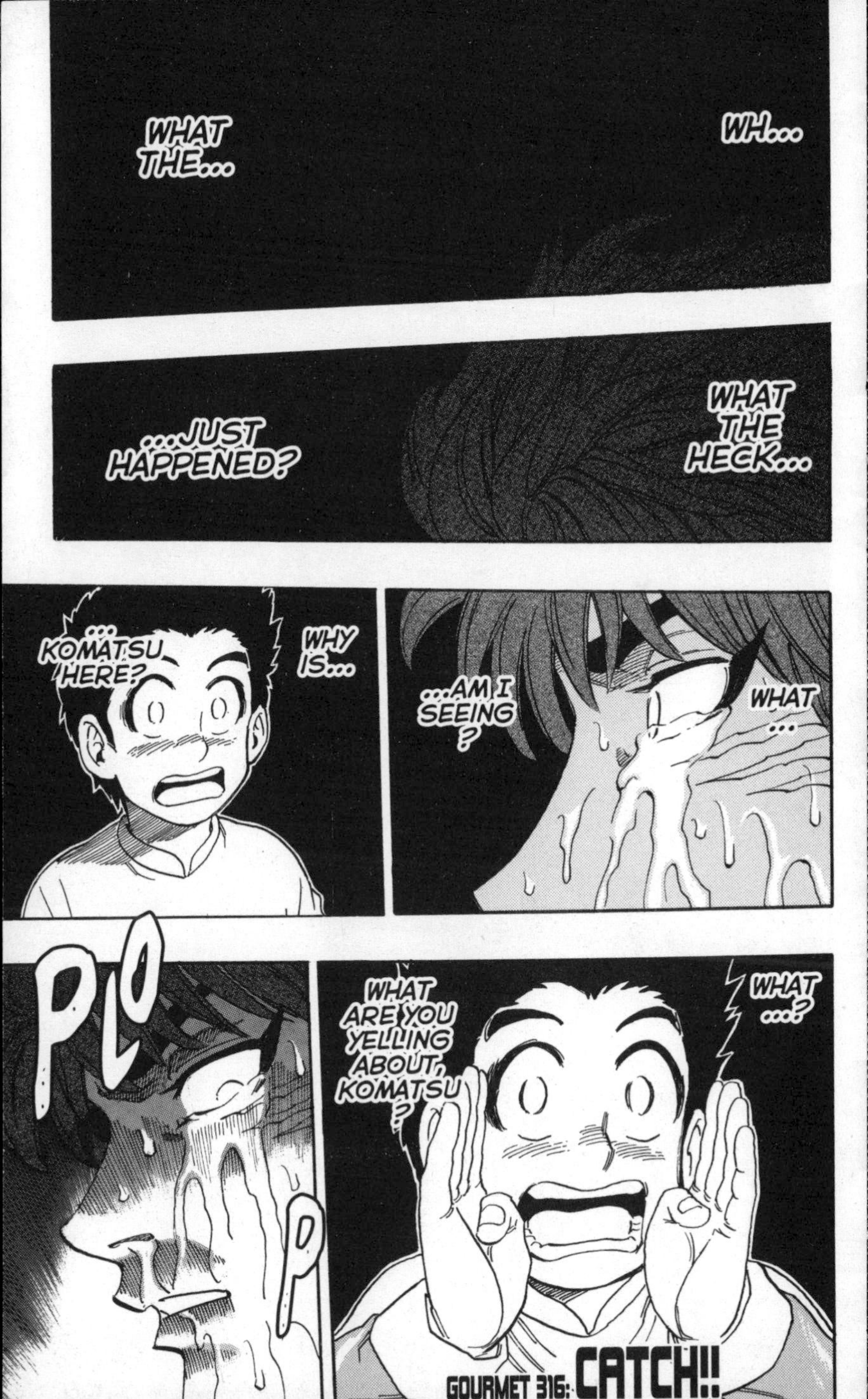
WH...
WHAT THE...
WHAT THE HECK...
...JUST HAPPENED?
WHAT...
...AM I SEEING?
WHY IS...
...KOMATSU HERE?
WHAT...?
WHAT ARE YOU YELLING ABOUT, KOMATSU?
PLOP
GOURMET 316: CATCH!!

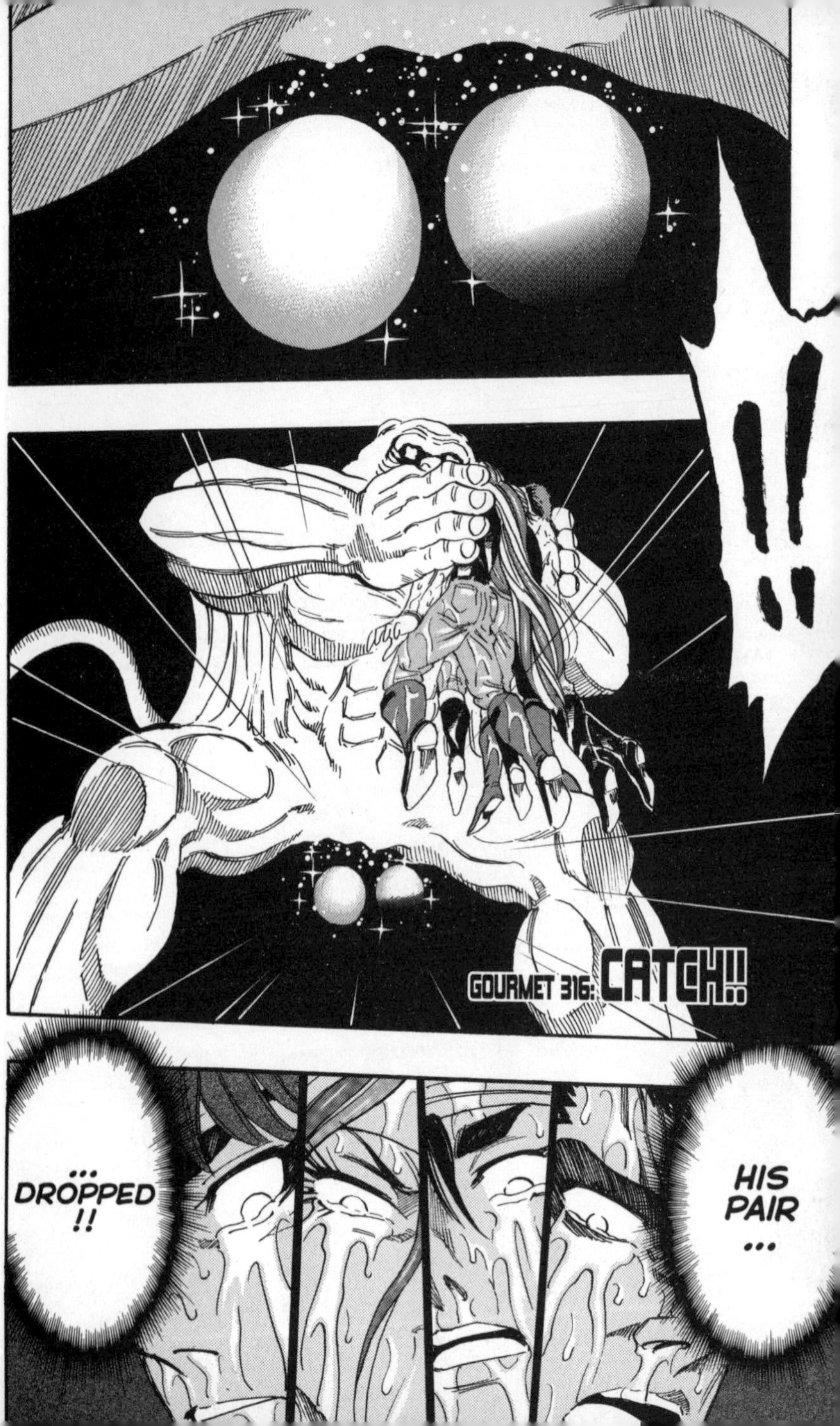
!!
GOURMET 316: CATCH!!
HIS PAIR...
...DROPPED!!

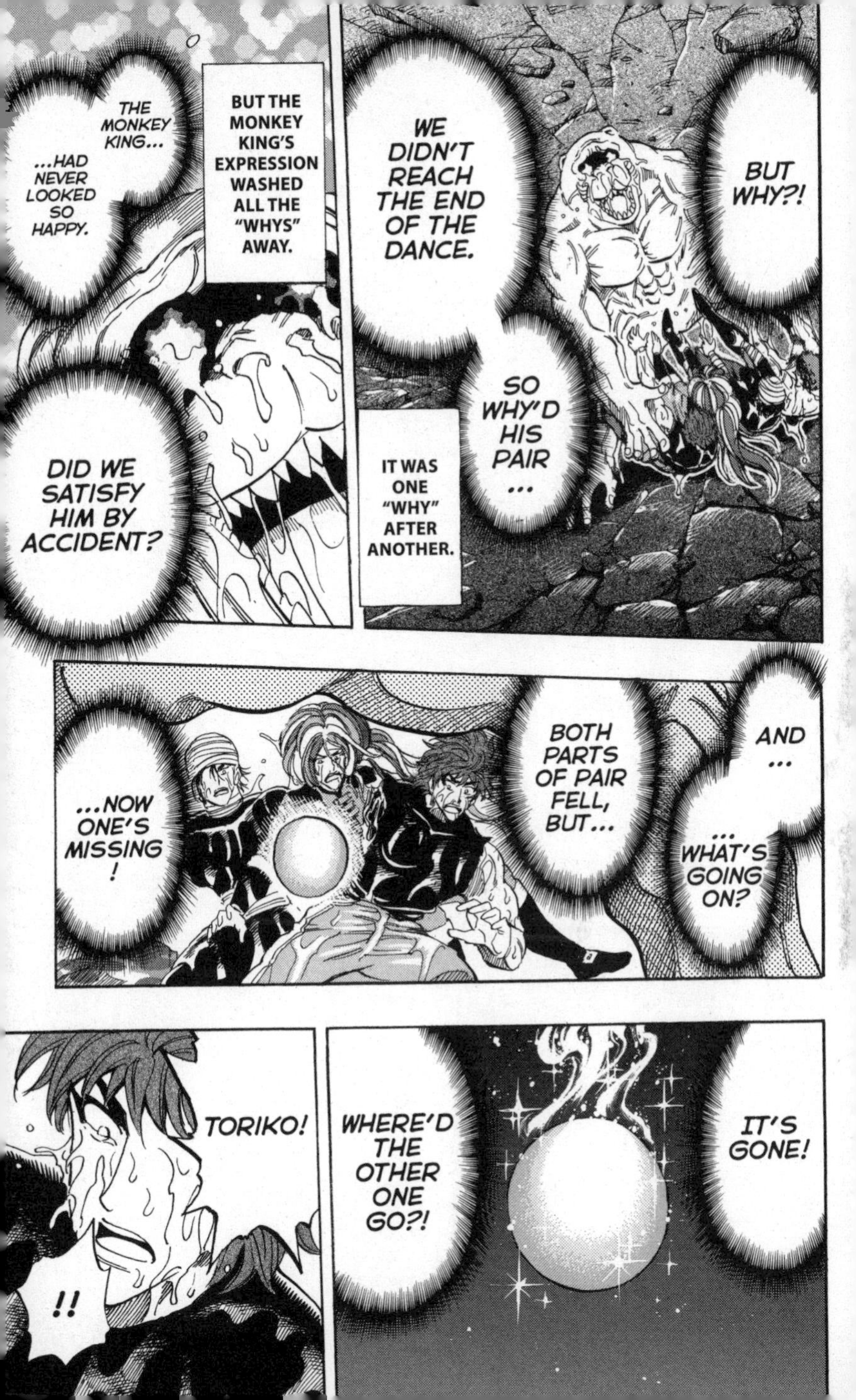
BUT WHY?!
WE DIDN'T REACH THE END OF THE DANCE.
SO WHY'D HIS PAIR ...
IT WAS ONE "WHY" AFTER ANOTHER.
BUT THE MONKEY KING'S EXPRESSION WASHED ALL THE "WHYS" AWAY.
THE MONKEY KING...
...HAD NEVER LOOKED SO HAPPY.
DID WE SATISFY HIM BY ACCIDENT?
AND ...
... WHAT'S GOING ON?
BOTH PARTS OF PAIR FELL, BUT...
...NOW ONE'S MISSING!
IT'S GONE!
WHERE'D THE OTHER ONE GO?!
TORIKO!
!!

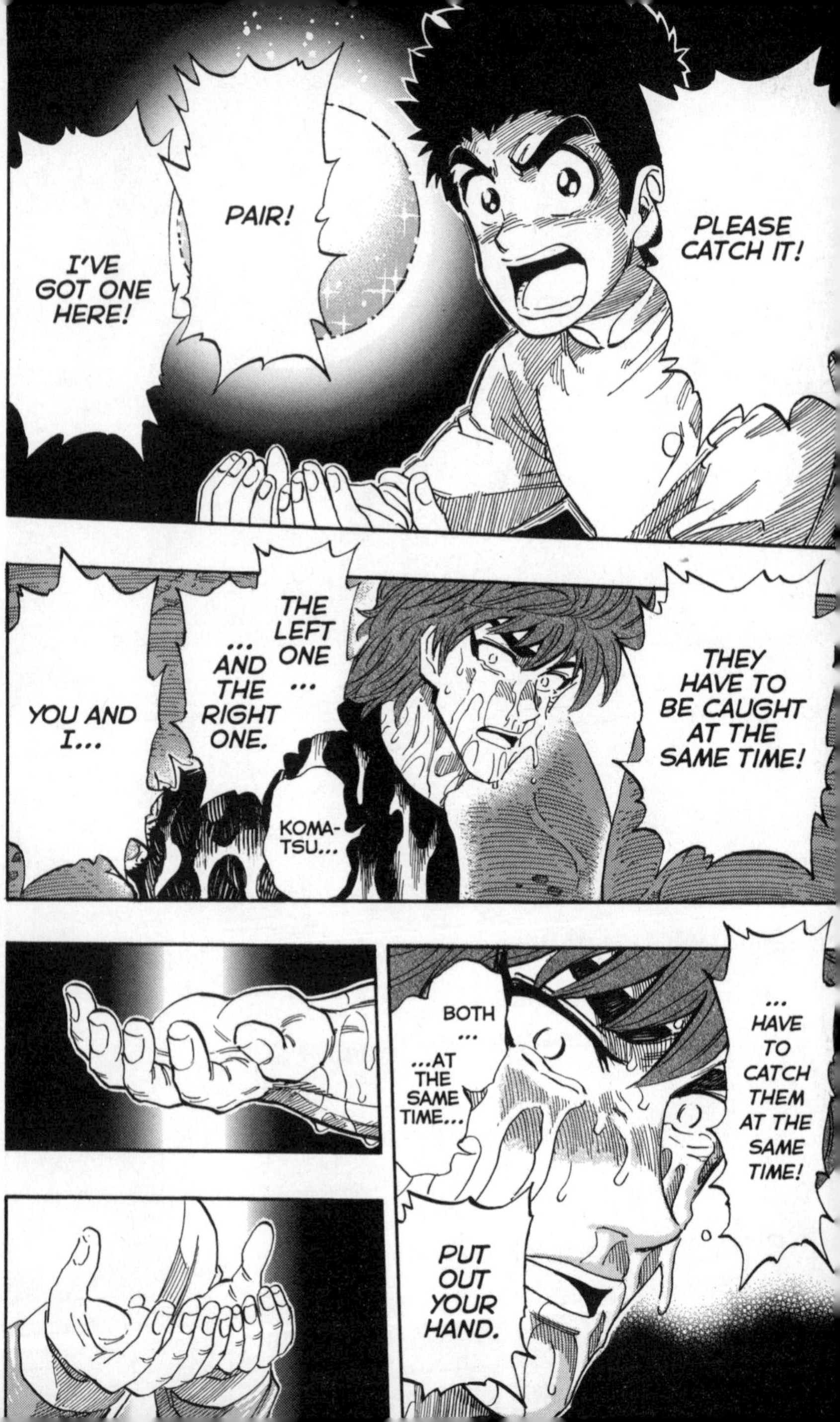
PLEASE CATCH IT!
PAIR!
I'VE GOT ONE HERE!
THEY HAVE TO BE CAUGHT AT THE SAME TIME!
THE LEFT ONE ...
... AND THE RIGHT ONE.
YOU AND I...
KOMA-TSU...
... HAVE TO CATCH THEM AT THE SAME TIME!
BOTH ...
...AT THE SAME TIME...
PUT OUT YOUR HAND.

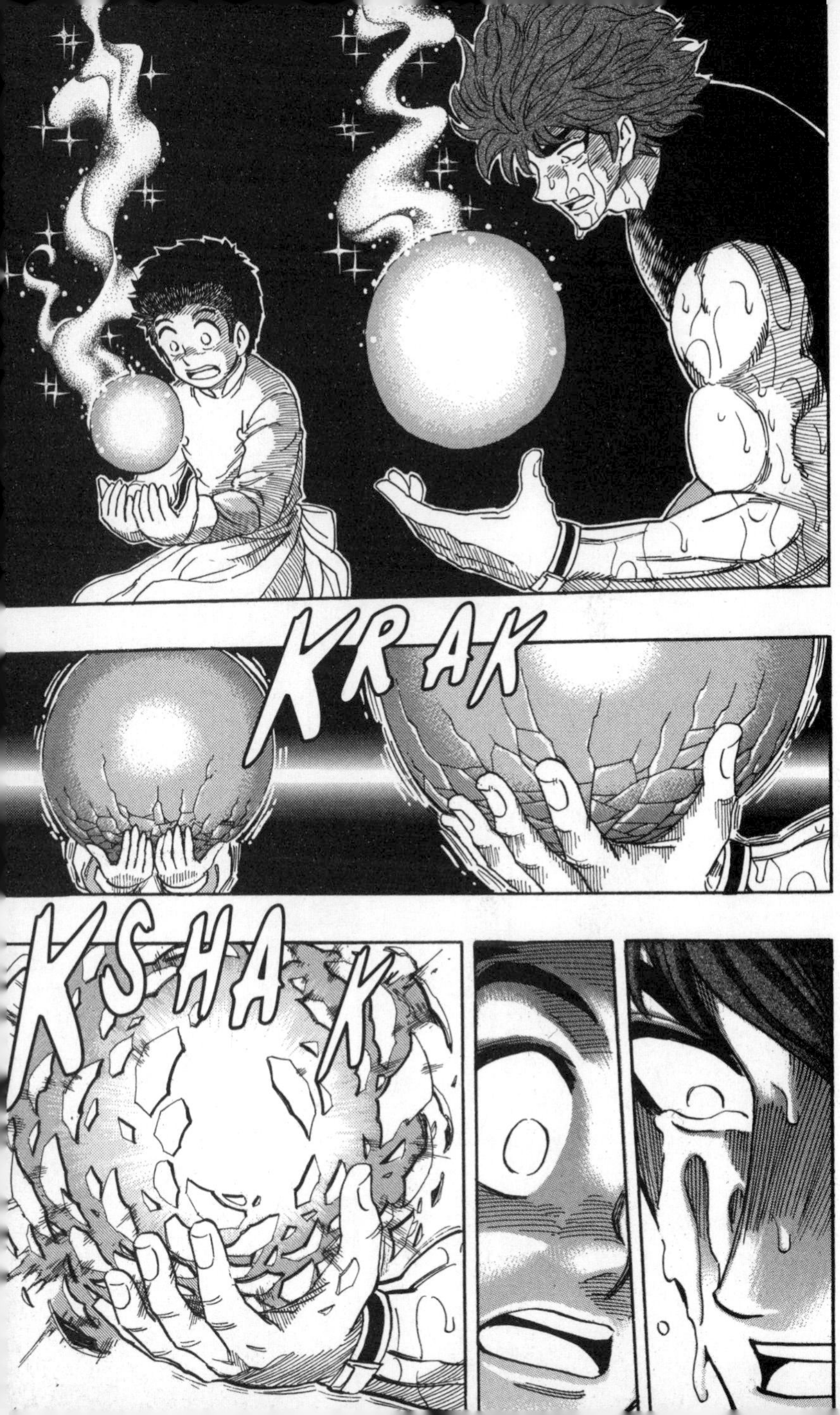
KRAK
KSHAK

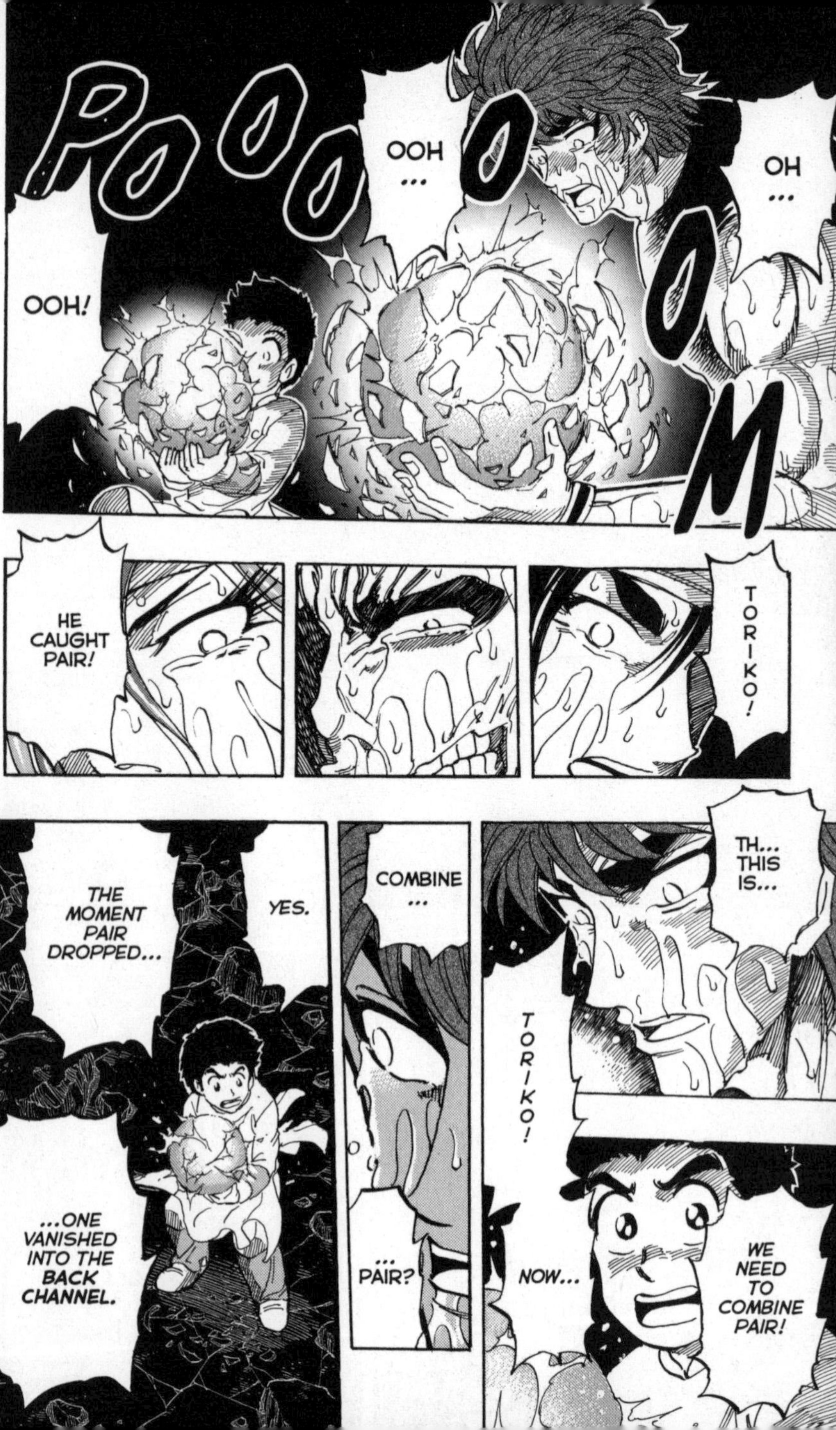
OH...
OOH...
OOH!
POOOOOOOM
TORIKO!
HE CAUGHT PAIR!
TH... THIS IS...
TORIKO!
WE NEED TO COMBINE PAIR!
NOW...
COMBINE...
...PAIR?
YES.
THE MOMENT PAIR DROPPED...
...ONE VANISHED INTO THE BACK CHANNEL.

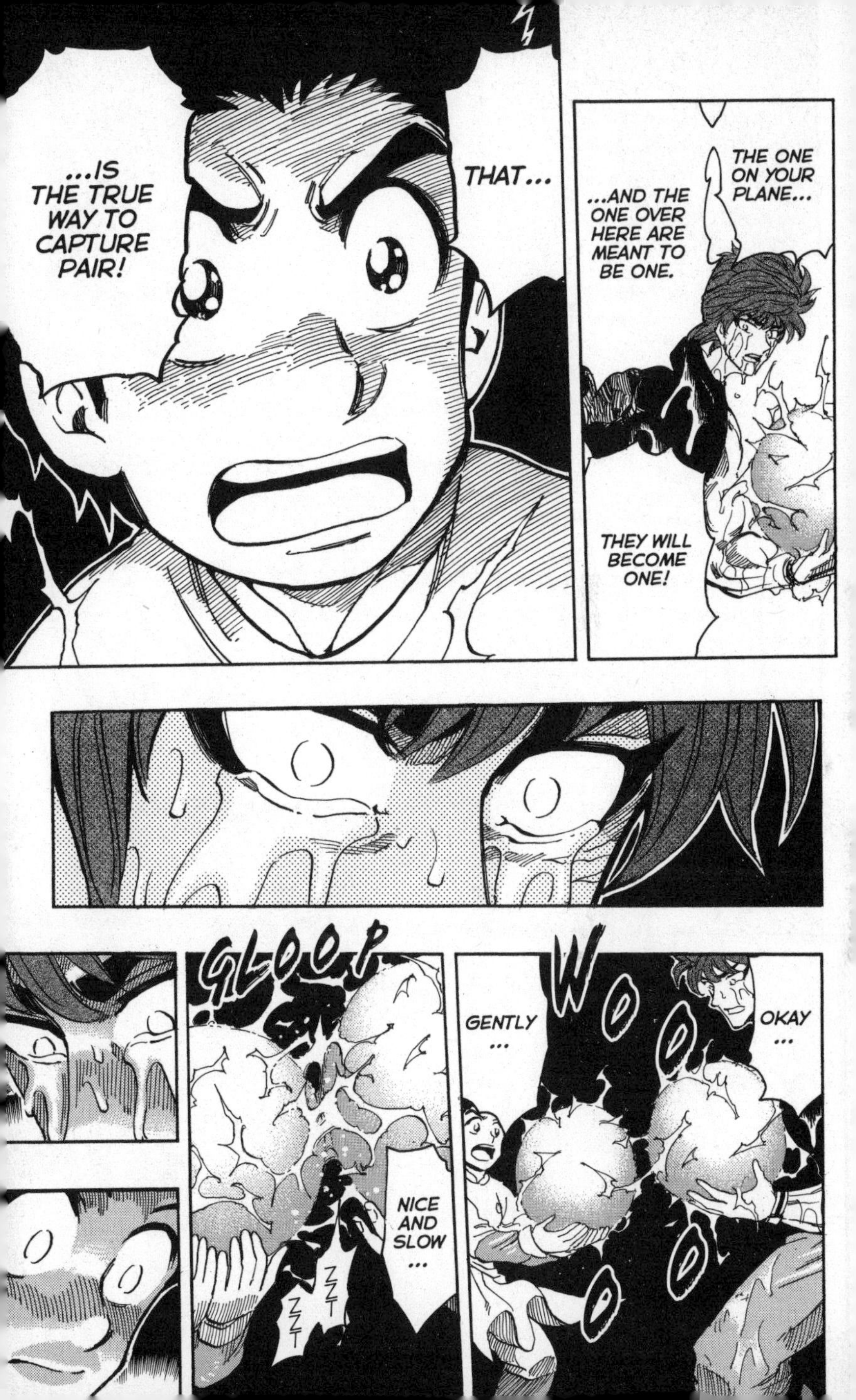
THE ONE ON YOUR PLANE...
...AND THE ONE OVER HERE ARE MEANT TO BE ONE.
THEY WILL BECOME ONE!
THAT...
...IS THE TRUE WAY TO CAPTURE PAIR!
OKAY...
WOOOOOOOO
GENTLY...
GLOOP
NICE AND SLOW...
ZZT
ZZT

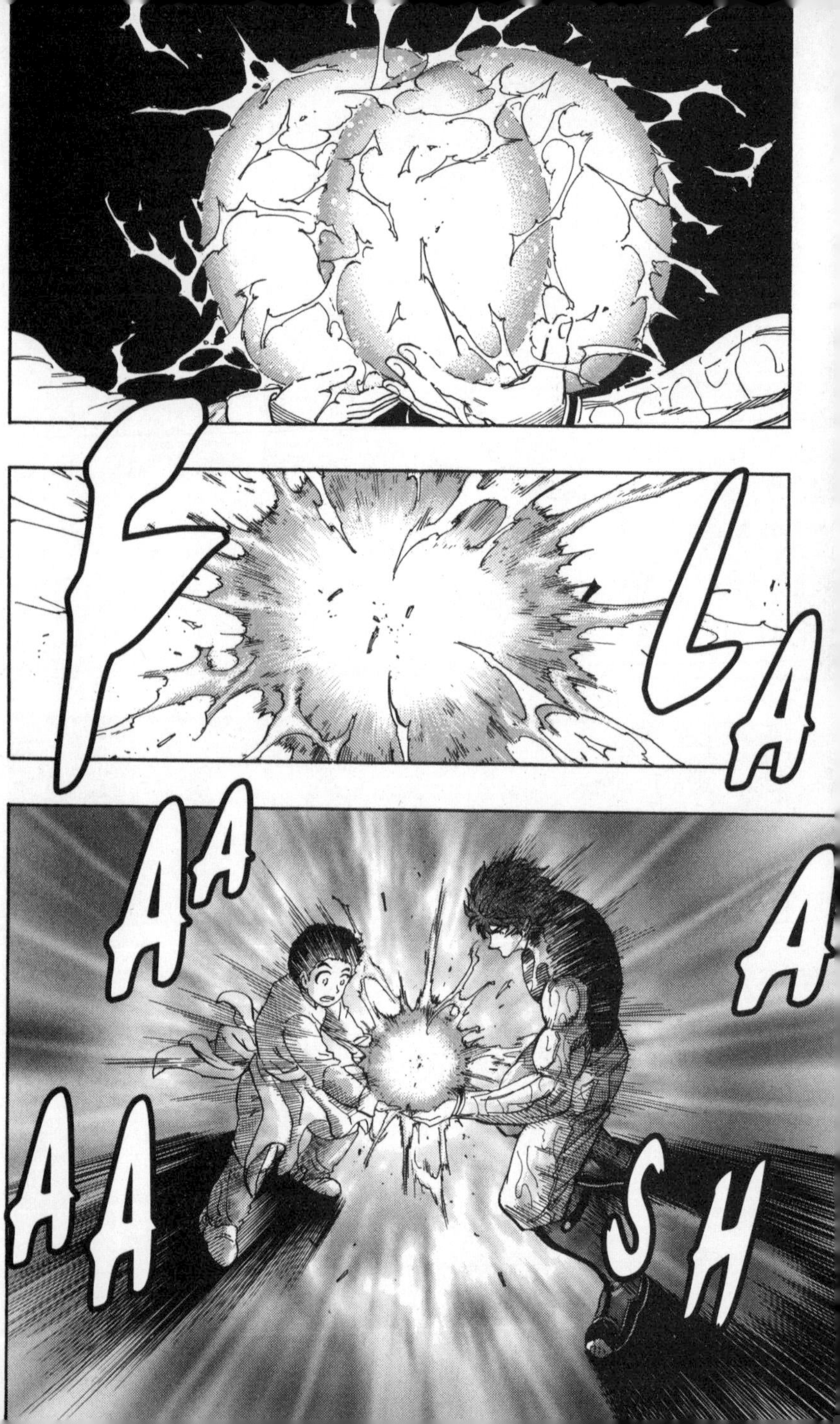
FLAAAAAASH

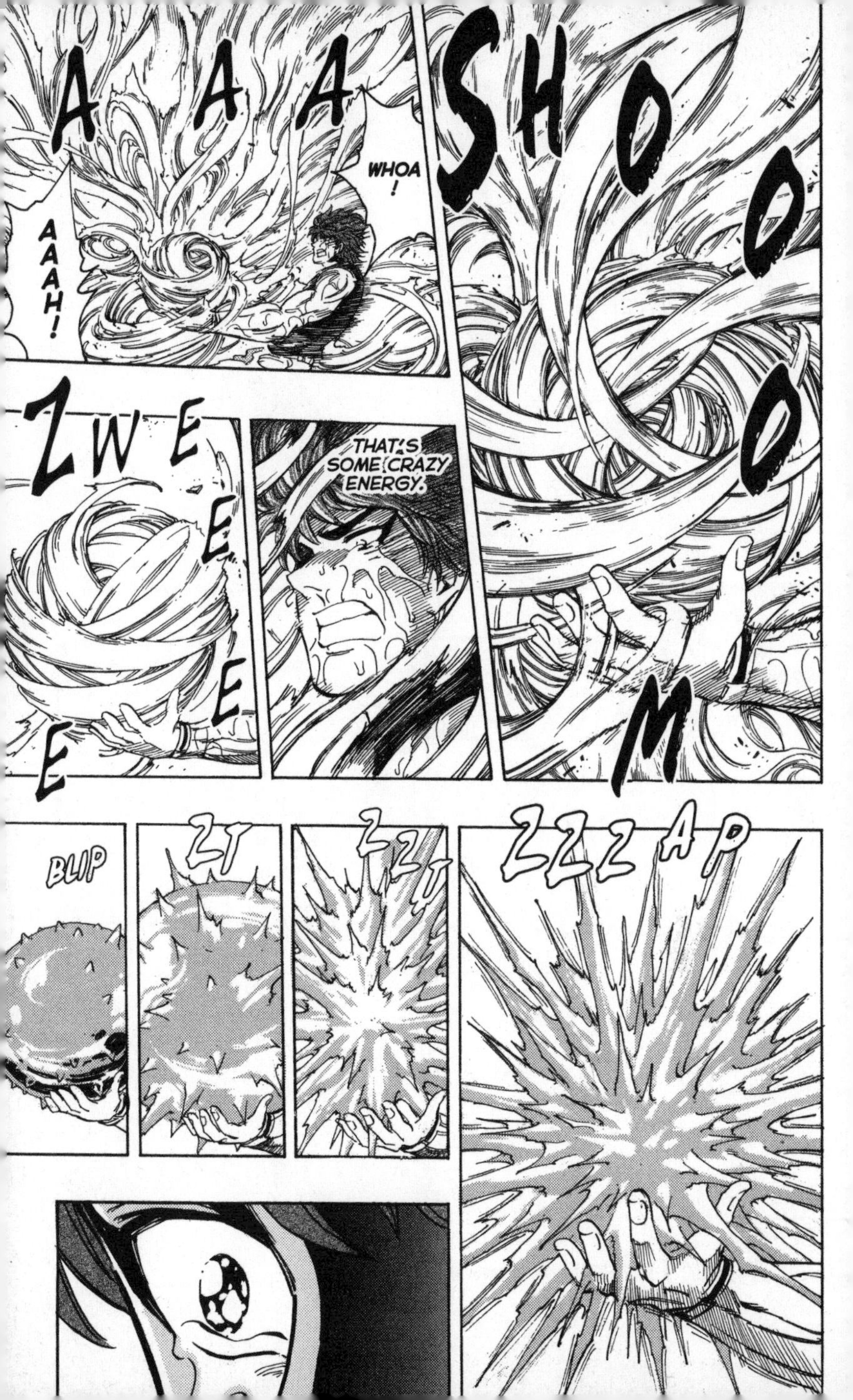
SHOOOM
AAA
WHOA!
AAAAH!
THAT'S SOME CRAZY ENERGY.
ZWEEEE
ZZZAP
ZZT
ZT
BLIP

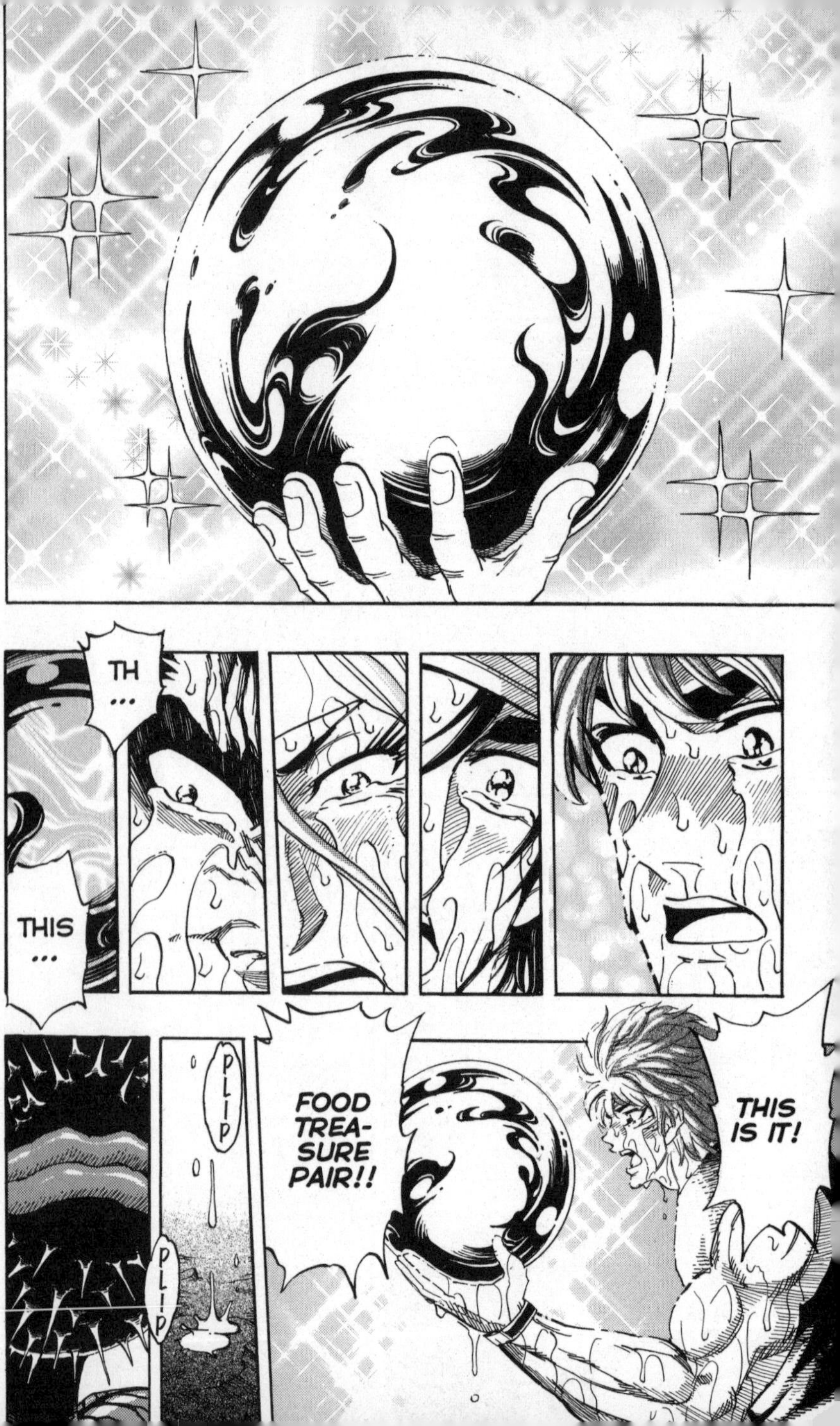
TH...
THIS...
THIS IS IT!
FOOD TREA-SURE PAIR!!
PLIP
PLIP

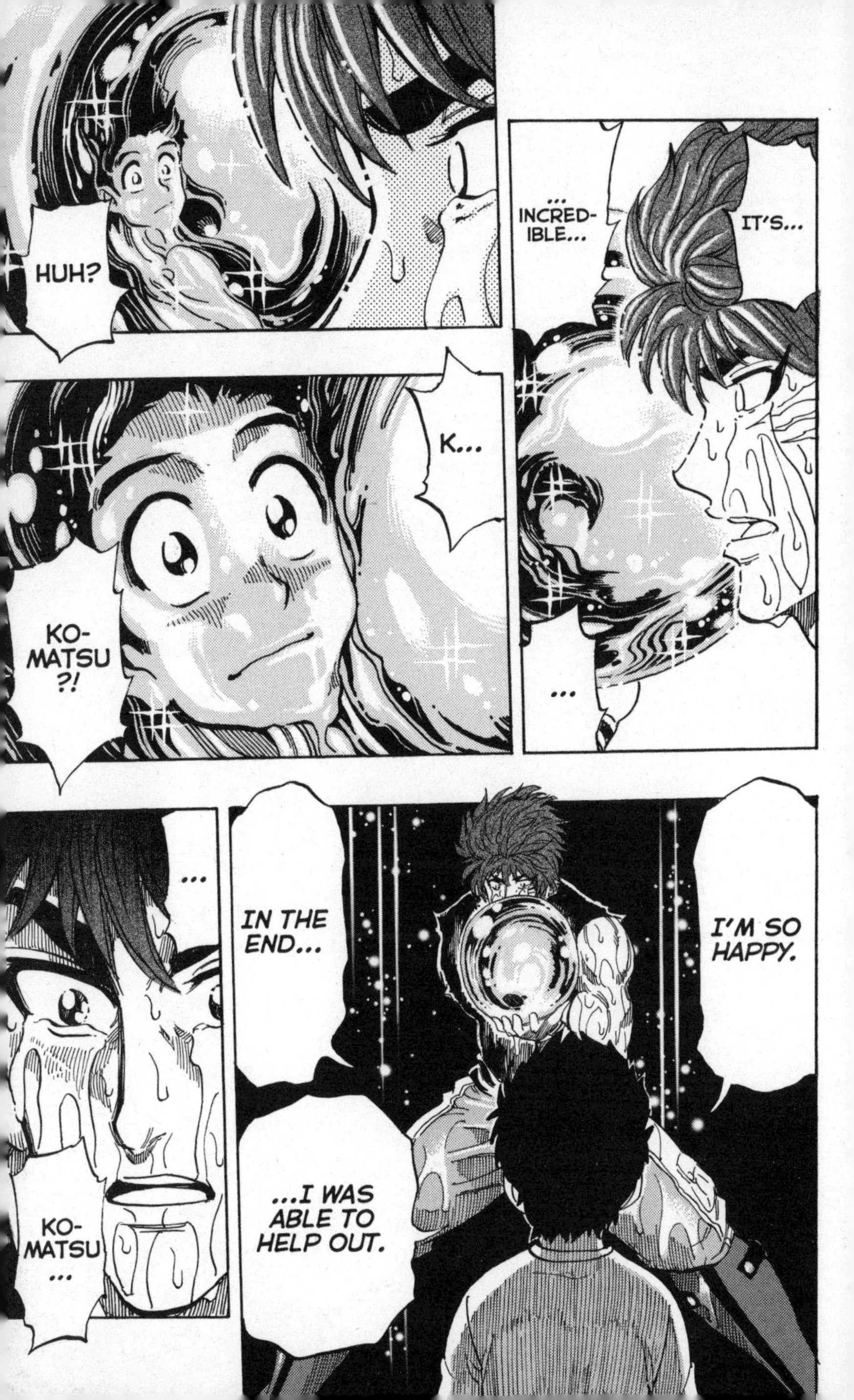
IT'S...
...INCREDIBLE...
...
HUH?
K...
KOMATSU?!
I'M SO HAPPY.
IN THE END...
...I WAS ABLE TO HELP OUT.
...
KOMATSU...

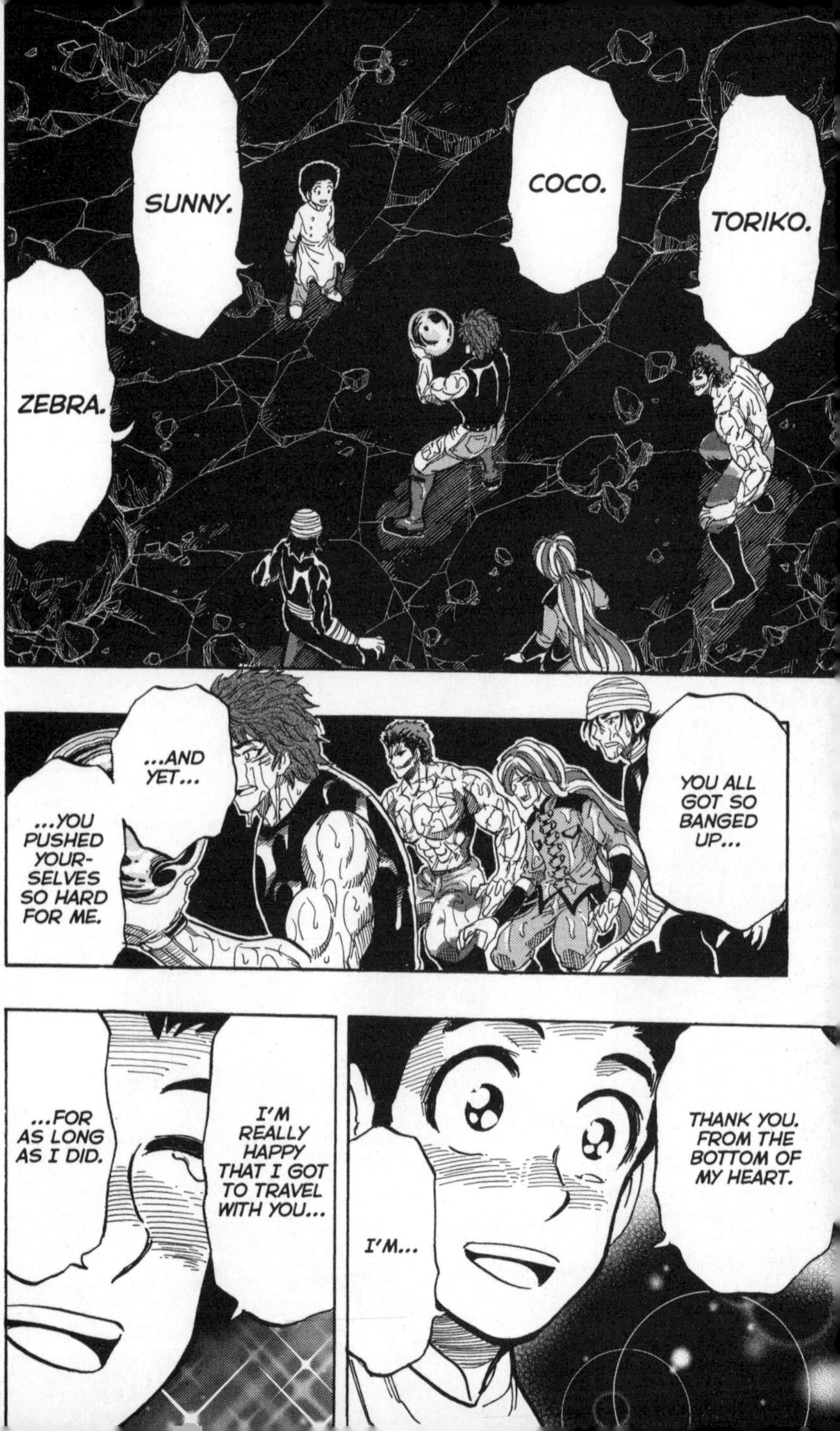
TORIKO.
COCO.
SUNNY.
ZEBRA.
YOU ALL GOT SO BANGED UP...
...AND YET...
...YOU PUSHED YOUR-SELVES SO HARD FOR ME.
THANK YOU. FROM THE BOTTOM OF MY HEART.
I'M...
I'M REALLY HAPPY THAT I GOT TO TRAVEL WITH YOU...
...FOR AS LONG AS I DID.

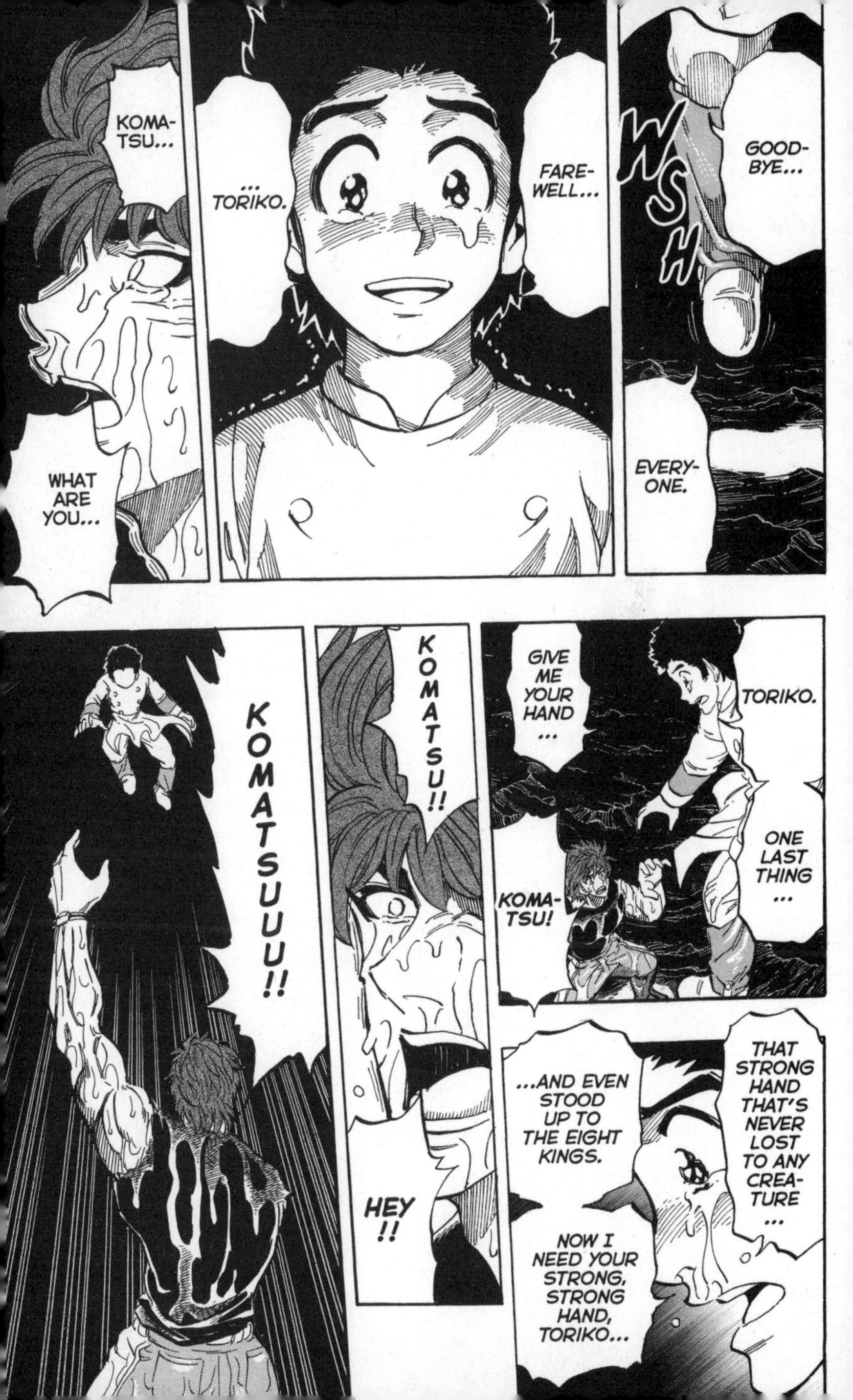
WSH
GOOD-BYE...
EVERY-ONE.
FARE-WELL...
...TORIKO.
KOMA-TSU...
WHAT ARE YOU...
TORIKO.
GIVE ME YOUR HAND...
ONE LAST THING...
KOMA-TSU!
THAT STRONG HAND THAT'S NEVER LOST TO ANY CREA-TURE...
...AND EVEN STOOD UP TO THE EIGHT KINGS.
NOW I NEED YOUR STRONG, STRONG HAND, TORIKO...
KOMATSU!!
HEY!!
KOMATSUUUU!!

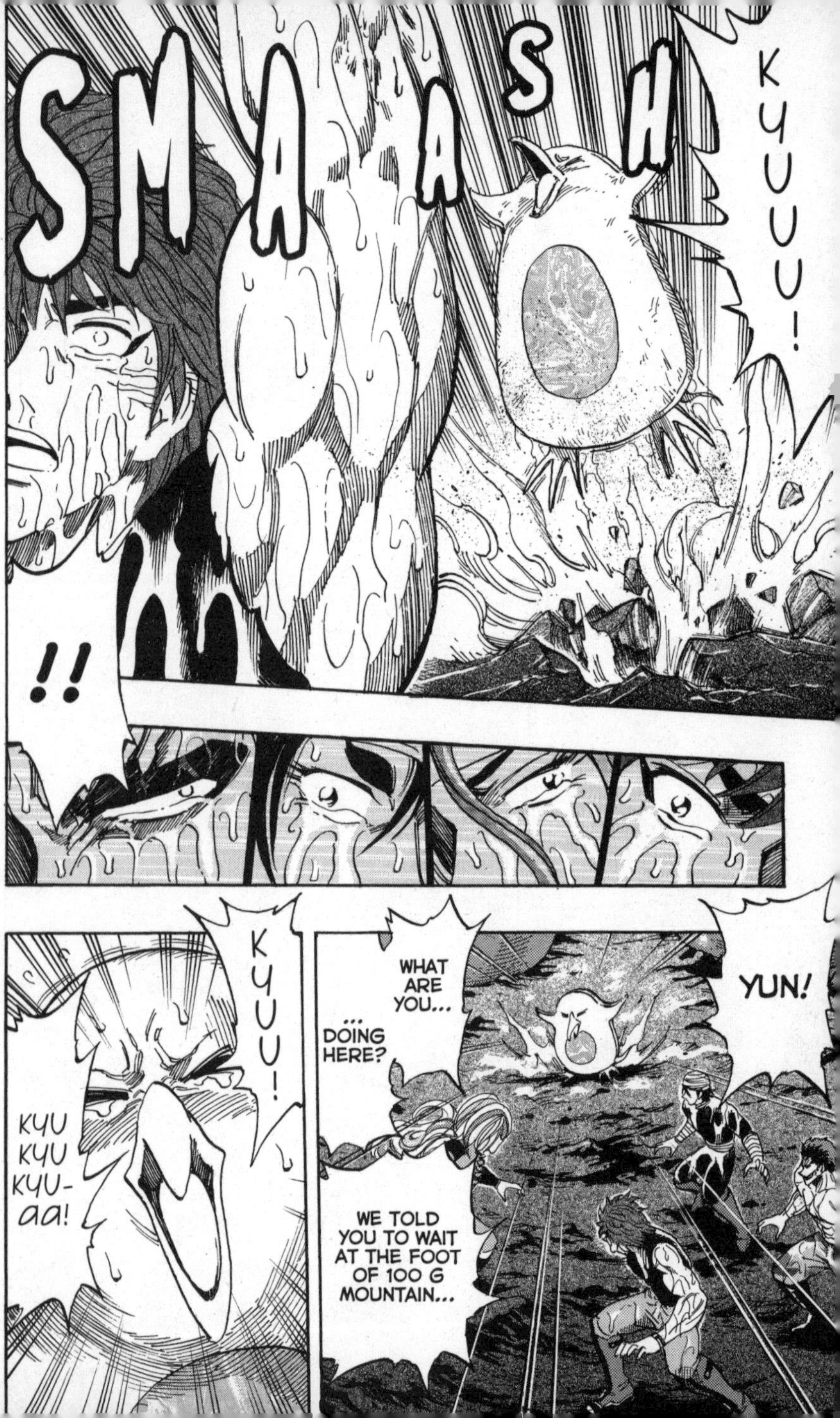
KYUUUU!
SMAASH
!!
YUN!
WHAT ARE YOU...
... DOING HERE?
WE TOLD YOU TO WAIT AT THE FOOT OF 100 G MOUNTAIN...
KYUUU!
KYU KYU KYU-aa!

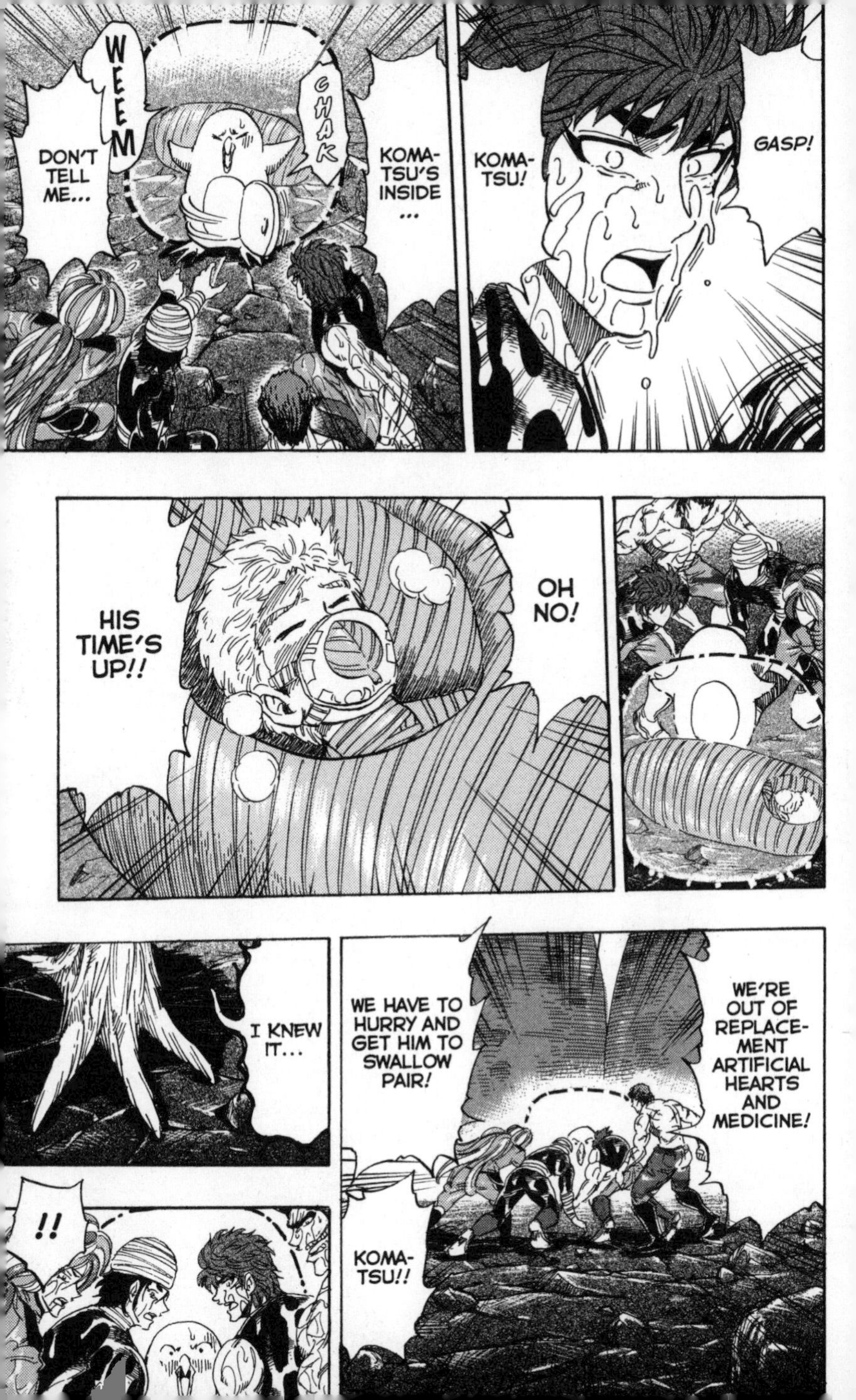
GASP!
KOMA-TSU!
KOMA-TSU'S INSIDE...
CHAK
WEEEM
DON'T TELL ME...
OH NO!
HIS TIME'S UP!!
WE'RE OUT OF REPLACE-MENT ARTIFICIAL HEARTS AND MEDICINE!
WE HAVE TO HURRY AND GET HIM TO SWALLOW PAIR!
KOMA-TSU!!
I KNEW IT...
!!

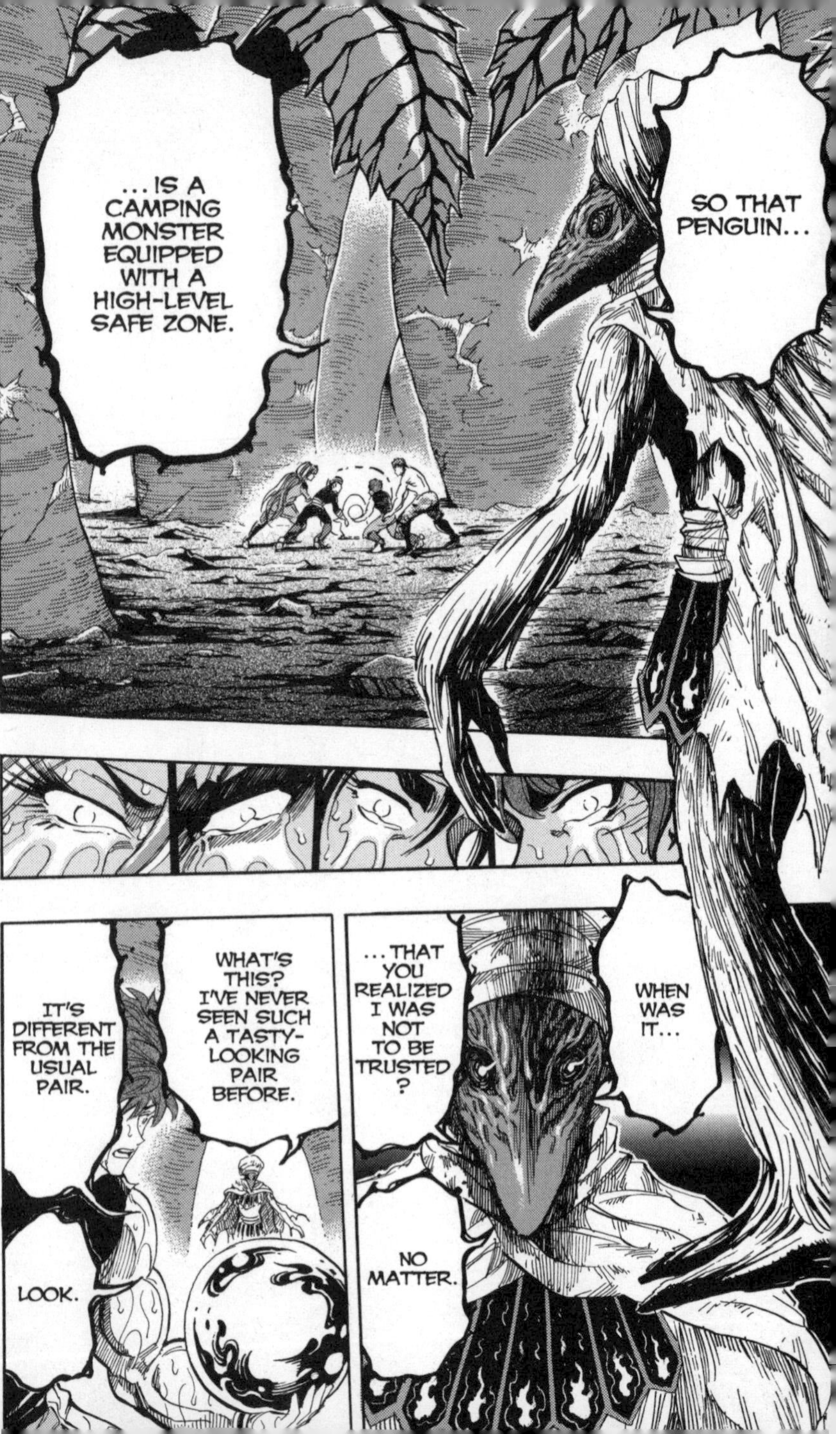
SO THAT PENGUIN...
...IS A CAMPING MONSTER EQUIPPED WITH A HIGH-LEVEL SAFE ZONE.
WHEN WAS IT...
...THAT YOU REALIZED I WAS NOT TO BE TRUSTED?
NO MATTER.
WHAT'S THIS? I'VE NEVER SEEN SUCH A TASTY-LOOKING PAIR BEFORE.
IT'S DIFFERENT FROM THE USUAL PAIR.
LOOK.

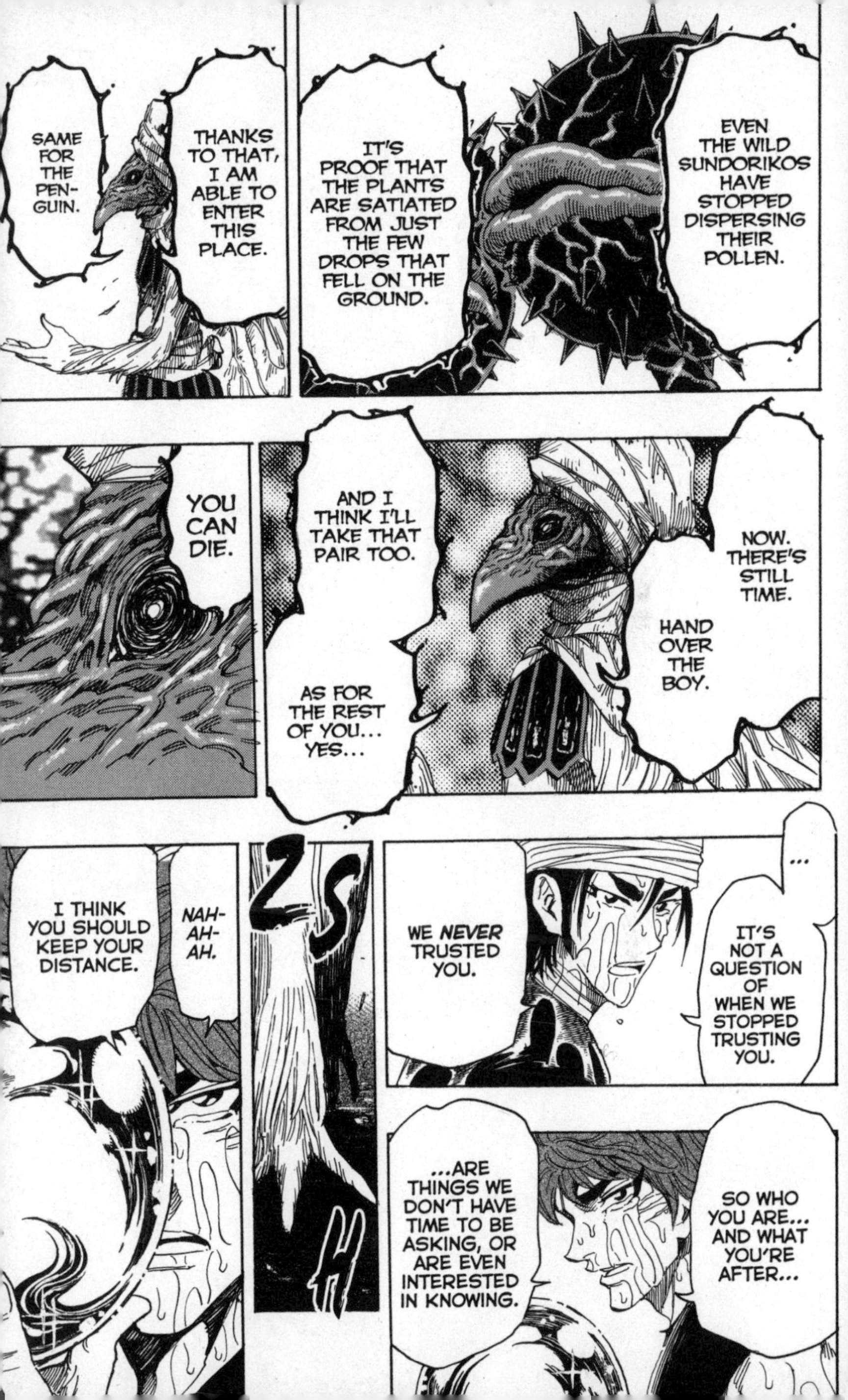
EVEN THE WILD SUNDORIKOS HAVE STOPPED DISPERSING THEIR POLLEN.
IT'S PROOF THAT THE PLANTS ARE SATIATED FROM JUST THE FEW DROPS THAT FELL ON THE GROUND.
THANKS TO THAT, I AM ABLE TO ENTER THIS PLACE.
SAME FOR THE PEN-GUIN.
NOW. THERE'S STILL TIME.
HAND OVER THE BOY.
AND I THINK I'LL TAKE THAT PAIR TOO.
AS FOR THE REST OF YOU... YES...
YOU CAN DIE.
...
IT'S NOT A QUESTION OF WHEN WE STOPPED TRUSTING YOU.
WE *NEVER* TRUSTED YOU.
SO WHO YOU ARE... AND WHAT YOU'RE AFTER...
...ARE THINGS WE DON'T HAVE TIME TO BE ASKING, OR ARE EVEN INTERESTED IN KNOWING.
ZS
H
NAH-AH-AH.
I THINK YOU SHOULD KEEP YOUR DISTANCE.

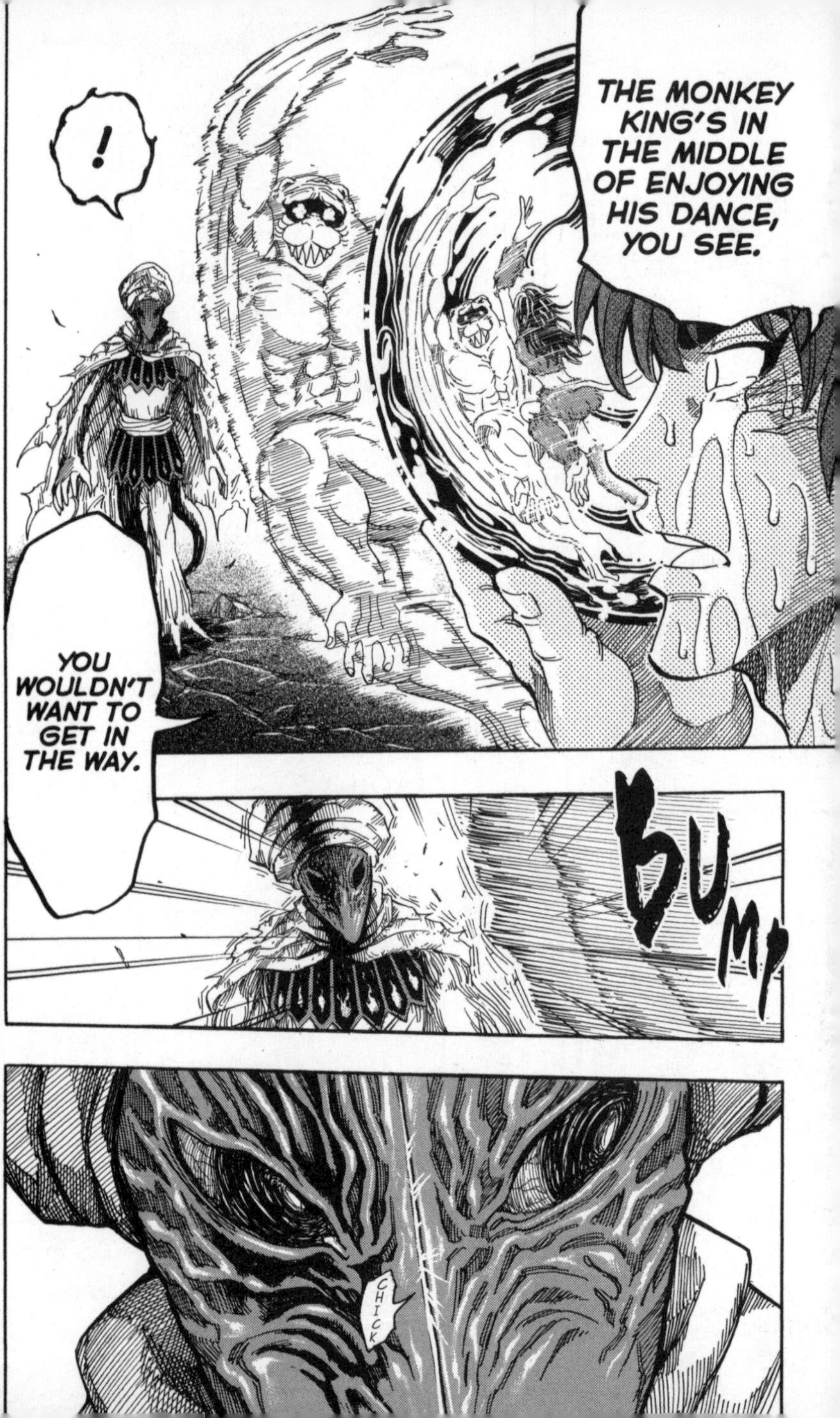
THE MONKEY KING'S IN THE MIDDLE OF ENJOYING HIS DANCE, YOU SEE.
!
YOU WOULDN'T WANT TO GET IN THE WAY.
BUMP
CHICK

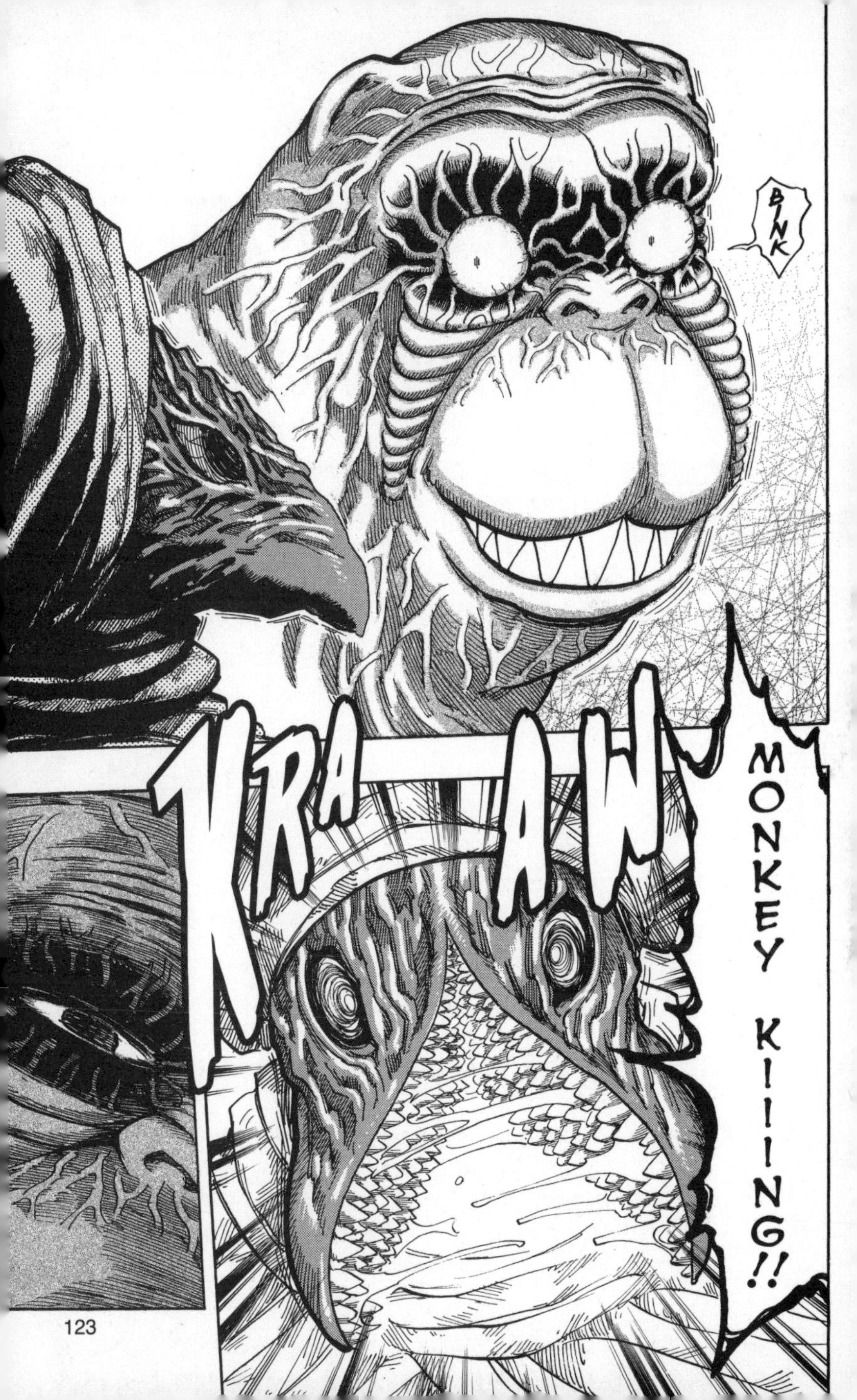
BINK
KRAAAW
MONKEY KIIING!!

TORIKO

GOURMET CHECKLIST

Vol. 342

PHANTOM SAKE
(ALCOHOL)

...THE ONE DRINK...
GLUB
...THAT ICHI LIKED.

CAPTURE LEVEL: LESS THAN 1

HABITAT: ARTIFICIALLY PROCESSED

SIZE: ---

HEIGHT: ---

WEIGHT: ---

PRICE: 1,000 YEN PER 750 ML BOTTLE

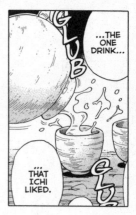

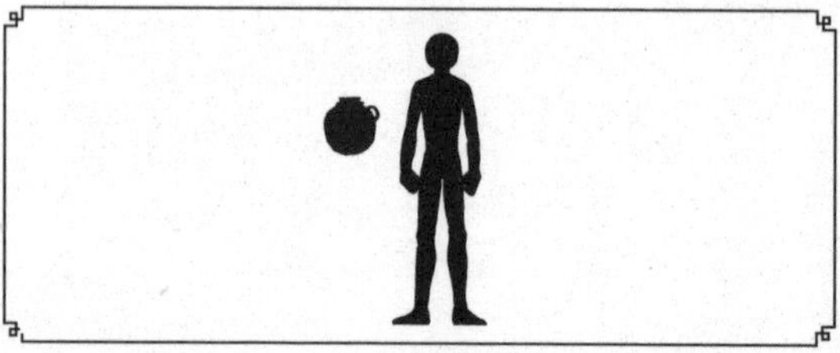

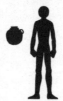

SCALE

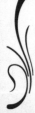

JIRO GAVE THIS ALCOHOL TO TORIKO TO CHEER HIM UP AFTER HE WAS DEFEATED BY STARJUN. IT'S THE ONE ALCOHOL THAT ICHIRYU ENJOYED. IT IS EASY TO FIND AND IS FAIRLY AVERAGE. DESPITE THIS, THERE'S SOMETHING NOSTALGIC ABOUT ITS TASTE AND IT PERFECTLY MEMORIALIZES THE LATE ICHIRYU. EVEN TORIKO TOOK SEVERAL SWIGS OF THIS MYSTERIOUSLY APPEALING DRINK.

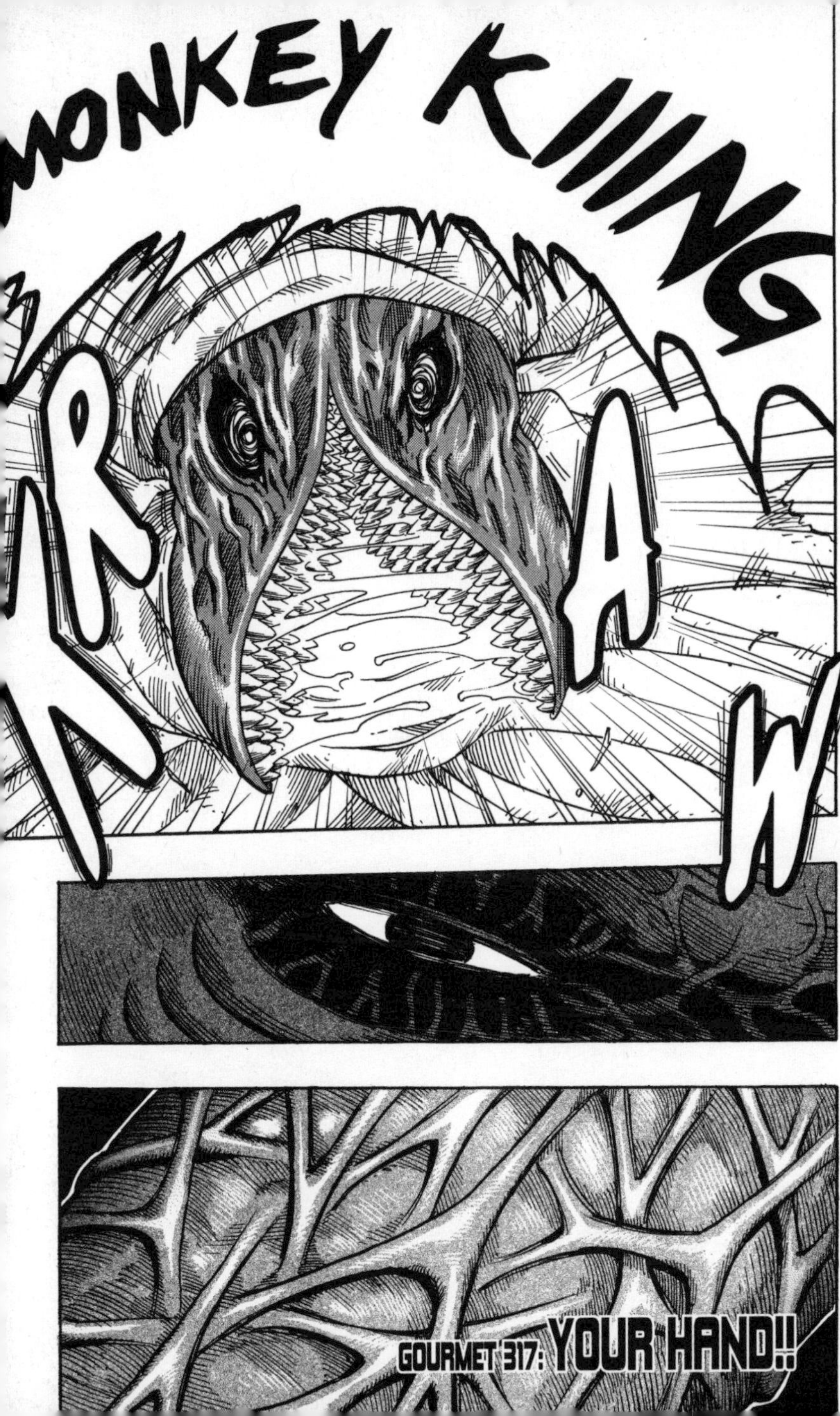
MONKEY KIIING

GOURMET 317: YOUR HAND!!

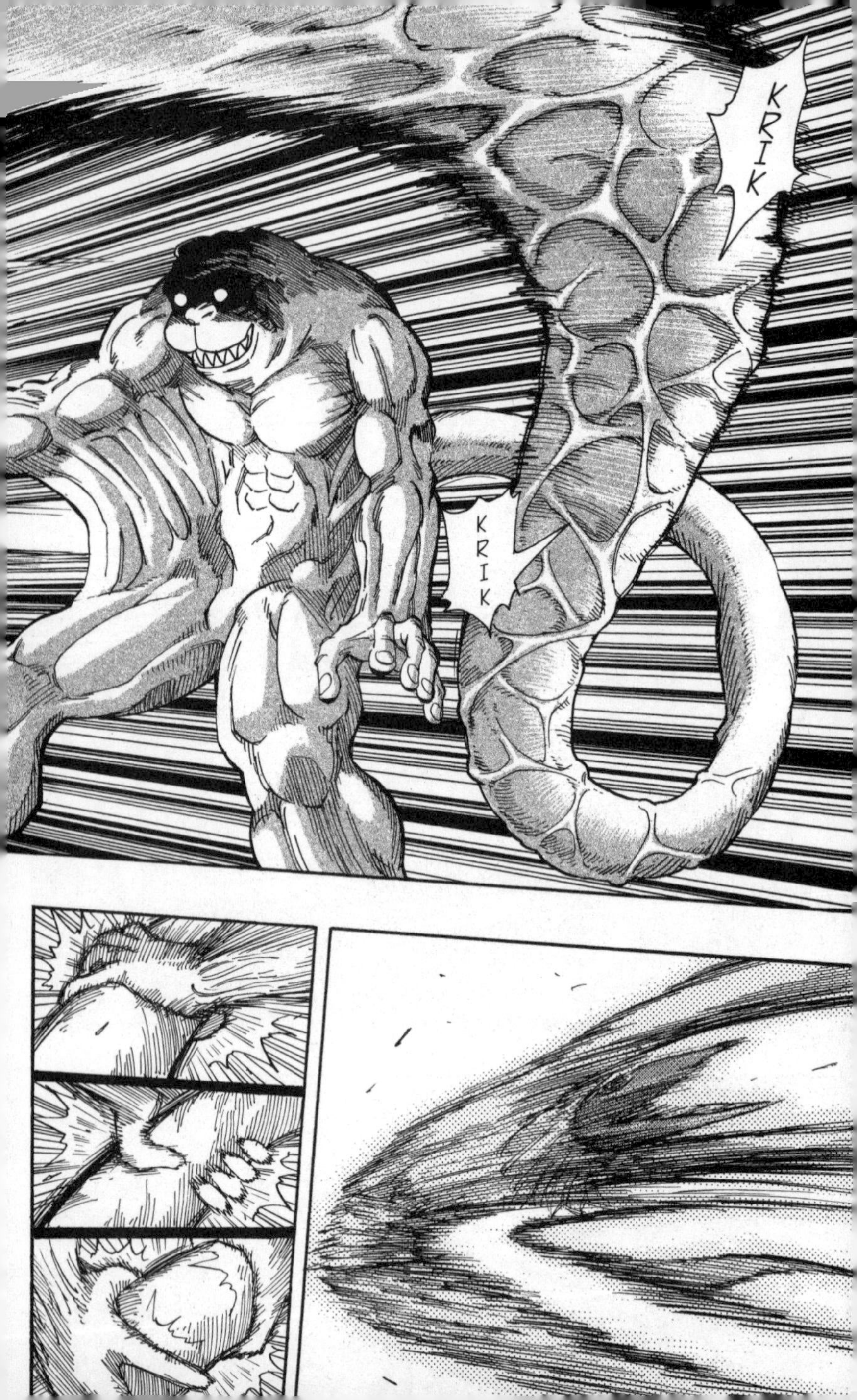
KRIK
KRIK

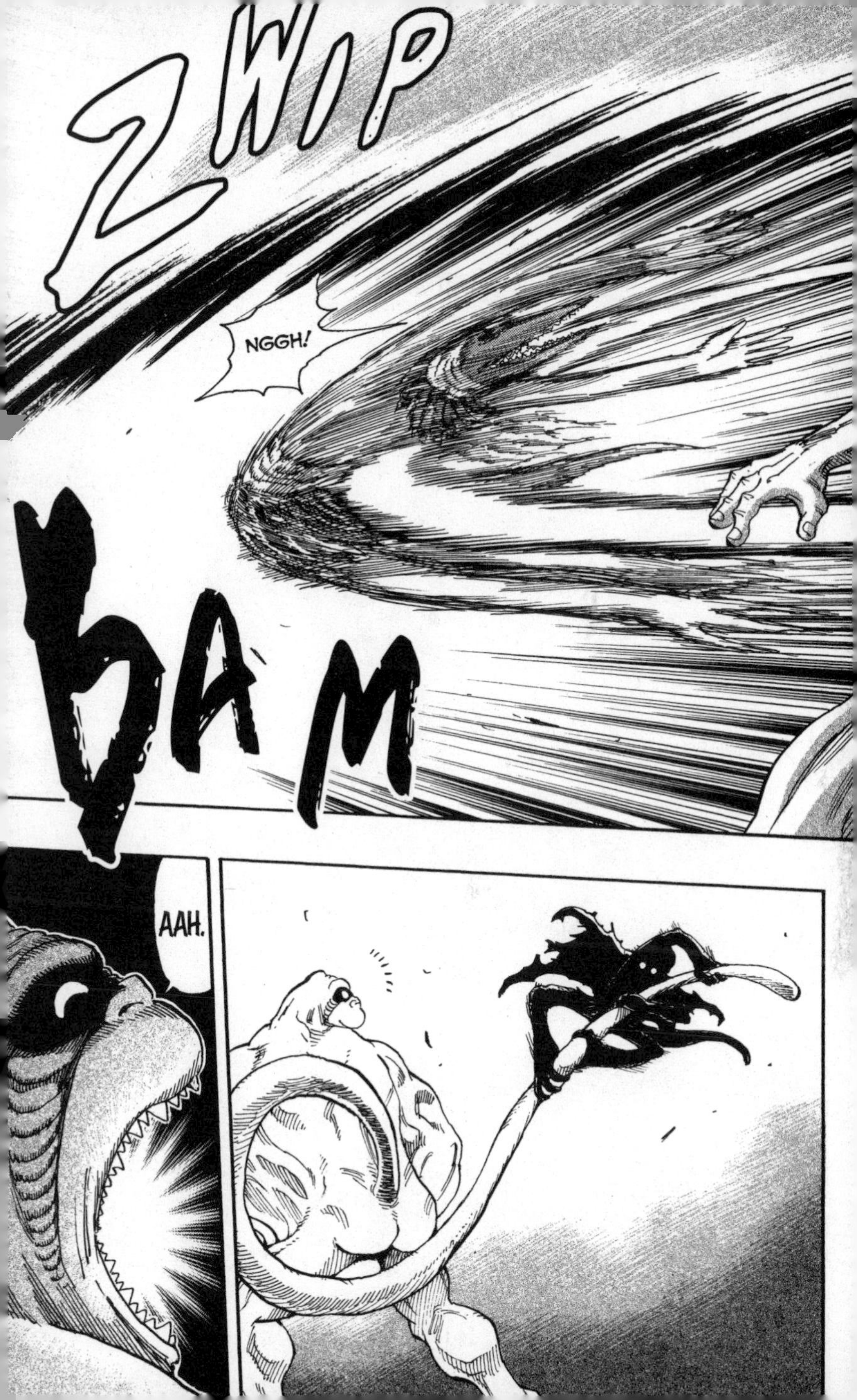
ZWIP
NGGH!
BAM
AAH.

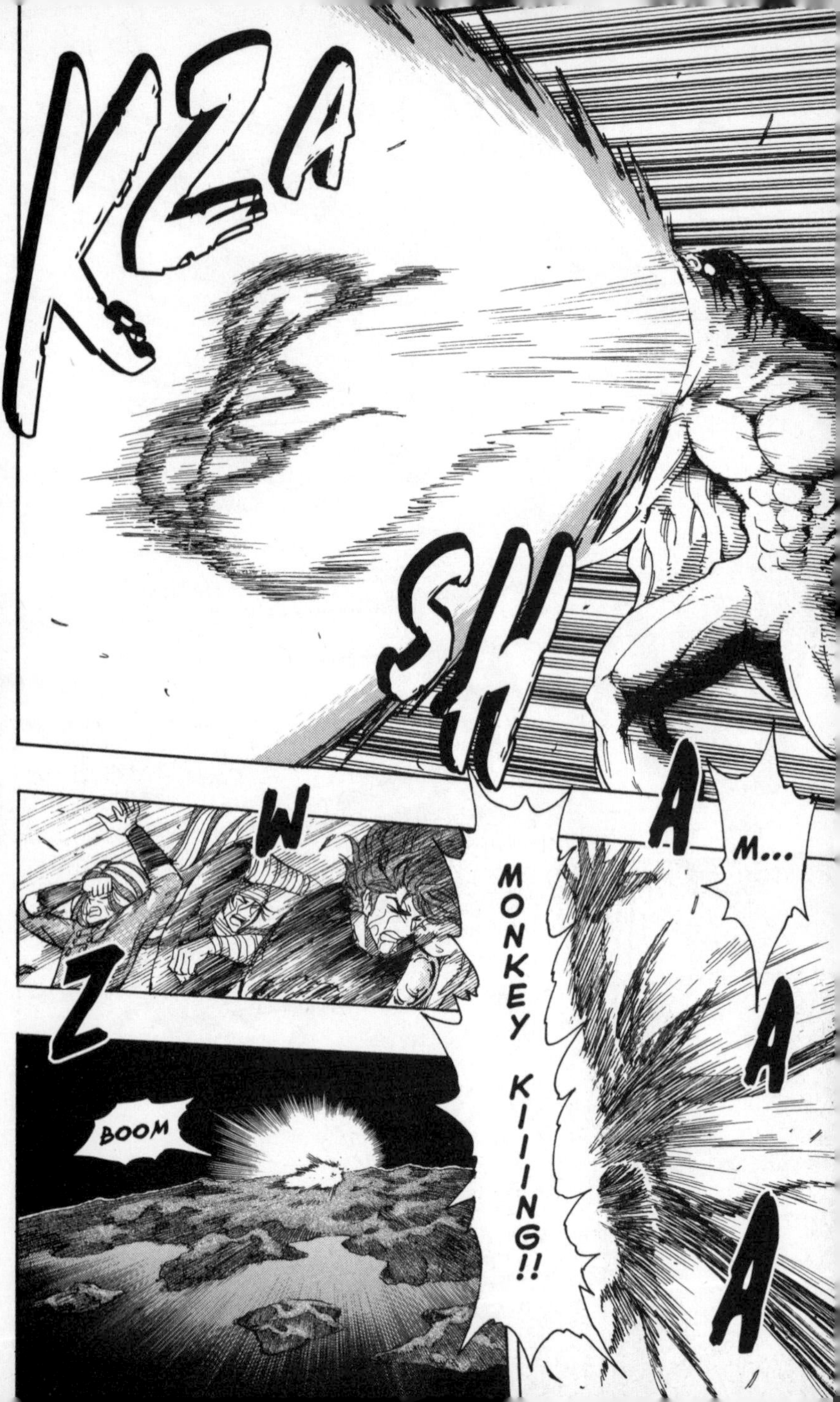
KRA
SH
W
Z
BOOM
M...
MONKEY KIIIING!!
AAAA

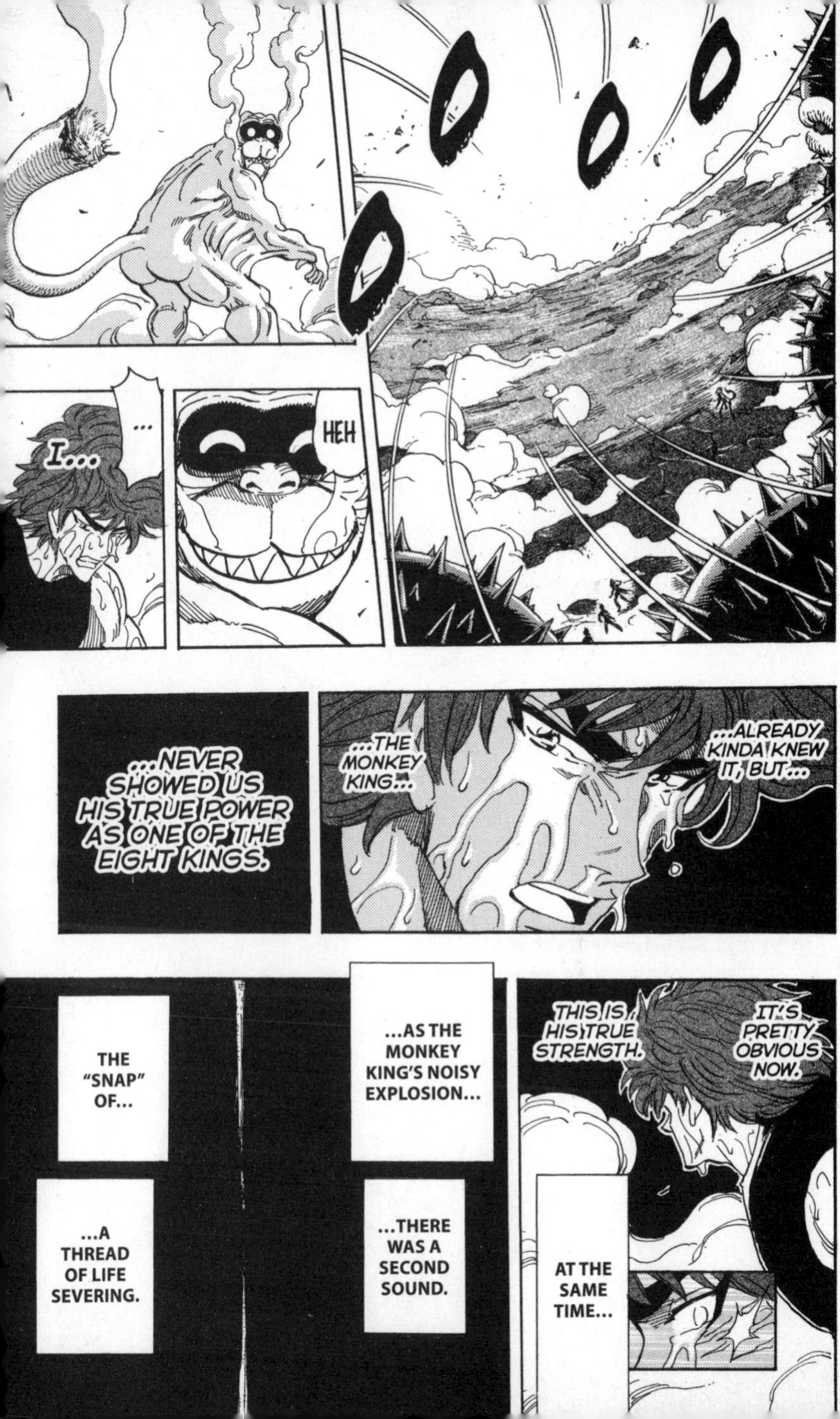
HEH
...
I...
...ALREADY KINDA KNEW IT, BUT...
...THE MONKEY KING...
...NEVER SHOWED US HIS TRUE POWER AS ONE OF THE EIGHT KINGS.
IT'S PRETTY OBVIOUS NOW.
THIS IS HIS TRUE STRENGTH.
AT THE SAME TIME...
...AS THE MONKEY KING'S NOISY EXPLOSION...
...THERE WAS A SECOND SOUND.
THE "SNAP" OF...
...A THREAD OF LIFE SEVERING.

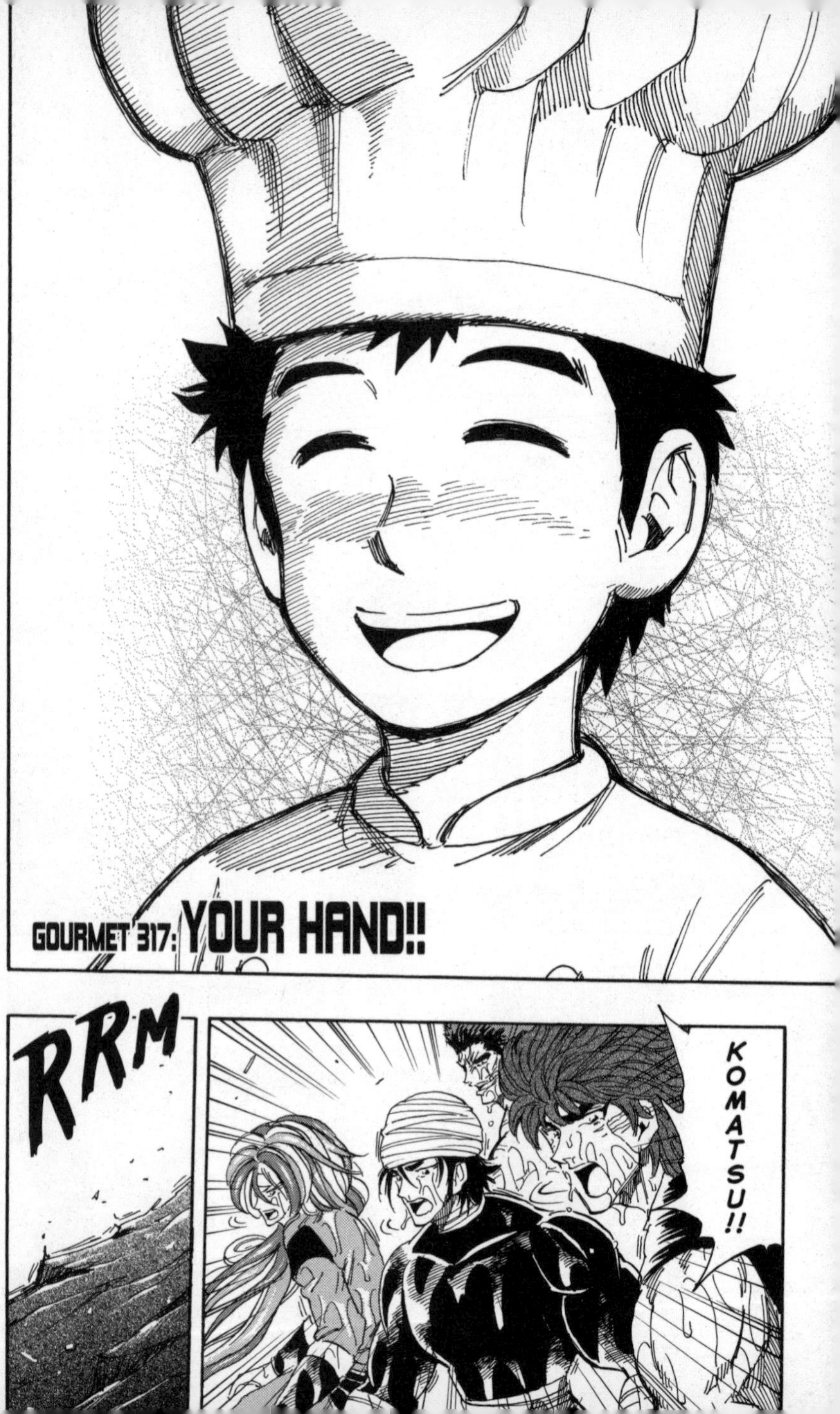
GOURMET 317: YOUR HAND!!
KOMATSU!!
RRM

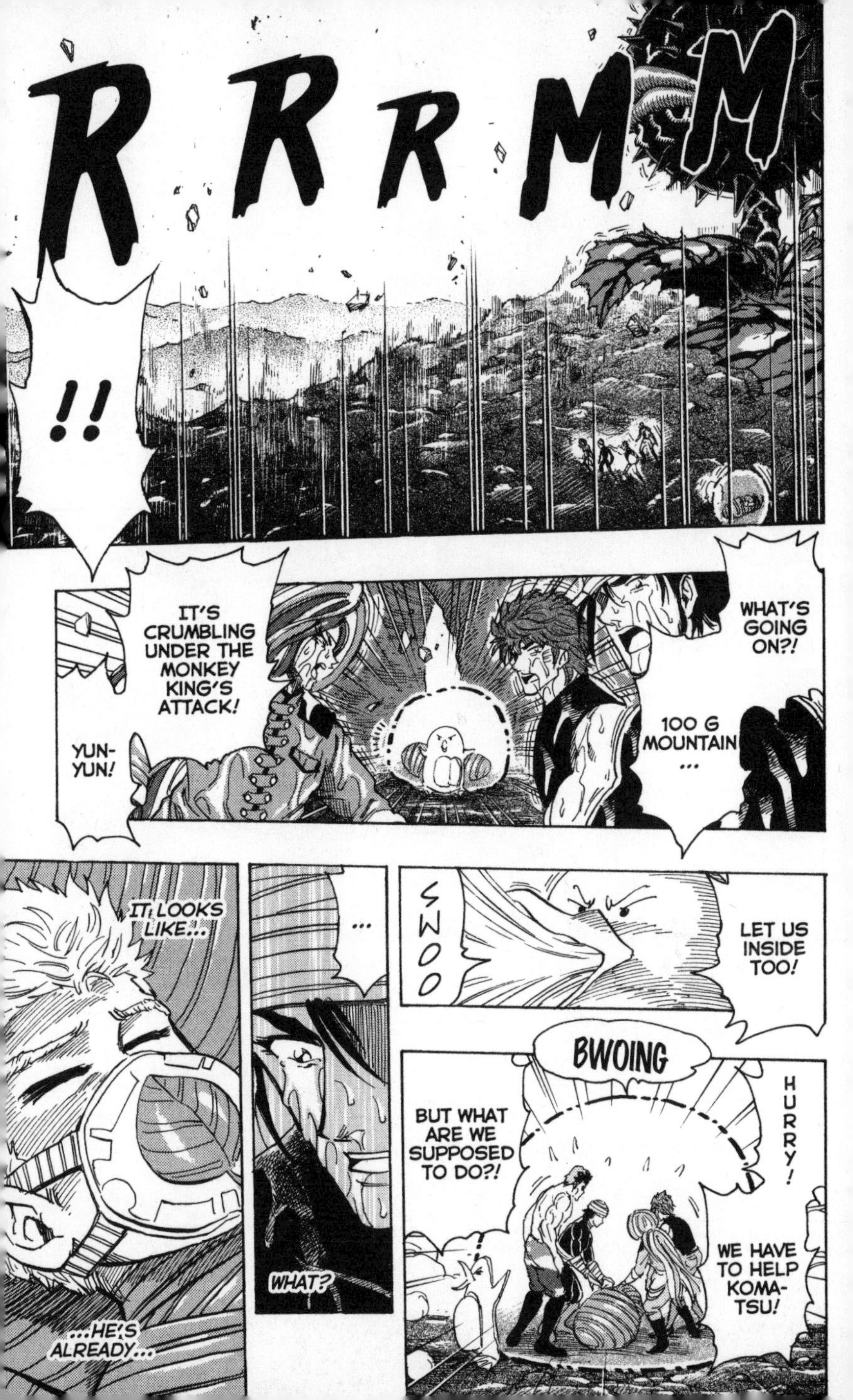
RRRMM
!!
WHAT'S GOING ON?!
100 G MOUNTAIN...
IT'S CRUMBLING UNDER THE MONKEY KING'S ATTACK!
YUN-YUN!
LET US INSIDE TOO!
SWOO
BWOING
HURRY!
BUT WHAT ARE WE SUPPOSED TO DO?!
WE HAVE TO HELP KOMATSU!
...
WHAT?
IT LOOKS LIKE...
...HE'S ALREADY...

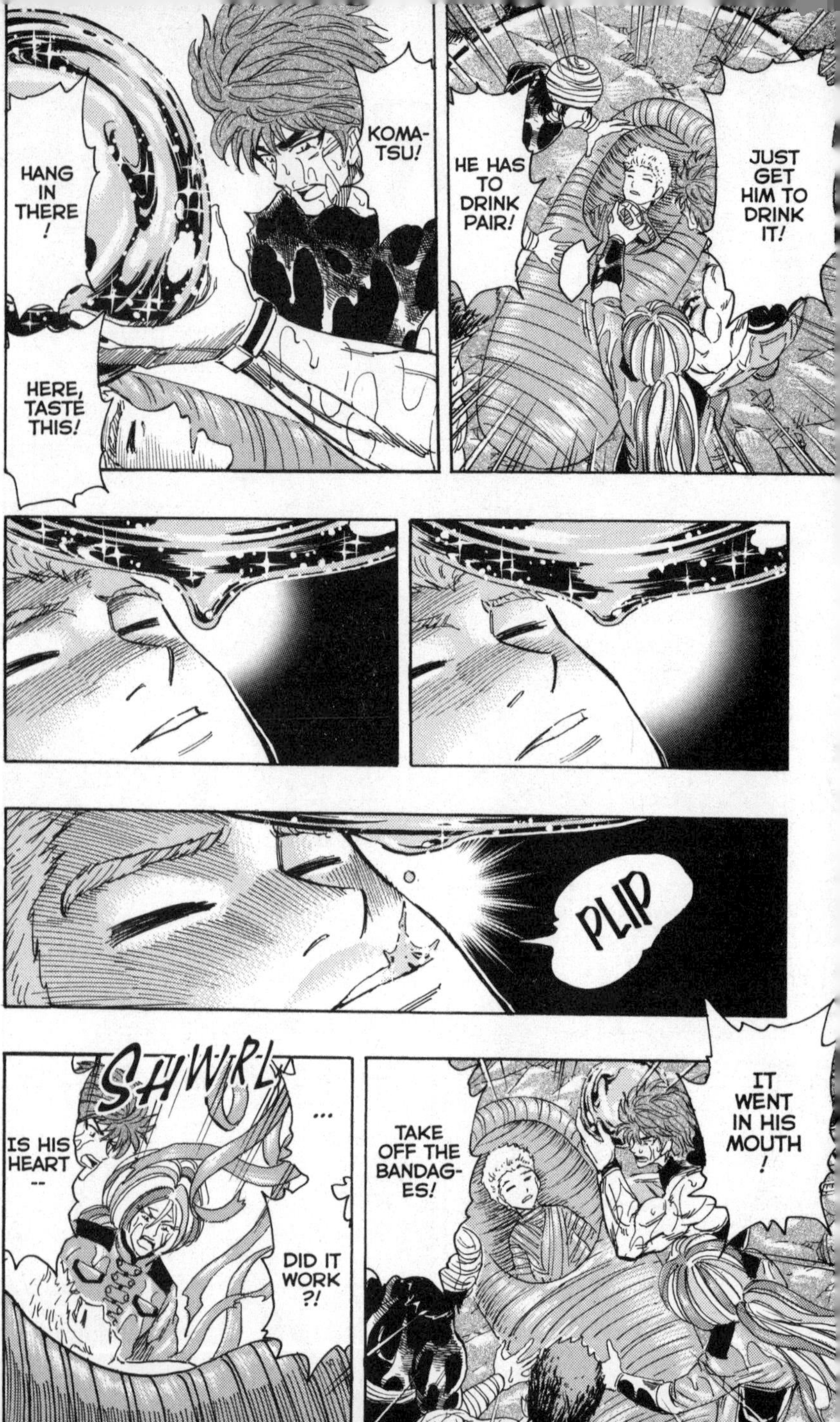
JUST GET HIM TO DRINK IT!
HE HAS TO DRINK PAIR!
KOMA-TSU!
HANG IN THERE!
HERE, TASTE THIS!
PLIP
IT WENT IN HIS MOUTH!
TAKE OFF THE BANDAG-ES!
SHWIRL
...
IS HIS HEART --
DID IT WORK?!

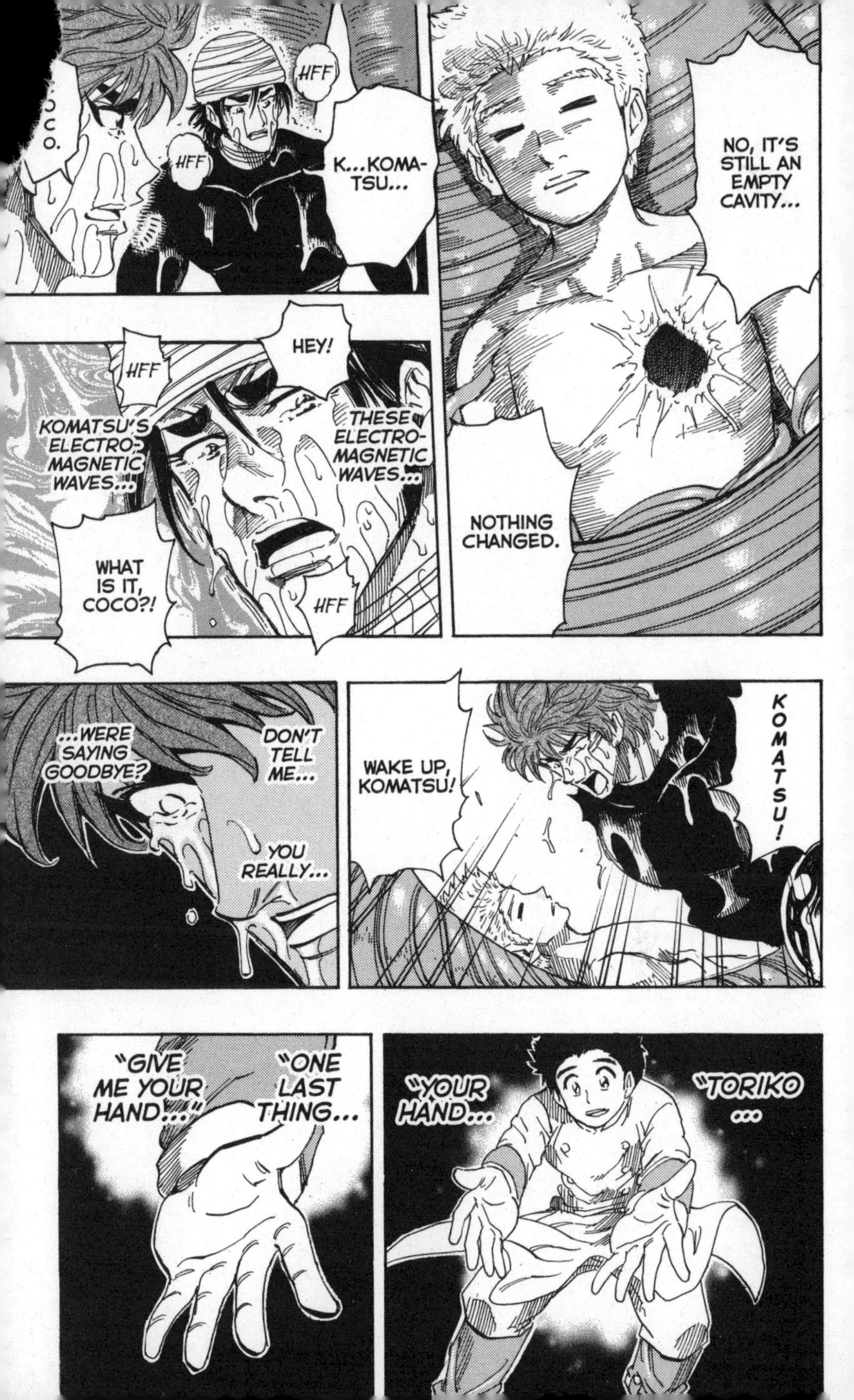
NO, IT'S STILL AN EMPTY CAVITY...
NOTHING CHANGED.
COCO.
HFF
K...KOMA-TSU...
HFF
HEY!
HFF
THESE ELECTRO-MAGNETIC WAVES...
KOMATSU'S ELECTRO-MAGNETIC WAVES...
WHAT IS IT, COCO?!
HFF
KOMATSU!
WAKE UP, KOMATSU!
DON'T TELL ME...
YOU REALLY...
...WERE SAYING GOODBYE?
"TORIKO...
"YOUR HAND...
"ONE LAST THING...
"GIVE ME YOUR HAND..."

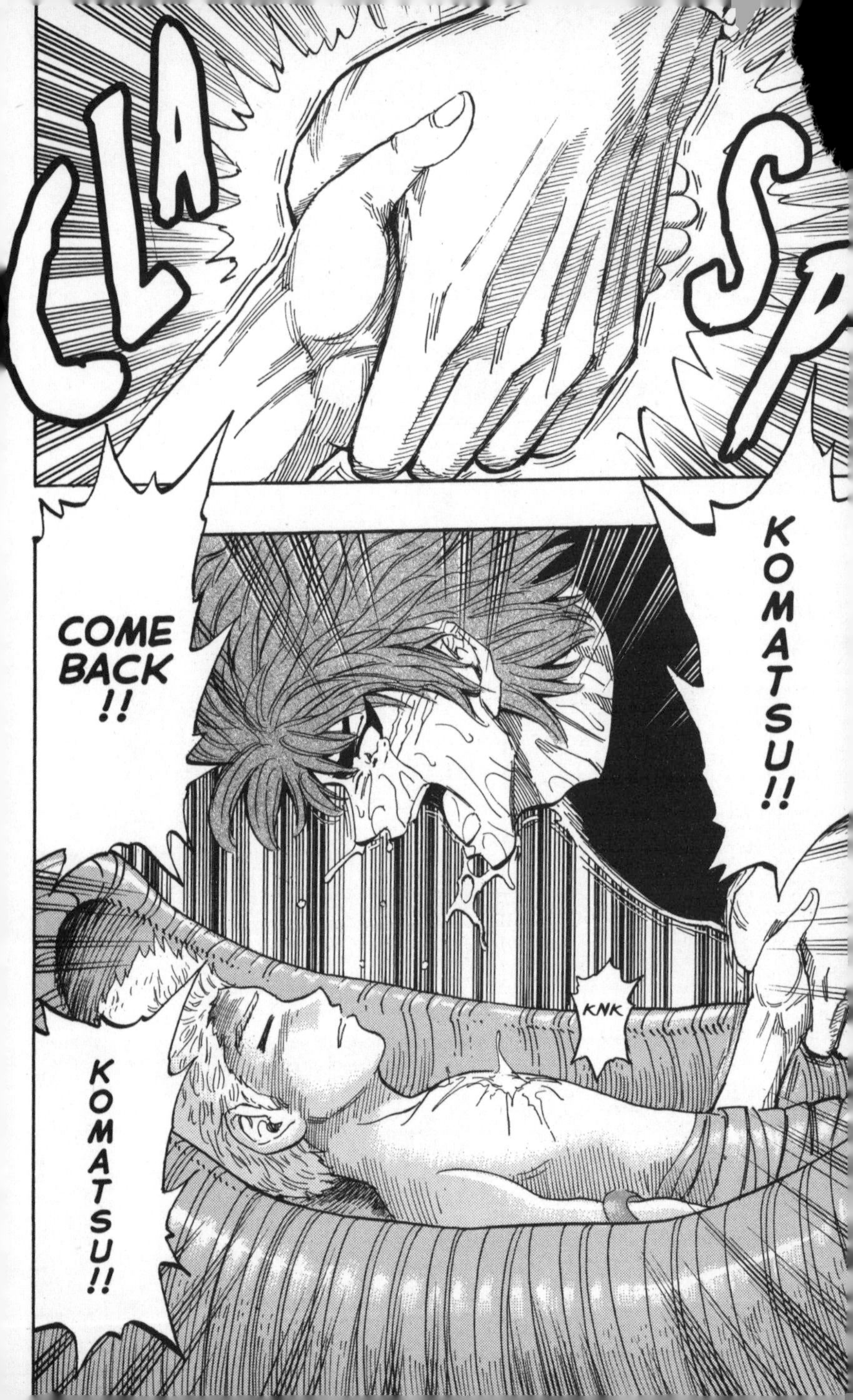
CLASP
KOMATSU!!
COME BACK!!
KNK
KOMATSU!!

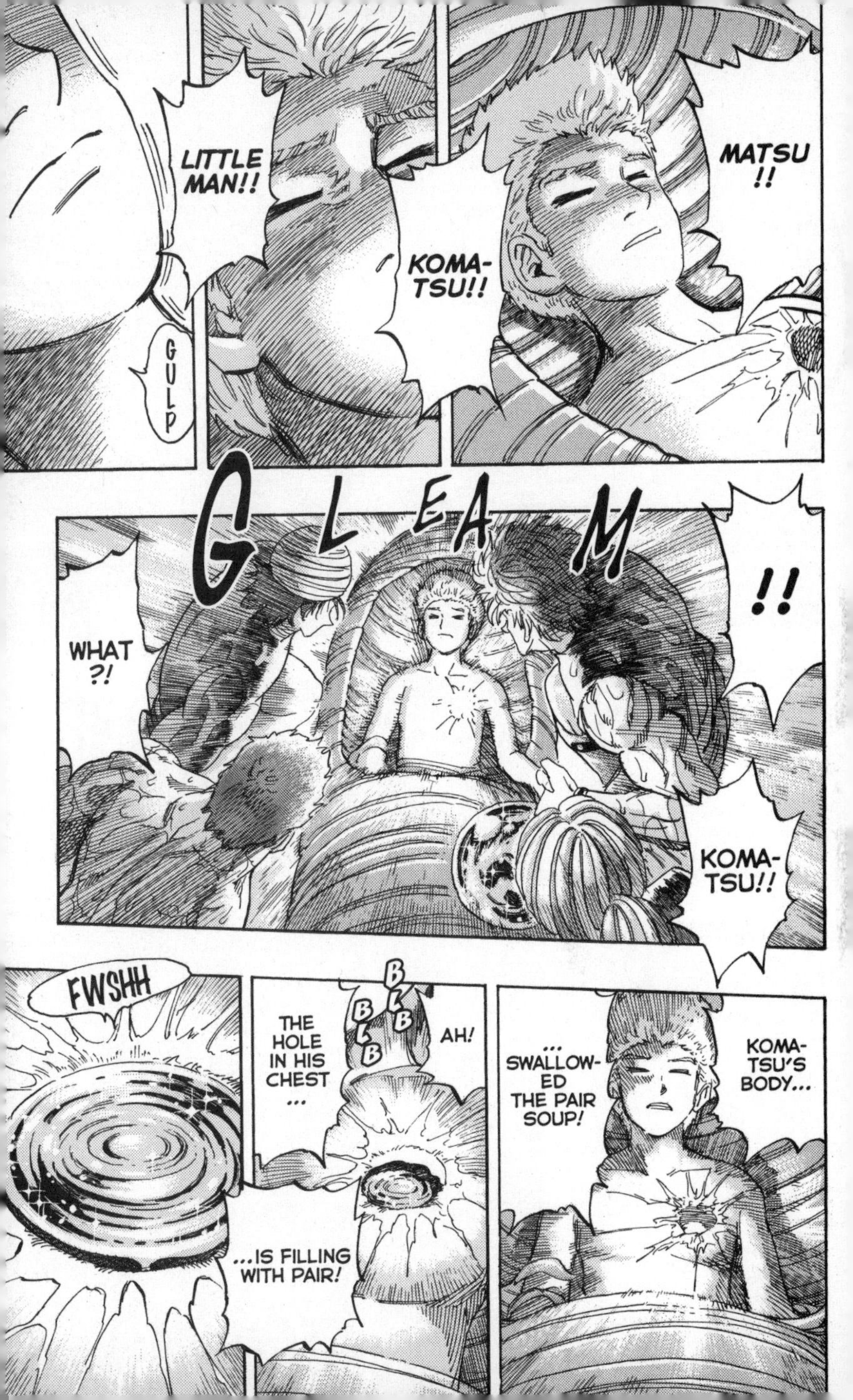
MATSU !!
KOMA-TSU!!
LITTLE MAN!!
GULP
GLEAM !!
KOMA-TSU!!
WHAT ?!
KOMA-TSU'S BODY...
... SWALLOW-ED THE PAIR SOUP!
AH!
BLB BLB
THE HOLE IN HIS CHEST ...
...IS FILLING WITH PAIR!
FWSHH

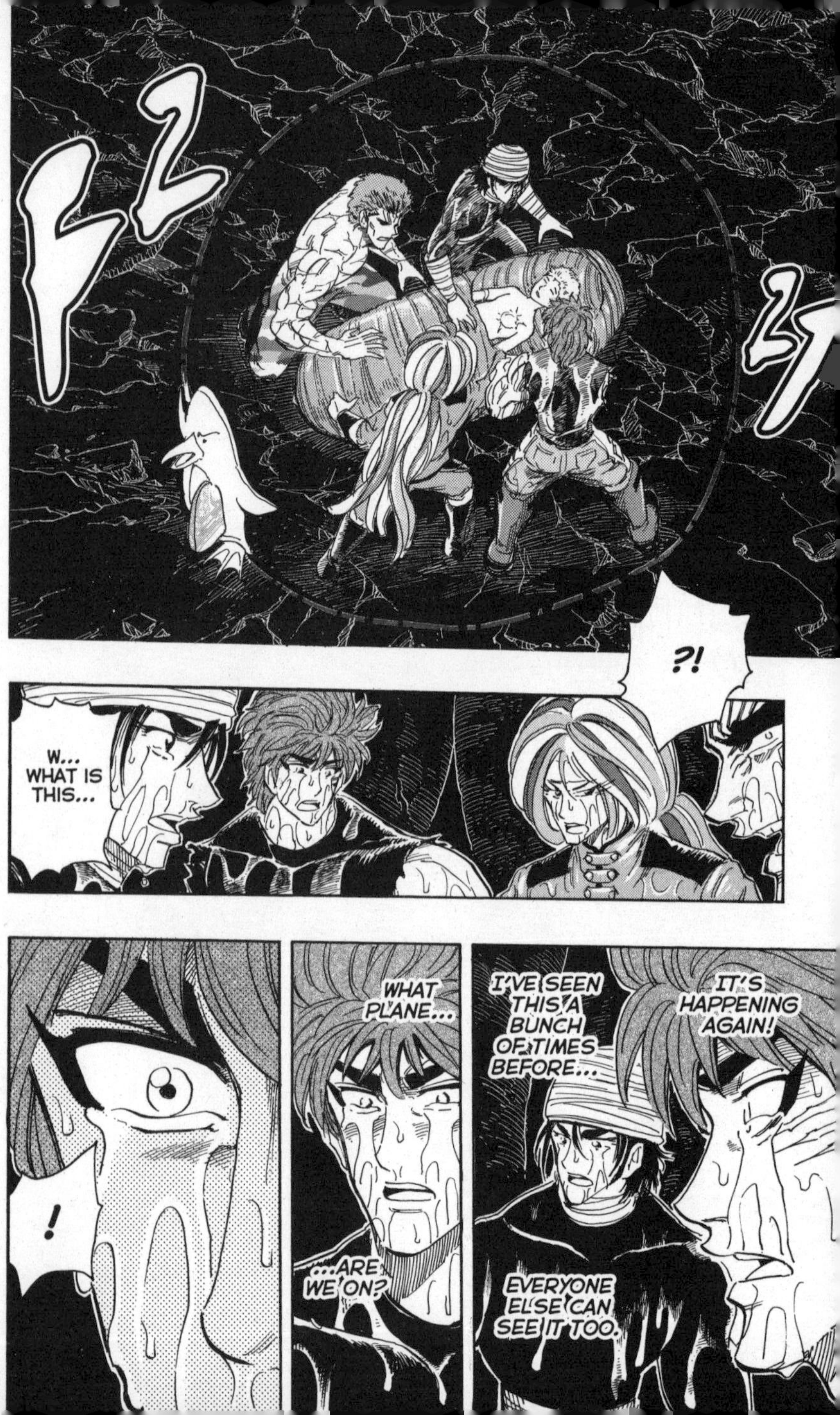
?!
W... WHAT IS THIS...
IT'S HAPPENING AGAIN!
I'VE SEEN THIS A BUNCH OF TIMES BEFORE...
EVERYONE ELSE CAN SEE IT TOO.
WHAT PLANE...
...ARE WE ON?
!

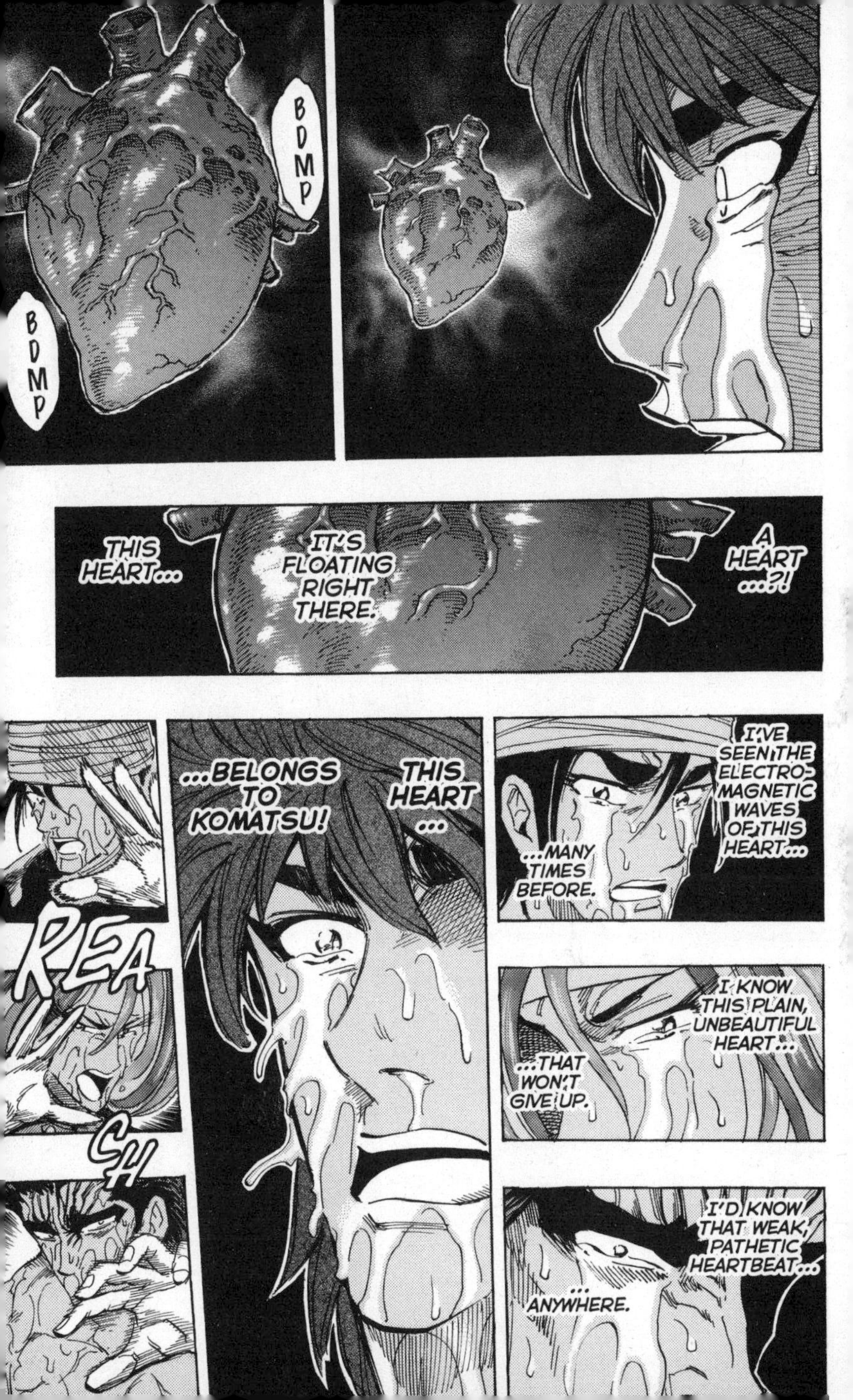
BDMP
BDMP
A HEART ...?!
IT'S FLOATING RIGHT THERE.
THIS HEART...
I'VE SEEN THE ELECTRO-MAGNETIC WAVES OF THIS HEART...
...MANY TIMES BEFORE.
I KNOW THIS PLAIN, UNBEAUTIFUL HEART...
...THAT WON'T GIVE UP.
I'D KNOW THAT WEAK, PATHETIC HEARTBEAT...
... ANYWHERE.
THIS HEART ...
...BELONGS TO KOMATSU!
REA
CH

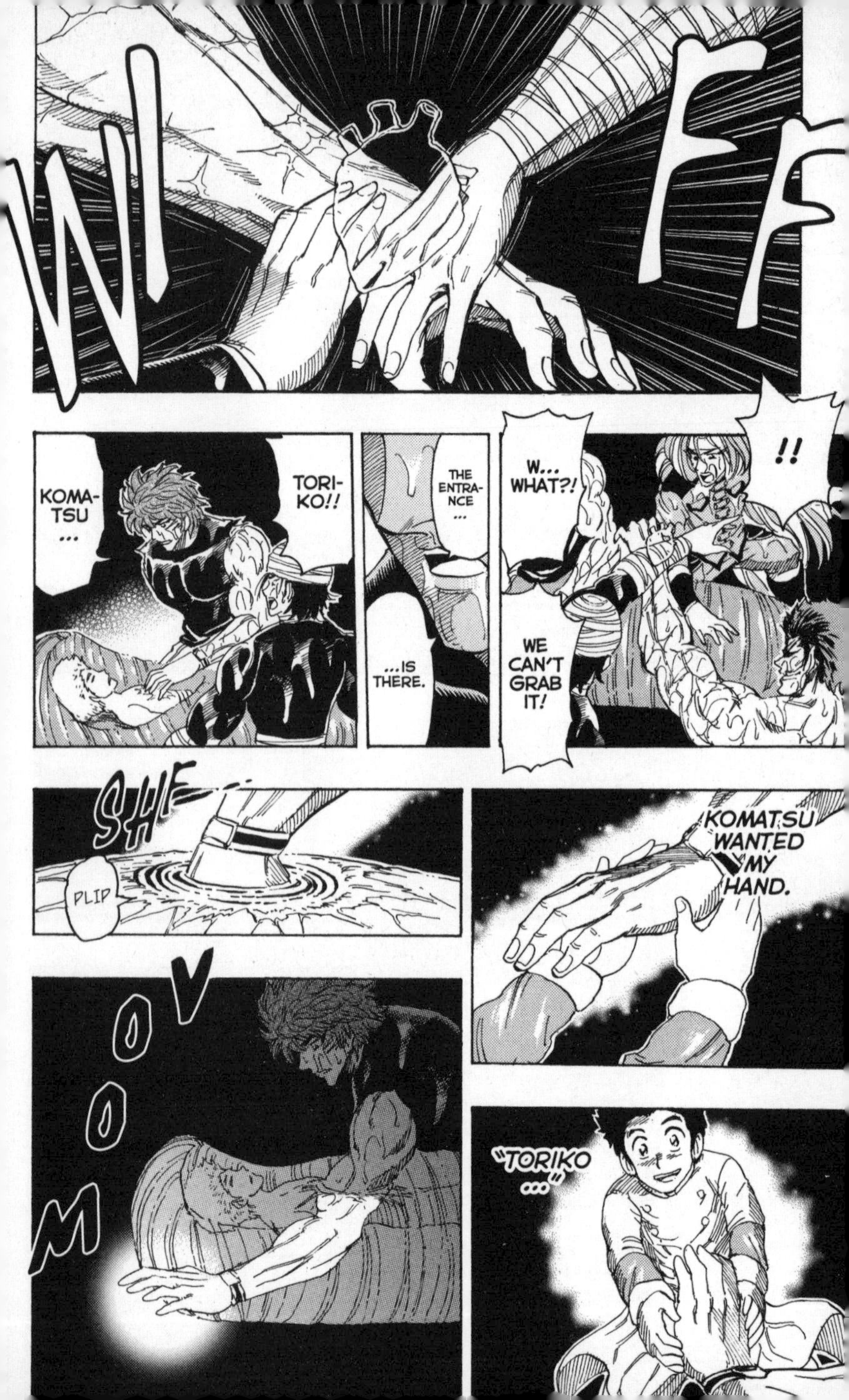
WIFF
!!
W... WHAT?!
WE CAN'T GRAB IT!
THE ENTRANCE...
...IS THERE.
TORIKO!!
KOMATSU...
KOMATSU WANTED MY HAND.
SHF...
PLIP
"TORIKO..."
VOOM

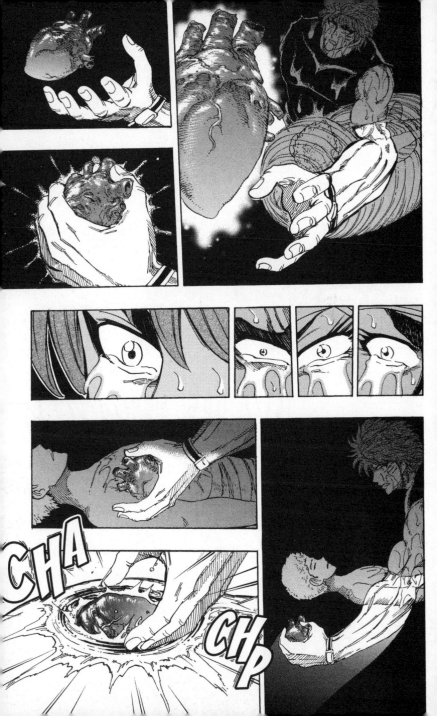

CHA

CHP

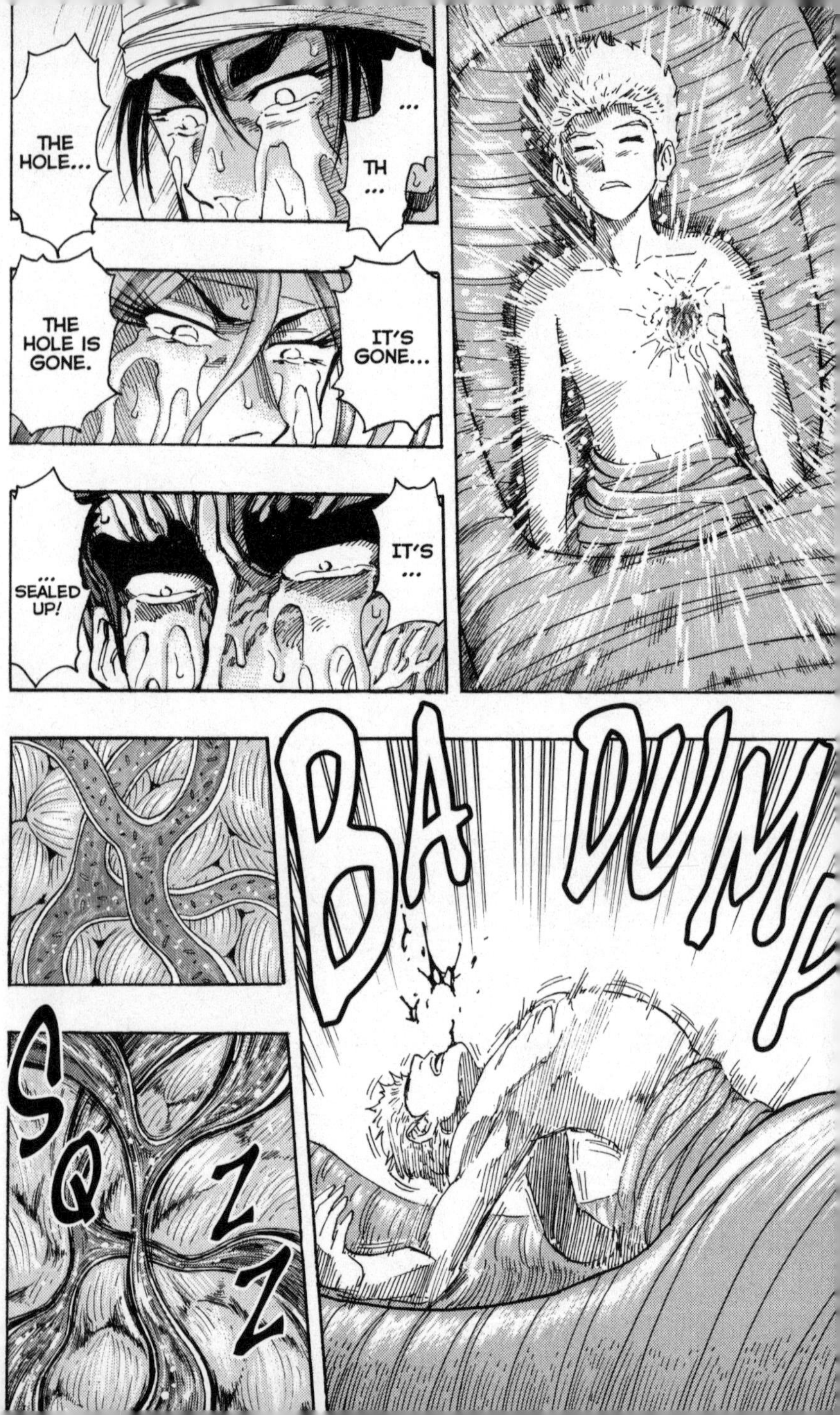
...
TH ...
THE HOLE...
IT'S GONE...
THE HOLE IS GONE.
IT'S ...
... SEALED UP!
BA DUM
SQZZ

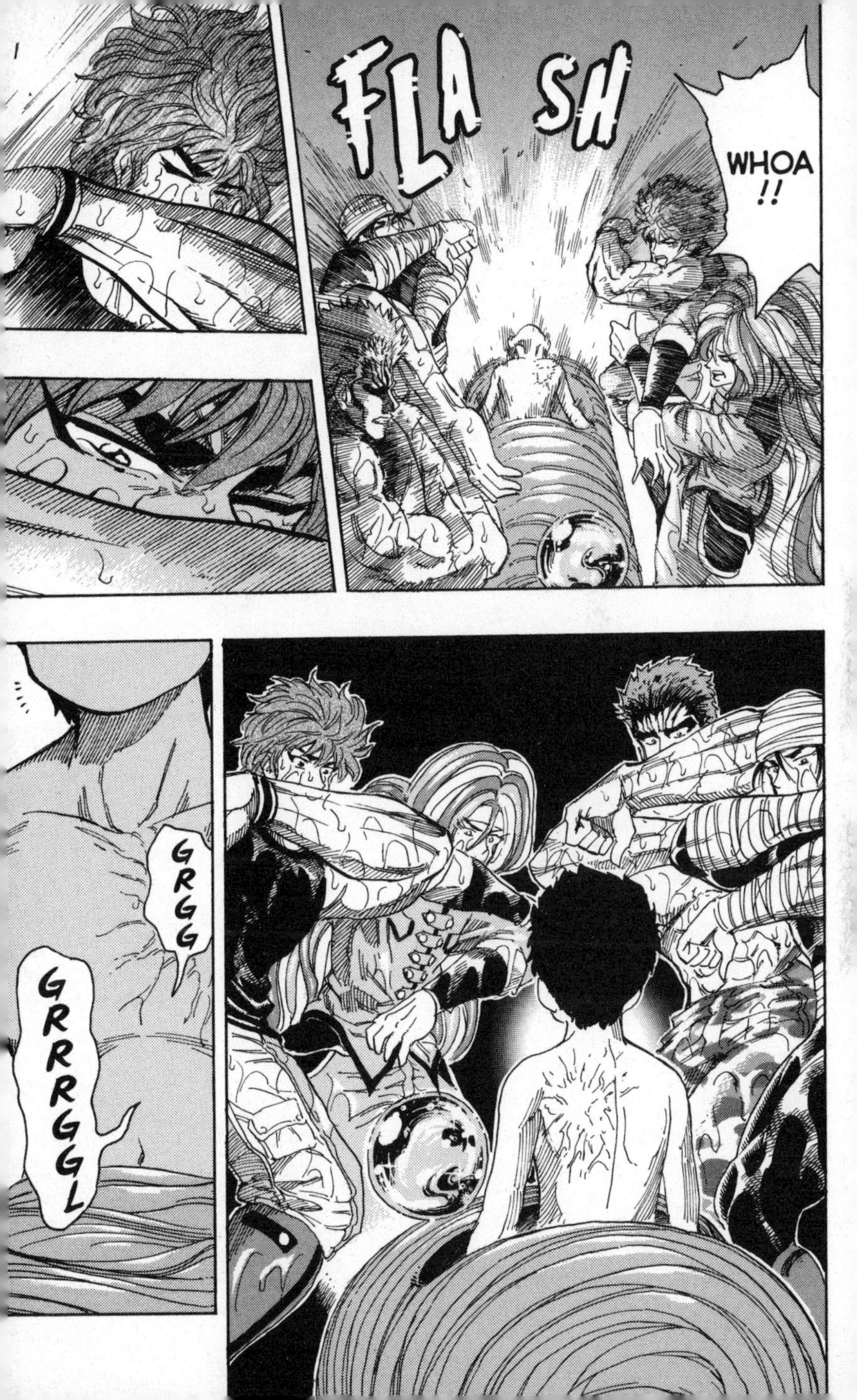
FLASH
WHOA !!
GRGG
GRRRGGL

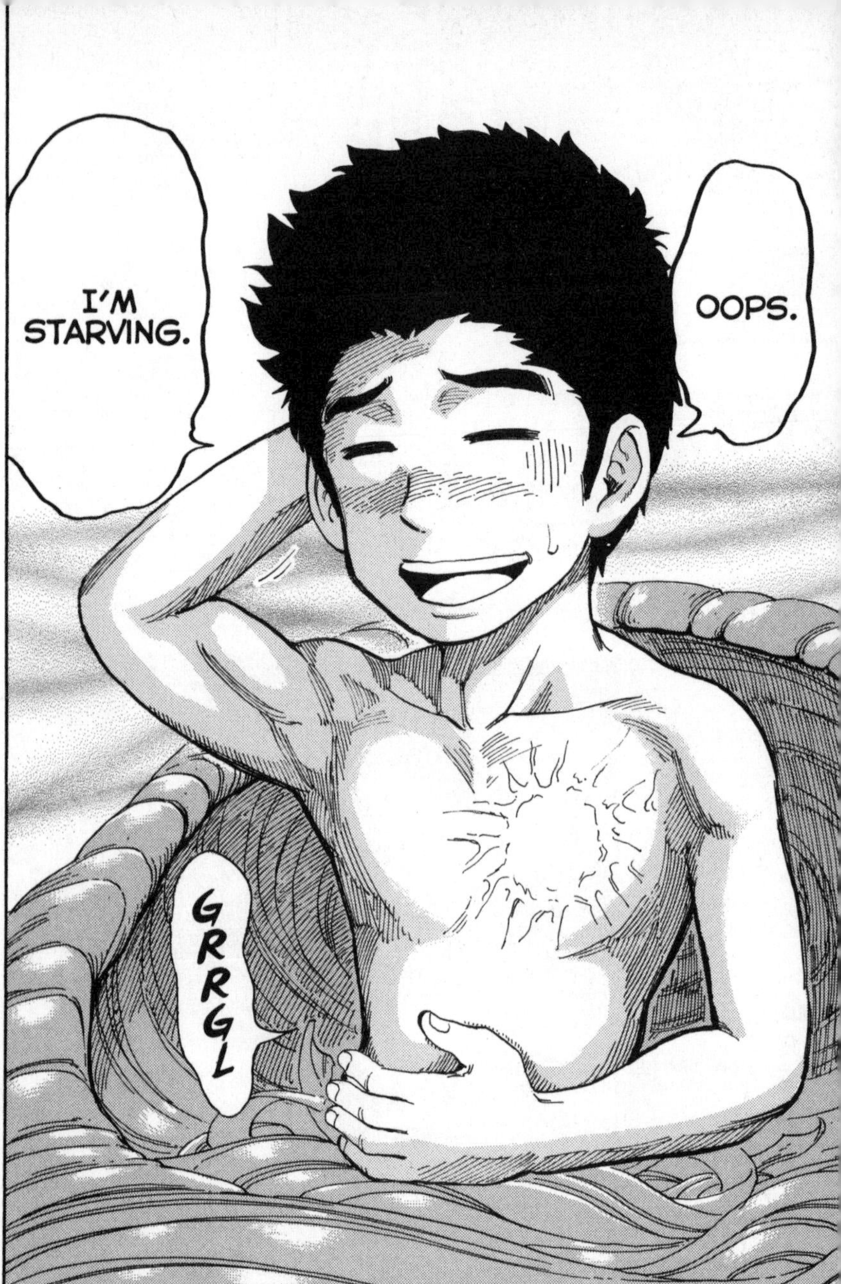
OOPS.
I'M STARVING.
GRRGL

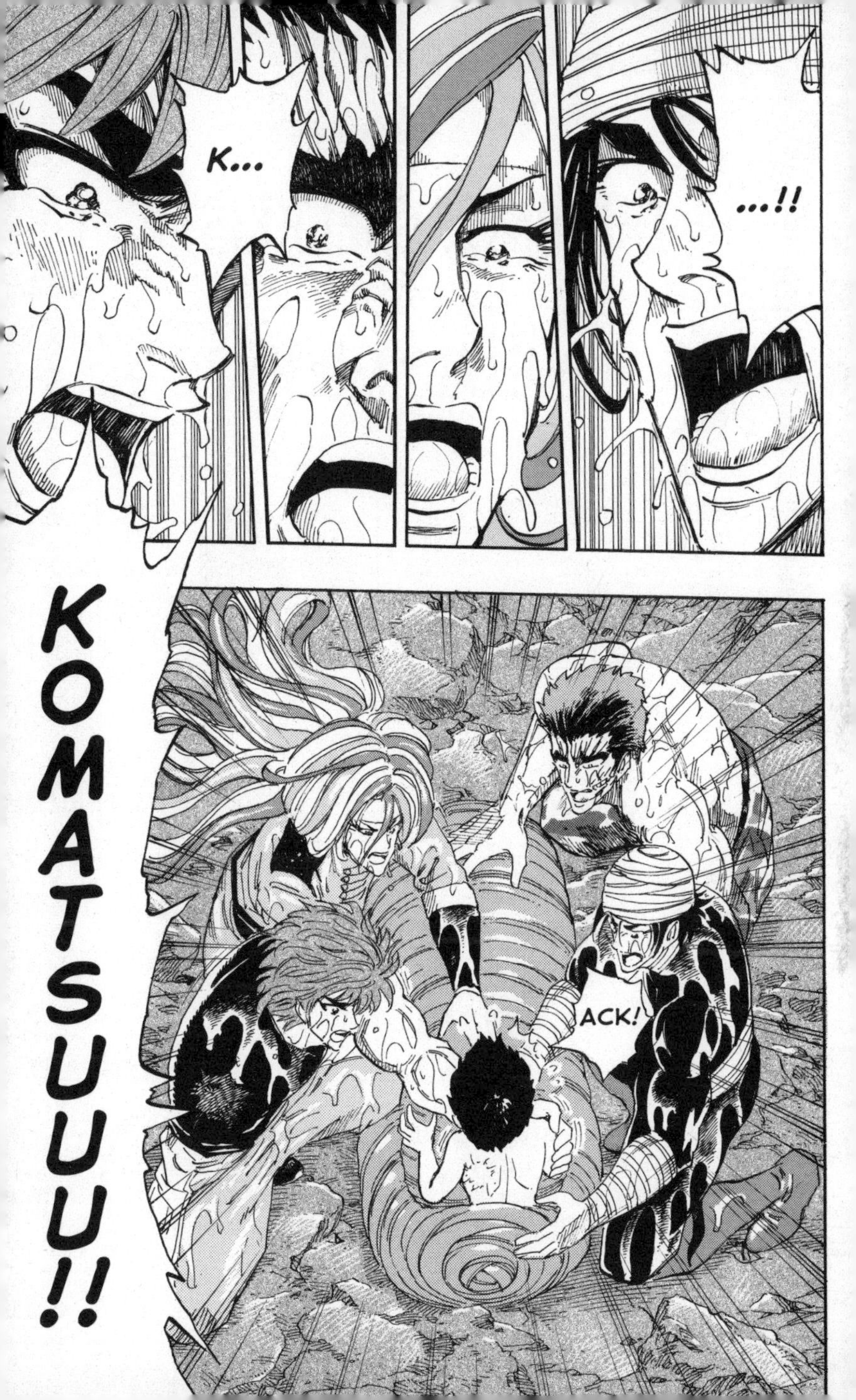
...!!
K...
ACK!
KOMATSUUU!!

TORIKO

GOURMET CHECKLIST

Vol. 343

WALLABY MOCHI
(MAMMAL)

CAPTURE LEVEL: 2
HABITAT: FOUND EVERYWHERE
SIZE: 1.5 M
HEIGHT: 1.2 M
WEIGHT: 60 KG
PRICE: 3,000 YEN PER KILOGRAM

WHEN I WAS IN GRADE SCHOOL I HATED SCHOOL... SO I'D ALWAYS SKIP CLASS.

BUT AFTER THE CAFETERIA STARTED SERVING WALLABY MOCHI...

...I STARTED GOING TO SCHOOL AGAIN.

SCALE

AN INGREDIENT THAT TORIKO DISCOVERED. IT'S A WALLABY WHOSE BODY IS MADE OUT OF MOCHI. SINCE IT'S TRANSPARENT, IT'S VERY DIFFICULT TO FIND, BUT IT'S DELICIOUS TO EAT WHEN CHILLED. THIS INGREDIENT IS SERVED IN SCHOOL CAFETERIAS AND THERE ARE MANY CHILDREN WHO COME TO SCHOOL JUST SO THEY CAN PARTAKE IN THIS TASTY TREAT.

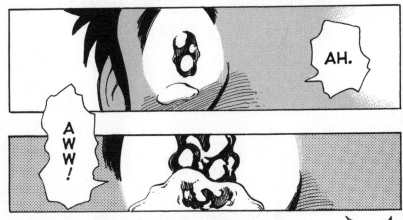

GOURMET 318: BAWL YOUR EYES OUT!!!

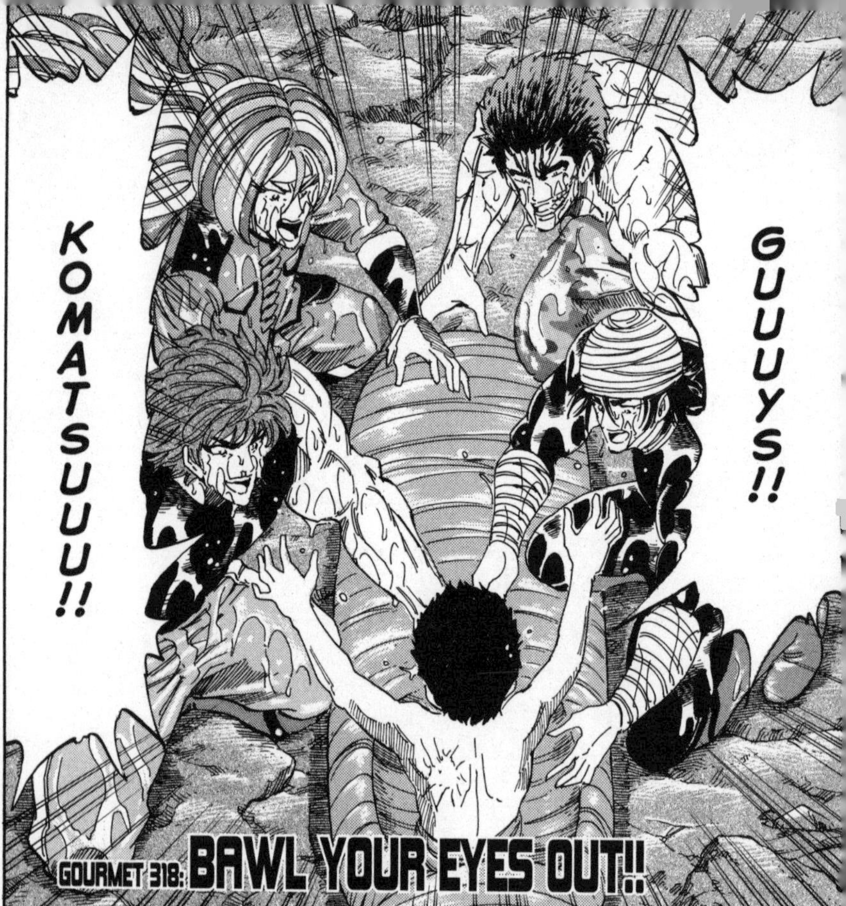
GUUUYS!!
KOMATSUUUU!!

GOURMET 318: BAWL YOUR EYES OUT!!

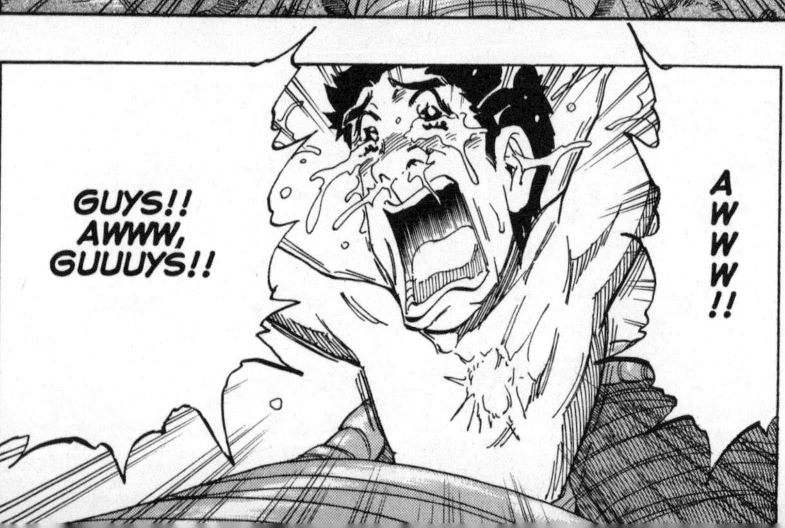
AWWW!!
GUYS!! AWWW, GUUUYS!!

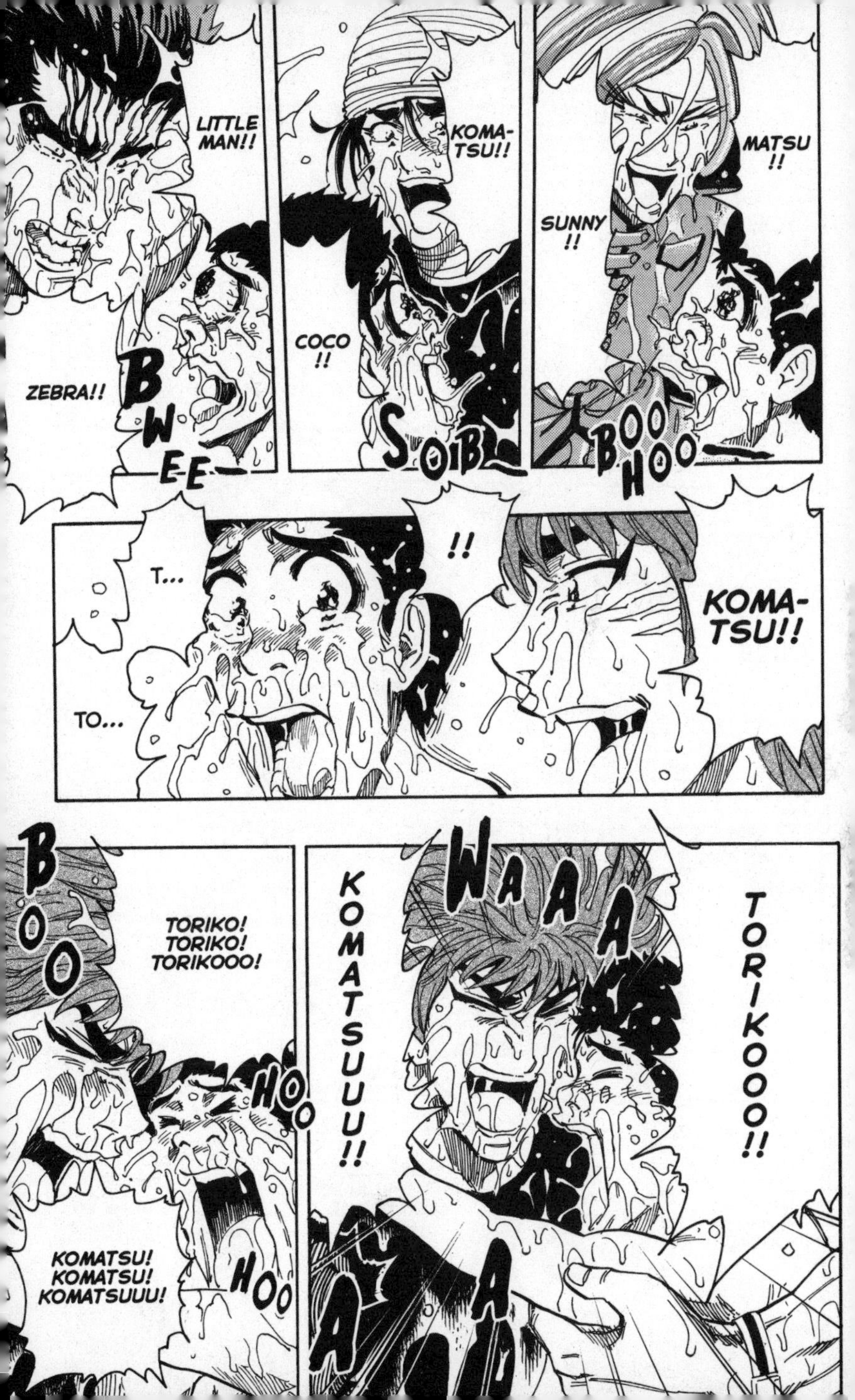
MATSU !!
SUNNY !!
BOO HOO
KOMA-TSU!!
COCO !!
SOB
LITTLE MAN!!
ZEBRA!!
BWEE
KOMA-TSU!!
!!
T...
TO...
TORIKOOOO!!
KOMATSUUUU!!
WAAAA
AAA
TORIKO! TORIKO! TORIKOOO!
KOMATSU! KOMATSU! KOMATSUUU!
BOO
HOO
HOO

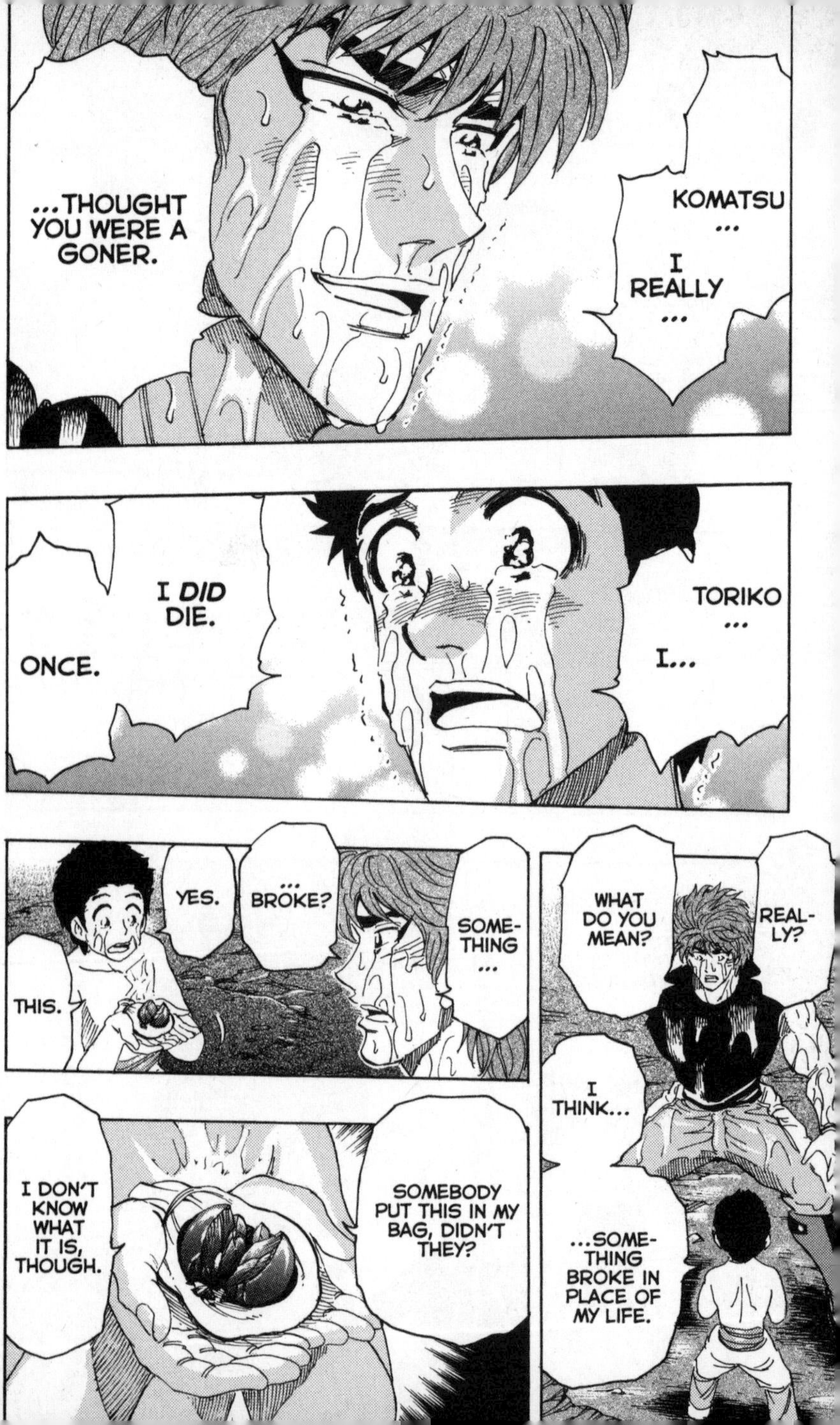
KOMATSU ... I REALLY ...
...THOUGHT YOU WERE A GONER.
TORIKO ... I...
I *DID* DIE.
ONCE.
REAL-LY?
WHAT DO YOU MEAN?
I THINK...
...SOME-THING BROKE IN PLACE OF MY LIFE.
SOME-THING ...
... BROKE?
YES.
THIS.
SOMEBODY PUT THIS IN MY BAG, DIDN'T THEY?
I DON'T KNOW WHAT IT IS, THOUGH.

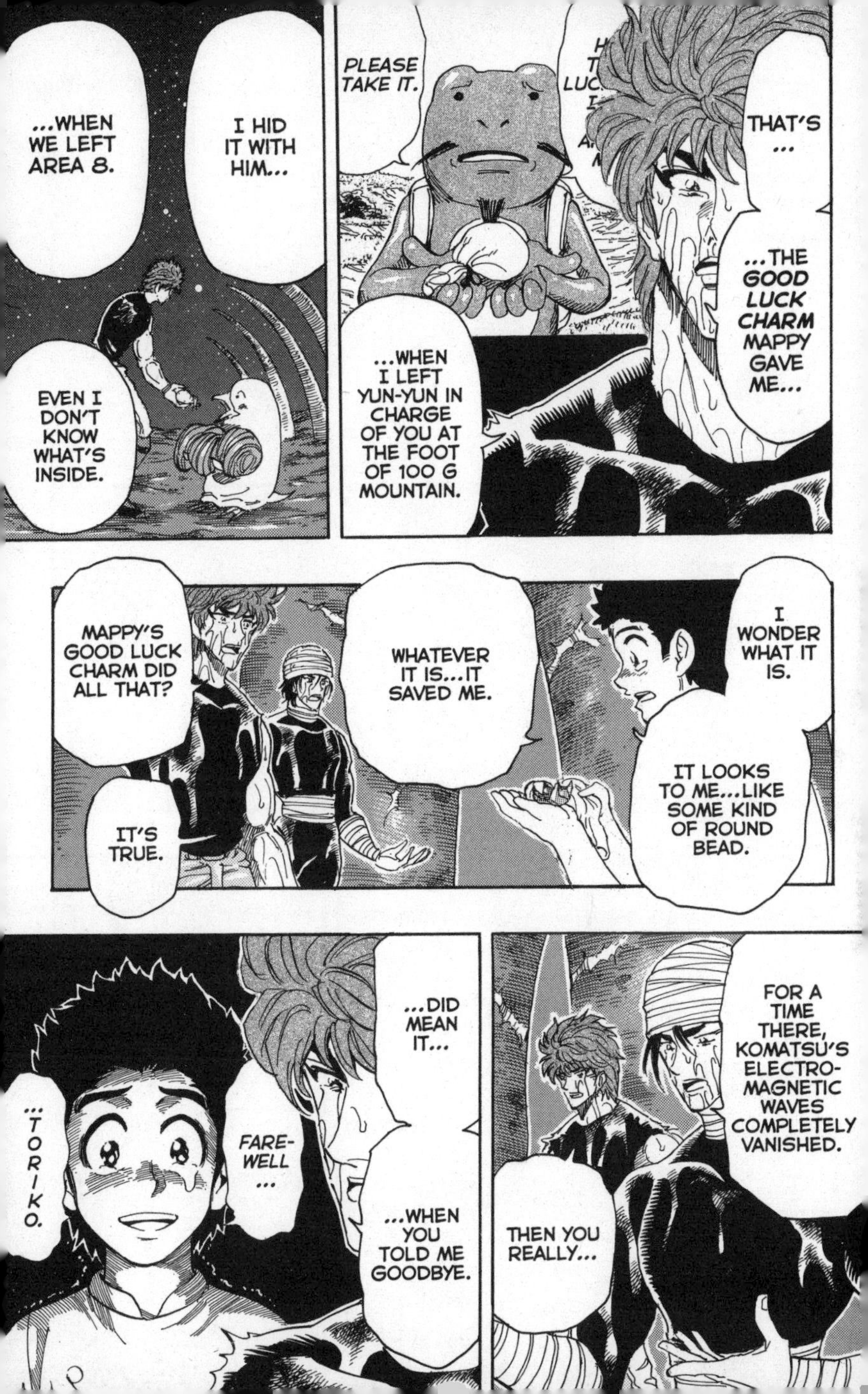
THAT'S...
...THE GOOD LUCK CHARM MAPPY GAVE ME...
PLEASE TAKE IT.
...WHEN I LEFT YUN-YUN IN CHARGE OF YOU AT THE FOOT OF 100 G MOUNTAIN.
I HID IT WITH HIM...
...WHEN WE LEFT AREA 8.
EVEN I DON'T KNOW WHAT'S INSIDE.
I WONDER WHAT IT IS.
IT LOOKS TO ME...LIKE SOME KIND OF ROUND BEAD.
WHATEVER IT IS...IT SAVED ME.
MAPPY'S GOOD LUCK CHARM DID ALL THAT?
IT'S TRUE.
FOR A TIME THERE, KOMATSU'S ELECTRO-MAGNETIC WAVES COMPLETELY VANISHED.
THEN YOU REALLY...
...DID MEAN IT...
...WHEN YOU TOLD ME GOODBYE.
FARE-WELL...
...TORIKO.

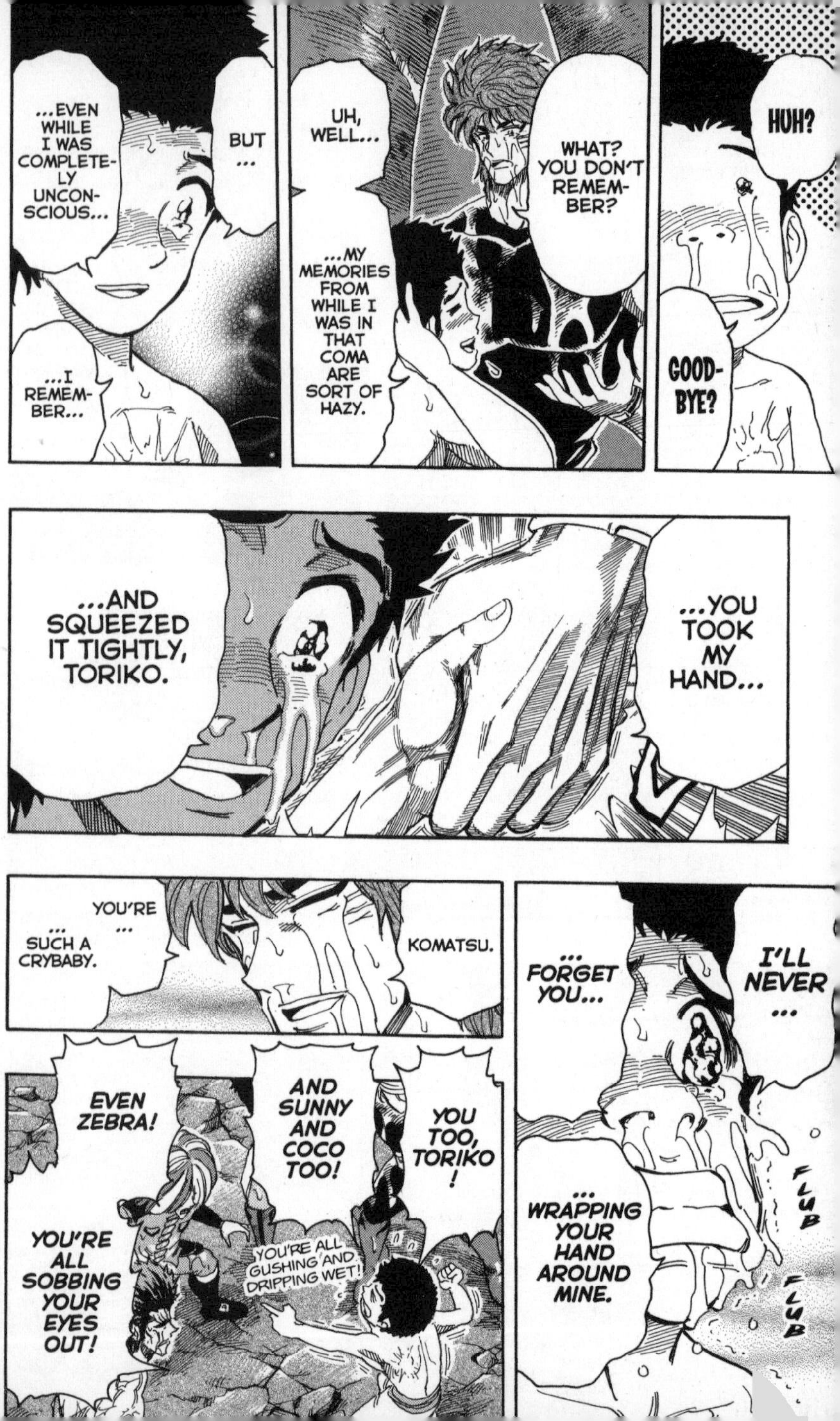
HUH?
GOOD-BYE?
WHAT? YOU DON'T REMEMBER?
UH, WELL...
...MY MEMORIES FROM WHILE I WAS IN THAT COMA ARE SORT OF HAZY.
BUT...
...EVEN WHILE I WAS COMPLETELY UNCONSCIOUS...
...I REMEMBER...
...YOU TOOK MY HAND...
...AND SQUEEZED IT TIGHTLY, TORIKO.
I'LL NEVER...
...FORGET YOU...
...WRAPPING YOUR HAND AROUND MINE.
FLUB
FLUB
KOMATSU.
YOU'RE...
...SUCH A CRYBABY.
YOU TOO, TORIKO!
AND SUNNY AND COCO TOO!
EVEN ZEBRA!
YOU'RE ALL GUSHING AND DRIPPING WET!
YOU'RE ALL SOBBING YOUR EYES OUT!

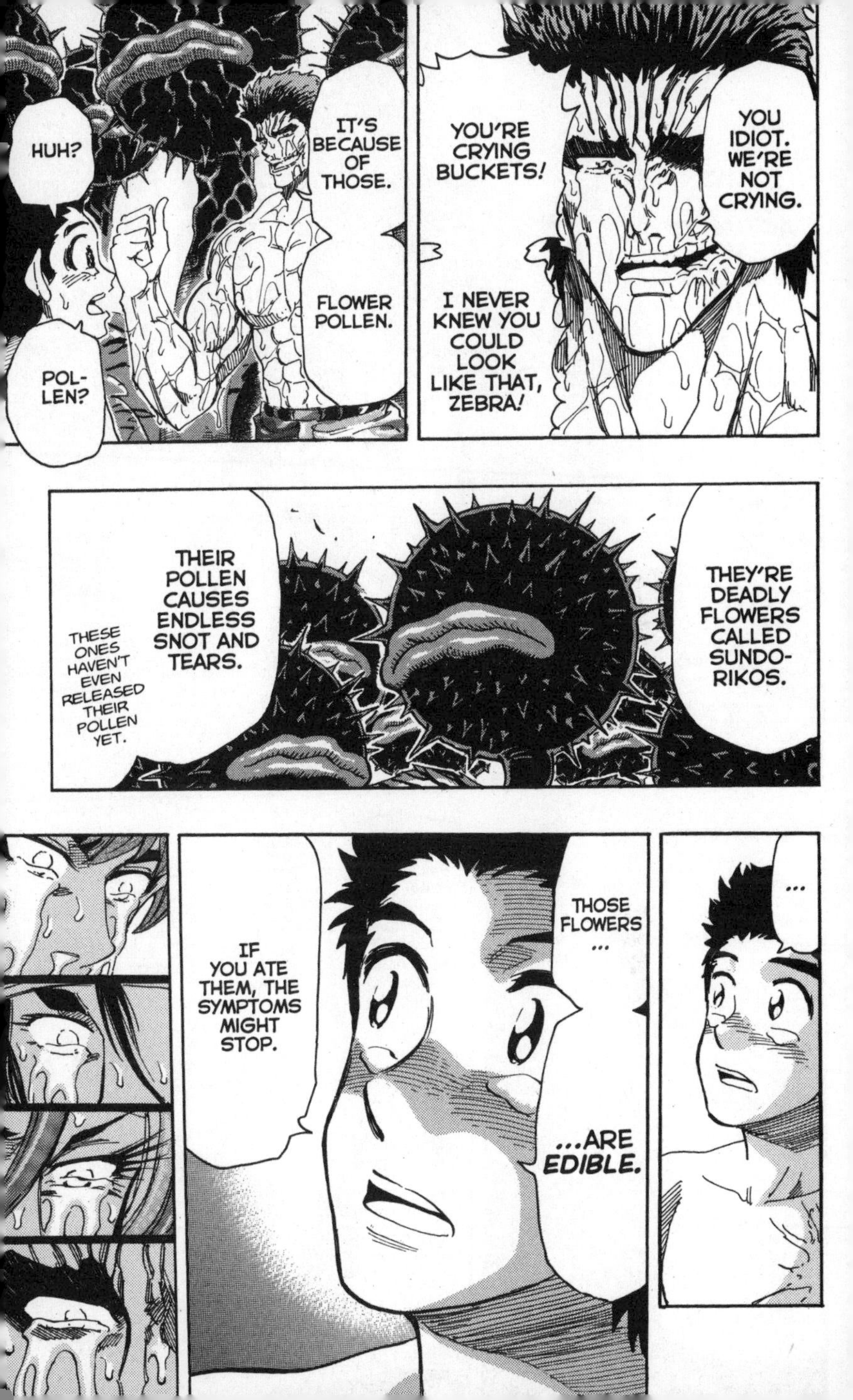
YOU'RE CRYING BUCKETS!
I NEVER KNEW YOU COULD LOOK LIKE THAT, ZEBRA!
YOU IDIOT. WE'RE NOT CRYING.
HUH?
IT'S BECAUSE OF THOSE.
FLOWER POLLEN.
POL-LEN?
THEY'RE DEADLY FLOWERS CALLED SUNDO-RIKOS.
THEIR POLLEN CAUSES ENDLESS SNOT AND TEARS.
THESE ONES HAVEN'T EVEN RELEASED THEIR POLLEN YET.
...
THOSE FLOWERS ...
...ARE *EDIBLE.*
IF YOU ATE THEM, THE SYMPTOMS MIGHT STOP.

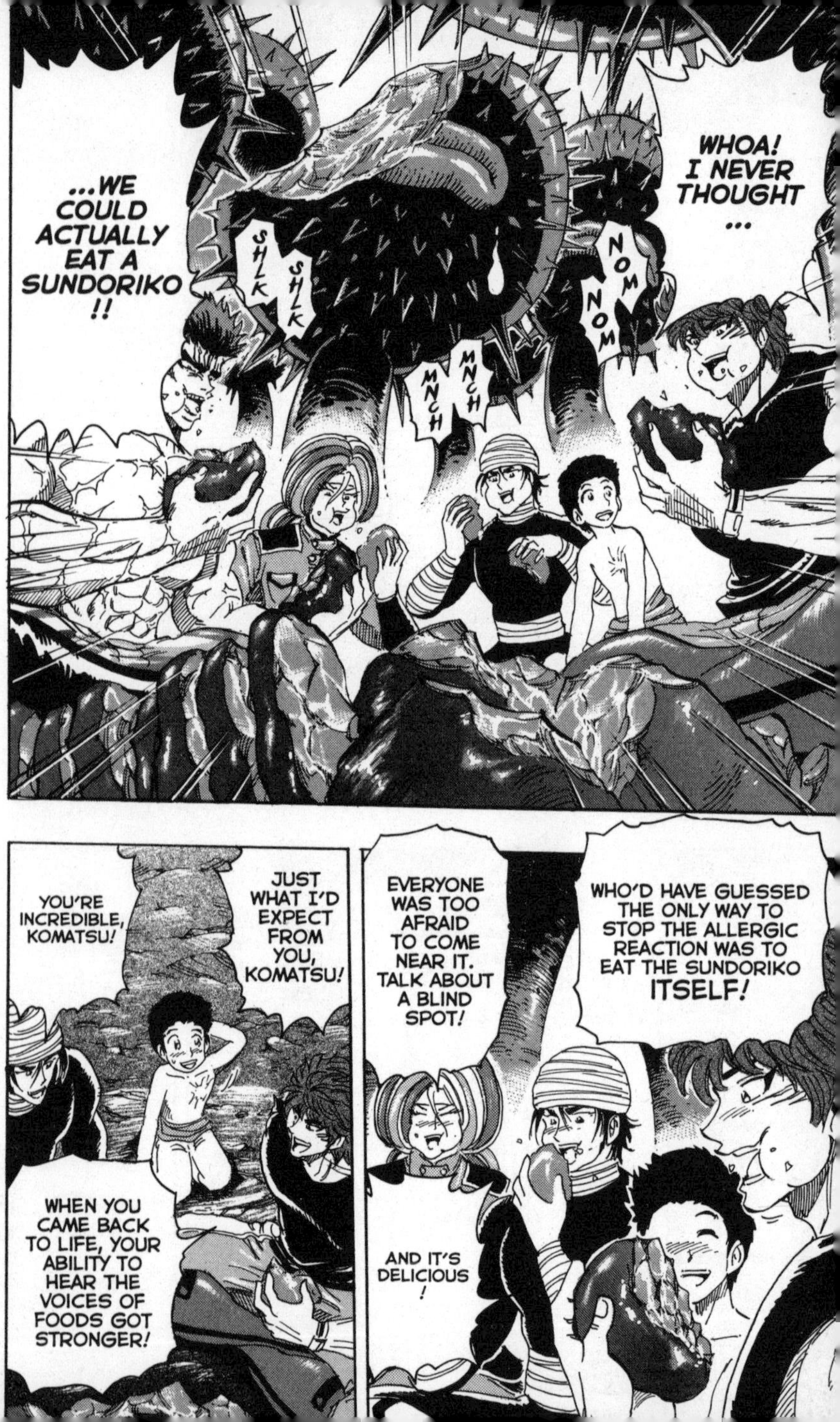
WHOA! I NEVER THOUGHT...
...WE COULD ACTUALLY EAT A SUNDORIKO!!
NOM NOM
MNCH MNCH
SHLK SHLK
WHO'D HAVE GUESSED THE ONLY WAY TO STOP THE ALLERGIC REACTION WAS TO EAT THE SUNDORIKO ITSELF!
EVERYONE WAS TOO AFRAID TO COME NEAR IT. TALK ABOUT A BLIND SPOT!
AND IT'S DELICIOUS!
JUST WHAT I'D EXPECT FROM YOU, KOMATSU!
YOU'RE INCREDIBLE, KOMATSU!
WHEN YOU CAME BACK TO LIFE, YOUR ABILITY TO HEAR THE VOICES OF FOODS GOT STRONGER!

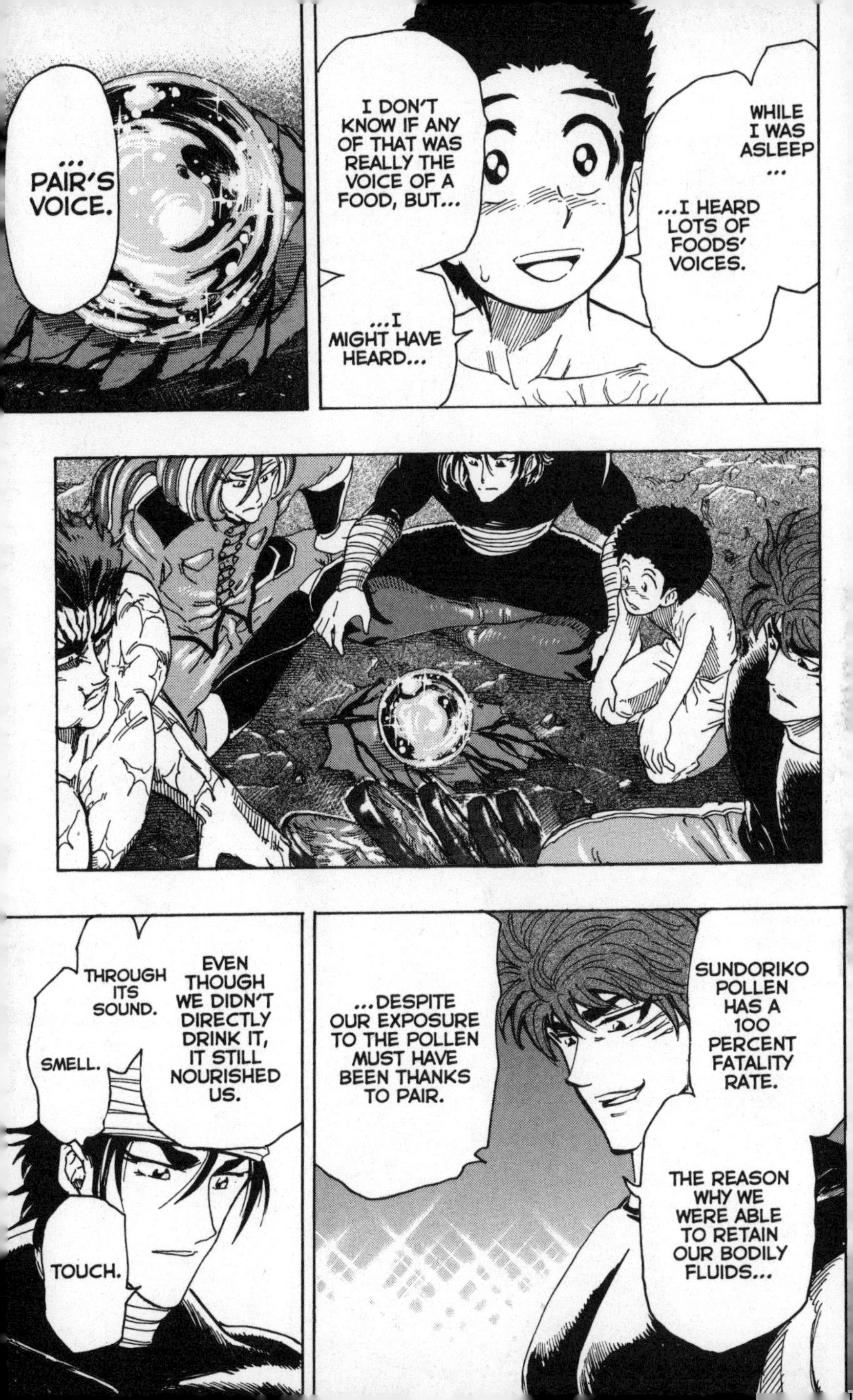
WHILE I WAS ASLEEP...
...I HEARD LOTS OF FOODS' VOICES.
I DON'T KNOW IF ANY OF THAT WAS REALLY THE VOICE OF A FOOD, BUT...
...I MIGHT HAVE HEARD...
...PAIR'S VOICE.
SUNDORIKO POLLEN HAS A 100 PERCENT FATALITY RATE.
THE REASON WHY WE WERE ABLE TO RETAIN OUR BODILY FLUIDS...
...DESPITE OUR EXPOSURE TO THE POLLEN MUST HAVE BEEN THANKS TO PAIR.
EVEN THOUGH WE DIDN'T DIRECTLY DRINK IT, IT STILL NOURISHED US.
THROUGH ITS SOUND.
SMELL.
TOUCH.

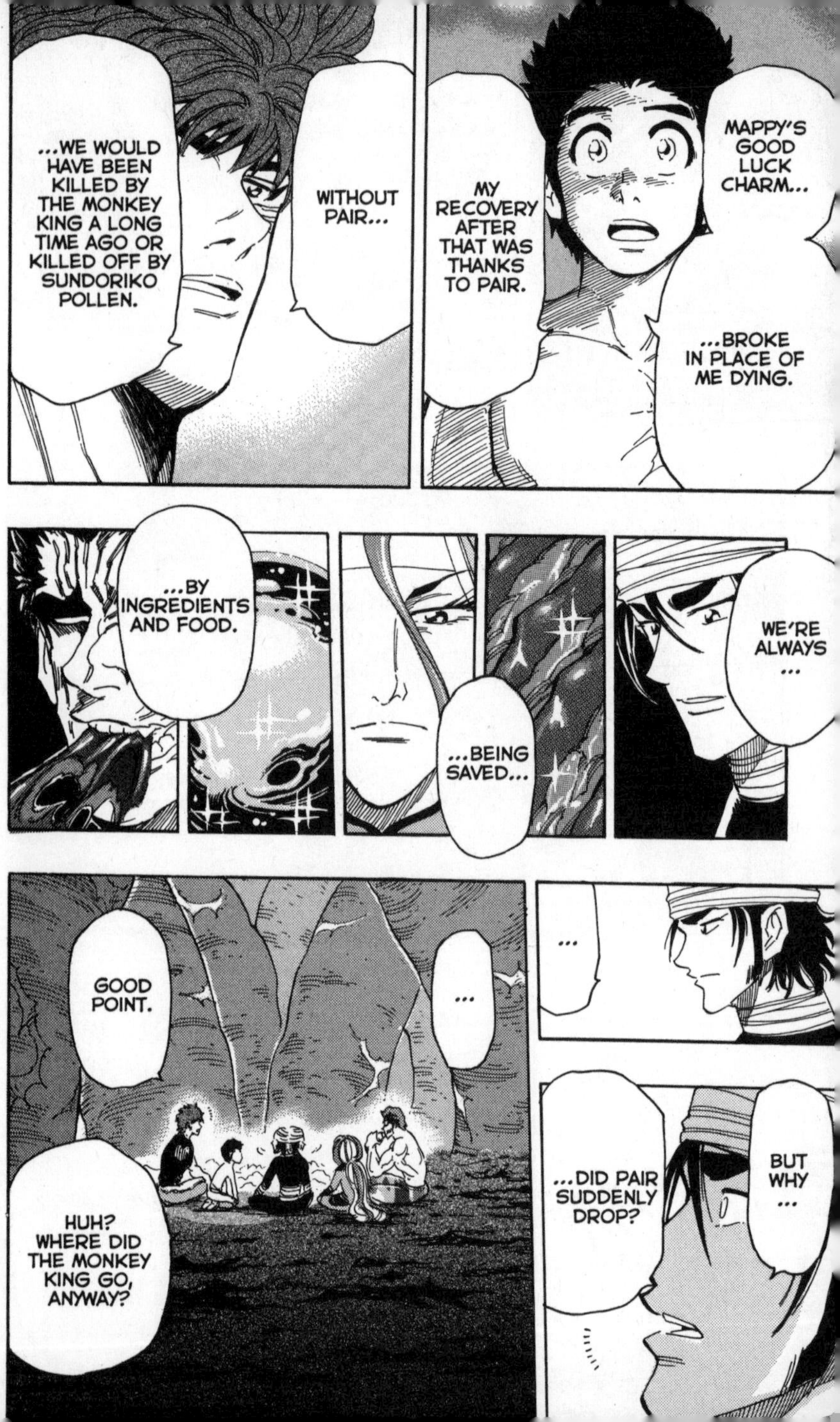
MAPPY'S GOOD LUCK CHARM...
...BROKE IN PLACE OF ME DYING.
MY RECOVERY AFTER THAT WAS THANKS TO PAIR.
WITHOUT PAIR...
...WE WOULD HAVE BEEN KILLED BY THE MONKEY KING A LONG TIME AGO OR KILLED OFF BY SUNDORIKO POLLEN.
WE'RE ALWAYS ...
...BEING SAVED...
...BY INGREDIENTS AND FOOD.
...
BUT WHY ...
...DID PAIR SUDDENLY DROP?
...
GOOD POINT.
HUH? WHERE DID THE MONKEY KING GO, ANYWAY?

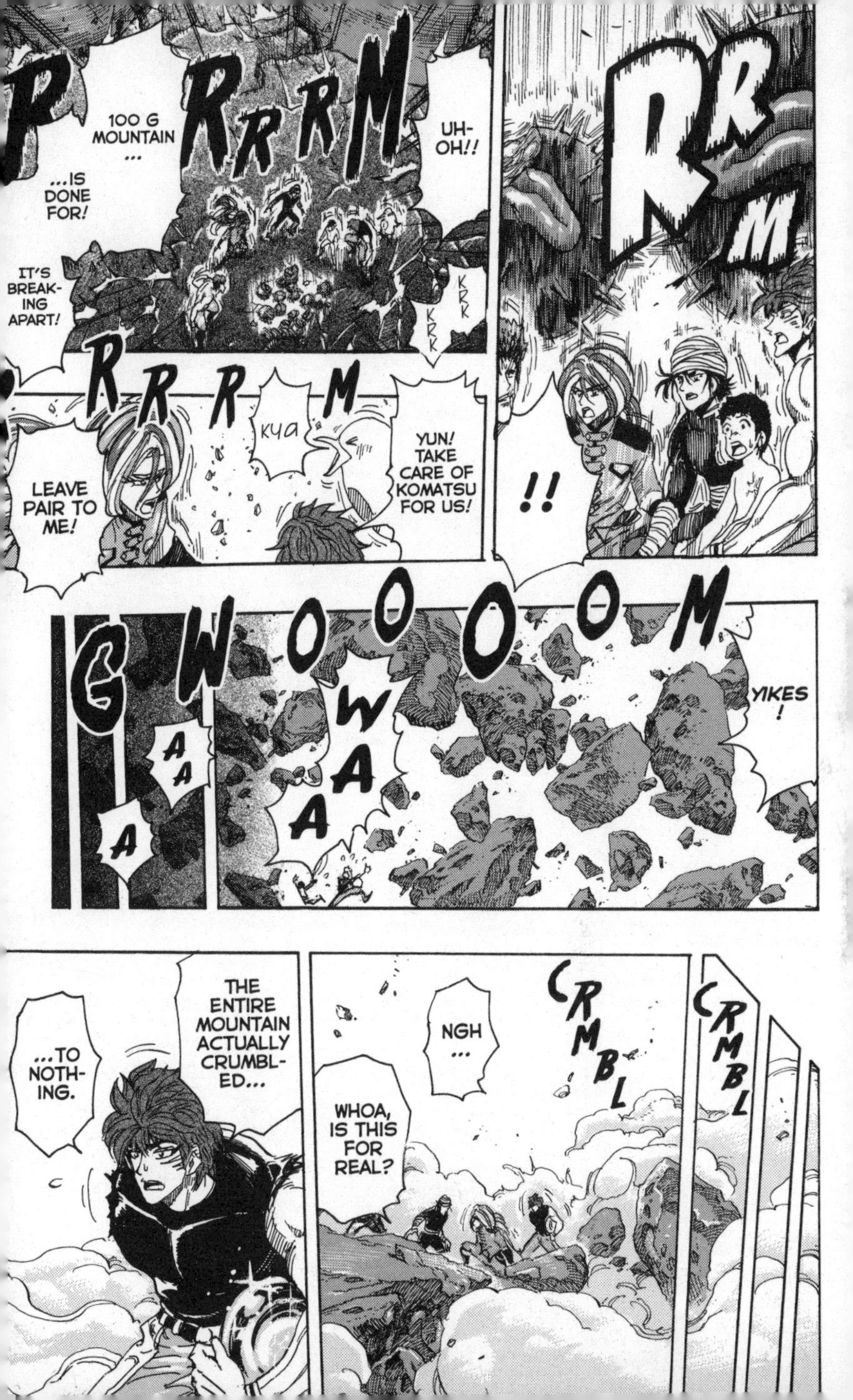
RRM
UH-OH!!
PRRRM
100 G MOUNTAIN...
...IS DONE FOR!
IT'S BREAKING APART!
KRK KRK
!!
YUN! TAKE CARE OF KOMATSU FOR US!
RRRM
KYA
LEAVE PAIR TO ME!
GWOOOOM
YIKES!
WAAA
AAA
CRMBL
CRMBL
NGH...
WHOA, IS THIS FOR REAL?
THE ENTIRE MOUNTAIN ACTUALLY CRUMBLED...
...TO NOTHING.

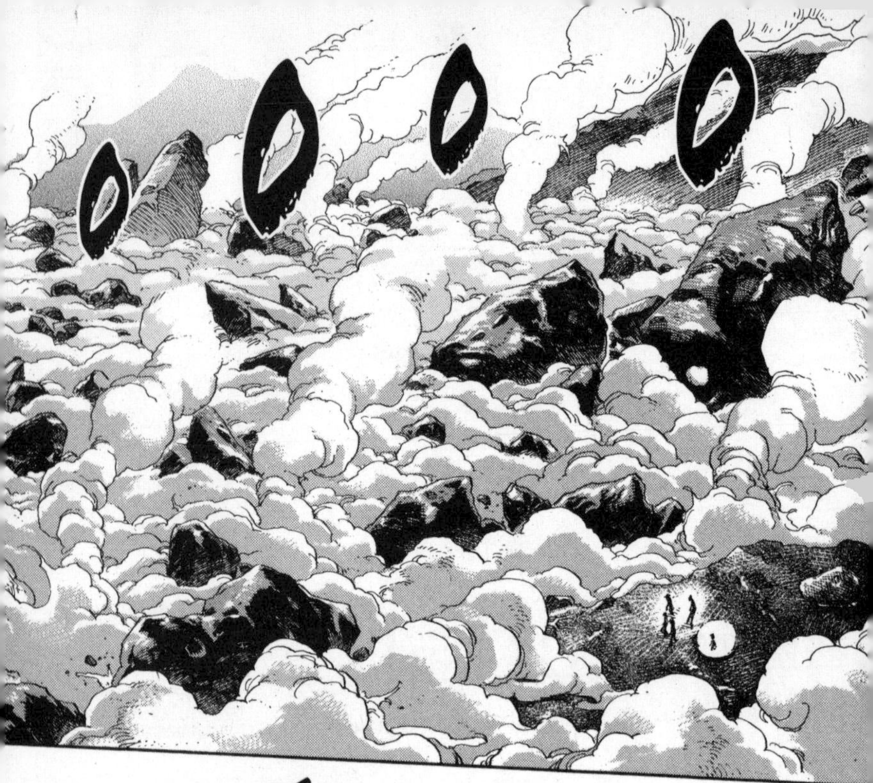

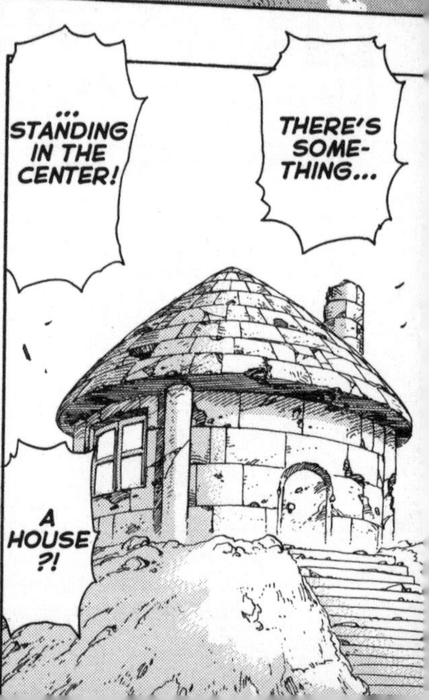
THERE'S SOME-THING...
...STANDING IN THE CENTER!
A HOUSE?!

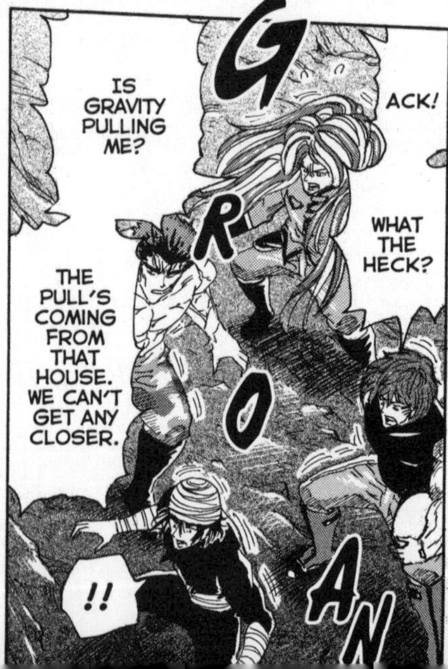
ACK!
WHAT THE HECK?
IS GRAVITY PULLING ME?
THE PULL'S COMING FROM THAT HOUSE. WE CAN'T GET ANY CLOSER.
GROAN
!!

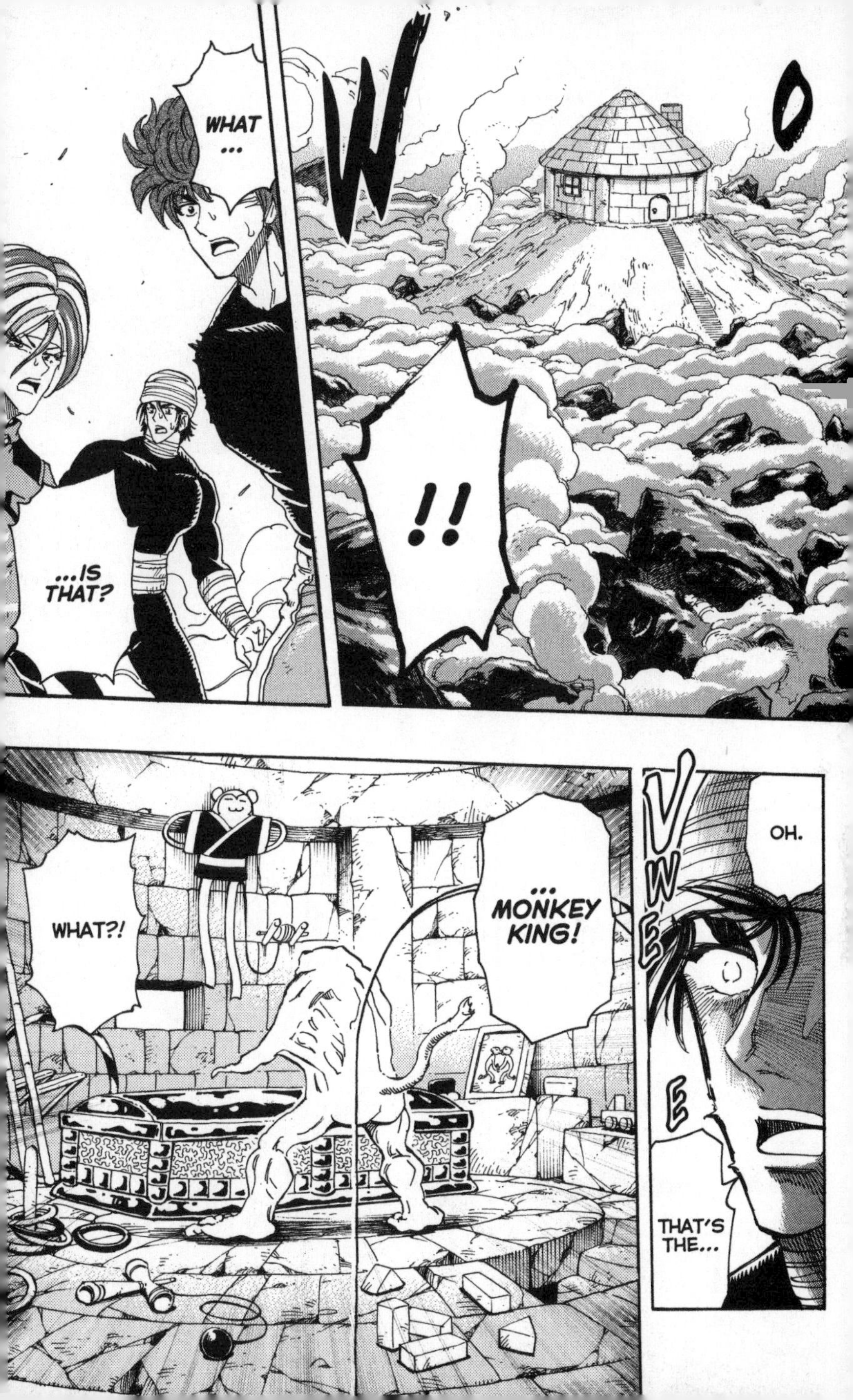
!!
WHAT ...
...IS THAT?
OH.
VWEE
THAT'S THE...
... MONKEY KING!
WHAT?!

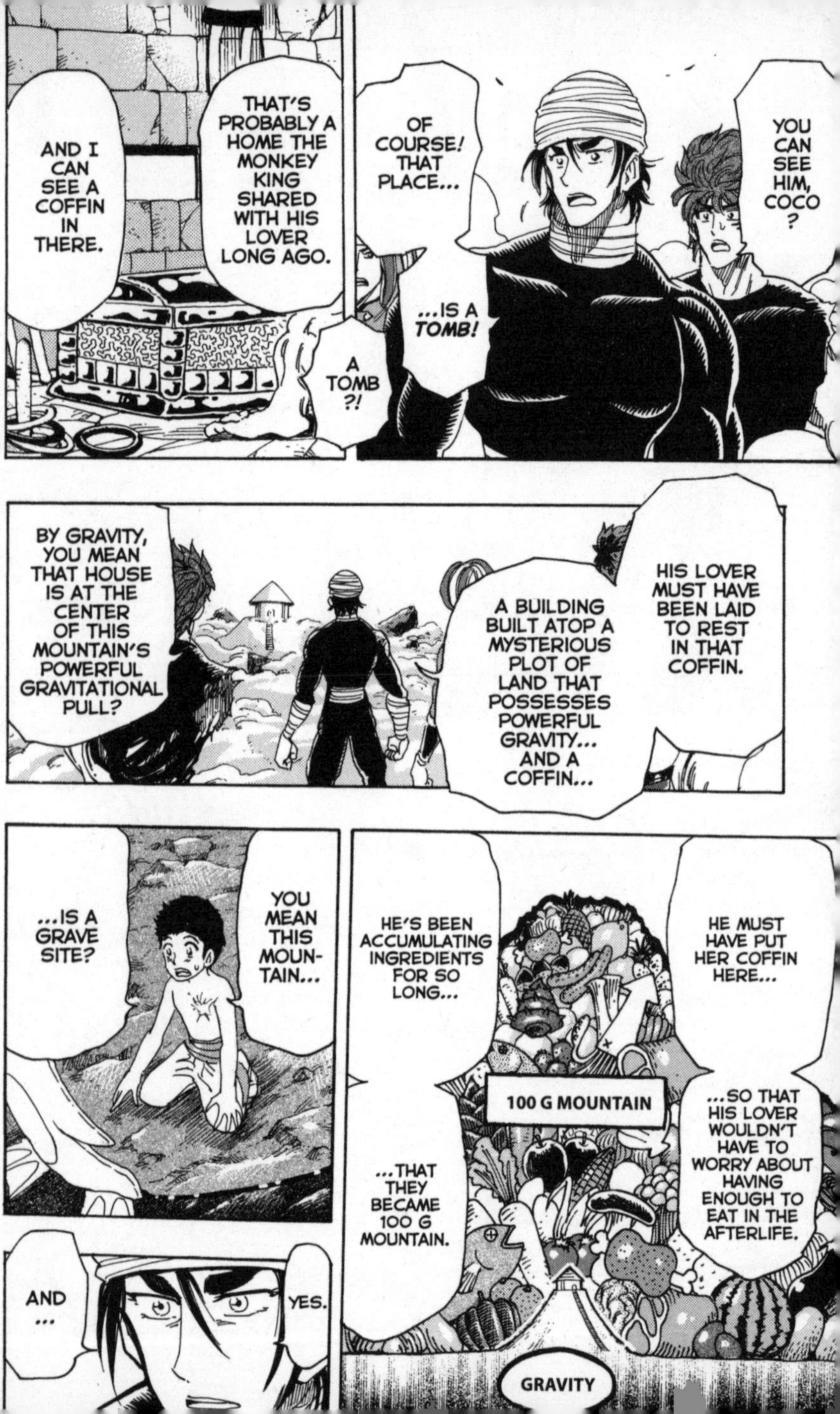
YOU CAN SEE HIM, COCO?
OF COURSE! THAT PLACE...
...IS A TOMB!
A TOMB?!
THAT'S PROBABLY A HOME THE MONKEY KING SHARED WITH HIS LOVER LONG AGO.
AND I CAN SEE A COFFIN IN THERE.
HIS LOVER MUST HAVE BEEN LAID TO REST IN THAT COFFIN.
A BUILDING BUILT ATOP A MYSTERIOUS PLOT OF LAND THAT POSSESSES POWERFUL GRAVITY... AND A COFFIN...
BY GRAVITY, YOU MEAN THAT HOUSE IS AT THE CENTER OF THIS MOUNTAIN'S POWERFUL GRAVITATIONAL PULL?
YOU MEAN THIS MOUN-TAIN...
...IS A GRAVE SITE?
YES.
AND ...
HE'S BEEN ACCUMULATING INGREDIENTS FOR SO LONG...
...THAT THEY BECAME 100 G MOUNTAIN.
HE MUST HAVE PUT HER COFFIN HERE...
...SO THAT HIS LOVER WOULDN'T HAVE TO WORRY ABOUT HAVING ENOUGH TO EAT IN THE AFTERLIFE.
100 G MOUNTAIN
GRAVITY

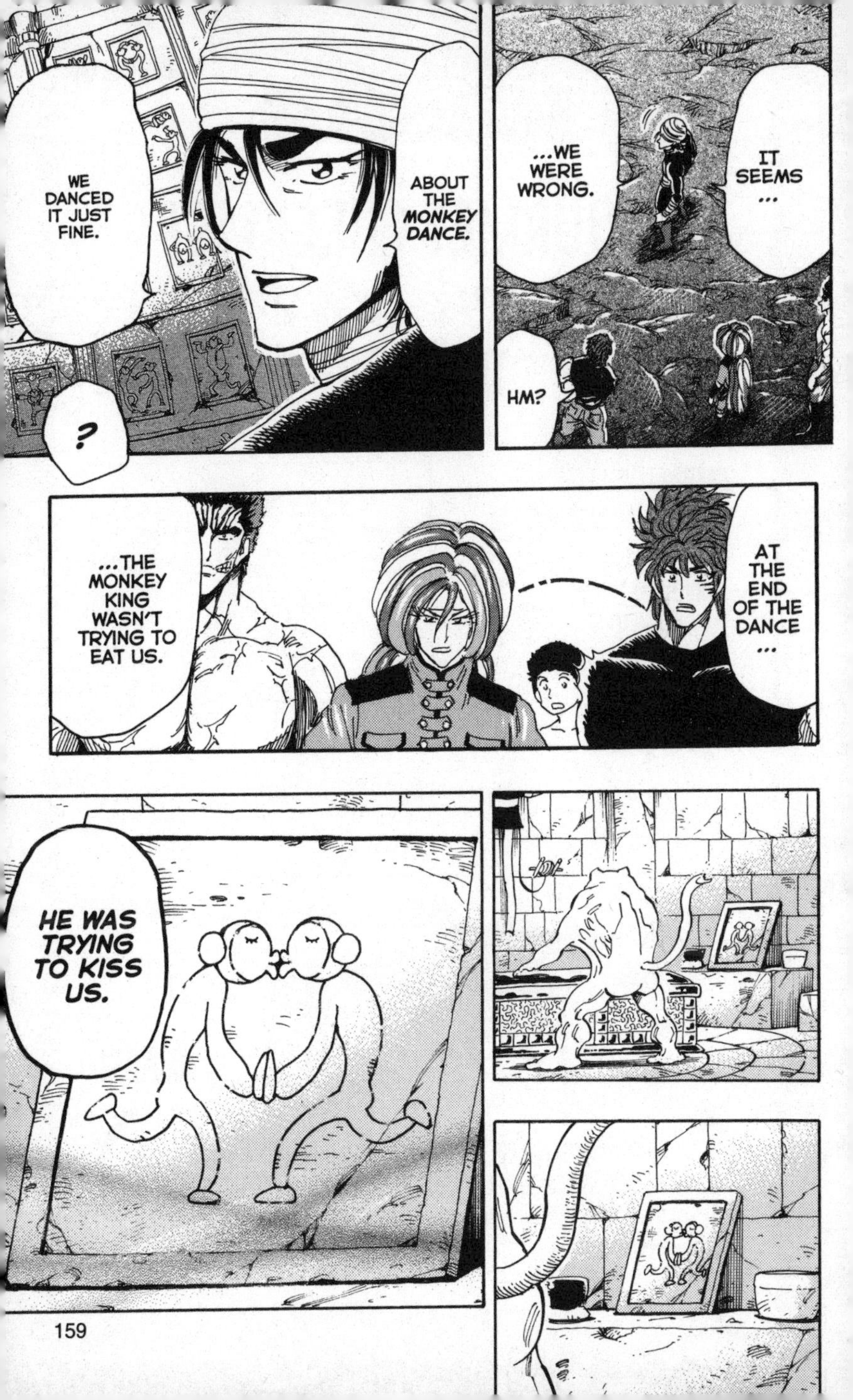
IT SEEMS...
...WE WERE WRONG.
HM?
ABOUT THE MONKEY DANCE.
WE DANCED IT JUST FINE.
?
AT THE END OF THE DANCE...
...THE MONKEY KING WASN'T TRYING TO EAT US.
HE WAS TRYING TO KISS US.

TORIKO

GOURMET CHECKLIST

Vol. 344

TIGER PIG
(MAMMAL)

CAPTURE LEVEL: 3
HABITAT: FOUND EVERYWHERE
SIZE: 3 M
HEIGHT: 2 M
WEIGHT: 2.5 TONS
PRICE: 200 YEN PER 100 G

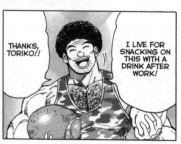

I LIVE FOR SNACKING ON THIS WITH A DRINK AFTER WORK!
THANKS, TORIKO!!

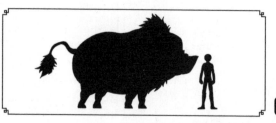

SCALE

AN INGREDIENT TORIKO DISCOVERED. IT HAS LONGER HAIR THAN A NORMAL PIG AND CAN GROW AS LARGE AS TWO TO THREE METERS LONG. IT IS A VERY CHEAP AND POPULAR INGREDIENT AND A PRECIOUS SOURCE OF CALORIES FOR MANUAL LABORERS.

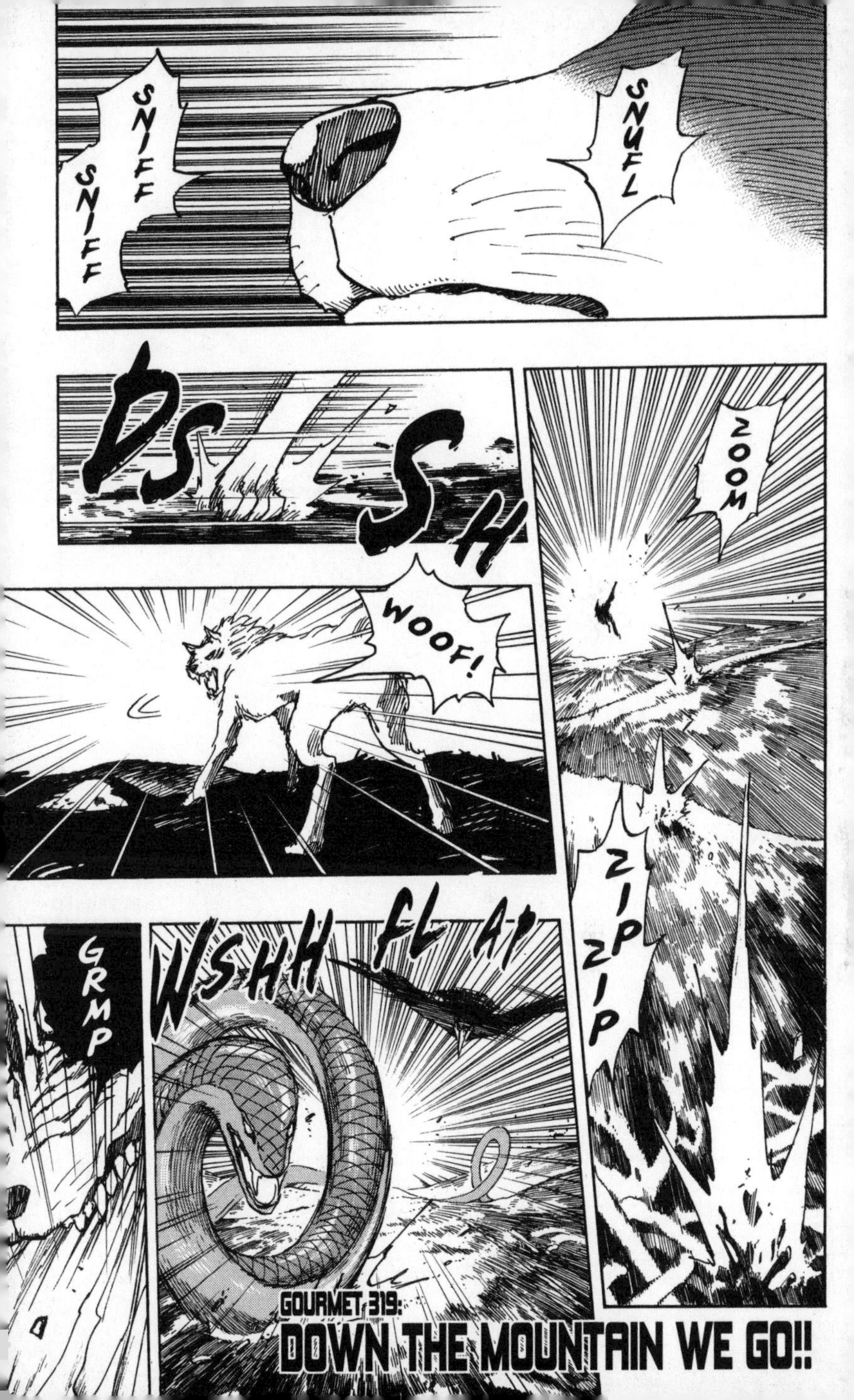
SNUFL
SNIFF SNIFF
ZOOM
ZIP ZIP ZIP
DSSH
WOOF!
WSHH FLAP
GRMP

GOURMET 319:
DOWN THE MOUNTAIN WE GO!!

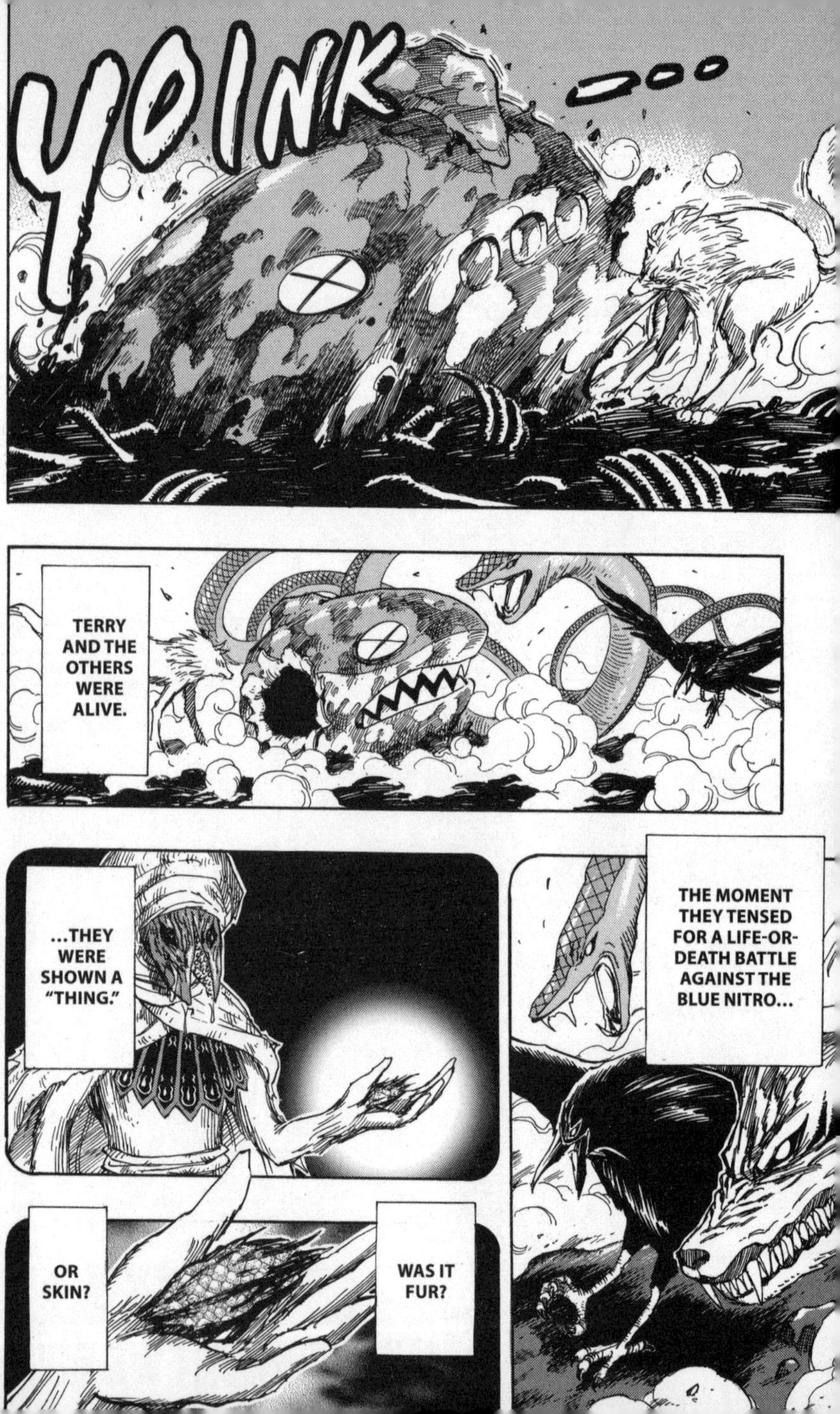
YOINK...
TERRY AND THE OTHERS WERE ALIVE.
THE MOMENT THEY TENSED FOR A LIFE-OR-DEATH BATTLE AGAINST THE BLUE NITRO...
...THEY WERE SHOWN A "THING."
WAS IT FUR?
OR SKIN?

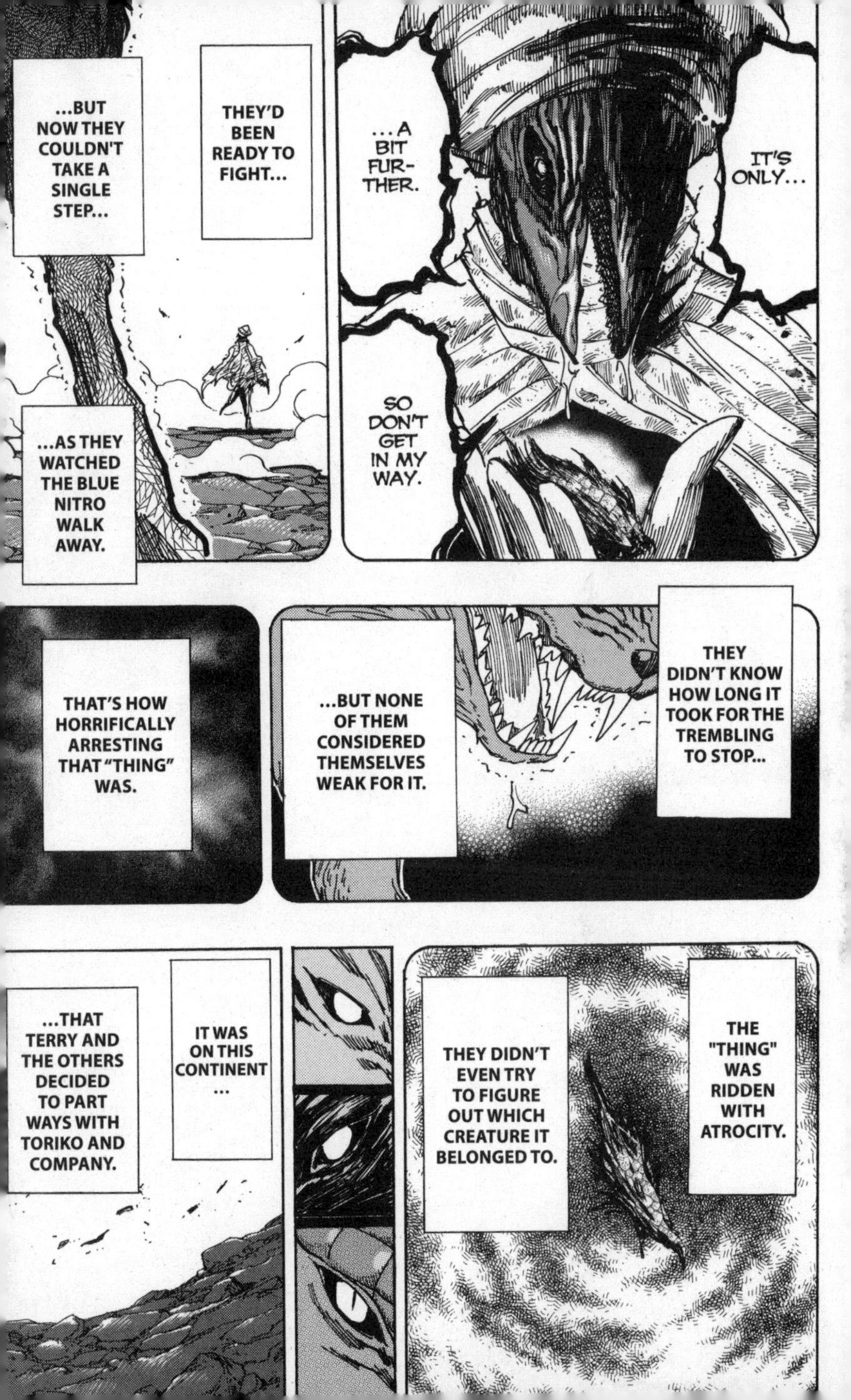
IT'S ONLY...
...A BIT FURTHER.
SO DON'T GET IN MY WAY.
THEY'D BEEN READY TO FIGHT...
...BUT NOW THEY COULDN'T TAKE A SINGLE STEP...
...AS THEY WATCHED THE BLUE NITRO WALK AWAY.
THEY DIDN'T KNOW HOW LONG IT TOOK FOR THE TREMBLING TO STOP...
...BUT NONE OF THEM CONSIDERED THEMSELVES WEAK FOR IT.
THAT'S HOW HORRIFICALLY ARRESTING THAT "THING" WAS.
THE "THING" WAS RIDDEN WITH ATROCITY.
THEY DIDN'T EVEN TRY TO FIGURE OUT WHICH CREATURE IT BELONGED TO.
IT WAS ON THIS CONTINENT...
...THAT TERRY AND THE OTHERS DECIDED TO PART WAYS WITH TORIKO AND COMPANY.

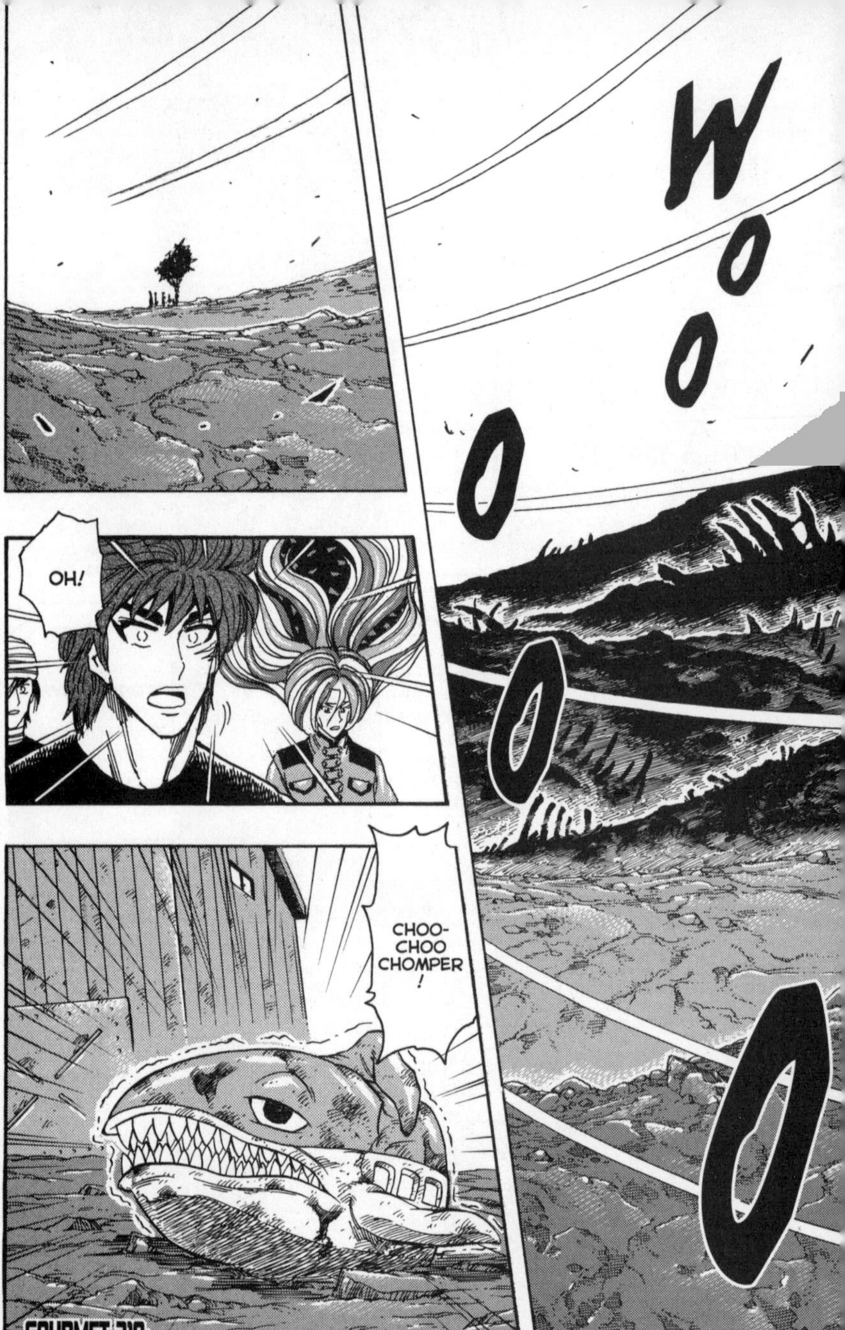
WOOOOOO
OH!
CHOO-CHOO CHOMPER!

GOURMET 319:
DOWN THE MOUNTAIN WE GO!!

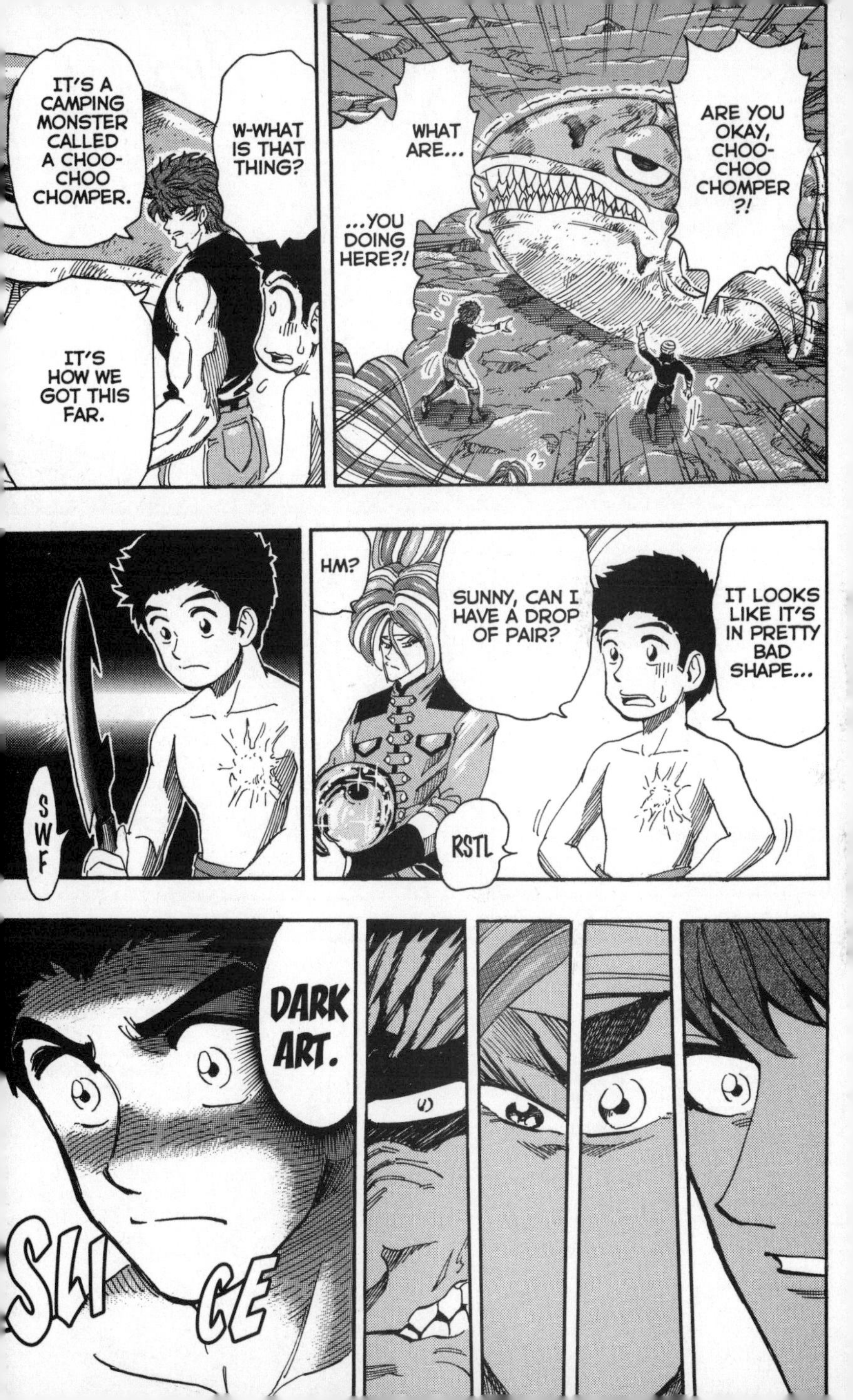
ARE YOU OKAY, CHOO-CHOO CHOMPER?!
WHAT ARE...
...YOU DOING HERE?!
W-WHAT IS THAT THING?
IT'S A CAMPING MONSTER CALLED A CHOO-CHOO CHOMPER.
IT'S HOW WE GOT THIS FAR.
IT LOOKS LIKE IT'S IN PRETTY BAD SHAPE...
SUNNY, CAN I HAVE A DROP OF PAIR?
HM?
RSTL
SWF
DARK ART.
SLICE

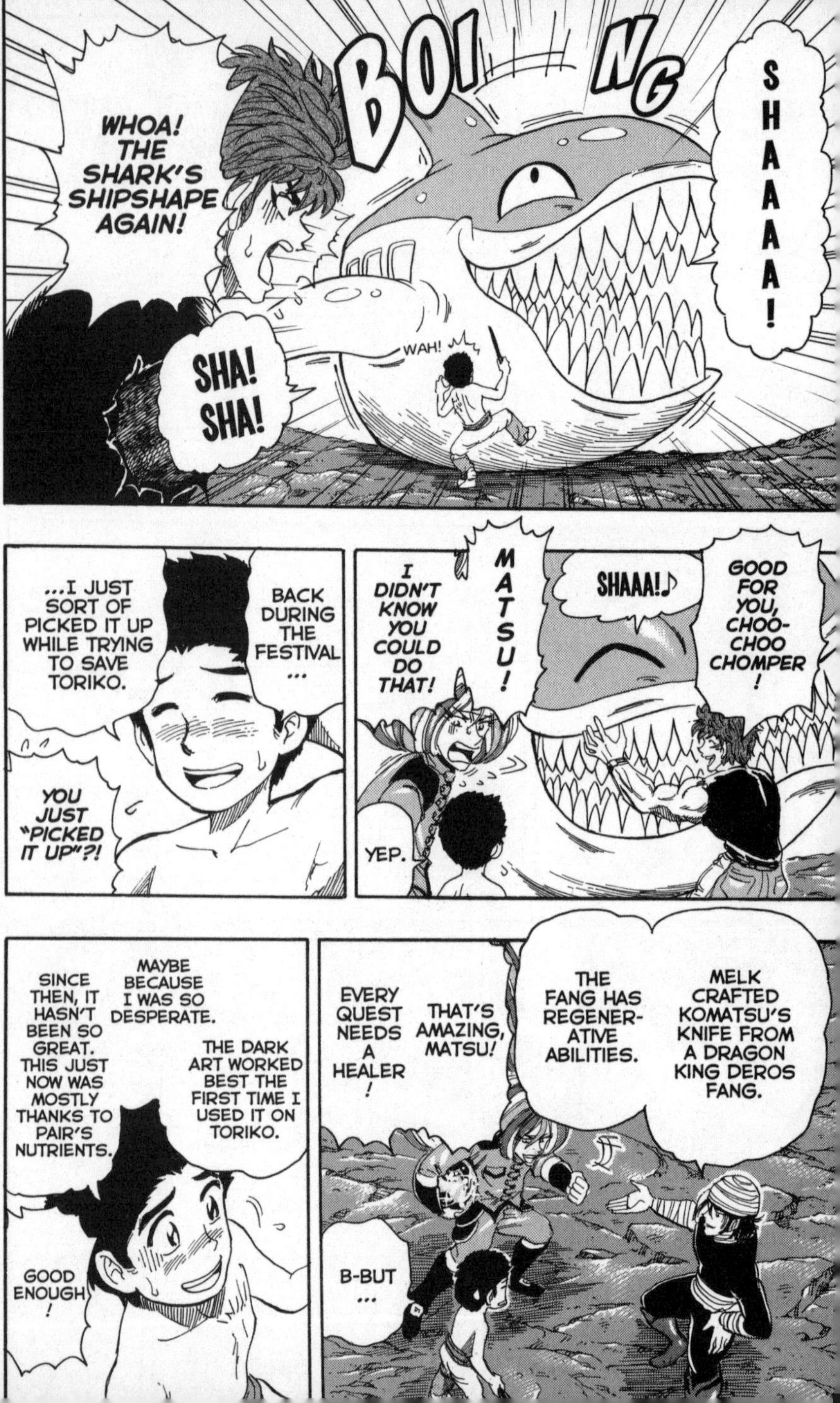
SHAAAAA!
BOING
WHOA! THE SHARK'S SHIPSHAPE AGAIN!
SHA! SHA!
WAH!
GOOD FOR YOU, CHOO-CHOO CHOMPER!
SHAAA!♪
MATSU!
I DIDN'T KNOW YOU COULD DO THAT!
YEP.
BACK DURING THE FESTIVAL...
...I JUST SORT OF PICKED IT UP WHILE TRYING TO SAVE TORIKO.
YOU JUST "PICKED IT UP"?!
MELK CRAFTED KOMATSU'S KNIFE FROM A DRAGON KING DEROS FANG.
THE FANG HAS REGENERATIVE ABILITIES.
THAT'S AMAZING, MATSU!
EVERY QUEST NEEDS A HEALER!
B-BUT...
THE DARK ART WORKED BEST THE FIRST TIME I USED IT ON TORIKO.
MAYBE BECAUSE I WAS SO DESPERATE.
SINCE THEN, IT HASN'T BEEN SO GREAT. THIS JUST NOW WAS MOSTLY THANKS TO PAIR'S NUTRIENTS.
GOOD ENOUGH!

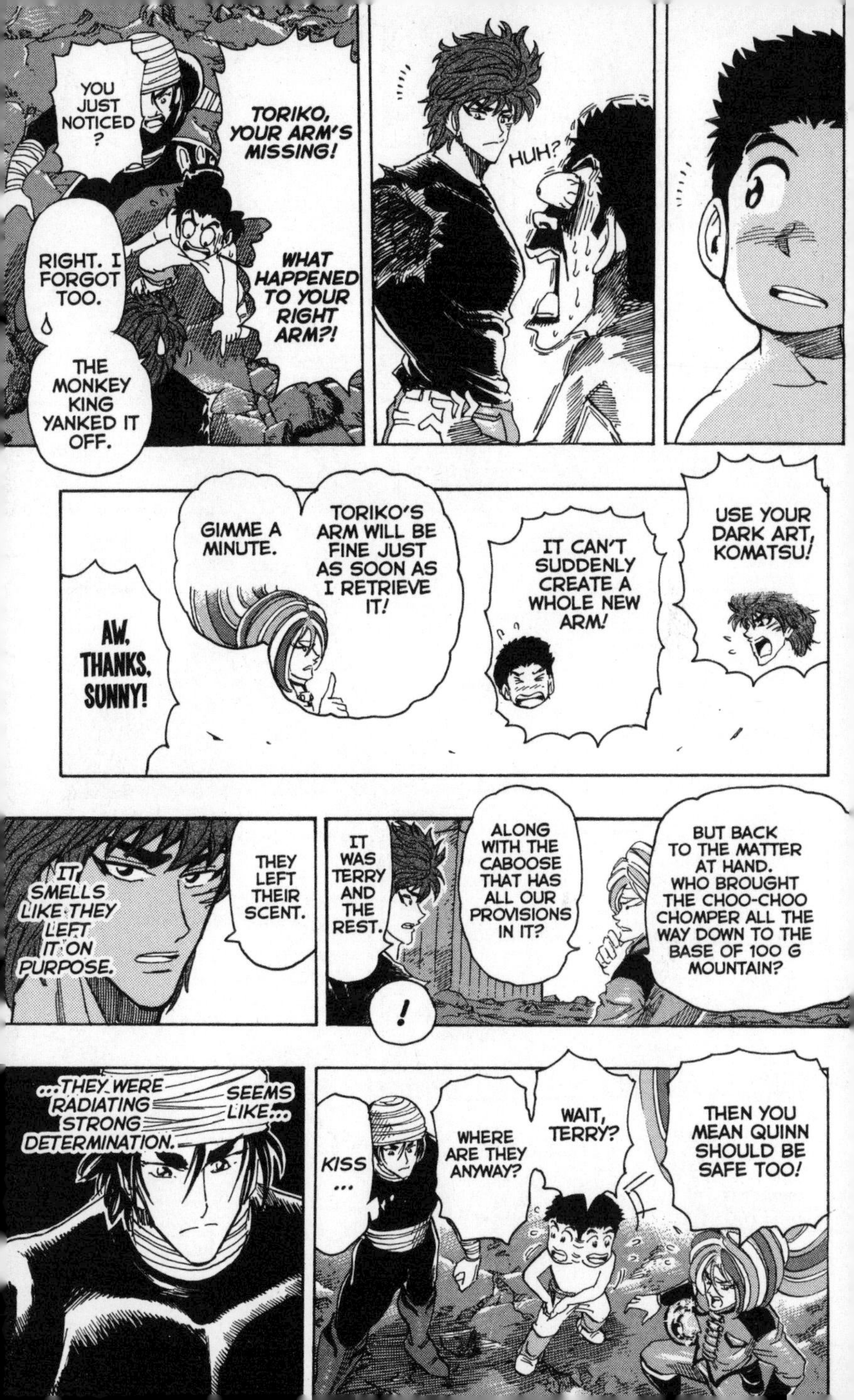
HUH?
TORIKO, YOUR ARM'S MISSING!
WHAT HAPPENED TO YOUR RIGHT ARM?!
YOU JUST NOTICED?
RIGHT. I FORGOT TOO.
THE MONKEY KING YANKED IT OFF.
USE YOUR DARK ART, KOMATSU!
IT CAN'T SUDDENLY CREATE A WHOLE NEW ARM!
TORIKO'S ARM WILL BE FINE JUST AS SOON AS I RETRIEVE IT!
GIMME A MINUTE.
AW, THANKS, SUNNY!
BUT BACK TO THE MATTER AT HAND. WHO BROUGHT THE CHOO-CHOO CHOMPER ALL THE WAY DOWN TO THE BASE OF 100 G MOUNTAIN?
ALONG WITH THE CABOOSE THAT HAS ALL OUR PROVISIONS IN IT?
IT WAS TERRY AND THE REST.
!
THEY LEFT THEIR SCENT.
IT SMELLS LIKE THEY LEFT IT ON PURPOSE.
THEN YOU MEAN QUINN SHOULD BE SAFE TOO!
WAIT, TERRY?
WHERE ARE THEY ANYWAY?
KISS ...
SEEMS LIKE...
...THEY WERE RADIATING STRONG DETERMINATION.

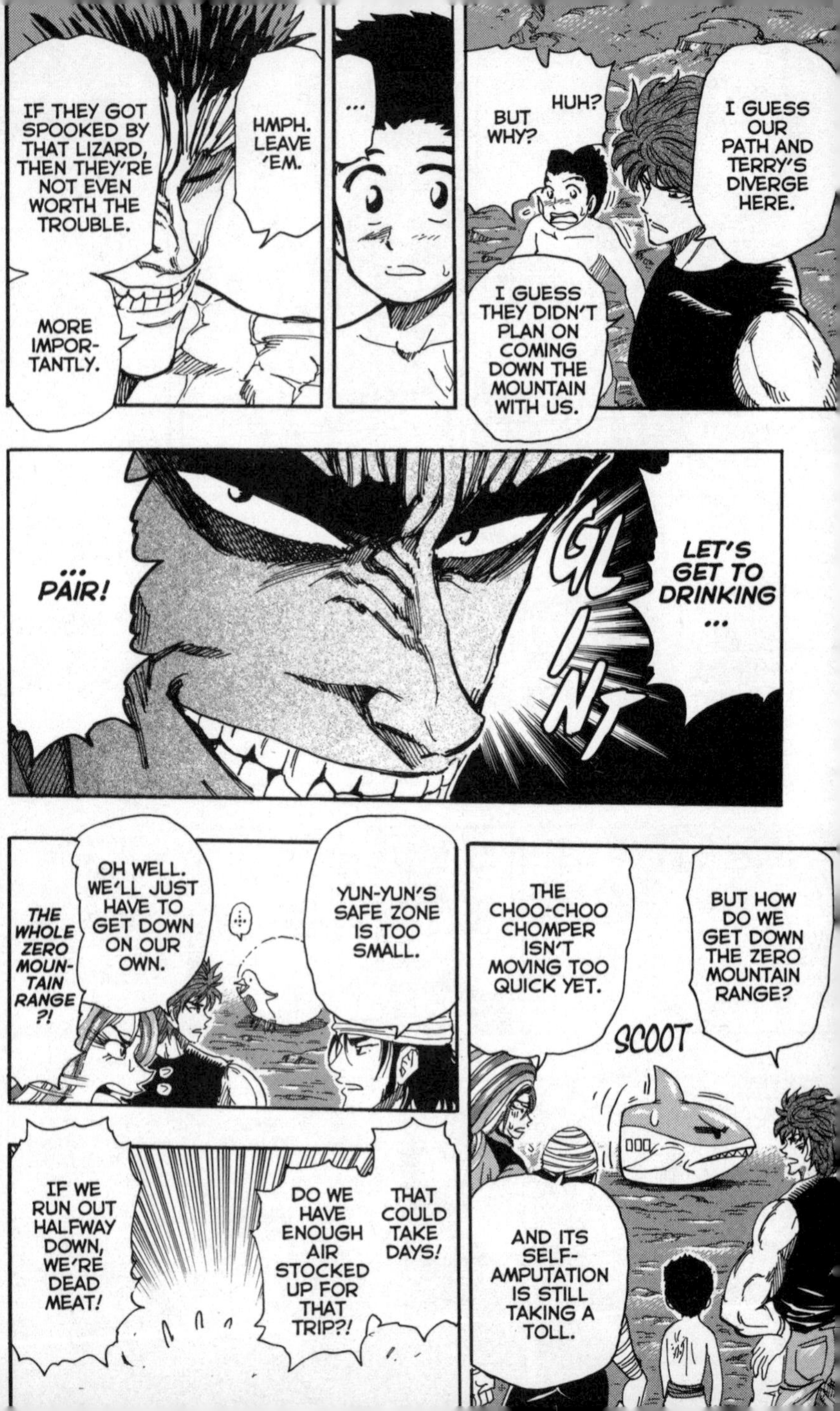
I GUESS OUR PATH AND TERRY'S DIVERGE HERE.
HUH?
BUT WHY?
I GUESS THEY DIDN'T PLAN ON COMING DOWN THE MOUNTAIN WITH US.
...
HMPH. LEAVE 'EM.
IF THEY GOT SPOOKED BY THAT LIZARD, THEN THEY'RE NOT EVEN WORTH THE TROUBLE.
MORE IMPORTANTLY.
LET'S GET TO DRINKING ...
GLINT
... PÄIR!
BUT HOW DO WE GET DOWN THE ZERO MOUNTAIN RANGE?
THE CHOO-CHOO CHOMPER ISN'T MOVING TOO QUICK YET.
SCOOT
AND ITS SELF-AMPUTATION IS STILL TAKING A TOLL.
YUN-YUN'S SAFE ZONE IS TOO SMALL.
OH WELL. WE'LL JUST HAVE TO GET DOWN ON OUR OWN.
THE WHOLE ZERO MOUNTAIN RANGE?!
THAT COULD TAKE DAYS!
DO WE HAVE ENOUGH AIR STOCKED UP FOR THAT TRIP?!
IF WE RUN OUT HALFWAY DOWN, WE'RE DEAD MEAT!

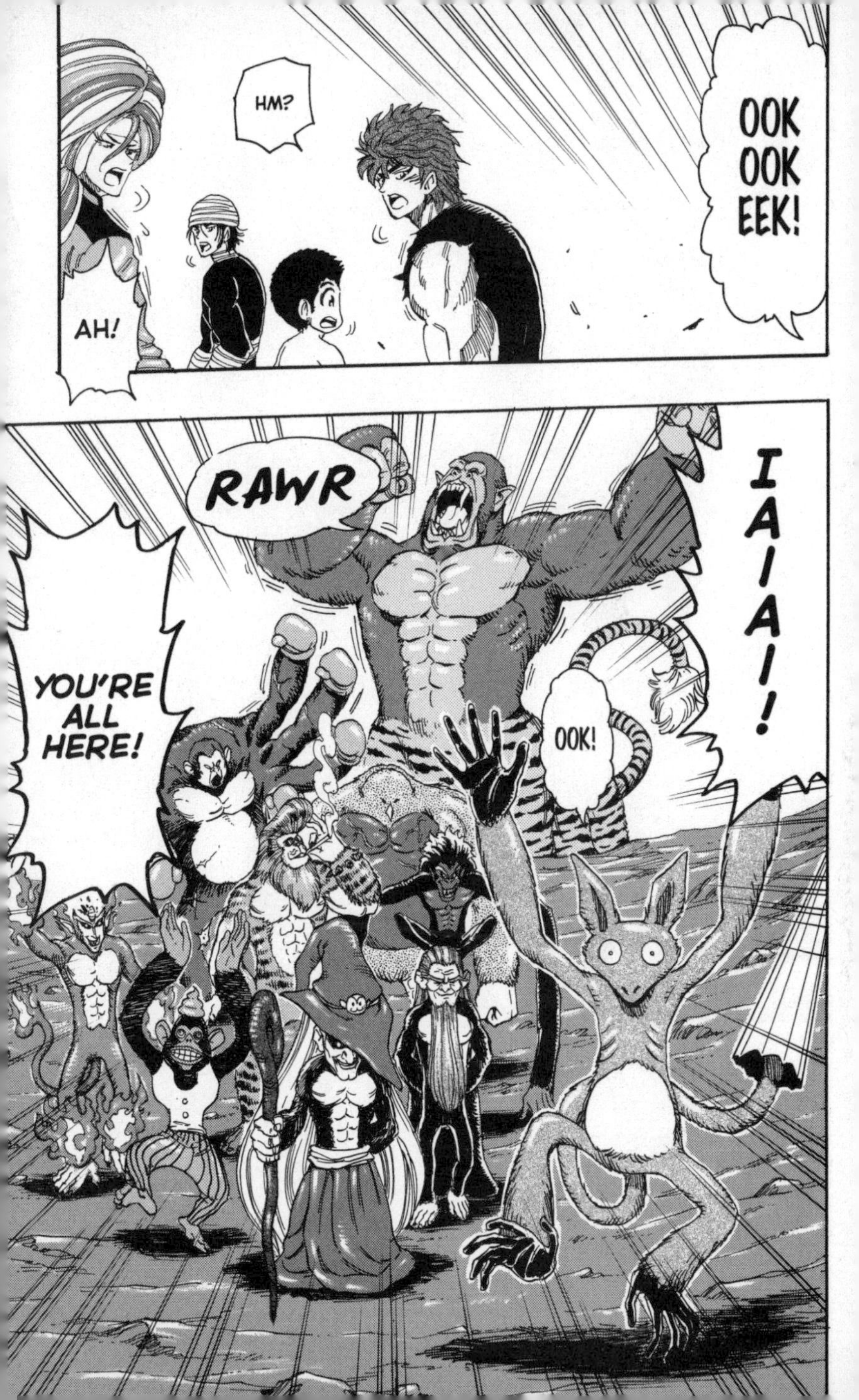
OOK OOK EEK!
HM?
AH!
IAIAI!
RAWR
OOK!
YOU'RE ALL HERE!

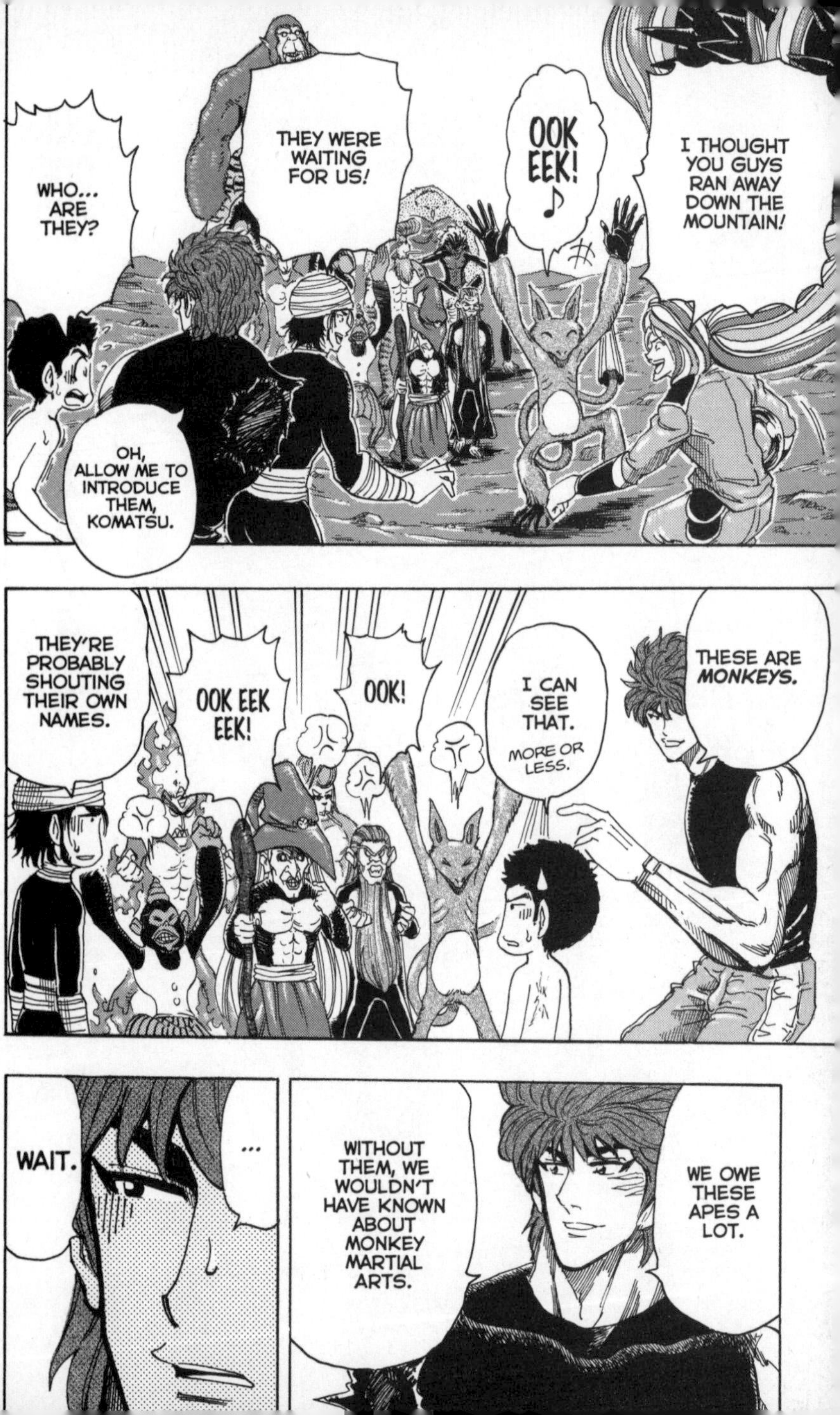
I THOUGHT YOU GUYS RAN AWAY DOWN THE MOUNTAIN!
OOK EEK! ♪
THEY WERE WAITING FOR US!
WHO... ARE THEY?
OH, ALLOW ME TO INTRODUCE THEM, KOMATSU.
THESE ARE *MONKEYS.*
I CAN SEE THAT.
MORE OR LESS.
OOK!
OOK EEK EEK!
THEY'RE PROBABLY SHOUTING THEIR OWN NAMES.
WE OWE THESE APES A LOT.
WITHOUT THEM, WE WOULDN'T HAVE KNOWN ABOUT MONKEY MARTIAL ARTS.
...
WAIT.

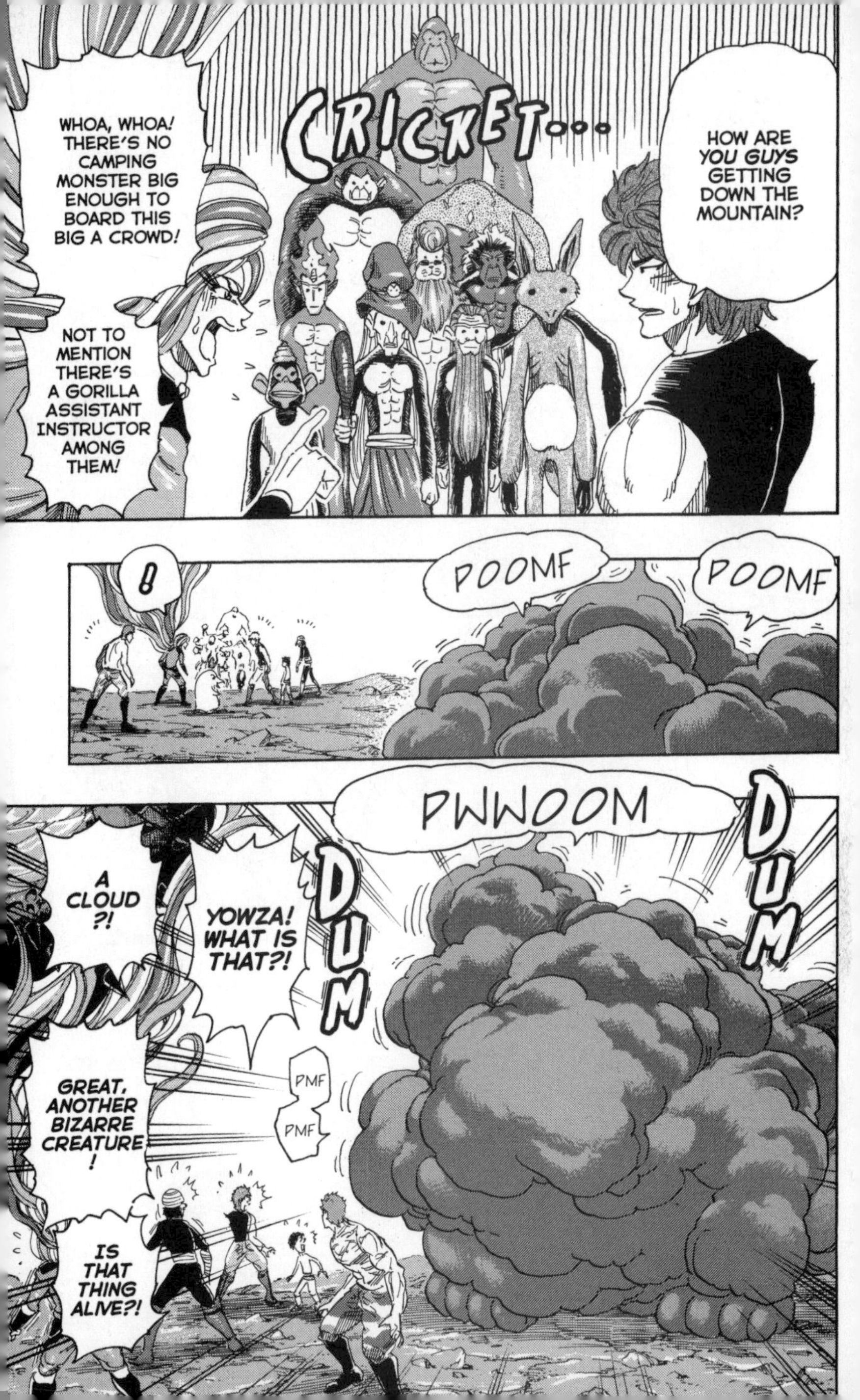
CRICKET...
HOW ARE YOU GUYS GETTING DOWN THE MOUNTAIN?
WHOA, WHOA! THERE'S NO CAMPING MONSTER BIG ENOUGH TO BOARD THIS BIG A CROWD!
NOT TO MENTION THERE'S A GORILLA ASSISTANT INSTRUCTOR AMONG THEM!
POOMF
POOMF
!
PWWOOM
DUM
DUM
YOWZA! WHAT IS THAT?!
A CLOUD ?!
PMF
PMF
GREAT, ANOTHER BIZARRE CREATURE !
IS THAT THING ALIVE?!

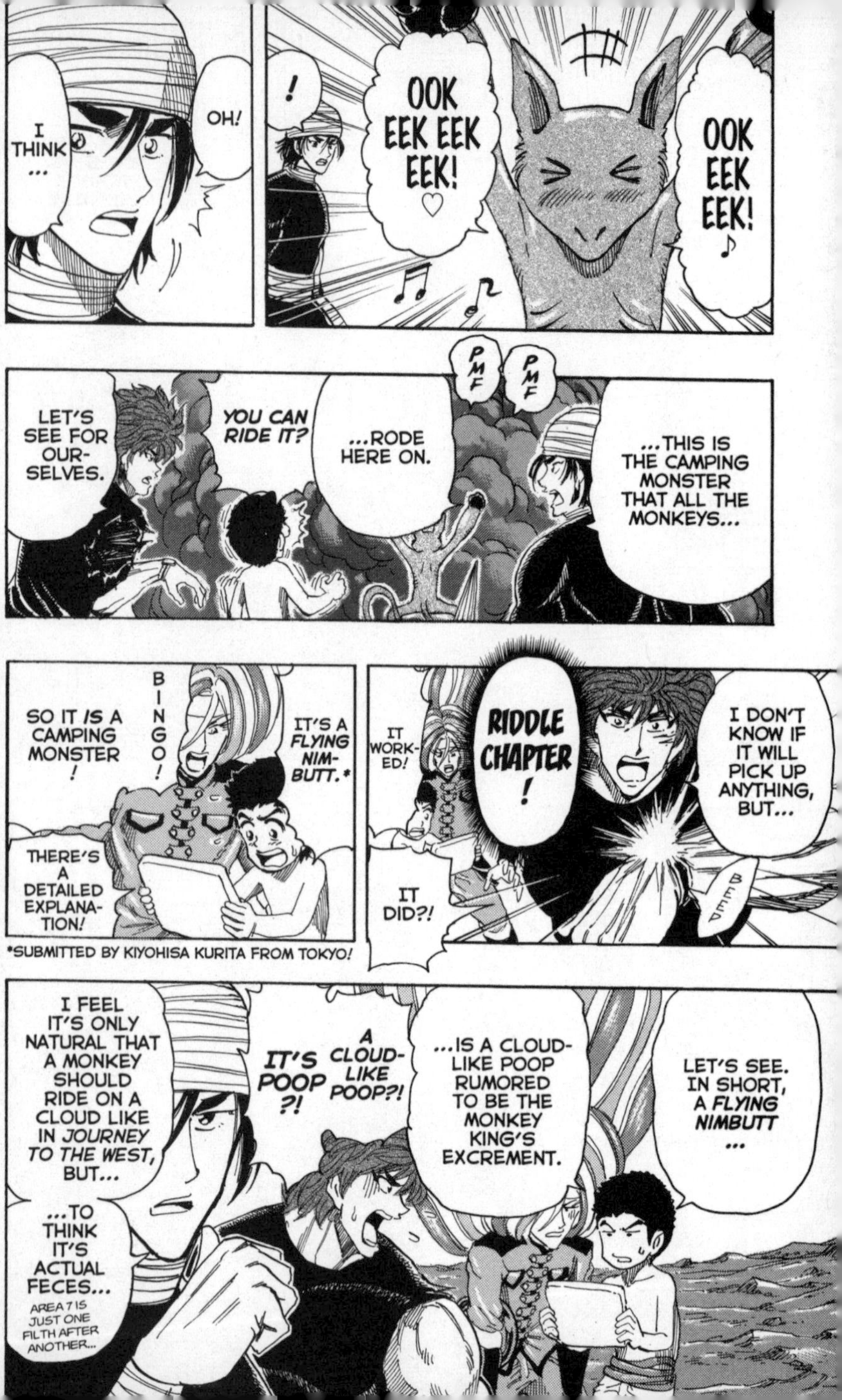
OOK EEK EEK! ♪
OOK EEK EEK EEK! ♡
!
OH!
I THINK ...
...THIS IS THE CAMPING MONSTER THAT ALL THE MONKEYS...
PMF
PMF
...RODE HERE ON.
YOU CAN RIDE IT?
LET'S SEE FOR OURSELVES.
I DON'T KNOW IF IT WILL PICK UP ANYTHING, BUT...
BEEP
RIDDLE CHAPTER!
IT WORKED!
IT DID?!
IT'S A *FLYING NIMBUTT*.*
BINGO!
SO IT *IS* A CAMPING MONSTER!
THERE'S A DETAILED EXPLANATION!
*SUBMITTED BY KIYOHISA KURITA FROM TOKYO!
LET'S SEE. IN SHORT, A *FLYING NIMBUTT* ...
...IS A CLOUD-LIKE POOP RUMORED TO BE THE MONKEY KING'S EXCREMENT.
A CLOUD-LIKE POOP?!
IT'S POOP?!
I FEEL IT'S ONLY NATURAL THAT A MONKEY SHOULD RIDE ON A CLOUD LIKE IN *JOURNEY TO THE WEST*, BUT...
...TO THINK IT'S ACTUAL FECES...
AREA 7 IS JUST ONE FILTH AFTER ANOTHER...

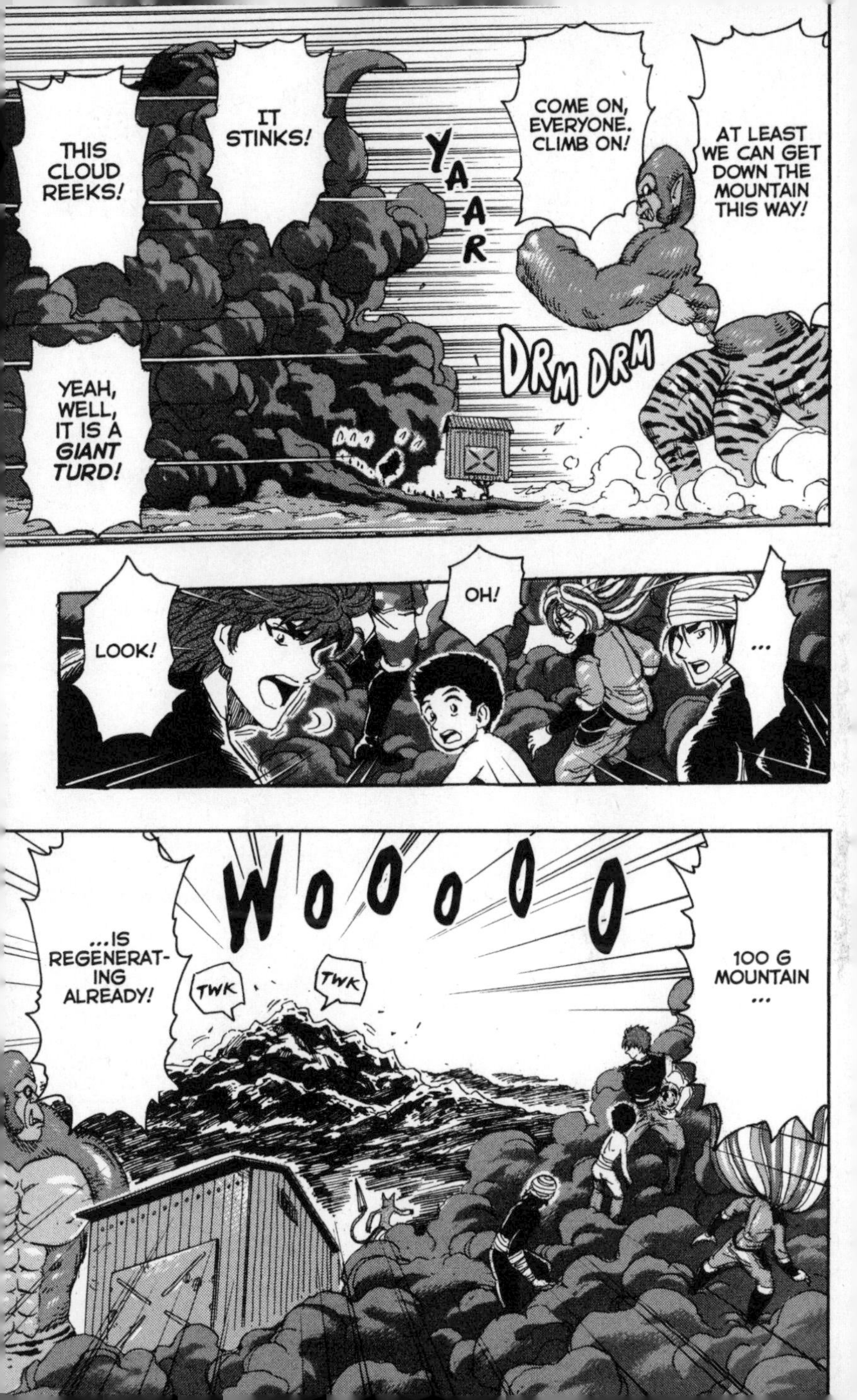

AT LEAST WE CAN GET DOWN THE MOUNTAIN THIS WAY!
COME ON, EVERYONE. CLIMB ON!
YAAR
DRM DRM
IT STINKS!
THIS CLOUD REEKS!
YEAH, WELL, IT IS A GIANT TURD!
...
OH!
LOOK!
100 G MOUNTAIN ...
WOOOOO
TWK
TWK
...IS REGENERAT-ING ALREADY!

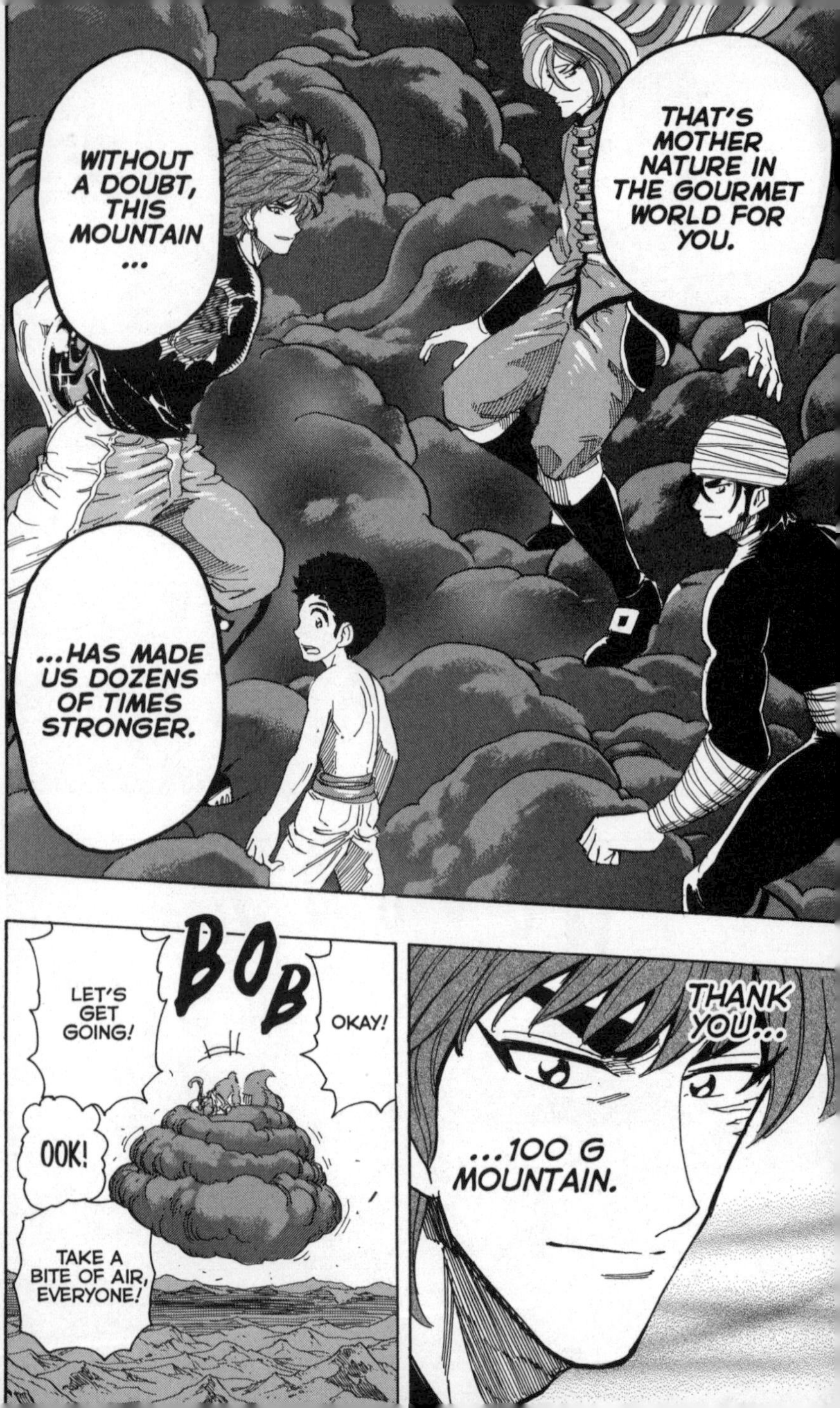
WITHOUT A DOUBT, THIS MOUNTAIN...
...HAS MADE US DOZENS OF TIMES STRONGER.
THAT'S MOTHER NATURE IN THE GOURMET WORLD FOR YOU.
THANK YOU...
...100 G MOUNTAIN.
LET'S GET GOING!
BOB
OKAY!
OOK!
TAKE A BITE OF AIR, EVERYONE!

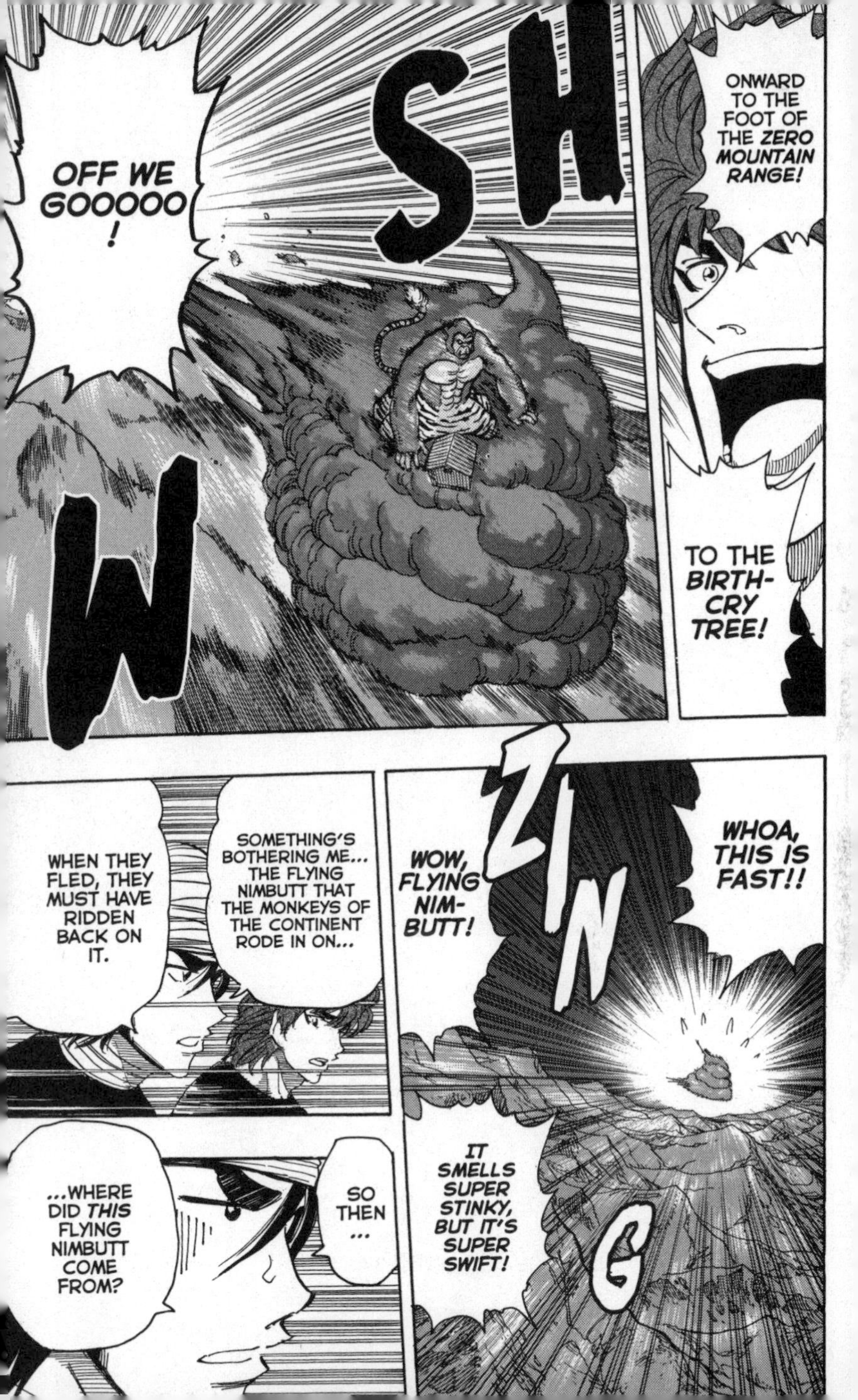
ONWARD TO THE FOOT OF THE *ZERO MOUNTAIN RANGE!*
TO THE *BIRTH-CRY TREE!*
OFF WE GOOOOO!
SH
W
WHOA, THIS IS FAST!!
ZING
WOW, FLYING NIM-BUTT!
IT SMELLS SUPER STINKY, BUT IT'S SUPER SWIFT!
SOMETHING'S BOTHERING ME... THE FLYING NIMBUTT THAT THE MONKEYS OF THE CONTINENT RODE IN ON...
WHEN THEY FLED, THEY MUST HAVE RIDDEN BACK ON IT.
SO THEN...
...WHERE DID *THIS* FLYING NIMBUTT COME FROM?

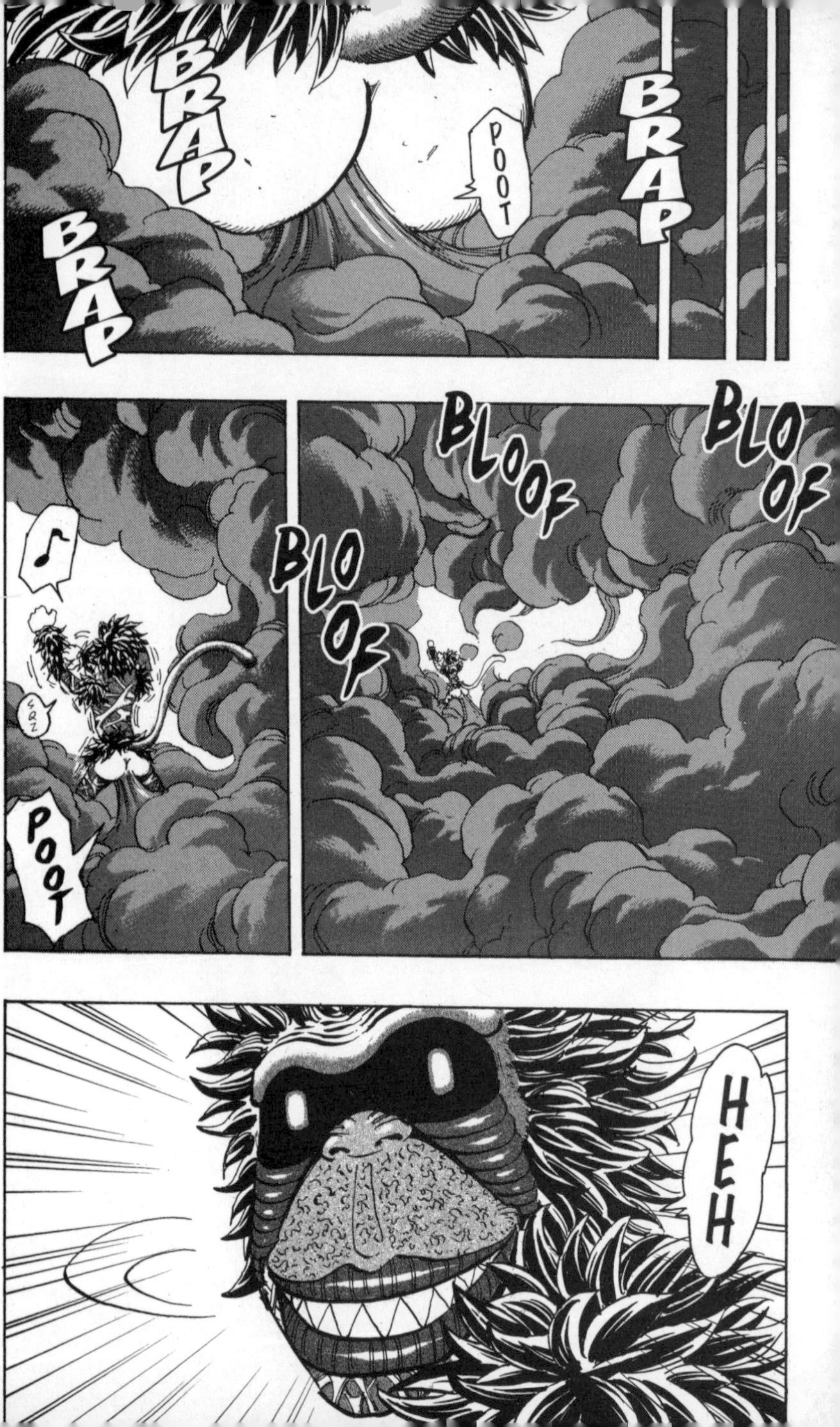
BRAP
POOT
BRAP
BRAP
BLOOF
BLOOF
BLOOF
♪
POOT
HEH

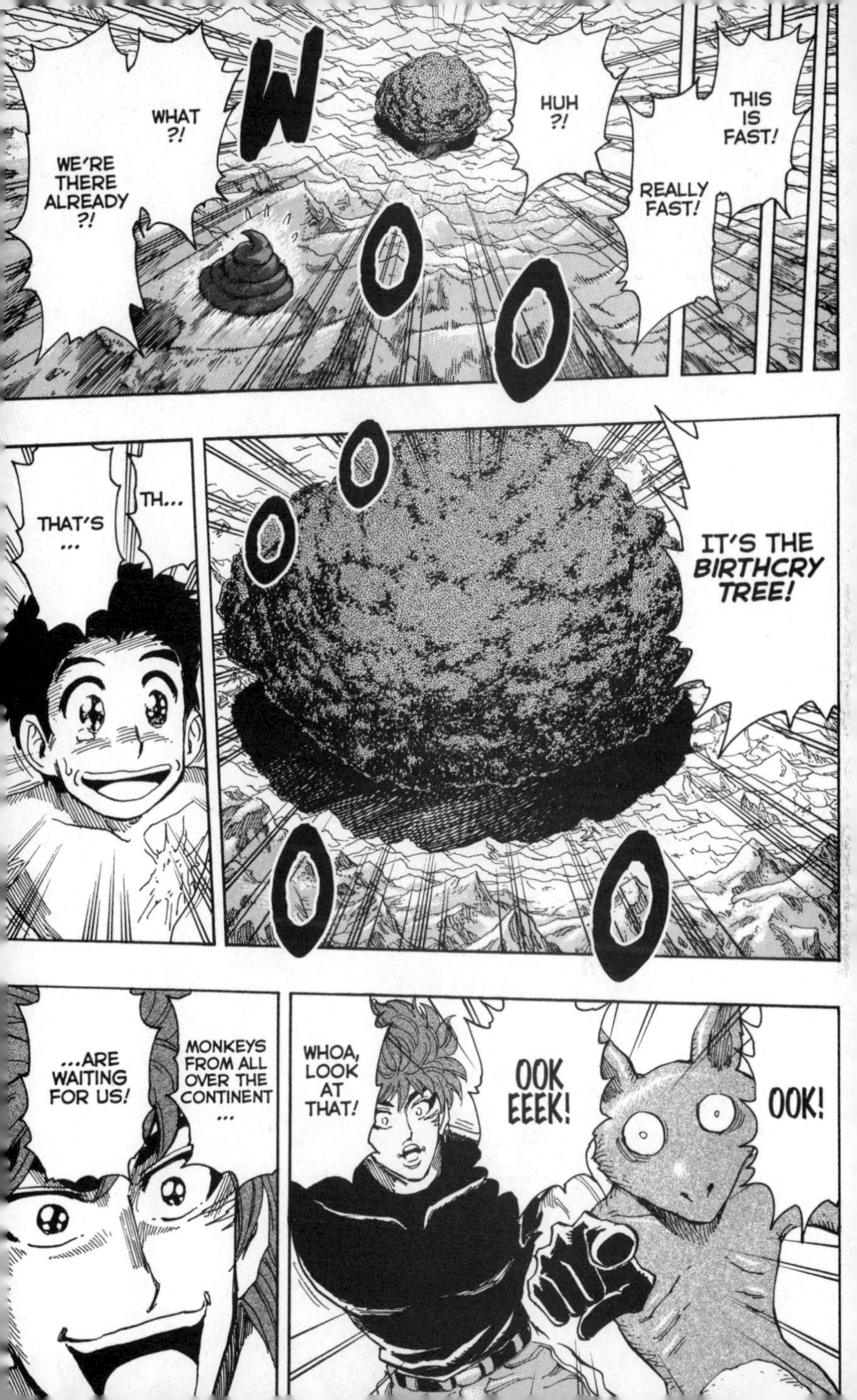
THIS IS FAST!
REALLY FAST!
HUH ?!
WOOO
WHAT ?!
WE'RE THERE ALREADY ?!
IT'S THE *BIRTHCRY* TREE!
TH...
THAT'S ...
OOK!
OOK EEEK!
WHOA, LOOK AT THAT!
MONKEYS FROM ALL OVER THE CONTINENT ...
...ARE WAITING FOR US!

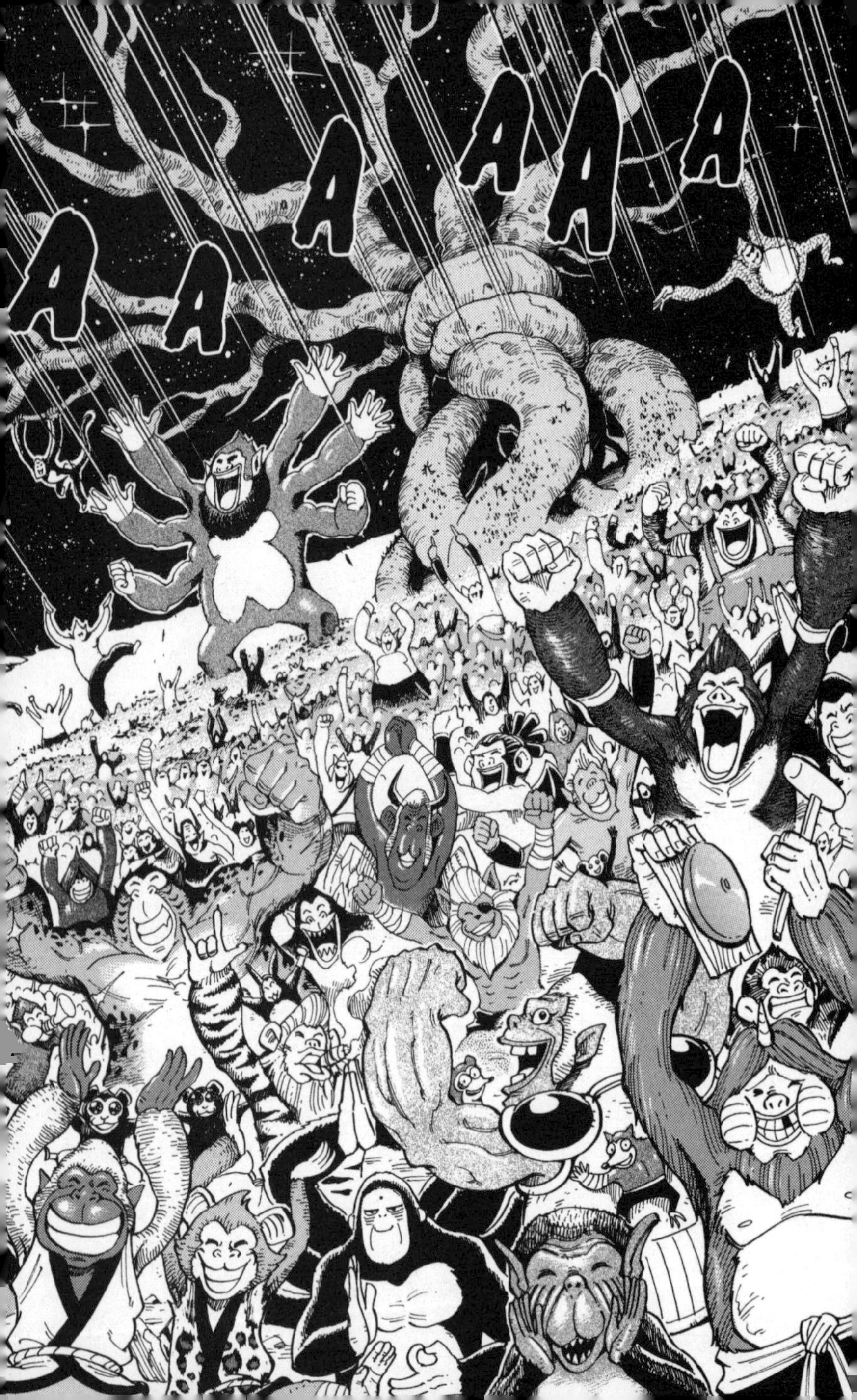
AAAAAAA

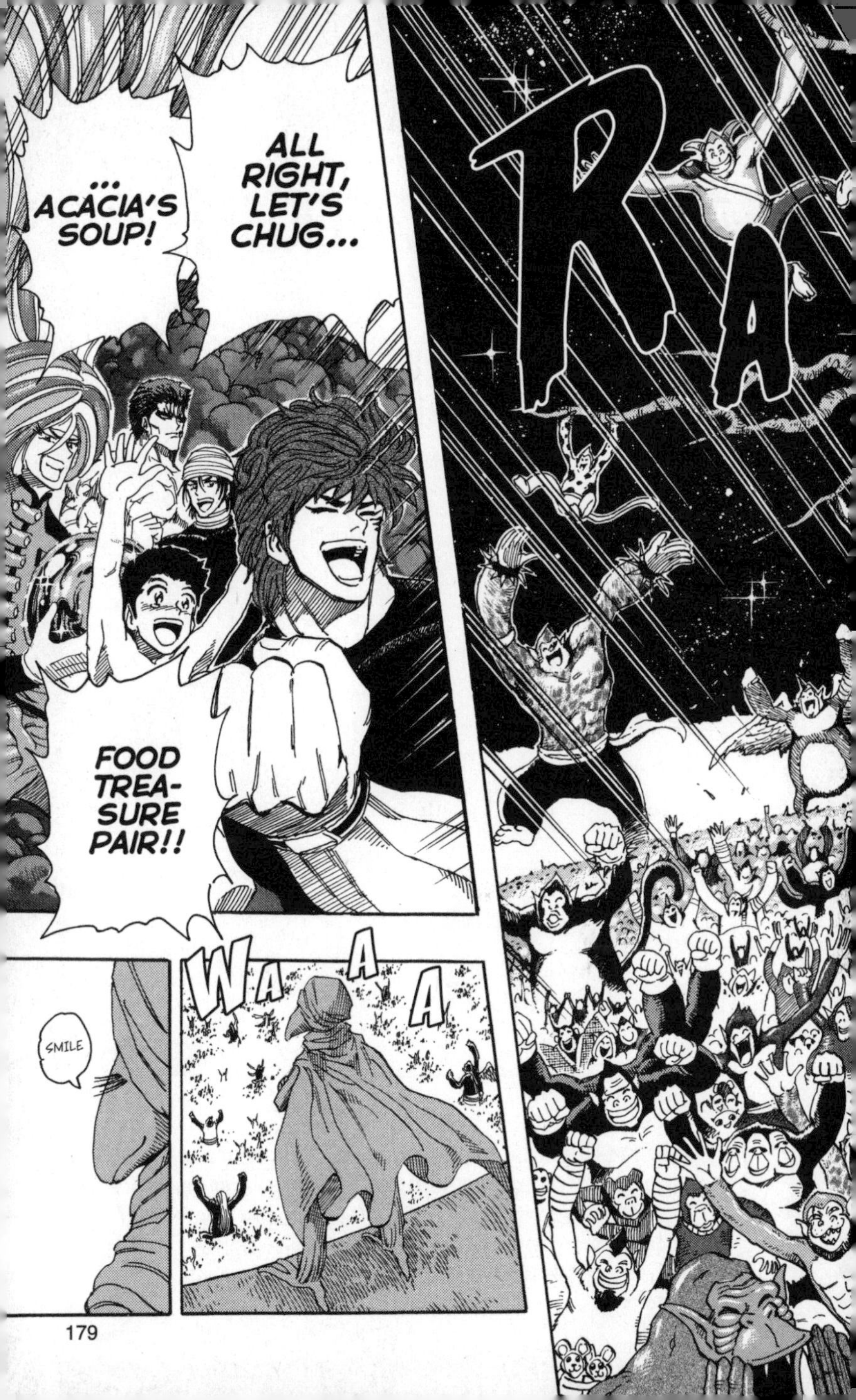
ALL RIGHT, LET'S CHUG...
... ACACIA'S SOUP!
FOOD TREA-SURE PAIR!!
WAAA
RA
SMILE

TORIKO

GOURMET CHECKLIST

Vol. 345

BONITO PEPPER
(PLANT)

CAPTURE LEVEL: 1
HABITAT: MILD CLIMATES
SIZE: ---
HEIGHT: ---
WEIGHT: ---
PRICE: 100 YEN PER ROLL

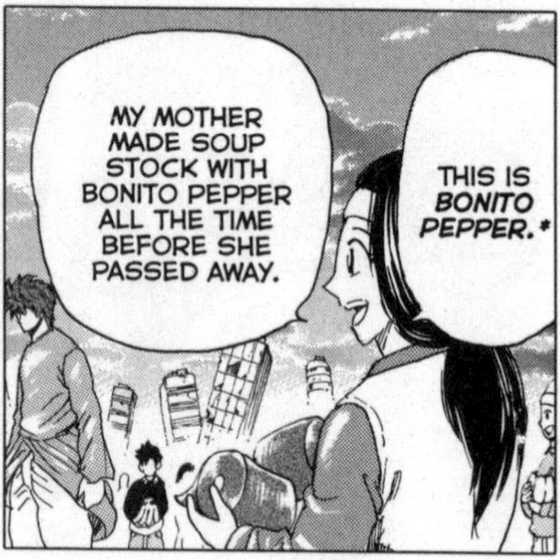
THIS IS BONITO PEPPER.*
MY MOTHER MADE SOUP STOCK WITH BONITO PEPPER ALL THE TIME BEFORE SHE PASSED AWAY.

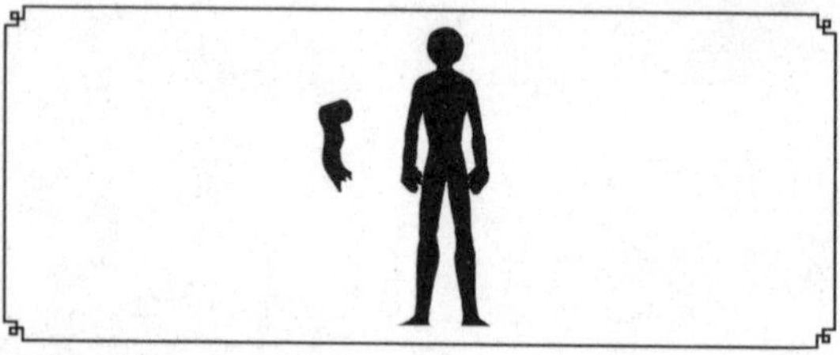

SCALE

AN INGREDIENT TORIKO DISCOVERED. THE BONITO FLAKES ARE SHAPED LIKE A TOILET PAPER ROLL AND GROW ON BONITO FLAKE TREES. THE BROTH DERIVED FROM THE FLAKES TASTES BETTER DEPENDING ON HOW DEEP THE FLAKES SOAK IN THE POT. YOU'RE BOUND TO FIND A ROLL OF THIS STUFF IN EVERY HOUSE. IT'S MOSTLY USED FOR MISO SOUP BROTHS, AND EVERY GOOD HOMEMAKER KNOWS HOW TO UTILIZE THIS DELICACY.

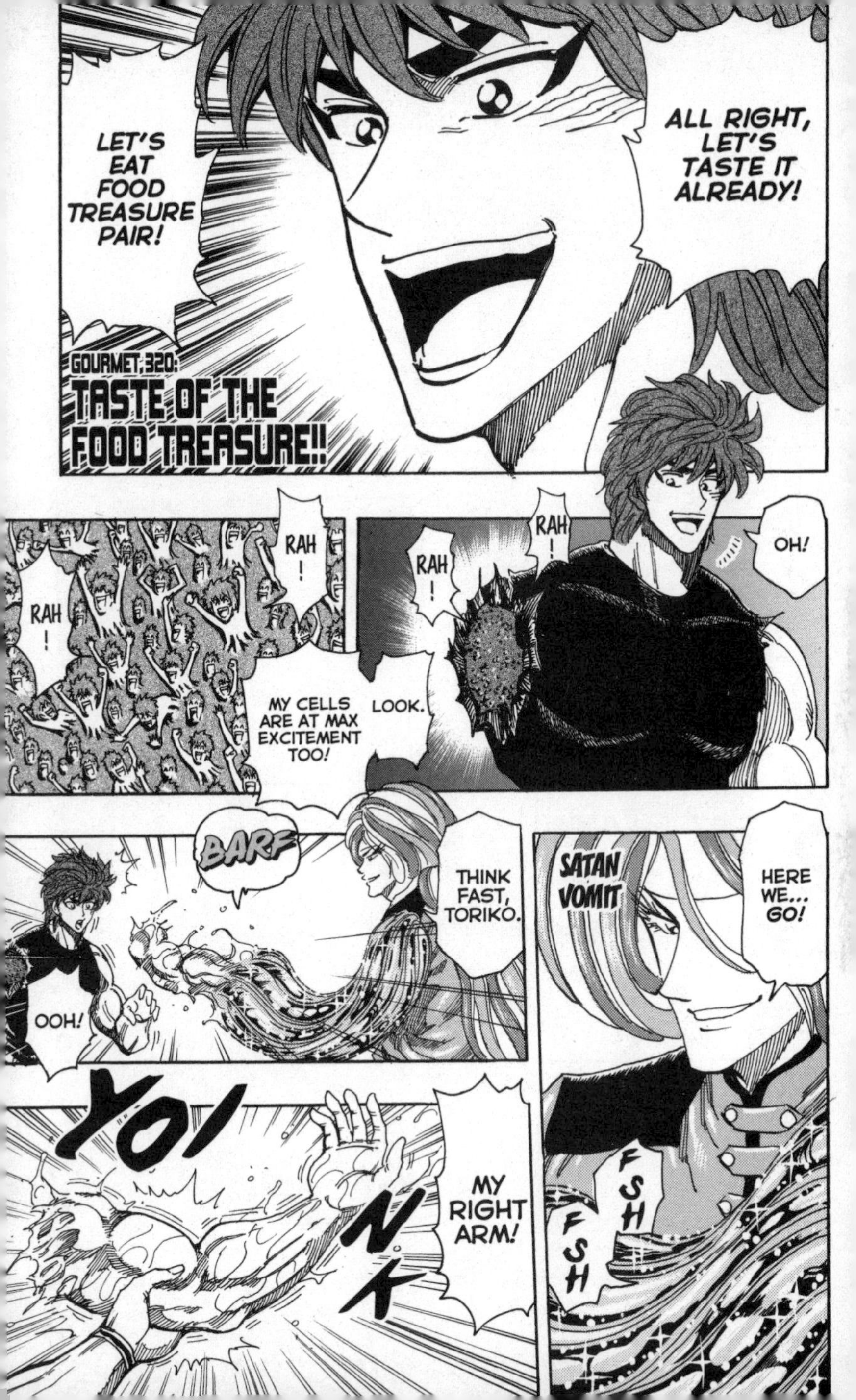
ALL RIGHT, LET'S TASTE IT ALREADY!
LET'S EAT FOOD TREASURE PAIR!
GOURMET 320:
TASTE OF THE FOOD TREASURE!!
OH!
RAH!
RAH!
LOOK.
RAH!
RAH!
MY CELLS ARE AT MAX EXCITEMENT TOO!
HERE WE... GO!
SATAN VOMIT
FSH
FSH
THINK FAST, TORIKO.
BARF
OOH!
MY RIGHT ARM!
YOINK

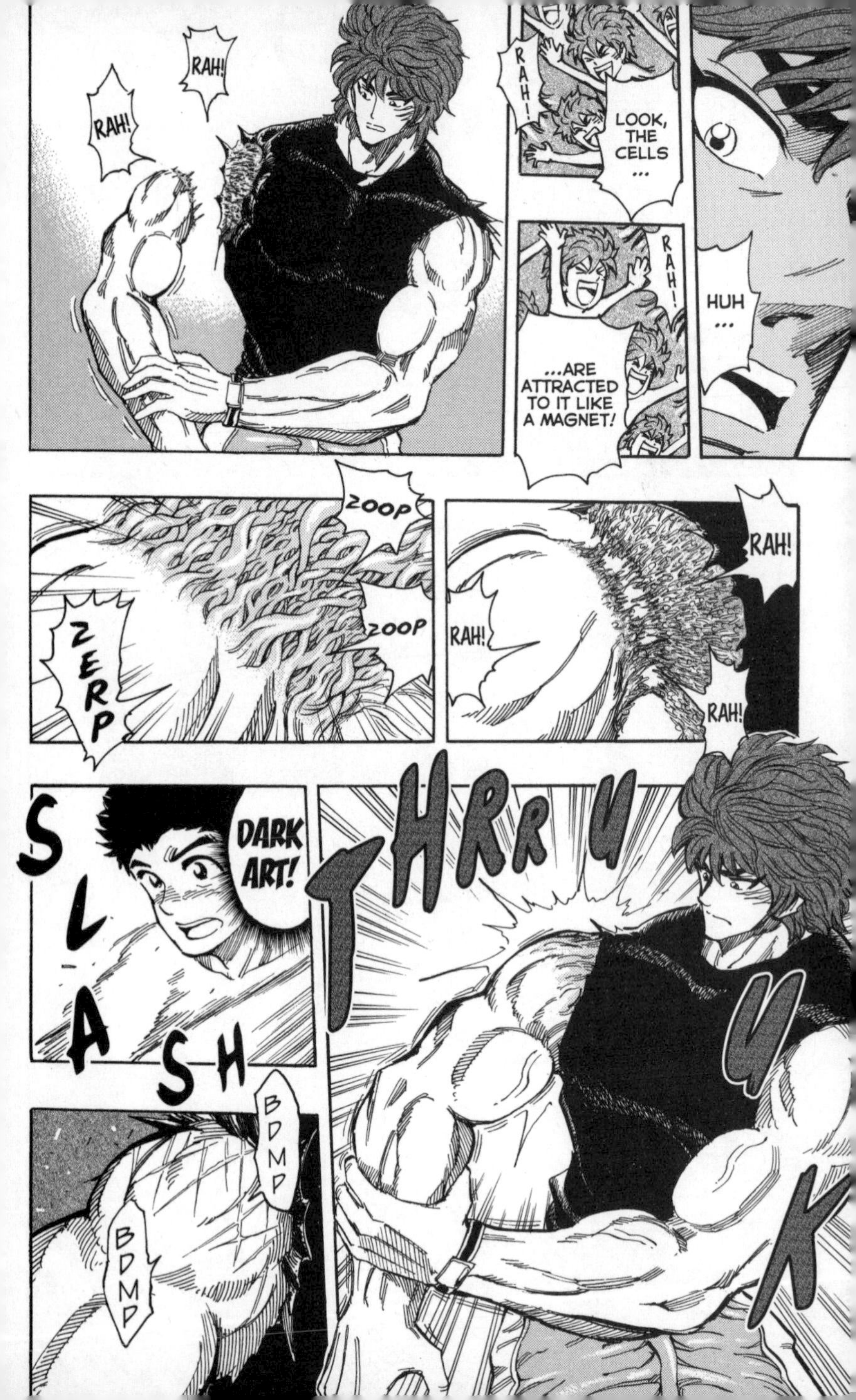
HUH...
RAH!
LOOK, THE CELLS...
RAH!
...ARE ATTRACTED TO IT LIKE A MAGNET!
RAH!
RAH!
RAH!
RAH!
RAH!
ZOOP
ZOOP
ZERP
THRRUUK
DARK ART!
SLASH
BDMP
BDMP

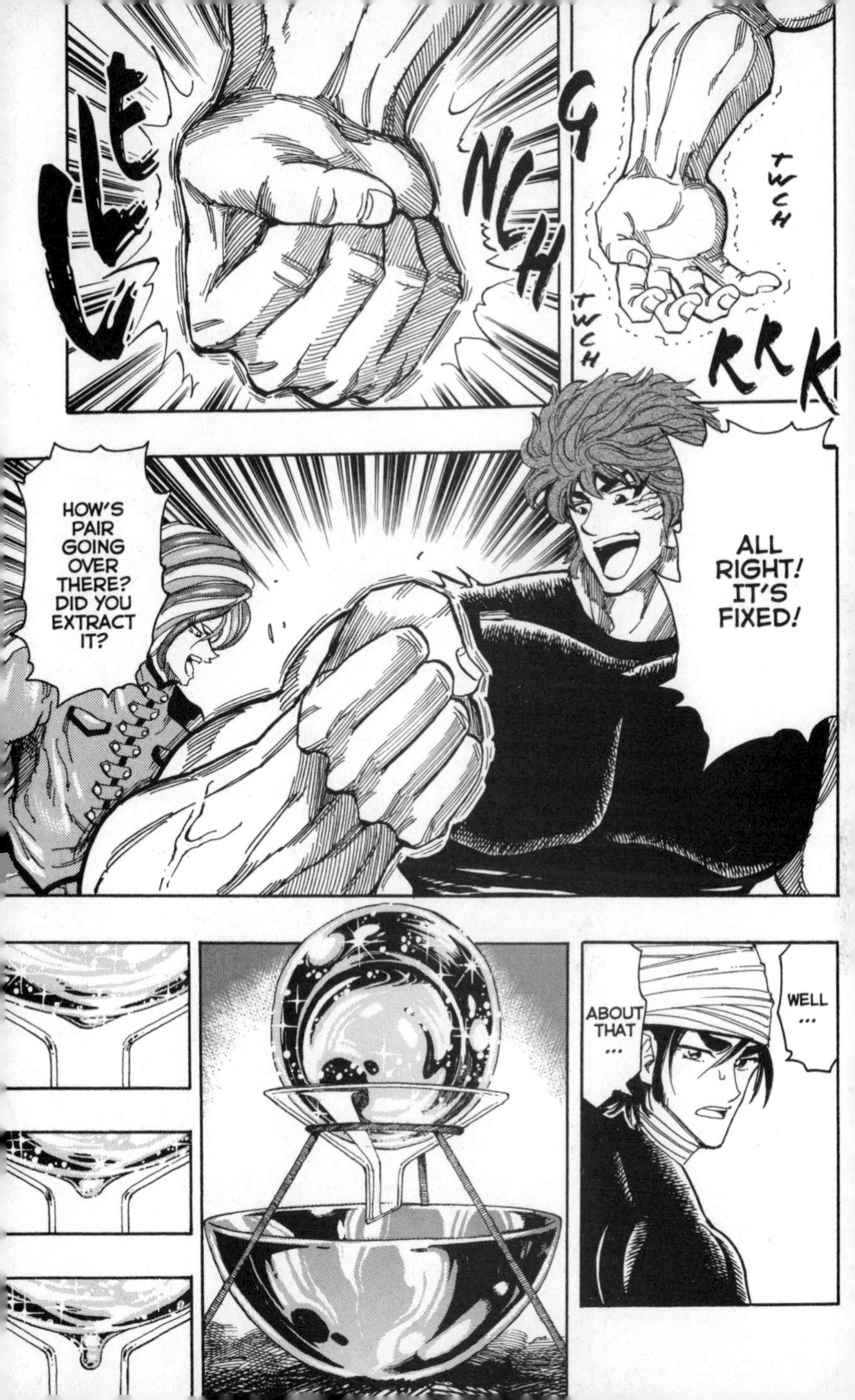
TWCH
TWCH
RRK
GNCH
ALL RIGHT! IT'S FIXED!
HOW'S PAIR GOING OVER THERE? DID YOU EXTRACT IT?
WELL ...
ABOUT THAT ...

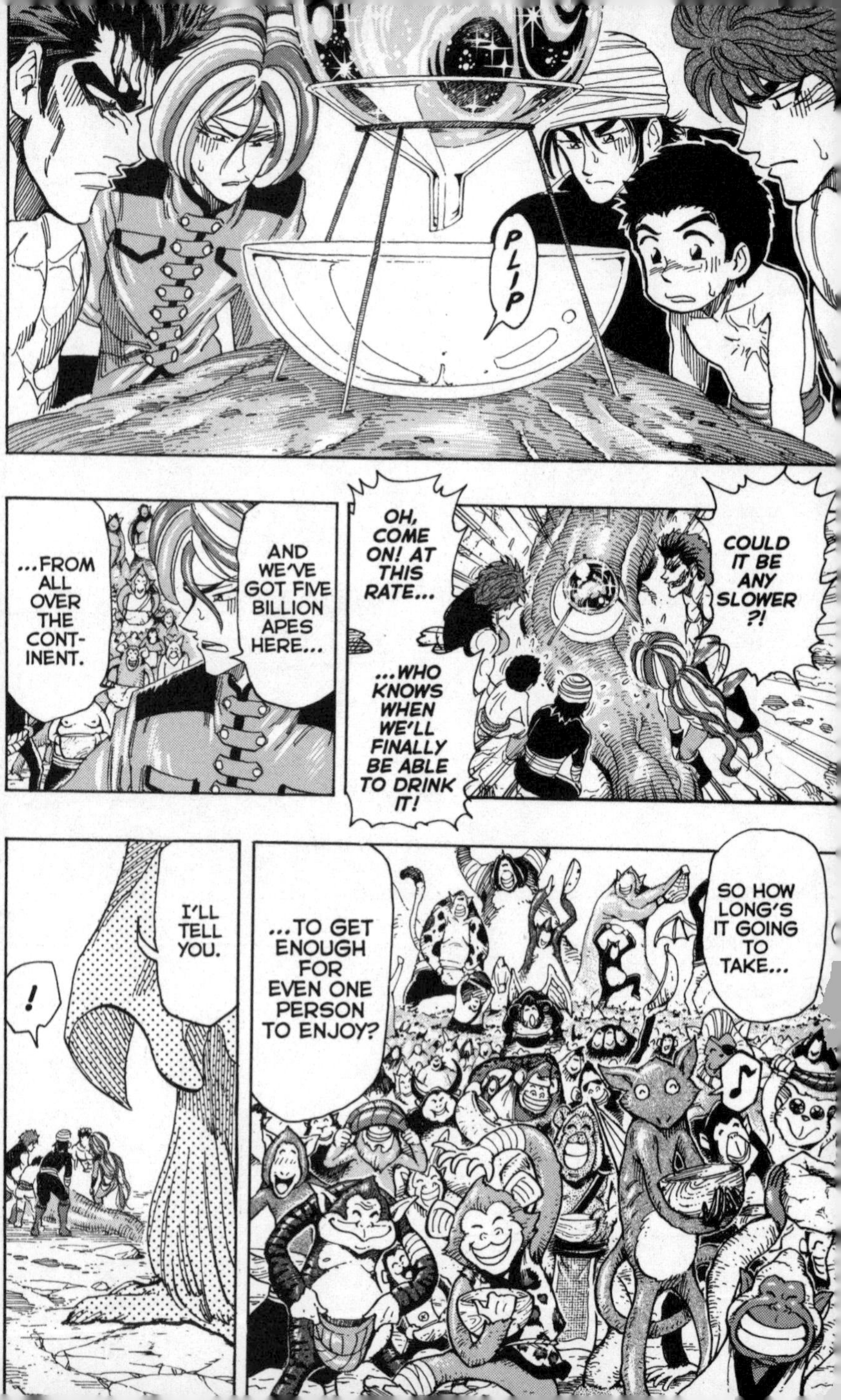
PLIP
COULD IT BE ANY SLOWER?!
OH, COME ON! AT THIS RATE...
...WHO KNOWS WHEN WE'LL FINALLY BE ABLE TO DRINK IT!
AND WE'VE GOT FIVE BILLION APES HERE...
...FROM ALL OVER THE CONTINENT.
SO HOW LONG'S IT GOING TO TAKE...
...TO GET ENOUGH FOR EVEN ONE PERSON TO ENJOY?
I'LL TELL YOU.
!

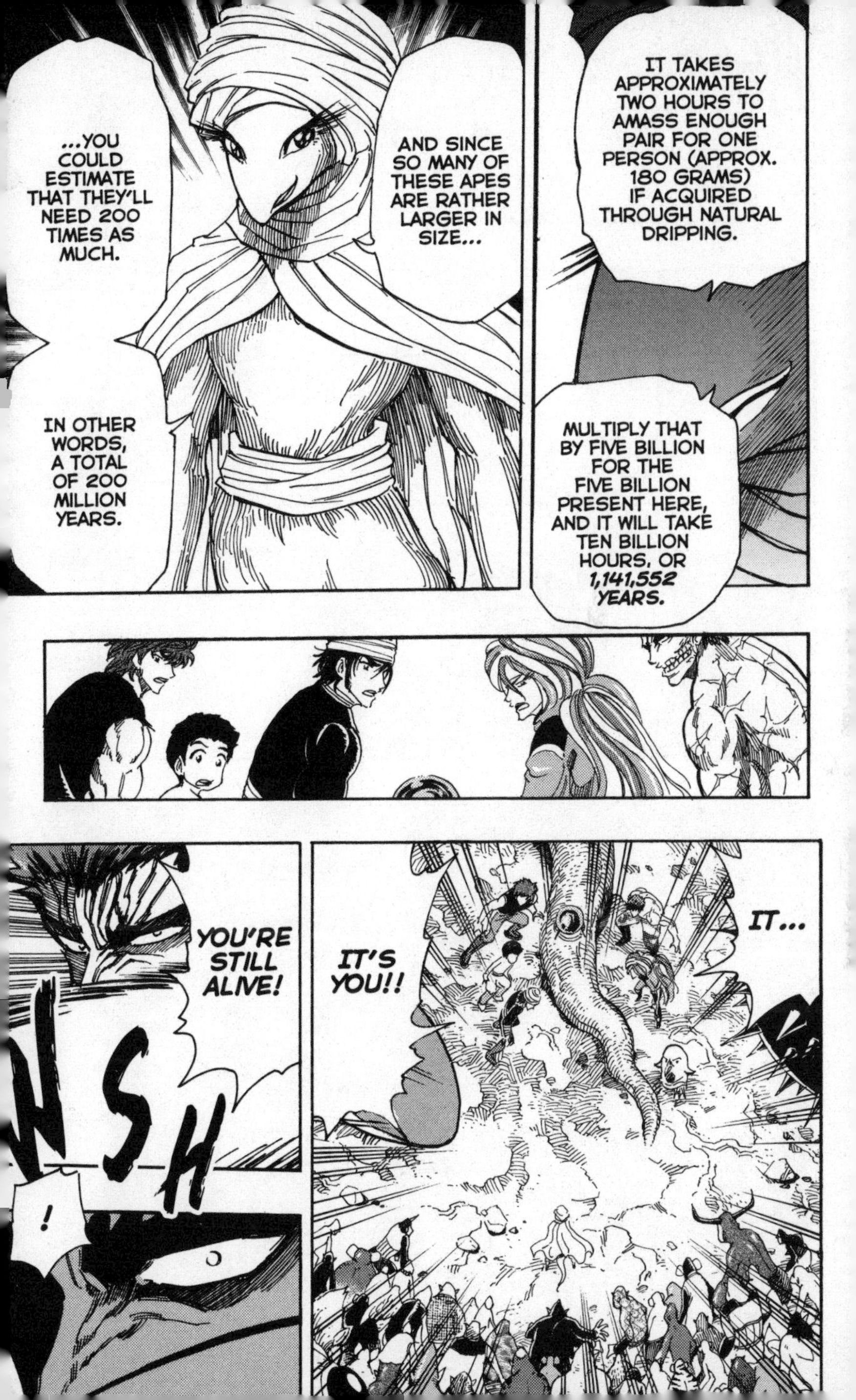
IT TAKES APPROXIMATELY TWO HOURS TO AMASS ENOUGH PAIR FOR ONE PERSON (APPROX. 180 GRAMS) IF ACQUIRED THROUGH NATURAL DRIPPING.
MULTIPLY THAT BY FIVE BILLION FOR THE FIVE BILLION PRESENT HERE, AND IT WILL TAKE TEN BILLION HOURS, OR 1,141,552 YEARS.
AND SINCE SO MANY OF THESE APES ARE RATHER LARGER IN SIZE...
...YOU COULD ESTIMATE THAT THEY'LL NEED 200 TIMES AS MUCH.
IN OTHER WORDS, A TOTAL OF 200 MILLION YEARS.
IT...
IT'S YOU!!
YOU'RE STILL ALIVE!
!

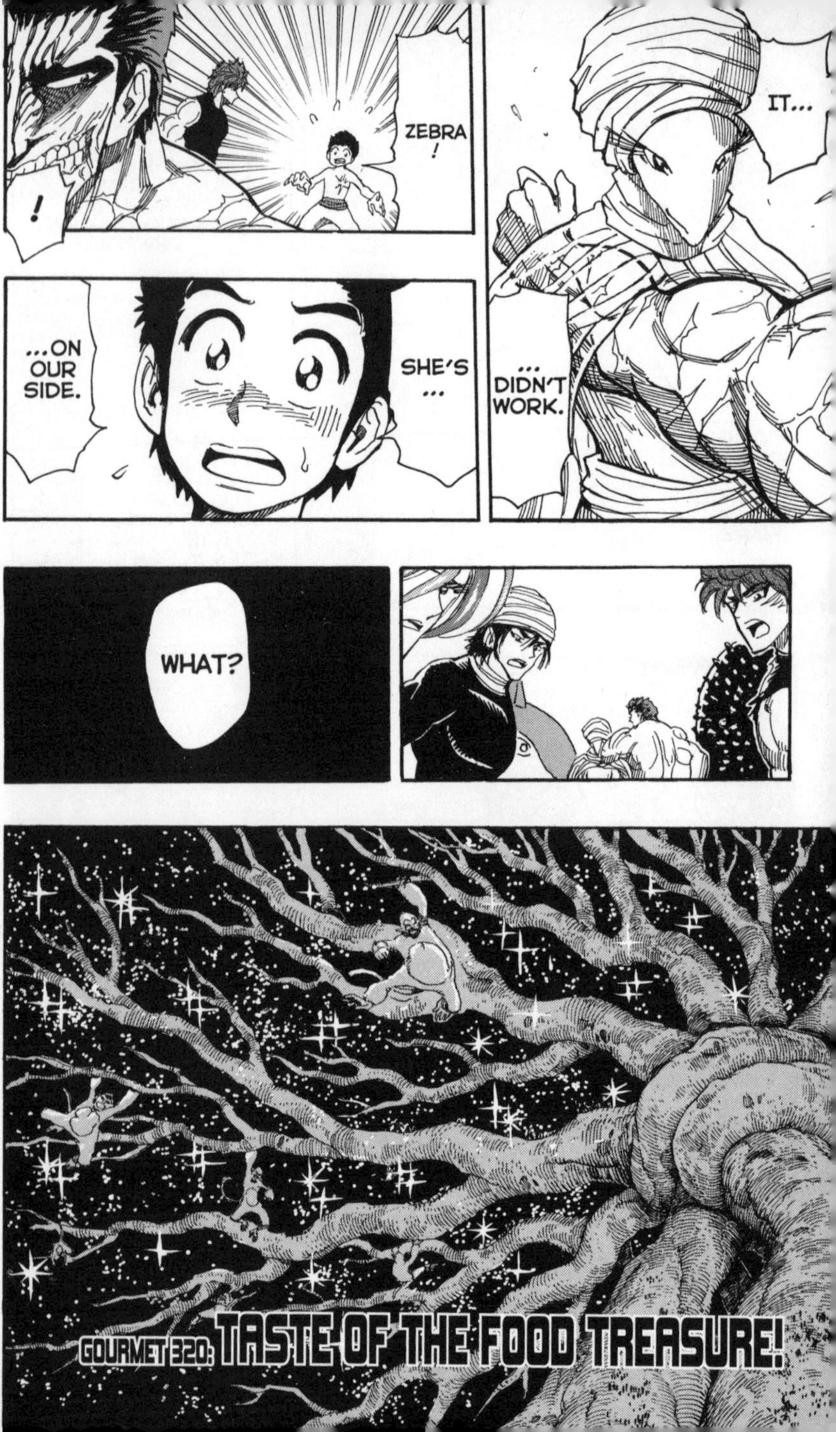
IT...
...DIDN'T WORK.
ZEBRA!
!
SHE'S...
...ON OUR SIDE.
WHAT?
GOURMET 320: TASTE OF THE FOOD TREASURE!

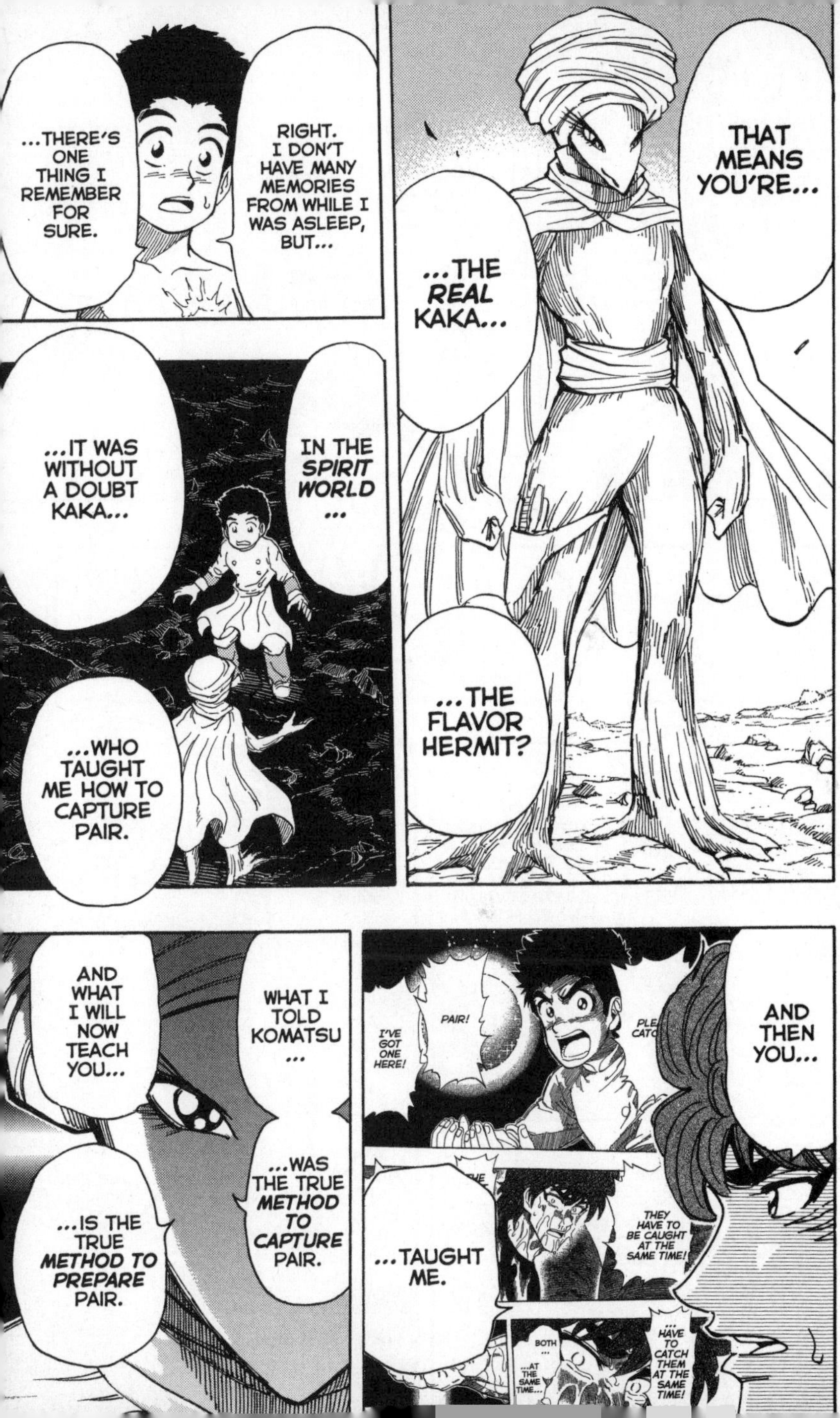
THAT MEANS YOU'RE...
...THE REAL KAKA...
...THE FLAVOR HERMIT?
RIGHT. I DON'T HAVE MANY MEMORIES FROM WHILE I WAS ASLEEP, BUT...
...THERE'S ONE THING I REMEMBER FOR SURE.
IN THE SPIRIT WORLD ...
...IT WAS WITHOUT A DOUBT KAKA...
...WHO TAUGHT ME HOW TO CAPTURE PAIR.
AND THEN YOU...
PAIR!
I'VE GOT ONE HERE!
...TAUGHT ME.
THEY HAVE TO BE CAUGHT AT THE SAME TIME!
...HAVE TO CATCH THEM AT THE SAME TIME!
BOTH ...
...AT THE SAME TIME....
WHAT I TOLD KOMATSU ...
...WAS THE TRUE METHOD TO CAPTURE PAIR.
AND WHAT I WILL NOW TEACH YOU...
...IS THE TRUE METHOD TO PREPARE PAIR.

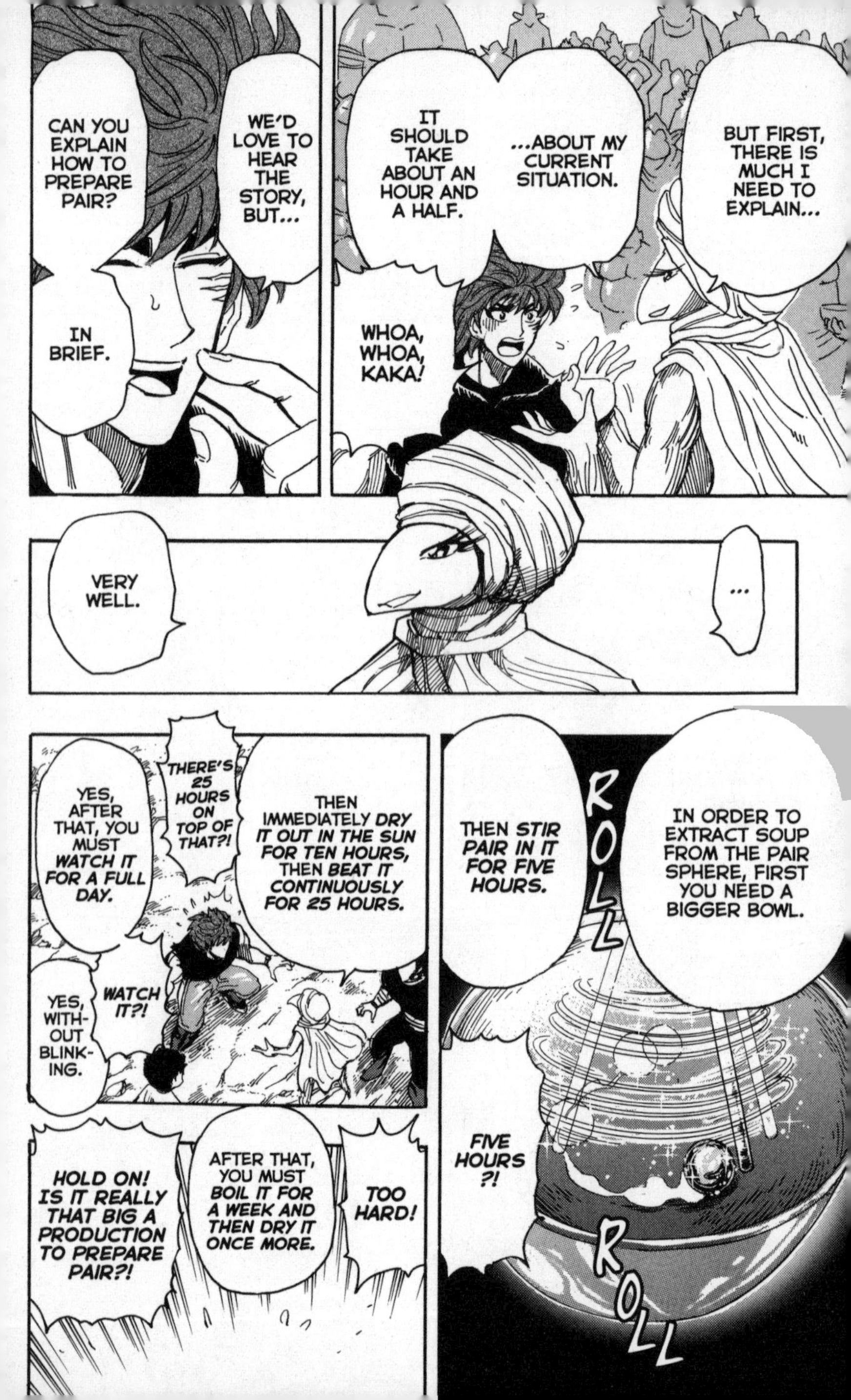
BUT FIRST, THERE IS MUCH I NEED TO EXPLAIN...
...ABOUT MY CURRENT SITUATION.
IT SHOULD TAKE ABOUT AN HOUR AND A HALF.
WHOA, WHOA, KAKA!
WE'D LOVE TO HEAR THE STORY, BUT...
CAN YOU EXPLAIN HOW TO PREPARE PAIR?
IN BRIEF.
...
VERY WELL.
ROLL
IN ORDER TO EXTRACT SOUP FROM THE PAIR SPHERE, FIRST YOU NEED A BIGGER BOWL.
THEN STIR PAIR IN IT FOR FIVE HOURS.
FIVE HOURS?!
ROLL
THEN IMMEDIATELY DRY IT OUT IN THE SUN FOR TEN HOURS, THEN BEAT IT CONTINUOUSLY FOR 25 HOURS.
THERE'S 25 HOURS ON TOP OF THAT?!
YES, AFTER THAT, YOU MUST WATCH IT FOR A FULL DAY.
WATCH IT?!
YES, WITH-OUT BLINK-ING.
AFTER THAT, YOU MUST BOIL IT FOR A WEEK AND THEN DRY IT ONCE MORE.
TOO HARD!
HOLD ON! IS IT REALLY THAT BIG A PRODUCTION TO PREPARE PAIR?!

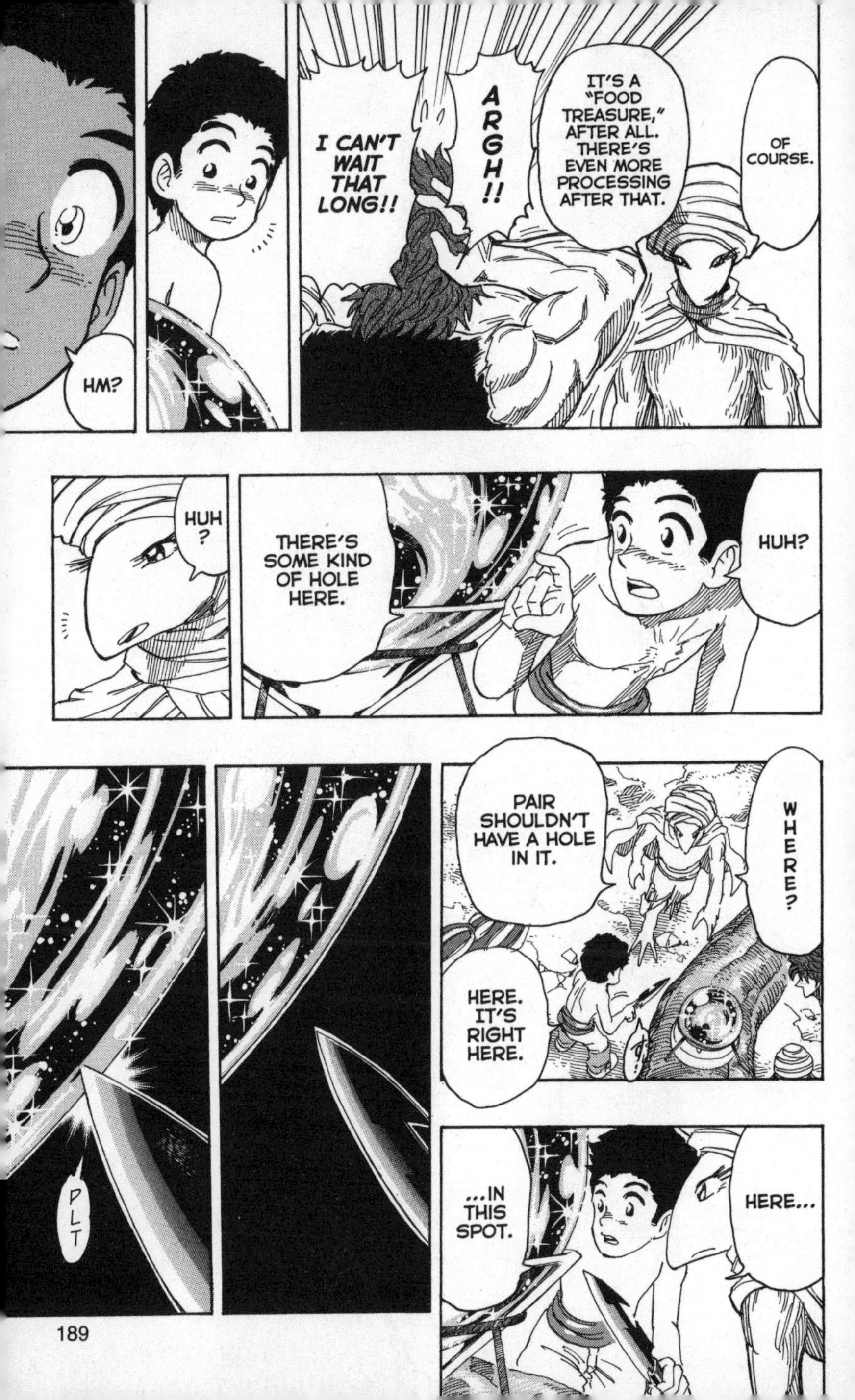
OF COURSE.
IT'S A "FOOD TREASURE," AFTER ALL. THERE'S EVEN MORE PROCESSING AFTER THAT.
ARGH!!
I CAN'T WAIT THAT LONG!!
HM?
HUH?
THERE'S SOME KIND OF HOLE HERE.
HUH?
WHERE?
PAIR SHOULDN'T HAVE A HOLE IN IT.
HERE. IT'S RIGHT HERE.
HERE...
...IN THIS SPOT.
PLT

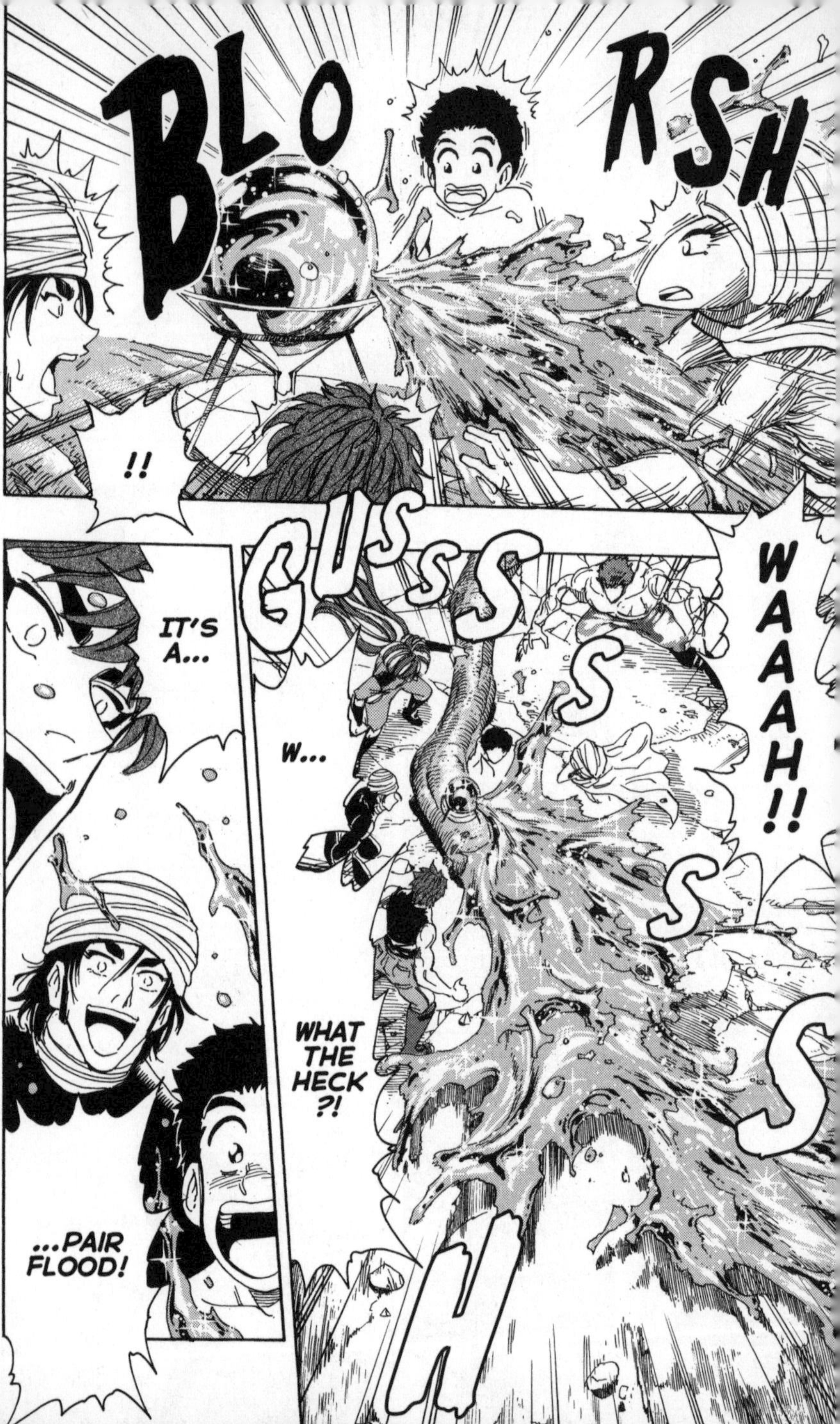
BLORSH
!!
GUSSSSSSH
WAAAAH!!
W...
WHAT THE HECK ?!
IT'S A...
...PAIR FLOOD!

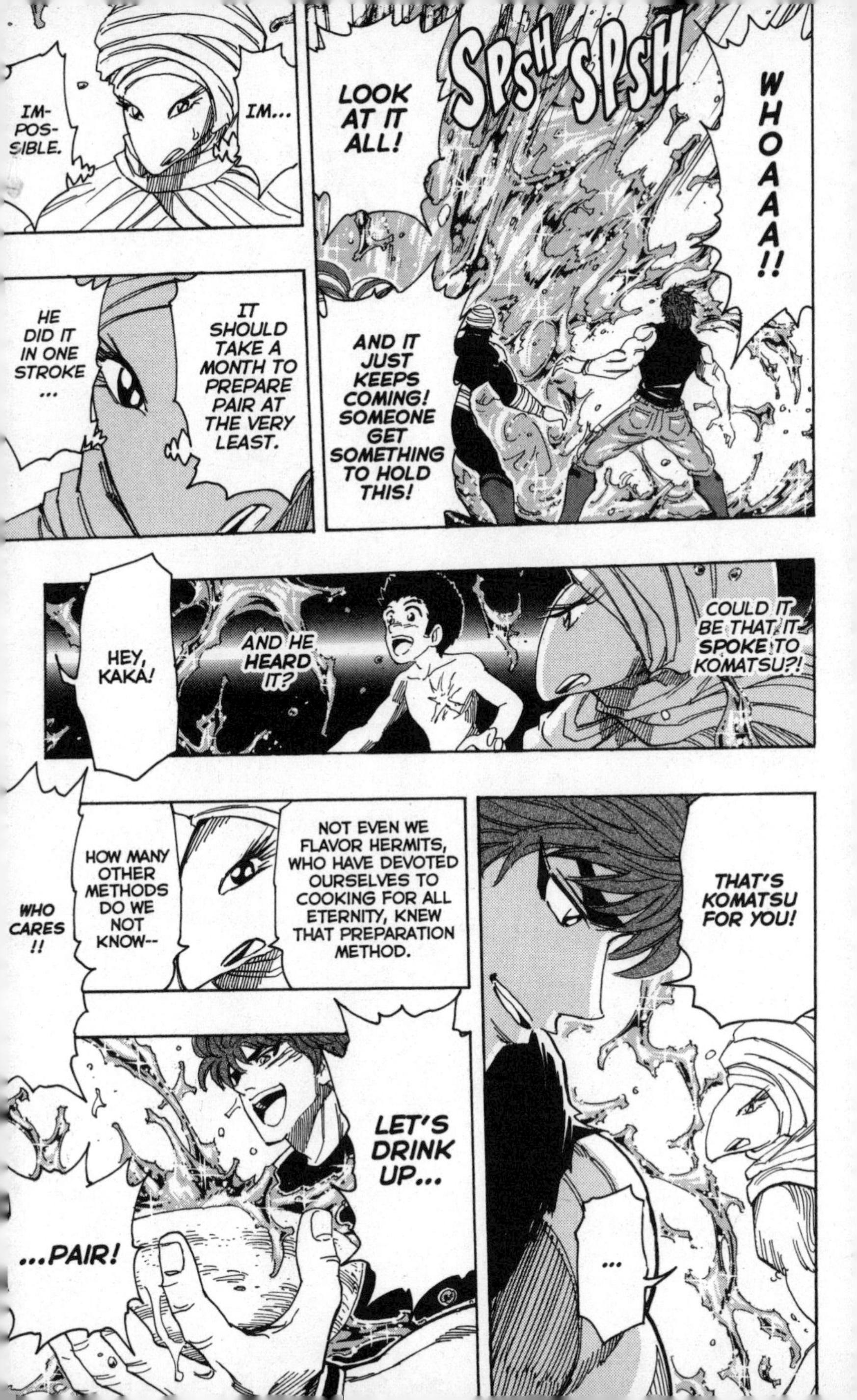
SPSH SPSH
WHOAAAA!!
LOOK AT IT ALL!
AND IT JUST KEEPS COMING! SOMEONE GET SOMETHING TO HOLD THIS!
IM...
IMPOSSIBLE.
IT SHOULD TAKE A MONTH TO PREPARE PAIR AT THE VERY LEAST.
HE DID IT IN ONE STROKE...
COULD IT BE THAT IT SPOKE TO KOMATSU?!
AND HE HEARD IT?
HEY, KAKA!
THAT'S KOMATSU FOR YOU!
...
NOT EVEN WE FLAVOR HERMITS, WHO HAVE DEVOTED OURSELVES TO COOKING FOR ALL ETERNITY, KNEW THAT PREPARATION METHOD.
HOW MANY OTHER METHODS DO WE NOT KNOW--
WHO CARES!!
LET'S DRINK UP...
...PAIR!

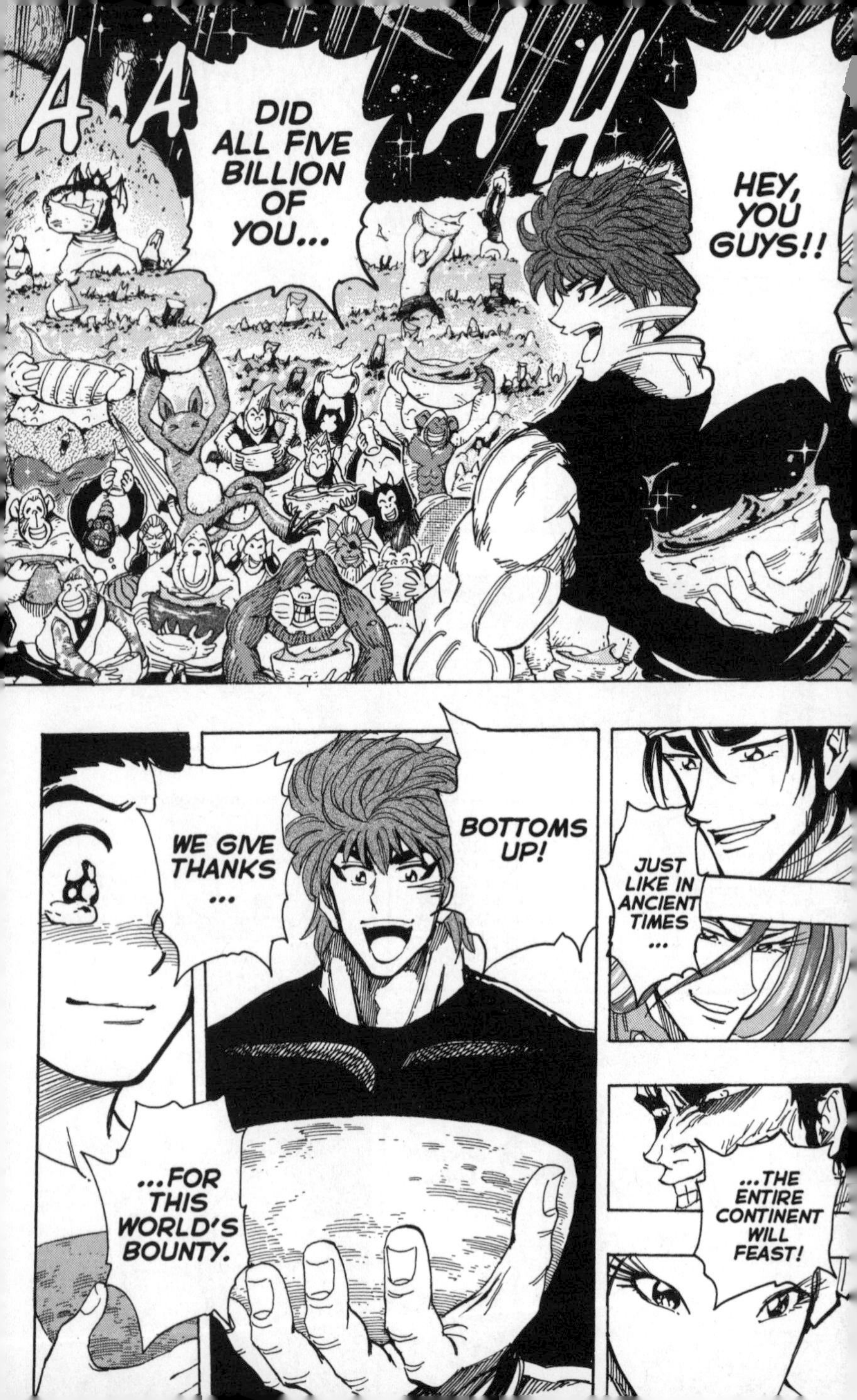
AAAH
HEY, YOU GUYS!!
DID ALL FIVE BILLION OF YOU...
JUST LIKE IN ANCIENT TIMES ...
...THE ENTIRE CONTINENT WILL FEAST!
BOTTOMS UP!
WE GIVE THANKS ...
...FOR THIS WORLD'S BOUNTY.

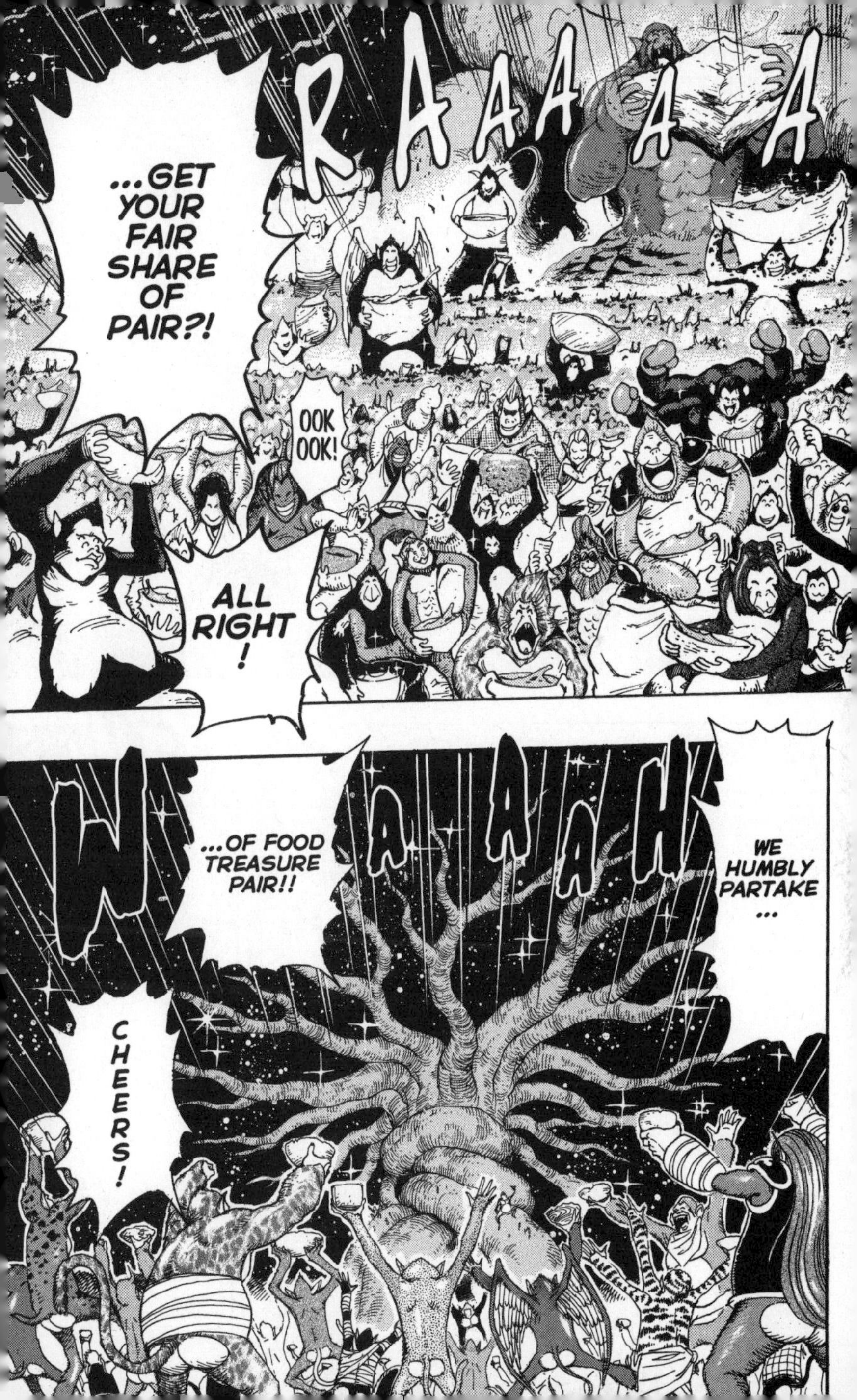
RAAAAA
...GET YOUR FAIR SHARE OF PAIR?!
OOK OOK!
ALL RIGHT!
WE HUMBLY PARTAKE...
...OF FOOD TREASURE PAIR!!
WAAAH
CHEERS!

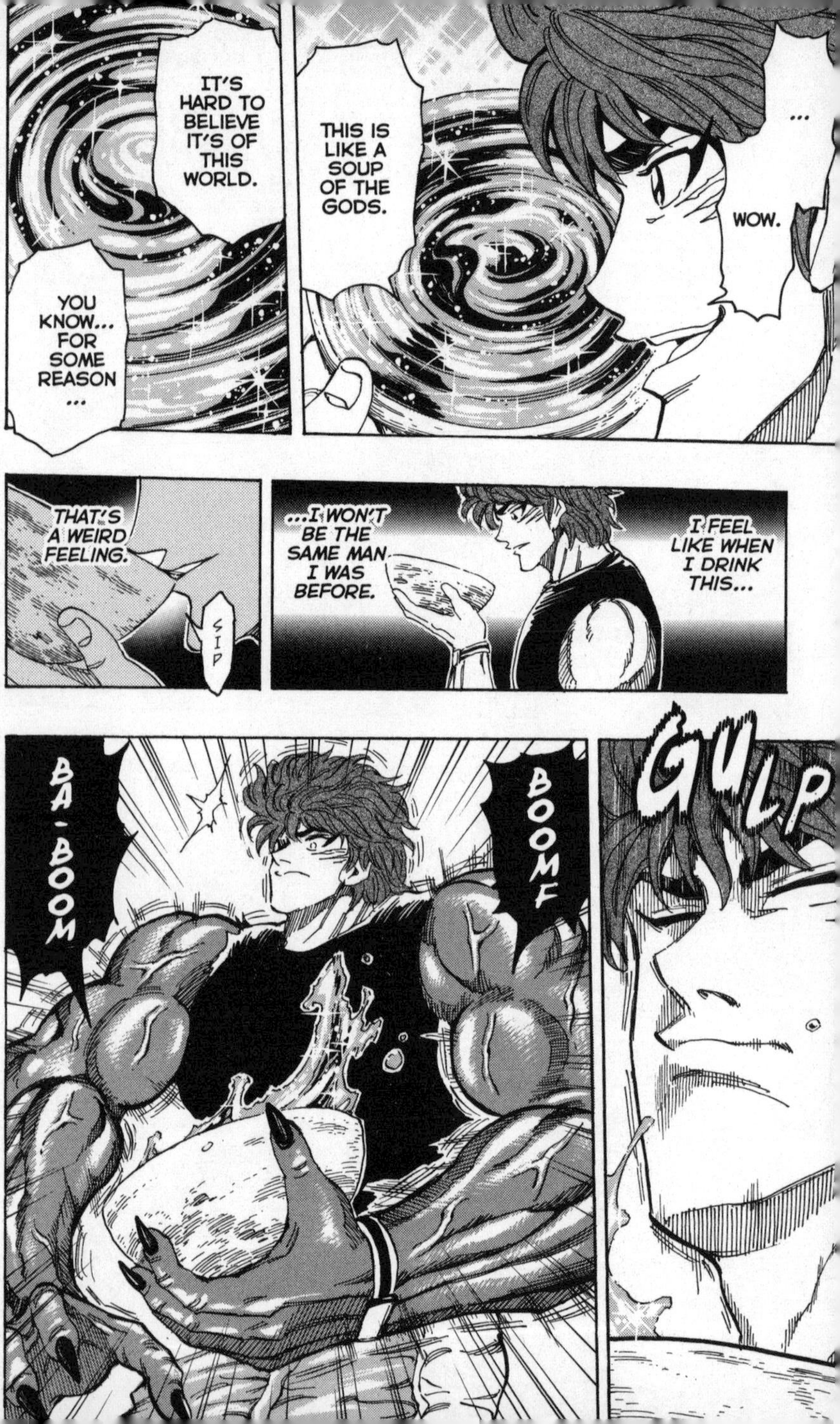
...
WOW.
THIS IS LIKE A SOUP OF THE GODS.
IT'S HARD TO BELIEVE IT'S OF THIS WORLD.
YOU KNOW... FOR SOME REASON...
I FEEL LIKE WHEN I DRINK THIS...
...I WON'T BE THE SAME MAN I WAS BEFORE.
SIP
THAT'S A WEIRD FEELING.
GULP
BOOMF
BA-BOOM

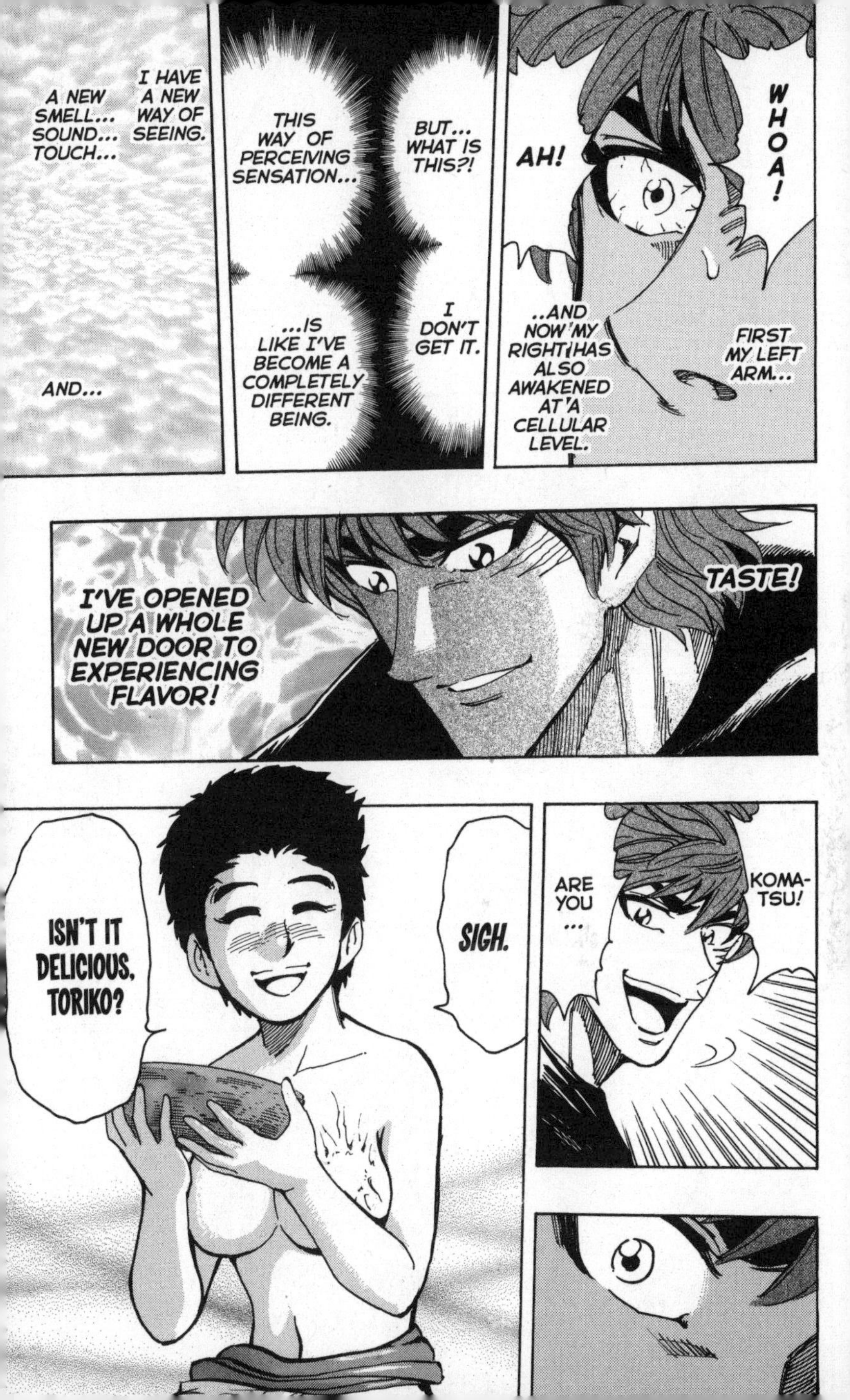
WHOA!
AH!
FIRST MY LEFT ARM...
..AND NOW MY RIGHT HAS ALSO AWAKENED AT A CELLULAR LEVEL.
BUT... WHAT IS THIS?!
THIS WAY OF PERCEIVING SENSATION...
I DON'T GET IT.
...IS LIKE I'VE BECOME A COMPLETELY DIFFERENT BEING.
I HAVE A NEW WAY OF SEEING.
A NEW SMELL... SOUND... TOUCH...
AND...
TASTE!
I'VE OPENED UP A WHOLE NEW DOOR TO EXPERIENCING FLAVOR!
KOMATSU!
ARE YOU ...
SIGH.
ISN'T IT DELICIOUS, TORIKO?

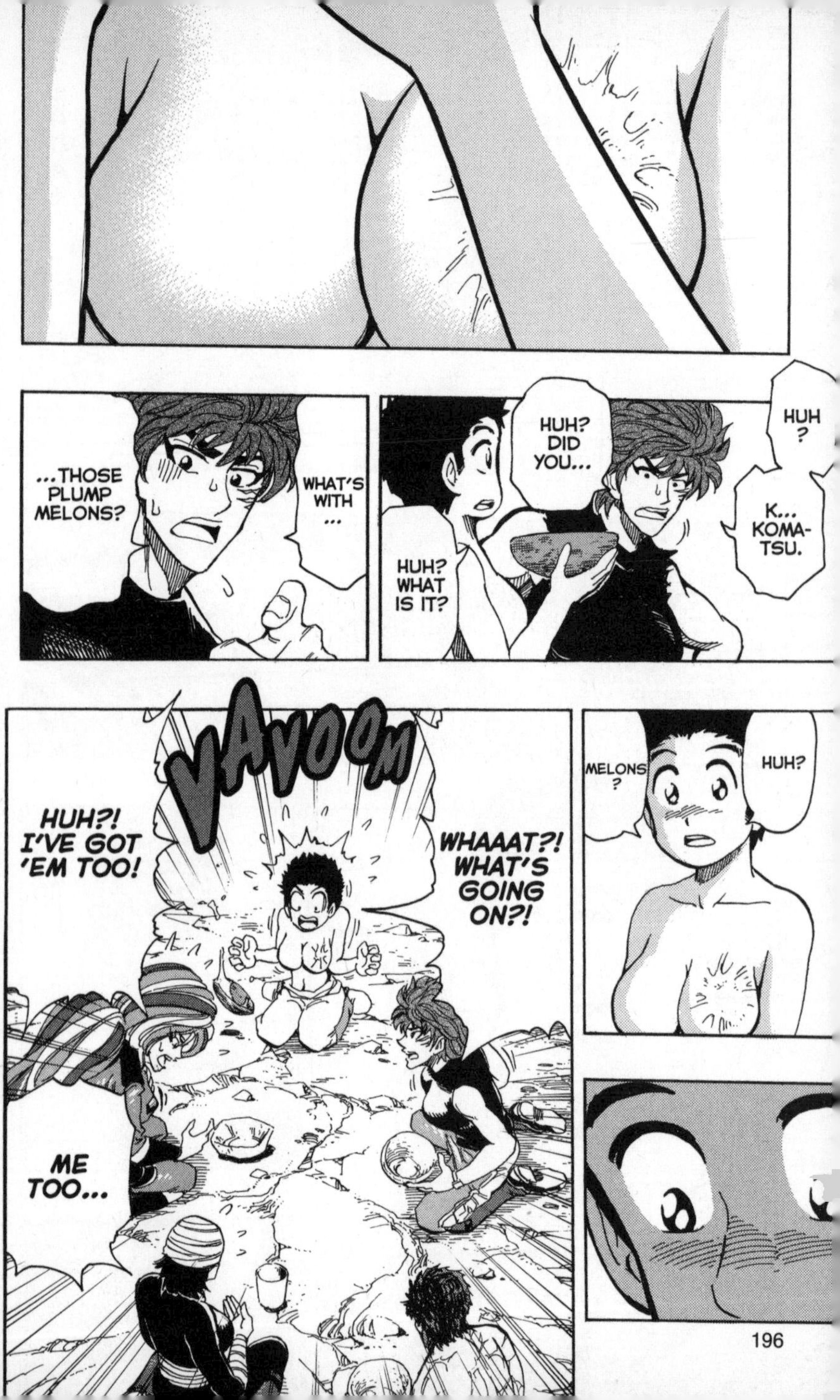
HUH?
K... KOMATSU.
HUH? DID YOU...
HUH? WHAT IS IT?
WHAT'S WITH ...
...THOSE PLUMP MELONS?
HUH?
MELONS?
VAVOOM
WHAAAT?! WHAT'S GOING ON?!
HUH?! I'VE GOT 'EM TOO!
ME TOO...

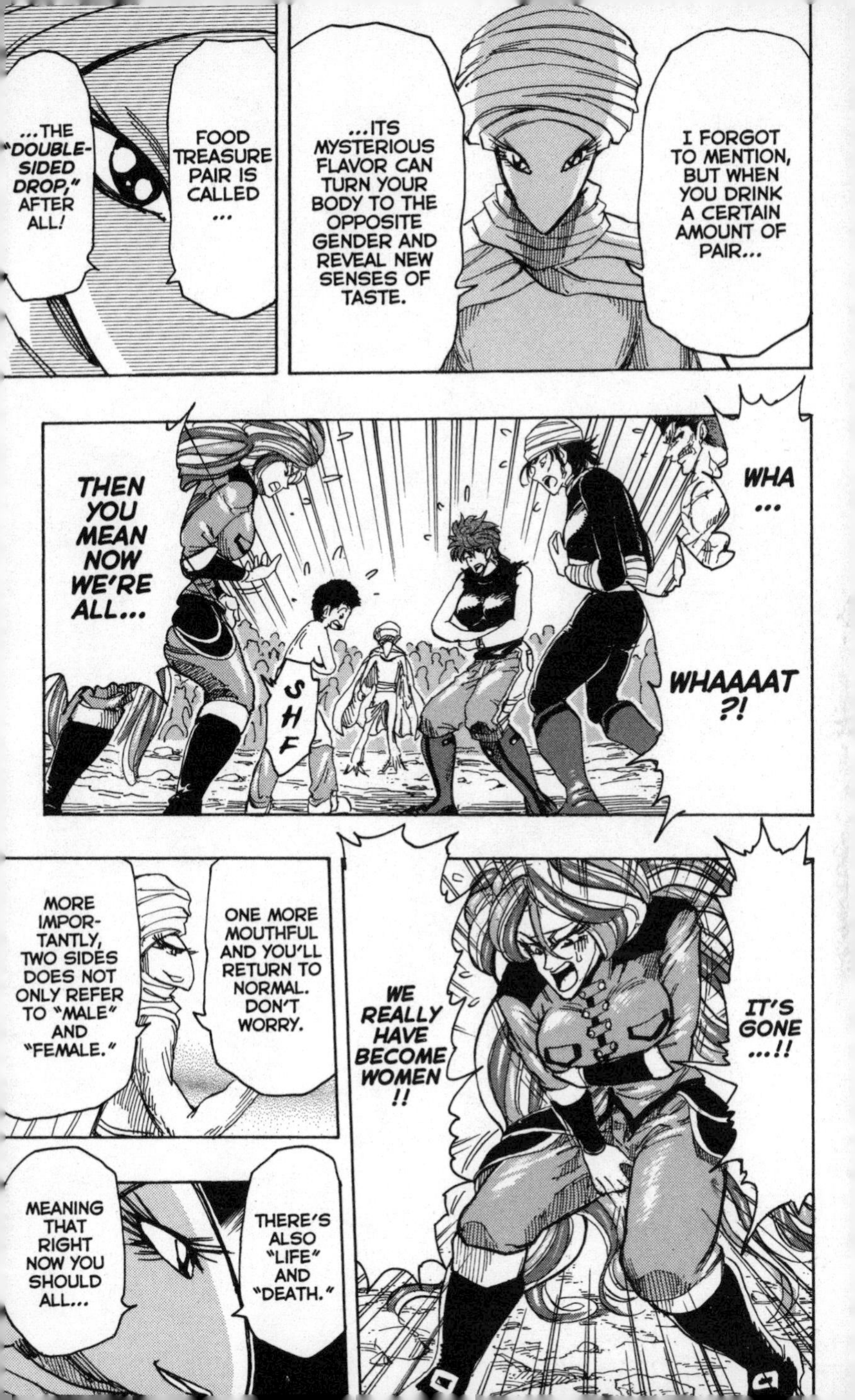

I FORGOT TO MENTION, BUT WHEN YOU DRINK A CERTAIN AMOUNT OF PAIR...
...ITS MYSTERIOUS FLAVOR CAN TURN YOUR BODY TO THE OPPOSITE GENDER AND REVEAL NEW SENSES OF TASTE.
FOOD TREASURE PAIR IS CALLED ...
...THE "DOUBLE-SIDED DROP," AFTER ALL!
WHA ...
WHAAAAT ?!
SHF
THEN YOU MEAN NOW WE'RE ALL...
IT'S GONE ...!!
WE REALLY HAVE BECOME WOMEN !!
ONE MORE MOUTHFUL AND YOU'LL RETURN TO NORMAL. DON'T WORRY.
MORE IMPOR-TANTLY, TWO SIDES DOES NOT ONLY REFER TO "MALE" AND "FEMALE."
THERE'S ALSO "LIFE" AND "DEATH."
MEANING THAT RIGHT NOW YOU SHOULD ALL...

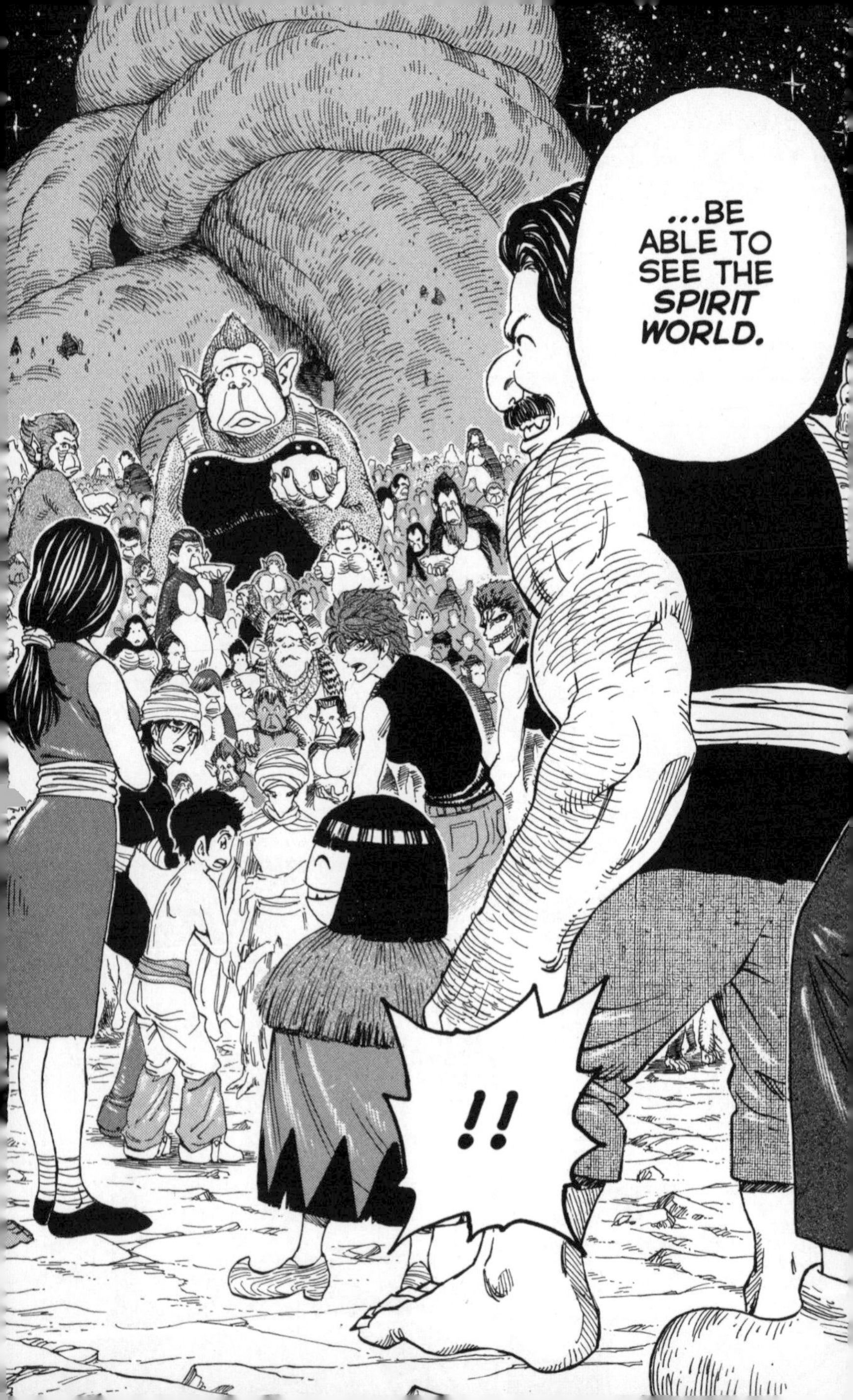
...BE ABLE TO SEE THE SPIRIT WORLD.
!!

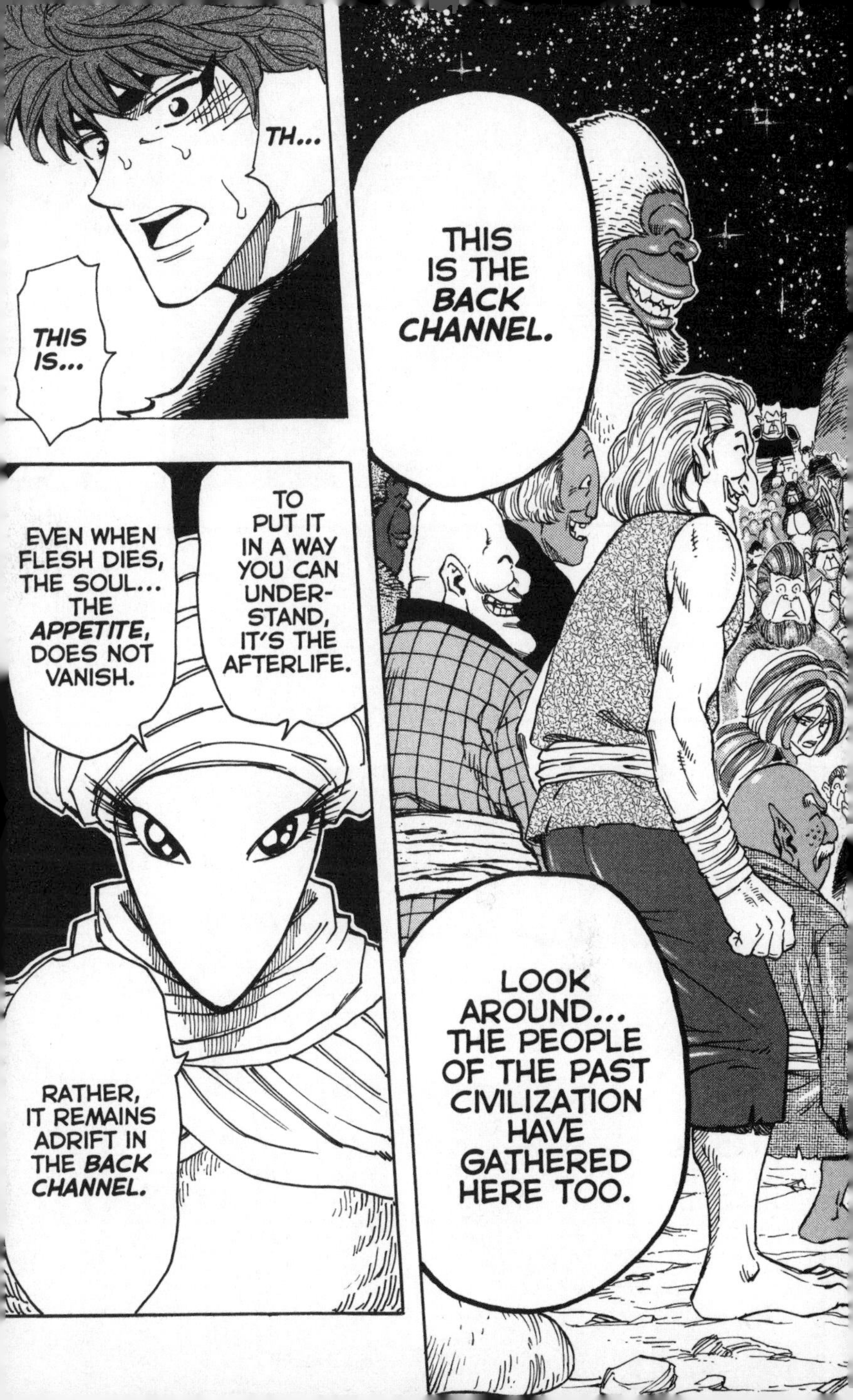
TH...
THIS IS...
THIS IS THE *BACK CHANNEL.*
TO PUT IT IN A WAY YOU CAN UNDER-STAND, IT'S THE AFTERLIFE.
EVEN WHEN FLESH DIES, THE SOUL... THE *APPETITE,* DOES NOT VANISH.
RATHER, IT REMAINS ADRIFT IN THE *BACK CHANNEL.*
LOOK AROUND... THE PEOPLE OF THE PAST CIVILIZATION HAVE GATHERED HERE TOO.

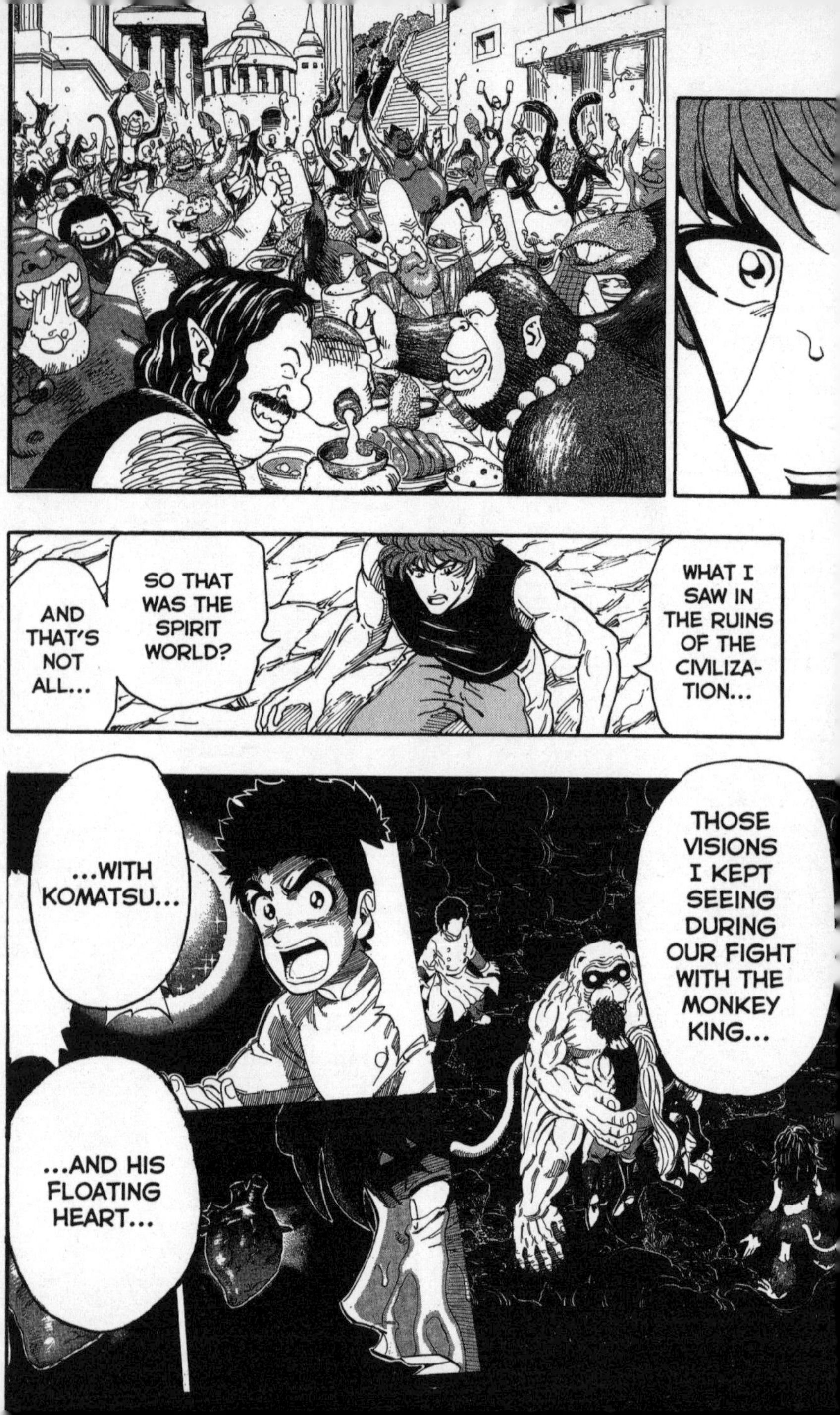
WHAT I SAW IN THE RUINS OF THE CIVILIZA-TION...
SO THAT WAS THE SPIRIT WORLD?
AND THAT'S NOT ALL...
THOSE VISIONS I KEPT SEEING DURING OUR FIGHT WITH THE MONKEY KING...
...WITH KOMATSU...
...AND HIS FLOATING HEART...

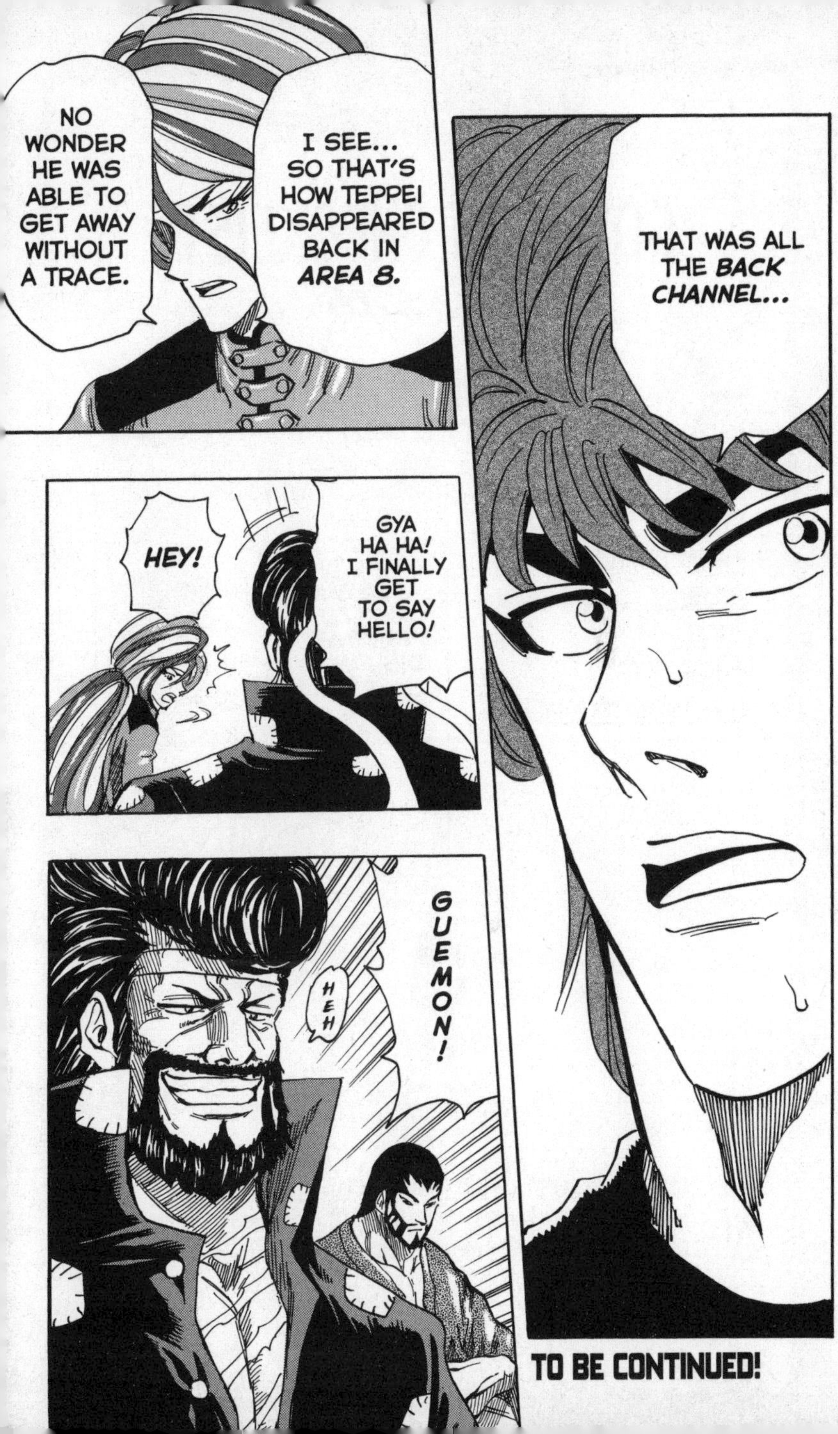
I SEE... SO THAT'S HOW TEPPEI DISAPPEARED BACK IN AREA 8.
NO WONDER HE WAS ABLE TO GET AWAY WITHOUT A TRACE.
GYA HA HA! I FINALLY GET TO SAY HELLO!
HEY!
GUEMON!
HEH
THAT WAS ALL THE BACK CHANNEL...
TO BE CONTINUED!

TORIKO

GOURMET CHECKLIST

Vol. 346

SIRLOIN POTATO
(ROOT VEGETABLE)

CAPTURE LEVEL: SYNTHETICALLY ENGINEERED
HABITAT: FERTILE FIELD
SIZE: 30 CM
HEIGHT: ---
WEIGHT: 500 G
PRICE: 150 YEN PER POTATO

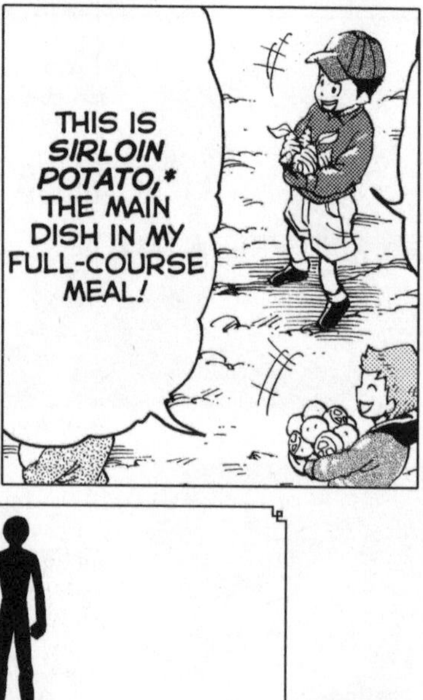
THIS IS SIRLOIN POTATO,* THE MAIN DISH IN MY FULL-COURSE MEAL!

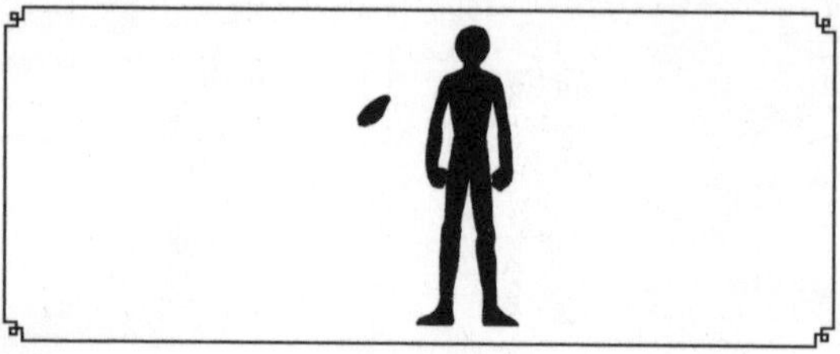

SCALE

AN INGREDIENT TORIKO DISCOVERED. IT TASTES LIKE BOTH SIRLOIN STEAK AND POTATO AND IS DELICIOUS WITH SOY SAUCE. IT'S SELECTIVELY BRED AND IS EASY TO CULTIVATE ON THE CHEAP. IT'S A POPULAR INGREDIENT FOR CHILDREN'S SNACKS.

TORIKO

GOURMET CHECKLIST

Vol. 347

SNAKE PASTA
(REPTILE)

CAPTURE LEVEL: 5

HABITAT: MILD CLIMATES

SIZE: 10 M

HEIGHT: ---

WEIGHT: 10 KG

PRICE: 5,000 YEN PER SNAKE

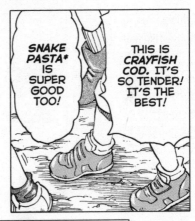

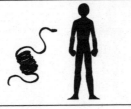

THIS IS CRAYFISH COD. IT'S SO TENDER! IT'S THE BEST!
SNAKE PASTA* IS SUPER GOOD TOO!

SCALE

AN INGREDIENT TORIKO DISCOVERED. IT COMES IN VARYING LENGTHS BUT CAN GROW AS LONG AS TEN METERS. THE HEAD HAS A VERY POTENT VENOM, BUT THE BODY IS PACKED WITH CARBS, MAKING IT A PERFECT ENERGY SUPPLEMENT. THIS INGREDIENT IS BELOVED BY ATHLETES FOR ITS RICH FLAVOR AND CALORIE COUNT.

TORIKO

GOURMET CHECKLIST

Vol. 348

COLA BROWN RICE
(GRAIN)

CAPTURE LEVEL: 42
HABITAT: HOT AND HUMID CLIMATES
SIZE: ---
HEIGHT: ---
WEIGHT: ---
PRICE: 150,000 YEN PER KILOGRAM

COLA BROWN RICE* IS SO GOOD!

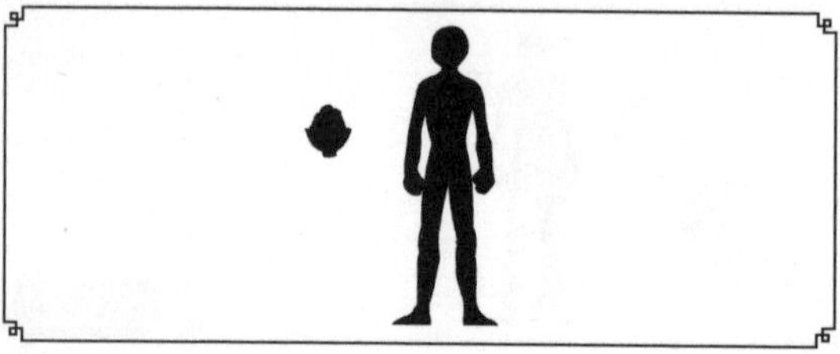

SCALE

AN INGREDIENT TORIKO DISCOVERED. THIS RICE IS FAT AND PUFFY LIKE COLLAGEN AND EACH AND EVERY GRAIN GLITTERS AND SHINES. WHEN YOU EAT IT, YOUR SKIN WILL ALSO FEEL PLUMP AND PERKY, SO IT'S A MUST-HAVE FOR WOMEN'S HEALTH AND BEAUTY REGIMENS.

TORIKO

GOURMET CHECKLIST

Vol. 349

REFRESHING MELON
(FRUIT)

CAPTURE LEVEL: 2
HABITAT: FERTILE FIELDS
SIZE: 25 CM
HEIGHT: ---
WEIGHT: 1.2 KG
PRICE: 5,000 YEN PER MELON

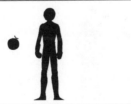

SCALE

AN INGREDIENT TORIKO DISCOVERED. WHEN YOU EAT IT, THIS MYSTERIOUS MELON WILL MAKE YOU FEEL REFRESHED. FOR THAT REASON, IT'S THE PERFECT INGREDIENT TO GIVE PEOPLE WHO ARE FEELING DEPRESSED AND IS A POPULAR GIFT FOR PEOPLE IN THE HOSPITAL.

TORIKO

GOURMET CHECKLIST

Vol. 350

RED-HOT ORANGE
(FRUIT)

CAPTURE LEVEL: UNKNOWN
HABITAT: SCORCHING LANDS
SIZE: 10 CM
HEIGHT: ---
WEIGHT: 200 G
PRICE: 3,500 YEN PER ORANGE

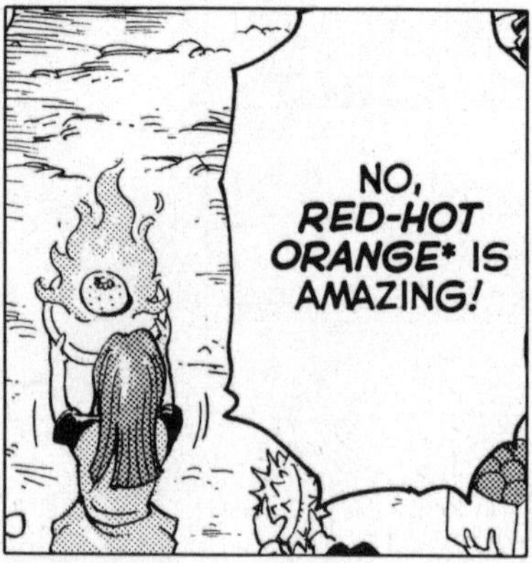
NO, RED-HOT ORANGE* IS AMAZING!

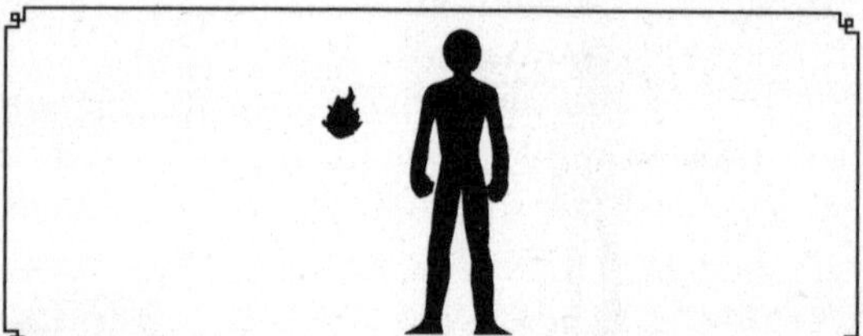

SCALE

AN INGREDIENT TORIKO DISCOVERED. SINCE ITS JUICES ARE LOADED WITH FAT, THIS ORANGE IS DANGEROUSLY FLAMMABLE AND REQUIRES SPECIAL PREPARATION. THE HIGHER THE TEMPERATURE, THE BETTER THE FLAVOR, BUT IT CAN ALSO BE TOO STRONG FOR PEOPLE WHO ARE SENSITIVE TO HOT FOODS.

COMING NEXT VOLUME

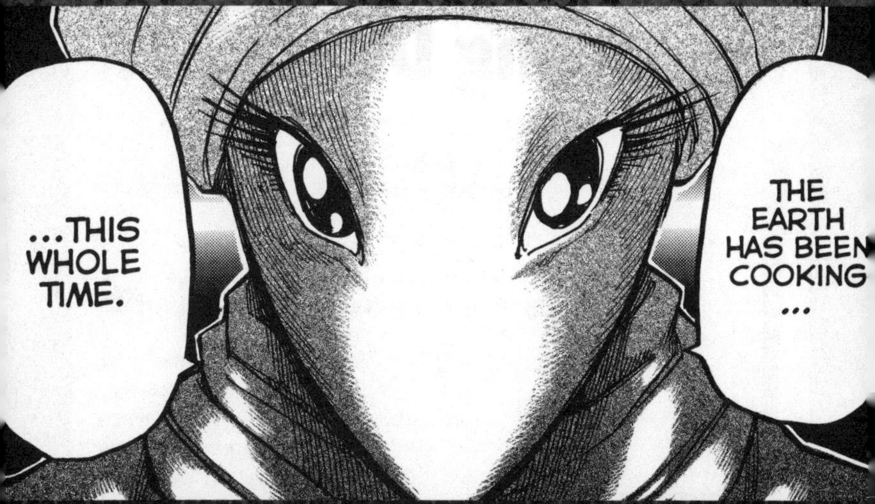
THE EARTH HAS BEEN COOKING...
...THIS WHOLE TIME.

DEPLOYMENT!!

The double-sided drop has plopped and Toriko and the gang drink deep from the fruit of their efforts—they finally get to taste Pair! The party is cut short when the real Kaka appears before them and reveals the turmoil boiling under the surface. The gang must continue on and capture the rest of Acacia's Full Course before the Gourmet Eclipse...which is only one month away!

AVAILABLE NOVEMBER 2016!

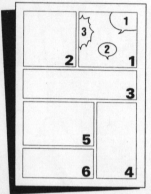

Whoops! Guess what? You're starting at the wrong end of the comic!

…It's true! In keeping with the original Japanese format, **Toriko** is meant to be read from right to left, starting in the upper-right corner.

Unlike English, which is read from left to right, Japanese is read from right to left, meaning that action, sound effects and word-balloon order are completely reversed… something which can make readers unfamiliar with Japanese feel pretty backwards themselves. For this reason, manga or Japanese comics published in the U.S. in English have sometimes been published "flopped"— that is, printed in exact reverse order, as though seen from the other side of a mirror.

By flopping pages, U.S. publishers can avoid confusing readers, but the compromise is not without its downside. For one thing, a character in a flopped manga series who once wore in the original Japanese version a T-shirt emblazoned with "M A Y" (as in "the merry month of") now wears one which reads "Y A M"! Additionally, many manga creators in Japan are themselves unhappy with the process, as some feel the mirror-imaging of their art skews their original intentions.

We are proud to bring you Mitsutoshi Shimabukuro's **Toriko** in the original unflopped format. For now, though, turn to the other side of the book and let the adventure begin…!

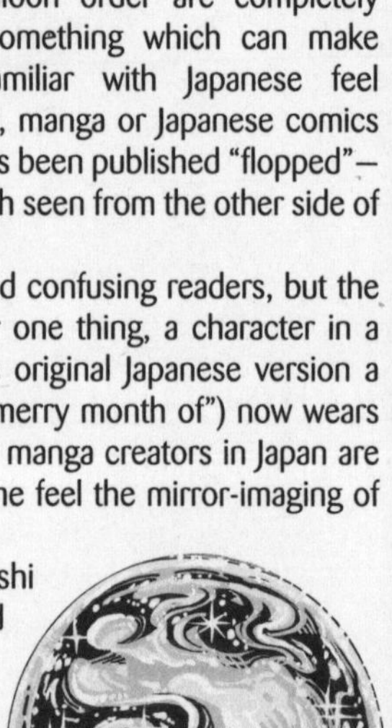